Opera Without Drama

Currents of Change in
Italian Opera, 1675-1725

Studies in Musicology

George Buelow, Series Editor
Professor of Musicology
Indiana University

Other Titles in This Series

Opera Without Drama

Currents of Change in
Italian Opera, 1675-1725

by
Robert S. Freeman

RESEARCH PRESS

Produced and distributed by
UMI Research Press
an imprint of
University Microfilms International
Ann Arbor, Michigan 48106

A revision of the author's thesis,
Princeton University, 1967

Library of Congress Cataloging in Publication Data

Freeman, Robert.
  Opera without drama.

   (Studies in musicology ; no. 35)
   "Currents of change in Italian opera, 1675 to 1725, and
the roles played therein by Zeno, Caldara, and others."
   Originally presented as the author's thesis, Princeton,
1967.
   Bibliography: p.
   Includes index.
   1. Opera—Italy—History and criticism. 2. Zeno, Apostolo,
1668-1750. 3. Caldara, Antonio, 1670-1736.   I. Title.
II. Series.

ML1733.F73   782.1'09   80-29133
ISBN 0-8357-1152-8

Contents

Preface

This study will not attempt to establish Caldara's operatic scores as a hitherto unrecognized turning point in musical history. There would, in fact, be no need for looking further into the operas of Caldara than did Alice Gmeyner in her 1927 dissertation[1] were one to consider Caldara only for his merits as an opera composer or for his role as an operatic innovator. Caldara's claim to attention as an opera composer rests primarily on his long-term connection in Vienna with the eighteenth century's two most popular authors of *opera seria* libretti, Apostolo Zeno and Pietro Metastasio. Both poets have been variously credited as reformers of the libretto; Caldara's virtual monopoly on the original musical settings of the more than two dozen libretti written by Zeno and Metastasio between 1718 and 1736 suggests a more than accidental relationship between Caldara and the two librettists.[2] The presumption of a possible community of musical-dramatic interests between Caldara and his librettists, the preservation in Vienna's Gesellschaft der Musikfreunde of an almost unbroken series of Caldara's actual composing scores (a most unusual phenomenon in early operatic history), and the inherent attractiveness of *opera seria* as a comparatively unexplored field were the original stimuli behind my interest in Caldara.

Once I had arrived in Vienna and had studied enough of Caldara's scores to form some impression of his development and strength as an opera composer and of his interest in musical-dramatic collaboration with Zeno and Metastasio, it became clear that I was dealing with a secondary figure whose relationship to Zeno and Metastasio had been no more than accidental. Unwilling to contribute still another study to the series "_____ als Opernkomponist," I was drawn to look further into the nature of Zeno's so-called reform in order to better understand his interest in *opera seria* and the goals towards which his libretti were directed. To a large extent, a book originally envisaged as a study on the operatic output of a particular composer thus turned into a general study on the history of the Italian libretto during the end of the seventeenth and beginning of the eighteenth centuries.

The following questions were posed during the early stages of the investigation. How were Zeno's earliest libretti different from those of his immediate predecessors both in Italy and in Vienna? To what degree did they differ from those written by his actual contemporaries, particularly those who, like Zeno, were early members of the Arcadian Academy, the group often credited with the reform of literary taste in Italy during the end of the seventeenth century? When and where did the historical tradition of "Zeno's reform" develop, and how familiar were the writers who founded it with the genre whose reform they attributed to Zeno? How did Zeno himself view his activities as a librettist? Did he consider at any point that he personally had brought anything new to the libretto? Is it meaningful to speak of the admitted difference between a Zeno libretto of 1720 and one by Minato or Aureli of, say, 1680 as the result of a reform? Was there, that is, a radical break at any point in either the form or the content of the libretto, with an attendant surge of criticism and hostility from those conservatives opposed to disturbing innovation? Or was the change a more gradual, evolutionary one? What was the relationship, with respect to the change, of Vienna to Venice? Did Zeno take something new to Vienna when he arrived there late in the summer of 1718, or did he merely continue something with which his predecessors in Vienna had already acquainted the Habsburg court before his arrival there? What was the relationship between the roughly simultaneous general changes around the turn of the eighteenth century in the construction of the libretto and in the composers' new manner of musical setting? How are we to understand Benedetto Marcello's famous satire, *Il teatro alla moda*, published in 1720? Are the inflexible customs it ridicules a meaningless exaggeration or were there frequent cases where, for example, the prima donna's mother dictated to the librettist on the placement, variety, and number of her daughter's arias? How are we to understand a dramatic or musical-dramatic reform in a context where the poet had so little to say about the final shape of an opera? Was the "Zeno reform" really without effect on such carryings on, or did the Marcello pamphlet describe a period several decades prior to its publication date? What were the forces which controlled Italian opera in Venice and in Vienna during the first decades of the eighteenth century? Was it apt to be the poet, the composer, or neither of them who determined the essential characteristics of the libretto and its setting? In particular, what was the relationship of Zeno and Metastasio to Caldara?

Since there is a notable lack of either musical or dramatic evolution between Caldara's earliest Viennese settings of Zeno texts from 1718 and his final settings of Metastasio texts in 1736, the year he died, my attention in the study of Caldara's operatic output was turned as much to the period of change which preceded his 1716 arrival in Vienna and to the consideration of the questions outlined in the preceding paragraph as to the relatively unchanging works of the period of his relationship with Zeno and Metastasio, 1718-36. This change of emphasis was undertaken in order to produce a more useful study, but it involved working with problems which would not have arisen for a study more concentrated on Caldara's Vienna operas. The Austrian National Library holds a very nearly complete run of copy scores and skeleton orchestral parts for the operas performed at various Habsburg residences in and around Vienna during the second half of the seventeenth and first half of the eighteenth centuries. Originally part of the emperors' personal libraries, these sources yield a more complete musical picture of the operatic life of baroque Vienna than has survived in one place for any other European city of the period, but their usefulness is impaired for reasons both physical and historical. Although, or perhaps even because, the Habsburgs were so careful about preserving orchestral scores and parts, they neglected to do much in the way of libretto collecting. Such Viennese libretti as were preserved in the city itself are now scattered among the various libraries of Vienna and among the several branches of the National Library. In the case of the National Library this proves to be a serious difficulty, for although the Music Division is well catalogued and easy to work with, the rest of the Library depends upon an often unreliable, largely pre-1800 slip catalogue generally unavailable to the public. It is ironic that the world's greatest collection of Viennese libretti for the period, part of the personal library of Zeno himself, resides 400 miles from Vienna in Venice's Biblioteca Marciana. Although it is not impossible to compare the Marciana libretti with the Viennese scores and parts, it is difficult enough to impede progress. The wonderful libretto collections of the Marciana and the Fondazione Cini are, similarly, not so useful as one might wish because of the weakness of Venice's collections of late seventeenth- and early eighteenth-century operatic scores. The relative scarcity of Venetian opera scores anywhere in the world from the period will always make it difficult to write anything definitive on the formal relationship of musical to poetic change in Italian opera during the closing decades of the seventeenth century. Venice seems to have been the center of the changes, but one lacks adequate source material. There is no problem about source material for late seventeenth-century Italian opera in Vienna, but the conservative domination there of Minato and Draghi kept out more progressive figures until after their deaths in 1698 and 1700, respectively. By the time composers like the two Bononcinis and librettists like Bernardoni and Stampiglia reached Vienna from Italy, the new formal structure of the libretto was no longer a novelty.

It seems doubly unfortunate for the study of Caldara that of his more than 60 extant full-length secular dramatic works, fewer than 10 percent come from that part of his career during which the style of the opera was changing most rapidly: the years before his permanent settlement in Vienna in 1716. One can infer a great deal more about musical change in the operas of a single composer, on libretti by one poet, sung by the same group of singers in the same theater than one can about a handful of works on new and old texts by a variety of poets in one city after another. The evolution of musical style in the former case is apt to mirror a composer's inner growth and changing musical ideals, but in the latter case there are liable to be so many conflicting extra-musical forces[3] at work on a composer that it is impossible accurately to distinguish among elements dictated by individual singers or by some impresario's impression of local taste—elements which, especially when one is dealing with scores prepared by copyists, often include unidentified scenes and arias by other composers. The degree to which we can follow the first quarter-century of Caldara's career as an opera composer is, then, seriously impeded not only by the sparseness and character of the musical sources but also by the dearth of secondary material on the backgrounds through which those sources came into being, the operatic milieus of early eighteenth-century Mantua, Macerata, Rome, Ferrara, Bologna, Milan, and Barcelona.

The history of opera in Italy from the death of Monteverdi through the middle of the eighteenth century has barely been touched, partly because of the gigantic tasks of ground-breaking still necessary and partly because of the reputed inferiority of the music involved. German dissertations have long exploited the possibility of studying the works of individual composers, but the usefulness of these works is in direct proportion to their authors' familiarity with the works of the predecessors and contemporaries of the composers under study. There are still all too few works which effectively place their subjects in any larger contexts, especially in those useful for further studies on similar subjects. One of the difficulties lies with the enormous quantities of material involved. Another concerns the bibliographical confusion created by all but a few of the reference works in the field. Libretti and scores with similar or even identical titles are often not the same works at all, even though the librettist and the composer are common to both. Operas with different titles, on the other hand, ostensibly the work of different librettists and composers, sometimes turn out to be identical, or nearly so. Works whose forewords claim that they are imitations of other works sometimes have little in common with their alleged ancestors. The bibliographical house of *opera seria* is all too often built on the sandy assumption that the information contained in title pages, dedications, libretto forewards, theater placards, and the like can all be taken at face value. It is tedious to check the veracity of such information and to compile alphabetic and thematic indices for the tracing of those arias which migrate from opera to opera and from city to city, but given the Italian public's constant demand for novelty and the impresario's concern for a financial profit, these and many other similar tasks of cataloguing will have to be undertaken if we are even to get below the surface in the history of *opera seria*.

The first of the two sections which constitute this study deals with an investigation of the genesis and significance of the "Zeno reform." The second, a study of Caldara's original settings between 1718 and 1736 of 23 full-length "reform" libretti by Zeno and Metastasio, concerns the musical-dramatic implications of the new directions in the libretto for an important *opera seria* composer of the period. Since J. H. VanderMeer, in his recent three-volume study of the operas of J. J. Fux[4] (Caldara's immediate superior in Vienna), has taken the revolutionary position that Fux and his contemporaries set *opera seria* texts, not hastily according to stereotypes but with painstaking and following explicit musical-dramatic principles set forth by a variety of rhetoricians, this is a question of special timeliness.

Much of the research for this study was conducted in Vienna at the Musiksammlung of the Nationalbibliothek and at the Archiv of the Gesellschaft der Musikfreunde. I am indebted to both institutions, and particularly to Frau Dr. Hedwig Mitringer, Director of the Gesellschaft Archiv, for special courtesy and helpfulness. I am grateful, too, to Pierluigi Petrobelli, who checked my transcriptions of documents discovered in the Archivio di Stato, Mantua, and to two former students, Robert Moreen and James Winn, who supplied material missing from my notes and needed for Appendix H. My work in Europe would not have been possible without a two-year fellowship from the Fulbright Program in Austria and a generous grant from the Martha Baird Rockefeller Foundation.

While conversations with Professor Oliver Strunk were responsible for my initial interest in *opera seria* and in Caldara's apparent connection with Zeno, I am equally indebted, for important advice and criticism, to Professors Arthur Mendel, J. Merrill Knapp, and Nino Pirrotta.

This study was completed in the early months of 1967. In the meantime I have spent five years as a faculty member at MIT and eight years as director of the University of Rochester's Eastman School of Music. For the past decade I have been active as a pianist, as an administrator, and recently as a developer of urban Rochester, roles which have left no time at all for scholarship. Accordingly, the materials here published do not take into account the scholarship of others published during the past 13 years. It is presented as an artifact of an earlier part of my life, and appears here essentially as it was written in 1967.

I

Testimony About the "Reform"

It is surely one of the greater ironies of musical history that opera, born in northern Italy during the closing years of the sixteenth century partly as the result of antiquarian interest in the musical dramas of ancient Greece, evolved so rapidly into a theatrical spectacular so different from the ideals it had set out to emulate. In place of a serious combination of poetry and music intended for the moving of souls and the improvement of human society, there quickly emerged an entertainment featuring virtuoso vocal display and fantastic scenic effects for an audience primarily concerned with the externals of performance. In place of the simple and dramatic libretti written by Ottavio Rinuccini, Alessandro Striggio and their colleagues for the earliest operatic productions in Florence and Mantua, composers were soon setting absurdly complicated texts involving large numbers of the most heterogeneous character types, ever-expanding numbers of mostly very undramatic musical arias, and long series of allegedly verisimilar accidents.[1] Giovanni Maria Crescimbeni blamed the degeneracy of Italian libretti during the second half of the seventeenth century on a vogue initiated by the Venice production of Cicognini's *Giasone* in 1649,[2] while others blamed everything from the Spanish romances which had preceded Cicogini[3] to the excessive restrictions of the commentators on Aristotle's *Poetics*[4] and the empty characterizations of Tasso and Guarini;[5] everything from the bombastic style of Giambattista Marino[6] and the introduction of dialects into Italian comedy[7] to the rapid development of Italian scenography,[8] the corruptibility of singers, the cupidity of impresarios, the stupidity of the public,[9] and the unnatural influence of foreign courts.[10]

Although eighteenth-century literary Italians were nearly unanimous in condemning the tastes of their seventeenth-century predecessors, hardly a voice was raised during the seventeenth century itself, except by the reactionary followers of Borromeo and Loyola, who systematically opposed all secular theater, whether musical or not.[11] Venetian librettists had begun at least by mid-century to complain from time to time about the bizarreness of Venetian taste and about the necessity of conforming to the whims of public fancy, but one has the impression that such claims to superior judgment, appearing in the forewords to libretti, were more in the nature of window dressing than of serious criticism.[12] Aurelio Aureli, one of those whose libretto forewords touch most often on the problems of Venetian caprice, was the consistent producer of Venice's most bizarre libretti. Confused plots, unexpected developments, unnatural characterizations, and occasional obscenities were taken as ornamental beauties which attracted extra business and not as disfiguring blemishes. The explicit aim of Aureli and his contemporaries, like that of the singers and machinists with whom they worked, was not to move an audience to tears or to virtue and noble conduct, but to astound, to impress, and, wherever possible, to overwhelm. When Marino in his epoch-making *Adone* wrote, "I know the rules better than all the world's pedants know them; but the most important rule is to know when to break rules . . . , accommodating oneself to current custom and to the taste of our century,"[13] he spoke in a sense for several generations of Italian librettists and impresarios.

Frugoni

The essay written by Francesco Fulvio Frugoni to accompany his own "opera melodrammatica," *L'Epulone*, published in Venice in 1675, is the first datable instance I have discovered during the second half of the seventeenth century in which a poet of serious literary aspirations deigned to criticize the literary sins of contemporary librettists. In *L'Epulone* Frugoni wrote a libretto to illustrate the critical ideas which he hoped would set a new standard in libretto writing, but despite his professed care in using the sort of rhymes which would endear his work to composers,[14] *L'Epulone* seems not to have made any special impression on the public for which he had intended it. Cardinal Giovanni Delfino, whose tragedies found praise from Frugoni and later from another operatic critic, Giovanni Maria Croscimbeni,[15] had evidently expressed an interest in *L'Epulone* before its completion, but no notice whatever was taken of the work in any of the forewords to conventional libretti printed in Venice around 1675.

Although *L'Epulone* itself is of negligible interest, Frugoni's 40-page essay indicates that a clearly articulated body of critical opinion against the normal operatic procedures of the day existed in Italy as early as 1675. Frugoni takes what he considers a moderate position somewhere between the conservative commentators on Aristotle, who allow music only a very circumscribed role in a drama constructed on the most rigid schemes, and the Venetian librettists, who hold the stage of 1675 with works permitting every license. The art of producing dramas, begins Frugoni, has become nothing but the art of ruining human society.[16] Instead of imitating nature for the ethical betterment of mankind, literature, painting, and the theater have become monstrous fantasies which corrupt. The musical theater in particular has elevated the means of expression to a position above that of the dramatic goals they are supposed to serve: scenery and stage machinery attract too much attention, and the singers, who are unjustly paid more than their intellectual superiors, the librettists, take no interest in the dramatic character of their roles, and behave obnoxiously as well.[17] Indeed, the characteristic weakness in contemporary Italian drama of all kinds, continues Frugoni, stems from the poet's inability to stand up for any reasonable dramatic ideals.[18] Too many unconnected episodes too often obscure the principal dramatic idea, if indeed the poet has even considered the possibility of building his work around a single idea.[19]

Frugoni realizes that Aristotle's *Poetics* is a problematic work,[20] and recognizes the foolishness of uncritical obedience to the regulations of the commentators on the *Poetics*, but he is equally critical of those who fail even to consider the applicability of Aristotelian principles. He sees nothing sacred about Aristotle's famous unities of time and place, but he abhors the frequency with which his contemporaries change setting and the liberties they take in prolonging the temporal limits of a drama to include the passage of 50 years or more.[21] Serious and comic characters should not be indiscriminately mixed in a work of art, and serious characters should never be permitted to behave or to speak like buffoons. The ostensible appropriateness of tone to character in *L'Epulone* is, in fact, one of the work's features of which Frugoni is particularly proud.[22] He does not contend that sung or spoken tragedy is the only worthwhile form of dramatic endeavor, but he distinguishes carefully between the kind of dialogue from which one can take pleasure in reading and the kind of slapstick humor which delights on the stage, but which seems senseless in print.[23] Far from disputing the possibility of an artistic combination of tragic and comic elements within a single drama, as did some of his successors, Frugoni interested himself in the problems of balance which tragicomedy (of which *L'Epulone* is an example) implies.

But despite his interest in seeing *L'Epulone* set to music and performed as an opera, he divided his work into five acts and preceded it with a prologue. Since, as Frugoni himself realized, operatic prologues and five-act libretti were no longer in fashion in 1675,[24] it is not surprising that *L'Epulone* seems never to have been set.[25] Although Frugoni's essay stated that he would not object to certain unspecified cuts in a work whose length was admittedly more impressive when read in private than when performed in public,[26] the average length of *L'Epulone's* lines of recitative would in itself have discouraged even the most sympathetic of Frugoni's composing friends.

French Influence in Italy

The French attacks on Italian poetry of all ages, which gathered momentum in 1674 with the publication of essays by Boileau and Rapin, did not at first concentrate the force of their onslaught on Italian opera. Like subsequent essays by Baillet, Bouhours, and the Italian Francophile, Padre Ettori, they aimed to glorify French culture at the expense of Italian by ridiculing the inflated style of Marino and his followers and by generally belittling even such classics of Italian poetry as Petrarch and Tasso.[27] Ambiguity, ostentation, inflated metaphors, dependence on or even plagiarism from French writers, and overuse of hyperbole, obscurity, and irrationality were the principal charges leveled at the Italians, but the lines which wounded the most deeply and antagonized the most bitterly were quotable barbs like the following, which irritated the already running sore of Italy's national pride:

> I pardon all these thoughts in a man from the other side of the mountains, but I do not know if I would pardon them in a Frenchman. (Bouhours, 1687)[28]

> The language now spoken in Italy is as much less like that of ancient Rome as it is more susceptible to corruption. If the former resembles the latter in some respects, it is not so much as a daughter resembles her mother as in the manner that monkeys resemble human beings. (Bouhours, 1671)[29]

> The modern Italians are satisfied to be enlightened by the same sun, to breathe the same air, and to inhabit the same land, which heretofore the ancient Romans inhabited; but they have left to history that severe virtue which the Romans practiced, and therefore think they have no need of tragedy to animate them to hard and difficult things which they have no mind to undertake. (Saint-Evremond, 1685)[30]

It seems to have been Saint-Evremond who was the first among the French to chastise Italy for her fondness for irregular and licentious libretti. Although he seems to have been fundamentally opposed to all opera, whether French or Italian, calling it "despicable in the disposition of both subject and verses," ". . . a bizarre affair made up of poetry and music, in which the poet and the musician, each equally obstructed by the other, give themselves no end of trouble to produce a wretched work,"[31] his pride as a Frenchman made it impossible for him not to prefer French opera to Italian: "The constitution of our operas cannot be more defective than it is. But it is to be acknowledged at the same time that no man can perform more than Lully upon an ill-conceived subject, and that it is not easy to outdo Quinault in what is required of him."[32] Besides Italy's lack of a composer or a librettist of the stature of either Lully or Quinault, she was to be pitied for what Saint-Evremond considered her lack of good taste in singing and the exaggeration of her musical passions, as well as for the total lack in Italy of anything comparable to the Tragédie française. It is a bad thing, according to Saint-Evremond, if opera is popular, but something infinitely worse if its popularity ruins all taste for spoken tragedy.[33]

Had all late seventeenth-century Italians been as culturally backward and isolated from the rest of Europe as some French critics liked to think, French insults would have gone unnoticed and given no offence. But although there were Italians who agreed with the French charge that Italy had no serious theater and in general no literary taste, it was not true that no one in Italy cared about the intellectual life of the rest of Europe or about Italy's European reputation.[34] Although Galileo's *Dialogue* had been suppressed by the Church the year after its publication in 1632, and the Roman Academy of the Lincei disbanded at the same time, Grand Duke Ferdinand II of Tuscany remained an active sponsor of experimental science, always eager for contact with the North. In 1657 he was instrumental in the foundation of Il Cimento, a Florentine academy devoted to the study of experimental science, which by 1660 was working in close cooperation with similar scientific associations in France.[35] Ferdinand's younger brother, Leo di Medici, who had worked in Rome on scientific studies with members of the disbanded Lincei, published an essay on those studies in 1667, the year in which he was elected a member of the College of Cardinals.[36] The freer intellectual climate of Rome, which had begun in 1667 with the papacy of Clement IX, was furthered in 1668 by the founding of the *Giornale dei letterati*, a periodical literary review which imitated and corresponded with the recently established (1668) *Journal des scavans* of Paris.[37] The medical authority of Galen was questioned in print by Leonardo di Capua in 1681[38] and, as we have seen, the validity of Aristotle's *Poetics* as the last word on tragedy was rejected.[39] Interest in the experimental philosophy exported from France seems also to have brought about a gradual improvement in the quality of Italian scholarship during the final years of the seventeenth century, especially through the influence exerted by two French historians who travelled extensively all over the peninsula—Mabillon in 1685-86 and Montfaucon in 1698-1701.[40]

Nor was the struggle between ancients and moderns joined in Italy only by students of the natural and social sciences. Italian opposition to Marino and his followers can be traced back even into the first half of the seventeenth century, but its influence spread in ever-widening circles during the second half of the century, particularly after 1665 through the insistence of poets like Francesco Redi on clarity and morality in Italian poetry. The explicit reaction to marinism in the works of such other mid seventeenth-century poets as Matteo Peregrini, Fulvio Testi, Scipione Herrico, Lorenzo Lippi, Lorenzo Mugalotti, Gian Nicio Eritreo, Traiano Boccalini and Tommaso Companella suggests that Italy had a literary conscience of her own,[41] but the existence in France of what many considered a superior culture must have acted as a powerful stimulus to that conscience.

Christina of Sweden[42] was the guest of honor at a 1656 performance in Rome of Corneille's *Heraclius*.[43] She visited France itself during 1656 and again during 1657-58.[44] None of her biographers records that French theater made any particular impression on Christina, but it is significant that she corresponded at length with Descartes and Corneille,[45] and that she was the founder and patron of a literary academy in Rome whose principal goal was the purification of Italian literary style.[46] (The Arcadian Academy itself met for the first time in the fall of 1690, more than a year after Christina's death, but its earliest members recognized her as their spiritual predecessor, and their literary goals continued to be those which Christina had cherished.)[47] It is not surprising that there were no performances in Italy of French tragedy or French opera in French, but one does find increasing numbers of published Italian translations of French tragedies[48] and in 1690 even an Italian translation of Quinault's libretto for *Armide*, for performance in Rome with Lully's original score.[49] Bertet, the French translator of *Armide*, tells us that he had made similar Italian translations of Lully's last six operas, but none of these seems ever to have been printed and, were it not for the memoirs of Coulanges, we could not be sure that even the *Armide* translation had ever actually been heard in performance.[50] The very fact of their existence points, nonetheless, to the growing determination of some French writers to cast Italy in the role of a literary satellite. The willingness with which late seventeenth-century Italians began to travel to Paris for advanced study and the degree to which knowledge of the French language spread in Italy[51] are evidence that disunited Italy's political inferiority complex with regard to the achievements of the "grand nation" had become a literary one as well.

Salvadori

Among those totally unconcerned about Italy's literary debt to France was Giuseppe Gaetano Salvadori, Neapolitan librettist and author of *Poetica toscana all'uso*, a book of prescriptions subtitled "how to compose sonnets, canzonas, madrigals, *ottave rime*, heroic poems, tragedies, and comedies, with and without music," which appeared in Naples in 1691. *Poetica toscana* is a volume whose clarity is often impaired by the awkwardness of its author's cumbersome prose, but it is nonetheless important for the light it sheds on several aspects of late seventeenth-century Italian opera not discussed by other writers.

Convinced that he is the first in the history of Italian literature to treat poetry written for music, and claiming personal familiarity with cultural currents all over Italy, Salvadori recognizes the existence of poetry as an independent art, but stresses the popularity of poetry for music and the practicality of writing it:

> If a man of understanding wishes to advance himself and to acquire the favor of a prince, rather than a sonnet, a canzona, or a heroic poem, let him present the prince with a *dramma per musica* or a collection of chamber cantatas, that will be immediately accepted, welcomed, and rewarded.[52]

He recognizes the existence of Italians who would criticize his ideas, identifying them as members of the Crusca "and other silly chatterers" and deriding their standards of criticism as outmoded and impractical, incapable of producing poetry that will please contemporary audiences.[53] A summary of Salvadori's dramatic credo is included here not only because it indicates the extent to which Italian librettists had become familiar even by the early 1690s with the reproaches directed against them by conservative Aristotelians and Francophiles, but also because it shows that many of the ideas considered by later writers to be part of a reform movement usually associated with Apostolo Zeno are actually to be attributed to the developing experience of singers, composers, and librettists of often bizarre tastes with a genre that was still relatively new.

In Salvadori's view, too much emphasis on morality is boring. Brevity is the password of dramatic success.[54] Exaggerations, hyperbole, the falsification of history, unintegrated episodes, and the use of improbable incidents are all justified if the audience approves.[55] Salvadori's only restriction on the use of the marvelous is the avoidance of spectacular effects that do not surprise. As he sees it, there is nothing improper about dramatic solutions through gods in machines, but it is senseless to use them too often:

> I will give (poets) the license not only to transform ships into shepherdesses, as did Virgil, but also for an ant to overturn the world, and for the stars, transforming themselves into oxen, to descend and plough the earth.[56]

There is no point, continues Salvadori, in arguing about sad and happy endings, for although the century prefers happy endings, either variety is acceptable.[57] There is no point, similarly, in insisting that every king be a serious figure and every peasant a buffoon, for the dramatic representation of comic kings and dignified peasants presents a welcome occasion for variety.[58] It is senseless for librettists to try to develop plots that seem verisimilar, for the public will believe what it chooses to believe. The invention of new dramatic ideas is entertaining, but a librettist pressed for time should not hesitate to purloin the ideas of others wherever he finds them.[59] Since Salvadori asserts, however, that allegories are no longer popular, he warns against them. Poets are advised to use a "clear, pure, and ornate style," but warned against the use of elements that might obscure meaning. The dances or intermedii used between acts may be dramatically connected with the plot of the drama or not, according to the discretion of the poet. One should seek in every instance to satisfy the public, for ". . . the world has changed; it is necessary to versify well and not to seek after so many sophistries and trifles under the veil of learning."[60]

Having addressed himself to problems common to various kinds of poetry, Salvadori turns during the final 20 pages of his essay to considerations peculiar to poetry for music. Musical texts should be written on sublime and magnificent subjects in a polished, clear, and resonant style, a point that Salvadori illustrates, as he does in other instances, with quotations from his own works and from those of Marino.[61] Dramatic texts for music, continues Salvadori, comprise two different kinds of poetry: recitatives and arias. The recitatives, whose individual words and syllables are never repeated in musical settings, consist of blank verse in lines of 7 and 11 syllables on which the composer takes no pains and from which the public receives no pleasure. Since the function of the recitative, according to Salvadori, is only to hold back the arias, passages of recitative should be as short as possible. Salvadori claims to limit his own recitative to six lines at a time, but admits that it is possible to use a few more if the individual speeches are all short. "Recitative is as necessary in musical dramas as is bread to man," but it is the arias, wherein words and syllables are often repeated, that make musical drama so popular.

Here Salvadori makes a point not encountered in any of the other writers reviewed here when he distinguishes between two kinds of aria: "natural" and "derived." Natural arias consist of several metrical, rhyming verses of four, six, or eight syllables each, and are intended by the librettist for musical setting as arias. "Arie cavate," however, are settings of a line or two which the poet intends as recitative but which the composer, sometimes taking advantage of the presence of a rhymed couplet, urged on perhaps by an ambitious singer, sets as arias.[62] Although Salvadori stresses the variety of aria forms available to contemporary librettists, the great majority of the poems he presents as examples of "natural" arias are four-line texts of two equal-length sentences each. Since, according to Salvadori, most settings of "natural" arias repeat the first sentence of each text after stating both sentences in their normal order, he advises librettists to arrange their aria texts in such a manner that each sentence constitutes a complete thought, and so that the first of these thoughts be capable of logical repetition after the statement of the second.[63]

Salvadori concludes his essay with a series of warnings "for librettists unfamiliar with music." Modern composers are men of power whose textual changes it is useless to resist. A prudent librettist familiarizes himself with the talents of the singers who will perform his work and collaborates wherever possible with the composer. Since arias are what the public desires, it is senseless to imitate those who try to include in their works as many as three or four scenes devoid of arias. In theory one can use arias at the beginnings of scenes, but experience shows that it is more effective to use recitative in that position. No individual singer should have more than three or four arias in succession, as happens in the libretti of some unthinking poets. It is unwise to write libretti that involve fewer than four or more than seven characters. One should avoid lengthy sentences and individual words whose accented syllables involve vowels other than "a" and "o," particularly in aria texts.[64]

Perrucci

More sensitive than Salvadori to French criticism of the Italian theater, but no more anxious than he to dispute the Italian public's right to determine the conventions of its own entertainment, was Salvadori's colleague, Andrea Perrucci, a Neapolitan librettist, impresario, and author of an informative treatise on theatrical production brought out in Naples in 1699, *Dell'arte rappresentativa premediatata ed all'improviso*. In the midst of a long list of contemporary Italian librettists and dramatists, Perrucci has special praise for Marchese G. G. Orsi of Bologna, a poet ". . . who has marvelously combined the rigidity of the antique style with the ease and grace of the modern, both in his own works and in those which he has translated (or rather beautified) from French originals."[65]

Perrucci realized that Orsi was fond of basing his works on French models and had enough national pride to assert (probably without knowing the French originals) that they were improvements on their models, but he saw no reason to dwell on the point. His essay deals rather with the most practical issues of opera production and he adopts as his principal standard the familiar impresario's maxim that the public is always right, that ". . . it is better to be wrong with the majority than correct with the minority,'' an indirect reference no doubt to the early stirrings during the 1690s of Italian librettists who aimed to lead public taste rather than follow it.[66] Perrucci finds it unfortunate that contemporary comedies are often obscene and often use as many as 40 or 50 characters each, but his objections are typically practical. Obscenity gives the theater a bad name, limiting its appeal to the poorer classes who are unable to support it, and bringing down the wrath of the Church, which can ruin an impresario by closing his theater or even tearing it down. No mention is made of any corrupting influence obscenity may exercise on public morals.[67] Forty or 50 characters in a single work are too many, not because of the difficulty of developing a unified dramatic action around them, but because they raise costs and create unnecessary confusion backstage, particularly with regard to entrances and exits.

The smooth movement of his characters on- and offstage is, in fact, a special concern of Perrucci's which helps to explain the care with which, as we shall see, some of his Italian contemporaries regulated entrances and exits in their dramas. Too often, writes Perrucci, actors enter in scenes where they do not belong or, even worse, collide while entering with actors who are exiting, leaving the stage empty, the worst sin of all. Perrucci takes pride in his manner of avoiding such problems: a cue sheet posted backstage and an invariable regulation that exits take place from the front of the stage while those entering do so from the rear. As a writer with experience in both sung and spoken theater, Perrucci adds the interesting comment that it is easier to cover up accidents in spoken theater than in opera, where collisions, missed cues, and failures of the machinery are much more embarrassing. All Italian actors, says Perrucci, are trained in the art of improvisation, but since opera singers have not learned the art of improvised recitative, the only escape from many a dilemma lies in ordering the orchestra to play a standby piece of instrumental music and in pretending that one has thus reached the end of an act. One may, in such an event, continue later as if the opera had been divided into five acts instead of into three, or simply maintain the three-act structure and divide the acts at places other than those indicated in the libretto.[68] Perrucci clearly lacked confidence in the memories of his singers, and considered the dramatic structure of contemporary libretti less important than the preservation of theatrical decorum. With most of the libretti that Perrucci must have used before 1699 such a procedure would not have made so much difference as it would have with the more carefully and conventionally structured libretti of the period which followed Perrucci's publication. It is unfortunate that no similar record of practical advice has yet been discovered from the period of Zeno and Metastasio.

Perrucci's advice on the staging of operas extends to most of the favorite points of the Aristotelian commentators, whose opinions he rejects as old-fashioned and stultified. Despite his willingness to use five acts in emergencies, he warns against using more than three when drawing up a libretto, and accuses those who insist on using five of obstinate opposition to the tastes of the modern public.[69] It is tedious, says Perrucci, if after the first act one is still obliged to sit through another four. Three or at the very most four hours should be the absolute maximum for any theatrical production. Anything longer ". . . runs counter to the hectic press of modern society."[70] Nor is there any point in insisting, as do some, on the complete separation of tragic and comic characters, Perrucci considering it adequate simply not to use persons of humble birth (shepherds, nurses, servants, and the like) as the *principal* characters in a tragedy and to avoid comic scenes of the kind which he claims most librettists no longer use: those which involve the satirizing of such physical defects as blindness or stuttering.[71] The neo-Aristotelians' avoidance of more than one set change per act and their fondness for long monologues are also criticized.[72] Perrucci's irritation at the stuffy Aristotelians who "do not realize that Italian librettists could easily write Aristotelian tragedies if they chose to do so," is matched by his dislike for the operatic hegemony which Venetian librettists (he mentions Melosio, Sbarra, Morando, Moniglia, Aurelii, Noris, Bussani, Arcoleo, and Corradi) exercise over all the other cities of Italy.[73] Although Perrucci never speaks of "Venetian opera" as such, it is clear that he would have had no trouble understanding that term had he come across it in a nineteenth- or twentieth-century history of opera. Perrucci was no expert on the operatic history of even his own day, but the picture he presents of Venetian libretti setting a standard which the rest of Italy tried to imitate is probably meaningful. The number of operas first performed in Venice and altered "to suit local taste" that one finds in looking through repertories of non-Venetian opera houses of the late seventeenth century is impressive.

Crescimbeni

Much more concerned than Perrucci about French attacks on Italy's literary heroes was Giovanni Maria Crescimbeni, poet and historian, resident of Rome, and virtual dictator of the famous Arcadian Academy which he had been instrumental in founding.[74] Meeting officially for the first time on October 6, 1690, the 14 original Arcadians set out to show the world—and especially the French—that Italy's literary tradition, although once infected with marinism, was sound again and as capable of demonstrating what the French called good taste as any other national literature.[75] It had become a vogue during the 1680s for marinist lyric poets to discover the error of their ways, to burn their flowery erotic verses, and to vow to devote their poetic futures to didactic and moral (often dramatic) poetry for the spiritual betterment of all Italians. Such conservative moralists of the early 1700s as Muratori, Martello, Vico, Maffei, Manfredi, Lemene, Maggi, and Zeno all admitted to an unsavory, Marino-influenced past, and so did most of the original Arcadians.[76] Their aim was to restore and maintain an ever more flourishing state of Italian literature, but their means of accomplishing that objective seem strange. To flee from the complexities of contemporary life to the simple existence enjoyed by humble shepherds was no more novel an idea than the founding of yet another Italian academy, but the elaborate thoroughness with which the early Arcadians carried out some of their ideas certainly was. Dividing the Greek province of Arcadia into pastures, one for each of the shepherds, they all exchanged their normal names for pastoral ones, swore to abide by the 10 laws of the Academy, and rapidly began to absorb other academies all over Italy as Arcadian colonies. So successful were Crescimbeni's recruiting techniques and so attractive the idea of assuming an Arcadian name that by early in the eighteenth century Arcadia's pan-Italian membership gave it a position of power and prestige never enjoyed by any other Italian academy before or since. Unfortunately for the anticipated reform of Italian style and taste, too many of the early Arcadians were more intrigued with their pastoral names and costumes than with the implementation of their original program. Instead of directing their attention to simplicity and directness of style, they so outdid each other in inventing pastoral symbols and metaphors that by the beginning of the eighteenth century Arcadia had split into two groups: those for whom the Academy meant an opportunity for make-believe and for extending Marino-like poetic fancies into the pastoral world, and those who belonged to Arcadia simply as a matter of professional convenience.[77]

Although Crescimbeni himself was a poet of ambition, his mark on eighteenth-century Italian literature, apart from his role in Arcadia, was made through the publication of a long compilatory history of Italian poetry, whose first edition appeared in six bulky volumes in 1698. Of significance for the history of the libretto is the appearance at the end of the second volume of a short description of 50 living poets credited by Crescimbeni as leaders in the revival of Italian poetry. Five of the 50 described are poets who had already written opera libretti, and the libretti of four of the five are specifically included by Crescimbeni among works worthy of mention: Abate Alessandro Guidi is praised for his *L'Endimione* (a dramatic poem completed with the collaboration of Queen Christina), Girolamo Gigli for his "various dramas," Paolo de' Conti di Campello for his "dramatic works," and Silvio Stampiglia for the "several dramatic works he has published."[78] Since Crescimbeni tries to soothe the feelings of those not included in his list of 50 with the remark that other significant poets will be similarly treated in subsequent volumes, we should not attach undue importance to the position granted here to Guidi, Gigli, Paolo di Capello, Lemene, and Stampiglia. It is, however, the first list in a general history of Italian literature in which libretti are accepted as objects of esteem; the names of Gigli, Lemene, and Stampiglia will appear again and again on similar lists throughout the first half of the eighteenth century.

The second occasion on which Crescimbeni treats what he considers the recent improvement in the form and content of the libretto occurs just before the end of the sixth section of his *La bellezza della volgar poesia*, a slim volume of Arcadian dialogues first printed in Rome in 1700. In a long speech put into the mouth of Paolo di Campello's nephew, Francesco Maria di Campello, Crescimbeni states what seem to be his own views on the history of Italian opera:

LOG. The art of acting, which flourished in Italy during the 16th century, has been in a state of decline ever since Rinuccini wrote his first libretti to be set to music; but it continued to exist at least until Giacinto Andrea Cicognini introduced the melodramatic genre with his work, *Giasone*, the first and most perfect melodrama that we have. Through *Giasone* he brought about the downfall of the art of acting, and as a consequence also the demise of the true and good sort of comedy, and of tragedy itself. In order better to attract with novelty the indolent taste of those theater goers to whom the rudeness of the comic and seriousness of the tragic were equally repugnant, the inventor of melodramas (Cicognini) combined elements of both in his works, monstrously linking kings, heroes, and other illustrious persons with buffoons, servants, and characters of the most humble birth. The confounding of character types brought about the total ruin of the rules of poetry, which fell into such disuse that attention was no longer given to the art of tragic declamation which, forced to serve music, lost its purity and became full of idiocy. The orderly handling of the poetic figures which dignify declamation, now restricted for the most part to the normal and familiar manner of speech more suitable for music, was neglected; and, finally, a combination of the too frequent use of those short poems, popularly called arias, and the excessive impropriety of making a stage personage speak by singing, utterly removed from poetic compositions the power of the *affetti* and the means of stirring an audience. The same Cicognini also manufactured prose comedies which became so popular in Italian theaters that in the end they reduced the art of acting to conversing only with the lowest sorts of people in shop windows and in public squares. This unhappy state of affairs grew worse and worse all over Italy through the course of forty years or more. Singers succeeded actors with more success than actors had ever enjoyed, and won incredible benefits, favors, and riches. But in the end, as is happening in other branches of poetry, it seems at present as if Italy is beginning to open her eyes, and to recognize the uselessness which comes from having abandoned her old traditions. And although she still has not reclaimed true comedy, nonetheless, choosing the lesser of two evils, she has corrected many man-

ifestations of that monstrous mixing of character types practiced till now, managing
at least to establish entirely serious melodramas like those used today in the theaters
of Venice, which do not use comic characters and which, by diminishing the excessive
number of arias, allow some opportunity in the recitatives for the *affetti*. In this
enterprise our members, the late Osino (Domenico David) and the most learned
Emaro (Apostolo Zeno), have been prime movers, and therefore, the honor of the
achievement is principally theirs. In Rome we have seen the return of tragedy which,
as everyone knows, although without music and full of sadness, has been much
honored and applauded by all Rome, especially since *Stilicone* and other tragedies
translated from French by our good friend Solero (P. D. Felippo Merelli) appeared
at the Theater of the Collegio Clementino. But, more than to any other person, the
honor of having brought back good taste to Italy is owed to our much-acclaimed
Crateo (Cardinal Pietro Ottoboni), author of a fine pastorale, *Amore eroico tra i
pastori*, which was the first to concern itself once more with the old rules, introducing
choruses and other qualities pertaining to good comedy.

EG. Then essentially you condemn all melodramas.

LOG. For my part I not only have not condemned any, but confess with freedom that I
take no little pleasure in listening to them, especially those of our fellow shepherds
Palmone (Silvio Stampiglia), Tirinto (Count Giulio Bussi), Nardilo (Giovanni Andrea
Moniglia), Panopo (Giacomo Sinibaldi), Cromiro (Pietro Antonio Bernardoni), Me-
tisto (Carlo Sigismondo Capece), and Amaranto (Girolamo Gigli), which seem to me
rather better than all the others I have heard. I admit, however, that the person who
invented melodrama would have done better not to have invented it and to have left
the world as he found it.

EG. Excuse me, Logisto, but it seems to me that you are too scrupulous, too unyielding
on this subject. Now I understand why Lacone is so right in asserting that whoever
does not wish to complete a melodrama on which he is working had best submit it
to your criticism.

LOG. One certainly cannot label a man scrupulous or unyielding who reasonably condemns
that which is not praiseworthy.

LIC. But in naming the best authors of melodramas, why did you fail to mention your
uncle, Egilo? [Paolo di Capello]

LOG. Modesty was my guide.

LIC. Then let us mention him, Logisto, for not only ought Egilo to have an honored place
among such authors, but in my opinion he is the best among writers of heroic-comic
melodramas, since in his libretti of that variety, besides his use of jokes and witticisms
from the mine of Plautus, there is such artifice that the comic quality interferes in
no way with the heroic. In his libretti one sees two genres united, as can be discerned
from reading *Pandolfo, Mario in Cartagine, Amor vuol gioventù*, and other works
already performed.[79]

Of particular interest for our understanding of the history of the Italian libretto around the turn of the eighteenth century are Crescimbeni's words of praise for David and Zeno, pointing as they do to two specific librettists and to two very specific changes in libretto construction which Crescimbeni felt were of special importance for the establishment of a more serious musical theater in Italy: the elimination of comic characters and a reduction in the number of arias. Crescimbeni's comments on these libretti probably stem, at least in the case of Zeno's, from personal familiarity with the libretti, for there are two letters in the published correspondence of Zeno which show that, at just the time when, as newly appointed head of the Arcadian colony in Venice, Zeno was negotiating with Crescimbeni about pastoral names for all the new Venetian Arcadians, Crescimbeni must have asked him to send on copies of his libretti. On May 17, 1690, Zeno reported that a Venetian Arcadian named Marcippo was to take care of mailing the libretti, but two weeks later, on May 13, Zeno wrote again to say that he was about to forward the libretti himself.[80] Since Zeno made no critical comments on his libretti in either letter, and is not known on any occasion to have mentioned either of the points included in *La bellezza della volgar poesia*, one presumes that Crescimbeni's remarks about the dropping of comic figures and the diminished number of arias were the result of his own observations or of remarks made to Crescimbeni by persons whose familiarity with Venetian opera he trusted. They cannot possibly have resulted from a familiarity with the contemporary Venetian operatic repertory as a whole, for when one compares the libretti written by David and Zeno during the 1690s with those of their Venetian contemporaries, it is apparent that the characteristics mentioned by Crescimbeni are not distinguishing characteristics. Comic characters appear in two of the four historical libretti of Zeno which had been produced in Venice before May 31, 1698,[81] and in all three of the David libretti produced there before that date.[82] And there were poets other than Zeno and David who wrote libretti for Venice during the 1690s which, although they contain no comic characters, are not mentioned by Crescimbeni.[83]

There are two occasions in the published correspondence of Zeno on which his feelings about comic figures in the melodrama have been preserved, and in neither of them does he take what could be called a strong stand against them. In a letter to Antonfrancesco Marmi, dated February 24, 1703, Zeno comments on the addition to his *Griselda* (for performance in Florence later in 1703) of raucously comic scenes for an octogenarian nurse who is madly in love with a male servant less than half her age: "I have read *Griselda*, and am extraordinarily well pleased by the comic scenes which Signor Gigli has made for you with so much skill. They are of so little consequence" (NB: the eight comic scenes in the 1703 version comprise just less than 20 percent of the length of the entire work) "that they have not bothered me in the least, nor have they made the work appear different from the manner in which I first published it."[84] Nearly 15 years later, in a letter to Marchese Giorgio Clerici of Milan, dated January 22, 1718, Zeno describes the tasks required of him in the post of imperial poet he is about to undertake in Vienna: "I shall not be involved in any comic works, since I have neither talent nor inclination to test myself in that direction. I beg Your Excellency to intercede in order that I may be excused from any poetic commissions beyond my theatrical labors, since these latter would distract me from my principal charge and since I would not be able to bear the double burden."[85]

David, who died on June 30, 1698, was not able to reply to Crescimbeni's words of praise, but Zeno, who courteously thanked Crescimbeni in a letter dated November 6, 1700, for his complimentary copy of *La bellezza*, had nothing to say about Crescimbeni's remarks on the melodrama,[86] and went on to write at least three more works with roles for servants.[87]

What then of David's and Zeno's ostensible roles in "diminishing the excessive number of arias and thereby allowing some opportunity in the recitatives for the *affetti*"? Here, too, Crescimbeni's remarks represent half truths apparently based more on hearsay than on a thorough knowledge of the recent Venetian repertory. Because of the dearth of musical sources for Venetian opera during the 1690s, because some Venetian librettists were in the habit of introducing occasional rhymes into their recitatives while failing to distinguish as unambiguously as did their eighteenth-century successors between the metrical patterns used in recitative and aria, and because late seventeenth-century Venetian printers of libretti made little apparent effort to distinguish typographically between arias and recitatives, it is impossible to make absolutely accurate calculations about the number of arias in any single Venetian opera of the period. So long, however, as such figures are taken to be accurate only within three or four integers, and so long as one does not neglect differing numbers of scenes (a rough index for overall length) from work to work when comparing differing numbers of arias, it is possible to make some general observations on the aptness of Crescimbeni's tribute to David and Zeno. Table A presents appropriate figures for all operatic works performed in the public theaters of Venice during the decade prior to the death of David and to Zeno's shipment of his own libretti to Crescimbeni in Rome.

Table A

Year	Title	Librettist	Composer	Theater[a]	No. of Scenes	No. of Arias	Ratio
1688	La fortuna tra le disgrazie	Cialli	Biego	A	49	42	.9
	Il Gordiano	Morselli	Gabrielli	B	44	48	1.1
	L'inganno regnante	Corradi	M. A. Ziani	C	56	55	<1.
	Orazio	?	G. F. Tosi	D	53	60	1.1
	La Corilda	"diversi"	A. F. Rossi	E	45	54	1.2
	Amazone corsara	Corradi	Pallavicino	C	53	61	1.1
	La pena degli occhi	?	A. F. Rossi	E	43	39	.9
	Carlo il Grande	Morselli	Gabrielli	D	59	58	<1.
1689	Il gran Tamerlano	Corradi	M. A. Ziani	C	51	52	>1.
	Amulio	Morselli	G. F. Tosi	D	52	57	1.1
	Il pertinance	?	Biego	B	47	53	1.1
	La Rosaura	Arcoleo	G. A. Perti	A	50	47	.9
	Le gare dell'inganno	P. E. Badi	Orgiani	E	58	65	<1.1
	La fortuna tra le disgrazie	Cialli	Biego	B	49	48	<1.
	Il trionfo d'amor	Badi	A. Lombardini	E	45	31	.7
	L'Argene	Badi	A. Caldara	G	41	40	<1.
1690	Pirro e Demetrio	Morselli	Tosi	D	40	50	1.3
	Brenno in Effeso	Arcoleo	Perti	B	53	53	1.
	L'amor di Curzio	Corradi	Algisi	C	55	53	<1.
	La Falsirena	Cialli	M. A. Ziani	A	47	54	1.1
	Il gran Macedone	Pancieri	Boniventi	F	50	72	1.4
	Trionfo della continenza	Corradi	Algisi	C	42	46	1.1
	Creonte	Cialli	M. A. Ziani	A	51	45	.9
1691	L'incoronazione di Xerse	Morselli	Tosi	D	41	48	1.2
	L'Almerinda	Pancieri	Boniventi	F	45	50	1.1
	L'inganno scoperto	Silvani	Perti	B	38	48	1.3

Year	Title	Librettist	Composer	Theater[a]	No. of Scenes	No. of Arias	Ratio
	L'Alboino	Corradi	Tosi & Pollarolo	C	42	53	1.3
	Marte deluso	Cialli	M. A. Ziani	A	45	52	1.2
	L'amante eroe	David	M. A. Ziani	B	52	47	.9
	La pace fra Tolomeo e Sel.	Morselli	C. F. Pollarolo	D	46	45	<1.
	La virtù trionfante	Silvani	M. A. Ziani	B	42	49	1.2
	L'Almira	Pancieri	Boniventi	C	44	57	1.3
1692	*L'Ibraim Sultano*	Morselli	C. F. Pollarolo	D	47	55	1.2
	Furio Camillo	Noris	Perti	B	50	53	>1.
	La Gelidaura	?	F. Quesdna	C	41	51	>1.2
	L'oppresso sollevato	?	G. Sebenico	C	37	64	1.7
	Onorio in Roma	Giannini	C. F. Pollarolo	D	54	46	.9
	La Rosalinda	Marchi	M. A. Ziani	A	64	51	.8
	Jole regina di Napoli	Corradi	C. F. Pollarolo	C	48	45	.9
1693	*La forza della virtù*	David	C. F. Pollarolo	D	47	46	<1.
	Il trionfo dell'innocenza	Cialli	A. Lotti	A	45	49	1.1
	Nerone	Noris	Perti	B	57	50	.9
	Gl'avvenimenti d'Erminia	Corradi	C. F. Pollarolo	C	52	51	<1.
	La fede creduta tradimento	M. A. Gasparini	G. Frezza	E	41	48	1.2
	Amage regina	Corradi	C. F. Pollarolo	A	49	51	>1.
1694	*Ottone*	Frigimelica	C. F. Pollarolo	D	40	69	1.7
	La moglie nemica	Silvani	M. A. Ziani	B	44	50	1.1
	L'amore figlio	Noris	M. A. Ziani	A	51	52	>1.
	Zenobia	Marchi	Albinoni	C	66	51	.8
	Alfonso Primo	Noris	C. F. Pollarolo	B	47	37	.8
	La schiavitù fortunata	Gualazzi	C. F. Pollarolo	A	43	43	1.
	Irene e Costantino	Frigimelica	C. F. Pollarolo	D	40	52	1.3

Year	Title		Composer				
1695	*Laodicea*	Noris	Perti	B	60	56	.9
	Prencipe selvaggio	Silvani	M. A. Gasparini	A	55	43	.8
	Il prodigo dell'innocenza	Gualazzi	Albinoni	C	44	53	1.2
	Il pastor d'Anfriso	Frigimelica	C. F. Pollarolo	D	37	59	1.6
	Rosimonda	Frigimelica	C. F. Pollarolo	D	40	48	1.2
	Gl'inganni felici	Zeno	C. F. Pollarolo	A	53	53	1.
1696	*La finta pazzia*	Noris	M. A. Ziani	B	48	58	1.2
	Basilio re d'Oriente	Neri	Navarra	F	43	53	1.2
	Sigismondo Primo	Grimani	Pignata	C	32	45	1.4
	Il Domizio	Corradi	M. A. Ziani	A	56	50	.9
	Ercole in cielo	Frigimelica	C. F. Pollarolo	D	41	49	1.2
	Eraclea	Godi	Sabadini	B	43	42	<1.
	L'Aamiro re	Pignata	Pignata	C	44	43	<1.
1696	*La costanza in trionfo*	Silvani	M. A. Ziani	A	43	41	<1.
	Zenone	Marchi	Albinoni	F	57	44	.8
	Il Tirsi	Zeno	"diversi"	B	41	49	1.2
	La Marianne	Burlini	Ruggieri	C	51	64	<1.3
1697	*Amor e Dover*	David	C. F. Pollarolo	D	46	40	< .9
	Erfile	Neri	Ariosti	B	47	44	.9
	Il Tigrane	Corradi	Albinoni	F	52	52	1.
	La forza d'amore	Burlini	C. F. Pollarolo	C	41	42	>1.
	Tito Manlio	Noris	C. F. Pollarolo	D	46	34	> .7
	I regi equivoci	Noris	C. F. Pollarolo	A	45	45	1.
	I rivali generosi	Zeno	M. A. Ziani	B	44	39	.9
	La promessa serbata	"diversi"	Caldara	C	47	47	1.
	Primislao Primo	Corradi	Albinoni	F	47	49	>1.
	Circe	Aureli	C. F. Pollarolo	C	46	42	.9
	Eumene	Zeno	M. A. Ziani	A	57	44	.8

Year	Title	Librettist	Composer	Theater[a]	No. of Scenes	No. of Arias	Ratio
1698	*L'ingratitudina castigata*	Silvani	Albinoni	F	35	38	< 1.1
	Marzio Coriolano	Noris	C. F. Pollarolo	D	49	38	.8
	Odoardo	Zeno	M. A. Ziani	A	52	38	> .7
	Tito Manlio	Noris	C. F. Pollarolo	D	47	34	> .7
	Camilla regina	Stampiglia	M. A. Bononcini	B	44	31	> .7
	L'Egisto re	Corradi	M. A. Ziani	F	47	48	> 1.
	Radamisto	Marchi	Albinoni	A	49	38	< .8
	La saggia pazzia	L. Lotti	Ruggieri	C	44	40	.9

a. The names of the theaters have been replaced by the following symbols:

A—Sant 'Angelo
B—San Salvatore
C—S. S. Giovanni e Paolo
D—San Giovanni Grisostomo
E—San Moise
F—San Cassiano
G—alli Saloni

On the basis of the figures in Table A one can state unequivocally that during the period in question neither David nor Zeno was in any way remarkable for an exceptionally low number of arias, either absolutely or in terms of the number of arias per scene. In the works of both poets there is a general decrease in the number of arias, both absolutely and in proportion to each libretto as a whole, but neither decrease is any more marked than in the cases of several other poets not mentioned by Crescimbeni and of no reputation as "reform" librettists. The general decrease is not connected with settings by specific composers or with works performed in specific theaters, but seems to be a general trend of the period, at least in Venice.

Although Crescimbeni made no changes of any consequence in his comments on recent operatic history in any of the subsequent editions of either *L'istoria della volgar poesia* or *La bellezza della volgar poesia*, he did add a good deal of new material in the chapter on opera included in the first volume of the supplement to his general history, *Comentarii intorno alla sua istoria della volgar poesia*. In this work, after repeating both the customary complaint about the evil effects wrought on Italian literature by the degeneracy of Italian libretti during the second half of the seventeenth century and the by now familiar view that conditions had finally begun to improve, Crescimbeni discusses in more detail than before his ideas on the ingredients of that improvement. The immoderate use of "arias whose insignificant length adds so much to the musical interest of a work but which are so injurious to its poetic eloquence" has begun to abate, as has the too frequent use of set changes. The ends of acts are still too often indicated by *intermezzi* and *balli* instead of by choruses, but in recent years, especially in Rome and Venice, poets have begun turning back more and more to the chorus, used in the Greek manner as a commentator outside the frame of the dramatic action. More attention has been given of late to restricting the action of each drama within reasonable temporal limits and, although the traditional operatic three-act division is still prevalent, some poets have turned back to the Aristotle-approved division into five acts. This time Crescimbeni calls for the early arrival of a savior for Italian dramatic poetry; he does not mention either David or Zeno, but stresses the dramatic merits lately to be found in the "favola pastorale," particularly in Cardinal Pietro Ottoboni's *Adonia*, "composed with the best antique taste and heard privately" (no doubt in Rome) "with the music of five of Italy's best composers, each of whom set one of the five acts into which the work is divided."[88]

Crescimbeni, then, is a critic of what he considers the operatic excesses initiated by Cicognini, but by no means an unalterable opponent of musical drama. He recognizes that the poetry which is most easily set to music is apt to violate what he considers the tenets of poetic good taste, but does not hesitate either to commend those Arcadians whom he considers successful as musical poets or even to undertake the composition of such poetry himself.[89] In the course of his writings on Italian literature Crescimbeni touches repeatedly on the subject of opera, crediting more than a dozen Arcadians with the composition of libretti which in one respect or another have brought about at least a partial *rapprochement* between the realities of the modern musical theater and the Aristotelian ideals for which he thinks it ought to strive. It is significant that Crescimbeni's praise goes only to Arcadians even though, as we have seen, the libretti of other non-Arcadian poets show some of the same attributes which Crescimbeni is so pleased to observe in the works of his fellow "shepherds." Arcadia's position of power and prestige in eighteenth-century Italy was impressive, but patriotism and an interest in the return of good taste to Italian literature were by no means Arcadian monopolies, as Crescimbeni seems to have thought. Andrea Perrucci, whose knowledge of operatic history was jumbled and confused but who, as an operatic impresario must have had a much more intimate knowledge of opera during the 1690s than did Crescimbeni, mentioned in 1699 that Venetian libertti had recently begun to reduce the number of their arias, but did not single out any individual librettist for special mention. For Crescimbeni "aria" meant an unnecessary thought in a disruptingly different metrical form which, when read, was redundant and often so altered by the composer as to become incomprehensible as poetry, destroyed dramatic tension when heard in the theater. For Perrucci "aria" meant something quite different: a popular (and, hence, indispensable) part of the theater whose number per work became excessive only when extending an opera beyond the length which an audience could endure without boredom.

Muratori

Crescimbeni's view on arias was shared by another early Arcadian critic of Italian opera, L. A. Muratori, whose treatise on the reform of Italian poetry, *Della perfetta poesia italiana*, appeared in 1706, but whose correspondence with Zeno had included, for several years before, a running dialogue on libretti. The most conservative of the operatic critics thus far encountered, Muratori longed for the return to Italy of tragedy and comedy modelled on his own conception of theater in ancient Greece—spoken dialogue with austerely simple, unaccompanied vocal music used only in the unison choruses which closed each act. But he was enough of a realist to know that opera had become too popular in Italy to permit its replacement by anything so stark as his own ideal. So he did not demand the elimination of opera, but pleaded instead that the balance of its constituent elements be redressed. Music should step back somewhat from its position of dictatorial absolutism and should, in a much simpler form, aim at a total dramatic effect by supporting, wherever possible, the intentions of both poet and scenographer.[90]

Muratori wrote no libretti of his own, devoting his energies to exhaustive histories of Italian literature and to his duties as librarian of the Duke of Modena. But, at least before the publication of *Della perfetta poesia*, Apostolo Zeno seems to have held his critical judgment on libretti in special esteem, and there is a good deal one can learn from studying that portion of the Zeno–Muratori correspondence which deals with libretti. The first letter of interest is addressed by Muratori to Zeno from Milan and dated May 20, 1699:

> Let us be frank, Sir. You have acquired great honor among poets with your noble dramas that please me so exceedingly, but now it appears that you have made a great step forward, penetrated even to Parnassus, so that before long you will be able to claim that crown which till now no Italian has attained. *Faramondo* is an exquisite drama, and even though it is difficult to be brief while satisfying the demands of the singers and thousands of other obstacles with which the French do not have to contend, you have fulfilled the demands of both poetry and drama. I rejoice exceedingly with you, with your epoch, and with the world. You will cultivate this rare talent and I am confident that you will be even better in the future. Sir, your manner of writing and your intellect seem to me most fortunate, with regard both to the strong feelings and to the characters you have used in *Faramondo*, even beyond those used by the French. I wish that you would undertake a drama, or rather a tragedy, without the obligation of actually staging it, for I know you would produce a splendid result. In such a work you would be able to construct with greater ease those plots which now are suffocated by the necessity of having to be brief and which, therefore, are often in part improbable. Our friend Maggi does not approve of the modern taste for so much complication of plot and is better satisfied with the purity of the ancients, of the kind often used by Corneille—I specify Peter because the other (Thomas) usually proceeds differently. I do not altogether agree with this opinion, since the construction of an involved plot in a verisimilar manner is undoubtedly worthy of greater praise. And this one certainly owes to *Faramondo*, for the gift of which I send you, Sir, a thousand thanks for having pleased me so extraordinarily.[91]

Although Zeno thought less and less of his earliest libretti as he grew older—so little, in fact, that in later years he did not even wish to recognize two of the six texts which had preceded *Faramondo* as his own works[92]—it is clear that between 1695 and 1699 he had already acquired a reputation as one of those dedicated to the new goals towards which some poets had begun to direct the Italian libretto. One sees from what is preserved of Zeno's correspondence during the 1690s that while he did his best to please the operatic impresarios and their public, his libretti were directed as well to an audience whose pleasure came from studying them at home—a dual purpose which contrasts strikingly with the ideals pursued by most of the other famous librettists in the history of opera, but a state of mind characteristic of serious Italian librettists from the end of the seventeenth century through the death of Metastasio. The best librettists before Zeno and after about 1780 have usually been so aware of the extent to which an ideal text for music differs from a text intended for performance in the spoken theater that they have been loath to see their works considered apart from the opera house. There are collected editions for the libretti of Moneglia,[93] Bernardoni,[94] Gigli,[95] Silvani,[96] and even several "complete" editions for those of Zeno[97] and Metastasio,[98] but nothing of the sort for Aureli, da Ponte, Piave, or Illica, to mention only a few of the better known librettists over the course of Italian operatic history.

That libretti of literary aspiration were being written in Italy before any of the works of David or Zeno and before the founding of the Arcadian Academy in 1690 is evident from the preface to an opera produced in Florence during 1689, *La serva favorita*, a work whose author clearly resents what he considers the pretentious airs displayed in the libretti of some of his contemporaries:

> If the censors of *belles lettres* severely punished any person of mature age who read Italian poetry, as Boccalini tells us, what would they have done had they found someone *reading* the libretto for an opera? This genre is designed to be heard in a different context, and poetry is required to clothe it with various defects in order to make them appear, in their proper context, like so many virtues, precisely in the manner of those painters who design in one plane what they wish to have appear as a three-dimensional image. And for this reason the more famous poets, in those of their works which are intended for musical setting, make a note of their intention, in order that the reader may know how these words are supposed to reach the ears of the public. Would it not be absurd if Aristarchus were to try to judge a distant painting with a microscope? The artifices of one variety of poetry are errors in another. A person who wished to use the lyric style in writing an epic, or epic style in writing a text for music, would surely commit a serious mistake. There are, for this reason, many muses—and they do not all play the same instrument.[99]

Zeno himself differentiated between what is effective in print and what makes sense in a musical setting on the stage as early as his apologetic preface to *Il Tirsi* (1696) for the literary sins he felt he had committed in that work:

> The style with which I have made the actors speak I have tried to make easier, not more ornamental; with respect to the sentiments expressed I have affected tenderness

of expression rather than unusualness of conception. In this manner I have adapted myself both to the nature of my shepherds and to the low estate of my own talent. Many things which when read will seem to you either too vulgar or hardly necessary to the story, will perhaps in the theater itself seem more pleasant because of the music, and more marvelous because of the machinery.[100]

Although Zeno and several of his contemporaries tried to achieve equal degrees of literary and popular success by writing libretti whose character developments and plots would be complicated enough and whose style dignified enough to please Arcadian tastes, but understandable enough on the stage not to antagonize the theatrical public, they realized that some of their works were more successful for one group than for the other. Muratori[101] and the author of a review in the *Giornale dei letterati d'Italia*[102] agreed that the dramas of Pier-Jacopo Martello were too complicated for the stage but of the greatest profit for the study of "intelletti," while in a letter of November 12, 1721, to Giuseppe Bini, Zeno expressed the fear that his drama *Ormisda* depended too heavily on the effects of scenery and staging to be as impressive as he had hoped when read in private.[103] In sending his comic *Don Chisciotte nella Sierra Morena* to Marchese Rangone, Pietro Pariati apologizes that ". . . this sort of composition is more effective when performed than when read,"[104] while Zeno writes of precisely the same work that it should give as much pleasure when read as when performed.[105]

But if the printing of single libretti was intended for two audiences, the publication of complete and collected editions was directed towards the litterateurs alone. The *da capo*-indicating addition under an aria of its first word or line was an almost unvarying characteristic of Venetian libretti after 1700, but in the collected editions these traces of music's formative influence on poetry were eradicated, as were all references to composers, scenographers, ballet masters, singers, and the like.[106] Neither Zeno nor Metastasio ever went so far as to eliminate any of the aria texts in the collected editions of their works, but there was a persistent undercurrent of literary opinion which speculated throughout the eighteenth century on the degree to which one could strengthen the best libretti by reducing or eliminating altogether the role of the aria and by expanding the scenes wherein strong emotions and noble characterizations played an important role. Zeno, no doubt encouraged by men like Muratori and Marchese Poleni,[107] certainly toyed with such an idea from time to time, particularly with regard to his oratorio texts,[108] and so, it would appear, did Metastasio.[109]

Muratori's already quoted letter on Zeno's *Faramondo* would have evoked sneers and cat calls from most Venetian opera goers, but Zeno's own interest in questions of plot, characterization, style, and the emulation of French tragedians like Corneille and Racine was stimulated by it, for in his note to Muratori of March 12, 1701, we find the explicit request for more such advice:

> Whatever be the judgment of those gentlemen on my drama, I am really glad to know that they have decided to restage *I rivali generosi* rather than risk uncertain success with *Aminta*, a labor of fresh inspiration which is not yet finished. I wish to complete it with as much perfection as I possibly can. But before that it would be both to my profit and to my pleasure to have your considered opinion of the work. I beg you to advise me without any scruple about whatever you find defective or wanting in it, either with regard to development or style, in order that by reforming my own weakness with the guidance of your most purified understanding I can allow my work to appear with less embarrassment under the eyes of his Serene Highness, at whose command it was conceived and shaped.[110]

Here once more Zeno returns, not to the question of a libretto using fewer arias and without comic characters, but to the problem of writing libretti in which both scenario and dialogue are more artfully developed. This is, in fact, Zeno's principal concern during his career as a librettist, the subject to which he returns whenever, in later years, he is asked to criticize the text of another poet.[111] We do not know whether Muratori ever offered the criticism on *Aminta* which Zeno had requested; but we do have the first use of the word "reform" in the Zeno–Muratori correspondence when, on July 15, Muratori writes to Zeno about his own latest literary project:

> At present I am working on that project of mine about which, on another occasion, I showed you a good deal of literary material. . . . I would like to demonstrate good taste in Italian poetry, and perhaps I shall end by entitling the work with a haughty line like "The Reform of Italian Poetry," aiming not only at praising and at defending but also at correcting the failings of our colleagues, for the profit of the young and of those who will follow us. With such a plan I shall examine the French Parnassus, and shall pay back, but without impertinence, those impertinences spoken of us by others.[112]

On July 23 Zeno replied that, looking forward to the completion of the work described in Muratori's previous letter, he fully approves the use of the term "reform," especially since modern criticism has shown itself so useful to Italian literature. But while criticism of Italy by Italians is proper, Zeno, like so many of his contemporaries, resents criticism from beyond the Alps:

> The French are worthy of your lashes: Rapin, Bouhours, Saint-Evremond, and others have with too much liberty made tribunals of themselves to pass judgment on our writers and on our works, which for the most part, to speak dispassionately, they understand very little or badly.[113]

Shortly thereafter Muratori must have asked Zeno for his opinion on contemporary libretti, for in a letter to Muratori during August, Zeno included those sentences which Muratori was to use so devastatingly five years later as the climax to his case against opera:

> To state sincerely my feelings about libretti, although I have written many of them, I would be the first to condemn them. Long experience has taught me that unless one uses many abuses, one misses the primary goal of such compositions—that is, pleasure. The more one wishes to insist on the rules, the more one displeases. And if the libretto is praised, the theater has little business.[114]

A month later Zeno reinforces that view with two sentences in the midst of another letter to Muratori, dated September 30:

> Whatever may be your judgment on libretti, do not worry about what some of those miserable poetasters will have to say about it. Utter it securely with that liberty which is fitting for gallant men of literary affairs.[115]

Five years later Muratori's book finally appeared in print under the title *Della perfetta poesia italiana*, and Apostolo Zeno, by that time well on his way towards the honorary title, "reformer of the libretto," wrote to Muratori thanking him for having printed the excerpt just quoted from Zeno's letter of August 1701:

> ". . . it serves me as a public apology against the criticisms of those who either do not understand the business of writing libretti or who think that they understand it too well.[116]

Public apology it may have been, but despite the bitter attacks on Italian tastes initiated in 1705 by the French journalists of Trévoux, and despite Zeno's prominent role in defending Italy against those attacks,[117] there was no slackening in his production of opera libretti. Between the beginning of Zeno's career as a librettist in 1696 and the 1706 publication of his letter against libretti in Muratori's treatise, Zeno had written at least 15 libretti, and he equalled that output during the decade which followed, if one counts the works on which he collaborated during that period with Pietro Pariati.[118] Muratori's essay was intended for an audience which looked askance at the world of opera and whose good opinion Zeno valued. But Zeno held no regular position in Venice and was in constant need of funds, not only for the support of his family but also for the proper pursuit of his expensive antiquarian interests in the collection of inscriptions, coins, rare books, and manuscripts. It was a need which even during the later 1690s Zeno discovered he could most easily supply through the composition of occasional libretti, but though he struggled throughout his career as a librettist to improve the literary quality of his works, he never overcame his embarrassment at earning his livelihood in a manner which he felt compromised his integrity as a writer and degraded him in the eyes of his literary compatriots.[119]

This curiously ambivalent attitude with respect to his own libretti was characteristic of Zeno, even during his final 20 years when, after 1729, he was able to retire to the antiquarian studies which interested him most. We have already seen that during the earliest part of his career he did not shrink from requesting Muratori's criticism of his libretti, but nonetheless wrote Muratori a letter condemning the genre in which he excelled, and claimed to be delighted when Muratori later published that letter. During the first decade of the eighteenth century he twice turned down offers from Vienna which would have made him imperial poet, first under Leopold I and then under Joseph I, being reluctant on both occasions to separate himself from the scene of his literary endeavors in Venice and to see his name connected in so official a way with the composition of libretti.[120] But after nearly a decade as principal editor of Italy's most important literary journal of his day, *Il Giornale dei letterati d'Italia*, he enthusiastically accepted a third offer from Vienna in 1717 to serve under Charles VI.[121] After refusing the title of First Imperial Poet in order not to offend his old friend Pariati, who had preceded him to Vienna and on whose assistance he counted for the completion of unwanted theatrical assignments, Zeno began to intrigue for the title of Imperial Poet *and Historian*, a designation he considered "more honorable and advantageous."[122] But he was nonetheless eager for the success of his libretti in Vienna, and even to his literary friends in Italy he reported with pride the praise that Charles VI and the court showered on his earliest works there.[123]

In Vienna there were no impresarios and no meanly educated public to satisfy as there had been in Italy. The ruling emperor and empress alone settled on the choice of libretto subject, and passed at successive stages on the acceptability of the scenario, the libretto, and the musical setting; the audience permitted to attend court performances was personally approved by them as well. Such was the confidence of Charles VI and his consort, Elizabeth Christine, in the judgment and ability of Apostolo Zeno that after his arrival in Vienna this traditional method of Habsburg control was lifted.[124] Charles VI was, moreover, a man of broad education and refined tastes. Fluent in Latin, Italian, Spanish, and French as well as German, a particular student of mathematics and architecture, an avid collector of books and manuscripts, a composer capable of directing any of the operas staged in his theaters, patron of Arcadia's Viennese colony,[125] Charles VI fully approved of nobility of character and seriousness of plot in the libretti Zeno wrote for his court.[126] So long as Zeno satisfied Habsburg custom by making it clear that the hero or heroine of each libretto personified virtues which characterized the Habsburger whose birth- or name-day was being celebrated,[127] he could be as antiquely serious as he pleased. The amorous intrigues which had assumed primary importance in Zeno's Italian productions were replaced by conflicts between such forces as a woman's chastity and the protection of her child, loyalty to state and devotion to family, or preservation of the principle of primogeniture and the fortune of a preferred younger son. Nor was there, as in Italy, any necessity of brevity, since Charles placed no limits on the length of works performed under his auspices; he is actually quoted by Zeno as having said that the longer the opera, the greater his pleasure.[128] Perrucci had written in 1699 that three to four hours was the maximum length for any opera in Italy,[129] but in Vienna works of five or six hours were not unusual.[130] The custom of using quotation mark-like indications, known as *virgolette*, to preserve a librettist's text in print while notifying the reader where the text had been cut for performance, was common all over Italy during the last quarter of the seventeenth century. It had been introduced in Vienna at the turn of the century, after the deaths of Minato and Draghi,[131] but it was never used there during the reign of Charles VI. The complete absence of *virgolette* in the libretti printed in Vienna between 1712 and 1740, the attention of the composers who set the libretti to making absolutely complete settings of the texts they received,[132] the absence of cuts in the numerous performing parts which survive from the period in question, and the almost exact correspondence between individual libretti and those versions of the same libretti which later appeared in collected editions of works by Zeno and Metastasio, all indicate that there was little tampering during Charles's reign with the texts submitted by his poets.

Once Zeno had reached Vienna in 1718 he was, in fact, freed from the limitations and restrictions about whose existence in Italy he and Muratori had complained with such vehemence earlier. But despite the constant praise he received from Charles[133] and despite the considerable income and prestige that his Vienna position assured him, the ever-recurring thought that the writing of even the most esteemed libretti was an unworthy career for a man of serious literary intent finally helped drive Zeno to petition Charles for retirement.[134] Once he had been definitely replaced in Vienna by Metastasio and had returned to Venice for good in the fall of 1731, Zeno continued through 1737 to write an annual oratorio text for Vienna, but after his completion of *Cajo Fabbricio* during the fall of 1729, he never again considered work on a secular text.

Although embarrassed apologies for his long concern with secular libretti appear in his letters during the later 1720s like a refrain, in the fall of 1730 he wrote a long letter to a Marchese Gravisi of Capodistria, disputing the very judgment of Muratori on opera that Zeno had praised so unreservedly a quarter of a century earlier:

Signor Muratori's book, *Della perfetta poesia*, truly contains the best precepts and will always be useful for anyone who reads it carefully. On the subject of musical dramas he is right to become heated, but I fear that passion led him to say too much. I could certainly write much of interest on this subject, drawn from truth and from experience, but since such a discussion would require a little time, which for the moment I do not have, I shall restrain myself till another more opportune occasion. For now I shall say only that although I condemn musical dramas as irregular tragedies, I cannot resolve myself to call them, as did Signor Muratori, "monstrous unions of a thousand improbabilities," at least if we consider them in the manner that they have been treated by several worthy poets of recent times. I would be unjust if I were proudly to inveigh against a type of composition with which I have acquired a little reputation and a great deal of profit in both Italy and Germany, not to speak of the approval with which my works have been received by the greatest monarch of the world, by his illustrious court, and generally by all the princes of Italy—a statement I can make to you openly and without fear of boasting. The goal which Signor Muratori proposed in his book was the reform of Italian poetry, and a very excellent and laudable goal it is. In speaking of musical dramas he regards them as a variety of poetry which, because of its monstrousness, is incapable of reform—an opinion in which, I repeat, I think he errs in part. He would have been pleased to see (opera) driven altogether from the public stage. It would have been better had he moderated so severe a sentence. And perhaps, had he been obliged to write today on this subject, he would have shown himself less cruel a judge. When, in fact, I was in Modena last June, he was kind enough to urge me to collect and to revise both my secular and sacred dramas, and to publish them in a collected edition; and, making me believe in his regard for me, he tried to urge that they could be useful to the public in some manner and could open an approach to the regulation of musical dramas. There are, of course, a great many improbable things in musical dramas, but some of these stem from the necessity and the nature of the genre, such as the frequent changes of scenery. For these and for similar difficulties there is no remedy. But other problems derive from the insufficient care of the poet, who preserves neither the unity of action, nor the conformity of the characters, nor the decorum of the tragic stage, nor the purgation of the *affetti*, nor the movement of these to compassion or to terror, nor the proprieties of a dramatic development and of an untying of the dramatic knot that is adjusted to good rules. These evils can and ought to be removed from the musical theater and to these one would have to address the remedy for any commendable reform. If your excellency has ever read a libretto free in whole or in part from such detrimental attributes, and if in reading it you have felt yourself moved by that emotion which is usually awakened by tragic compositions, preserve that love for the work with which you have previously regarded it, and do not call it so quickly "a hateful monster of poetry." It is true that on modern stages of every order and condition there excessively prevails an effeminate passion—love—without which it appears that no plausible drama can be written. I, too, am of the opinion that this is very offensive and that there ought to be some compensating passion. But the evil is that such spectacles are made at the expense of private impresarios, who do not put them on for the public free of charge but in order to make good their expenses and to return a profit. The greatest business today comes from those who understand least and from the gentler sex, in whom the weakest *affetti* make an impression more strongly. They *could* be undeceived, but it is a difficult business and hazardous for the impressarios. *Merope* of Signor Maffei is the only work in my day that I have seen achieve the miracle of pleasing everybody without any admixture of amorous interests. My own *Merope*, which existed before Maffei's, uses love only in passing, as an episodic interest, but nonetheless pleased exceedingly, as did *Ifigenia* and several other dramas of mine in which not the effeminate but the strong and noble *affetti* are those which move the soul. And this is the reason why I nourish more affection for my oratorios, in which I preserve the unities of place, action, and time as well as nobility of characterization to such an extent that I could reduce them to good tragedies, rendering them free from the requirements of the music with which they have to be performed in the imperial chapel. But now it is time that I close this rambling statement, which turned out to be longer than I had in the beginning anticipated.[135]

One infers from this letter that Gravisi must have asked Zeno to evaluate his career as a librettist and to comment on the view of opera put forward by Muratori in his publication of 1706. Since it would have been senseless for a poet who wished to draw a full salary in retirement for nothing more substantial than an annual oratorio text to have belittled the libretti which had so endeared him to Charles, the letter to Gravisi cannot be taken as an absolutely candid reflection of Zeno's views on opera. But it is important as the longest extant summary of those views.

In the preface to the 1735 collected edition of his oratorio texts (dedicated to Charles and to Elizabeth Christine) Zeno asserted the superiority of his Viennese works to those he had written before moving to Vienna. He attributed the improvement to the inspiration of Habsburg honor and virtue, and to the opportunity provided him in Vienna to abandon caricatures of the noble heroes of antiquity in favor of such dramatic motives as ". . . maturity of council in difficult affairs, magnanimity in the granting of pardons, moderation in prosperous times, fortitude in adverse circumstances, constancy in friendship and in conjugal love, courage in relieving the innocent, and generosity in treating the destitute."[136] Charles VI obviously enjoyed the dignity which Zeno's less love-centered plots lent to the prestige of Habsburg opera, but the musical arias and scenery changes which Zeno describes as inevitable problems stemming from the nature of opera were evidently features which Charles considered indispensable. Attention to the Aristotelian unities (especially that of action), reasonableness of dramatic development, and an approach wherever possible to the appearance and impact of spoken tragedy were the goals at which Zeno aimed, goals which he felt he and others had at least in part achieved. Although Zeno implies that both he and Muratori preferred his later, more serious works to those which Muratori included in his criticisms of 1706, Zeno's criticisms of Muratori suggest that he had been more offended by the operatic section of *Della perfetta poesia italiana* than he had ever previously admitted.

The career of a writer who could turn a handsome profit from a genre which both he and his most valued friends believed destroyed any basis for serious theater was clearly the cause of misgivings on Zeno's part which no effort to deepen the content of his libretti could eliminate. One sees these misgivings in his hesitancy to publish the collected edition of his works which by 1730 even Muratori had proposed,[137] and in his apparent insistence in 1744 that Gasparo Gozzi, the eventual editor of that edition, insert in his preface the quotation from the 1701 letter to Muratori which Zeno had long since repudiated in his letter of 1730 to Gravisi.[138] The libretti which contributed so much to Zeno's fame and fortune during his lifetime were, in fact, an embarrassment which followed him even to the grave. In a funeral oration delivered in Venice two weeks after Zeno's death on November 11, 1750, Antonio Valsechi praised Zeno's contributions to Italian nationalism, the painstaking nature of his scholarship, and the nobility of his character, but after criticizing him for having wasted so much of his life with the composition of libretti, finally absolved Zeno's sins by quoting his 1701 condemnation of all libretti from the familiar passage in Muratori's *Della perfetta poesia italiana*.[139]

Gravina

The severity of Muratori's criticism of musical theater in Italy during the early years of the eighteenth century was surpassed by an Italian only in Gianvincenzo Gravina's 1715 publication on tragedy. But because Gravina combined extreme views with liberal doses of self-adulation and had isolated himself from most of literary Italy by publicly breaking in 1711 with Crescimbeni's Arcadia, his later works stimulated more antagonism than admiration. They failed to make an impression not only on the librettists of Gravina's day but even on the future of his adopted son who, after Gravina's death in 1718, became the most famous librettist of the century, Pietro Metastasio.[140]

Gravina had not always been so outspoken a critic of opera. Twenty-five years before his book on tragedy he had in fact written an essay in support of a musical pastorale entitled *L'Endimione*, whose text by Alessandro Guidi had been completed with the collaboration of Queen Christina and performed in Rome during the summer of 1691 at a meeting of the early Arcadians.[141] In the essay published in both the Rome and Amsterdam editions of *L'Endimione* that appeared in 1692, Gravina defended those features of the work which he was certain would be opposed by Aristotelian fundamentalists: the use of love as a central dramatic idea, the poet's willingness to alter a well-known myth to suit his own dramatic purposes, the absence of dramatic development resulting from a cast of only three characters, and the poet's failure to distinguish between comedy and tragedy.[142] Curiously enough, the only idea in Aristotle's *Poetics* which Gravina eagerly defended in his *L'Endimione* essay was a point from which most Arcadian dramatists would have strongly dissented: the use of characters whose conduct is neither black nor white but the result of complex interactions of good and evil motivations.[143] (David, Zeno, and the others whose libretti we shall study later were proud of the consistency of characterization they brought to the libretto through heroes incapable of unvirtuous thoughts and villains whose scheming treachery could end only when overwhelmed—usually at the end of the final act— by an unexpected display of the hero's magnanimity.)

Gravina was convinced throughout his life that Italian theater could approach the Greek tragedies he so admired only when it abandoned the tinkling rhymes he detested and concerned itself with syllables of varying length, but, although *L'Endimione* utilized occasional rhymes and was written in blank verse interrupted only by accentual meters for musical arias, he did not object.[144] In Gravina's *Della ragion poetica* of 1708, he continued his advocacy of quantitative poetry and his attacks on rhyme,[145] but carried this critical survey of Italian literature no further than the sixteenth century, regarding the period since the advent of Tasso and Guarini as unworthy of serious consideration.[146] Unlike most of his Arcadian colleagues, Gravina admitted no improvement whatever in Italian taste during the closing years of the seventeenth century, relenting in his insistence on the insignificance of contemporary Italian literature only when joining the defense of literary Italy against the attacks of the French.[147] Contemporary Italian theater, described in *Della ragion poetica* as the unfortunate object of evil influences from foreign courts and the slave of a corrupted public,[148] was beneath Gravina's criticism in 1708.

It was by no means beneath his criticism in the essay on tragedy Gravina published in 1715. Here he supported the familiar Aristotelian view that the principal aim of the theater should be the moral enlightenment of the people, and explored in detail those elements in the theatrical practices of the early eighteenth century which he felt had turned Italian theater into what was at best an amoral entertainment. Although *Della tragedia* was obviously intended as an explicatory supplement to Gravina's publication of five of his own tragedies,[149] he tried to prove, not that tragedy in ancient Greece had been performed with little music, but that it had been given a complete musical setting. The trouble with modern opera, wrote Gravina, was not caused, as some maintained, by the intrusion of music into a sphere where it did not belong, but by an important change in the nature of music. In antique times Gravina imagines there to have been two distinct musical styles, one for use by declaiming soloists and another for unison choruses. Gravina wisely avoids becoming specific about stylistic details, but he states that the two styles must have been fundamentally different from either recitative or aria as practiced in his own day. The difference, asserted Gravina, lay in music's transformation from an effective means of projecting a text to a decorative element obscuring the meaning of a text—a transformation from a means for the enhancing of affective impact to a manner of weakening or even contradicting the affective intent of the poet. In antique times the authors of tragedy had been themselves the composers of the music and the designers of the scenery; they had created unified works of demonstrated dramatic effect. In modern times, however, there was no dramatic effect in Italian theater because, wrote Gravina, the poetry, the music, the scenery, and the production were all in the hands of men who understood nothing of each other's problems and who took no interest in active collaboration.[150]

In other respects Gravina's *Della tragedia* represents a peculiar mixture of conservative and liberal interpretations of Aristotle's *Poetics*, whose organizational plan Gravina admittedly followed.[151] He favors the strictest observation of Aristotle's three unities but is willing to admit the possibility of tragedies with happy endings.[152] He condemns those poets whose plots rely too heavily on amorous entanglements and unexpected developments, but accepts the untying of dramatic knots through recourse to a *deus ex macchina*.[153] The "recognition" plots which hard-line Aristotelians considered the only possible basis for tragedy are discussed by Gravina as one of several possibilities.[154] The protagonists of conflicting motivations which Gravina had supported in his *L'Endimione* essay are now rejected in favor of the incorruptible heroes and irredeemable villains of whom the eighteenth century was becoming increasingly fond.[155] Tragedies in three acts became as acceptable for Gravina, at least in theory, as those in five, and he admitted that the representation on stage of horror scenes in the Greek manner was too repugnant for contemporary audiences to be ethically effective.[156] But he opposed all verisimilitude-weakening scene changes, insisted that all acts end with choruses, and continued to maintain that Italian tragedies should be written and performed in syllables of varying length.[157] Rhyme, wrote Gravina, should be limited to the choruses.[158] True to his promise neither to praise nor to censure contemporary authors, he mentioned none of the other poets who were trying, just as he was, to bring some measure of antique dignity to the Italian theater.

Martello

Pier-Jacopo Martello, the author of several libretti during the closing years of the seventeenth century, an Arcadian since 1698, member of the Bolognese legation in Rome from 1708 to 1716, and Secretary of the Bolognese Senate from 1716 until his death in 1727,[159] was one of the poets who resented Gravina's haughty self-isolation most intensely. A friend of Gravina's before the Arcadian schism that Gravina had initiated in 1711, Martello was offended by the preface to Gravina's *Tragedie cinque* of 1712 in which the latter had taken all the credit for an alleged restoration of Greek tragedy. In *Della tragedia antica e moderna*,[160] a series of six dialogues between Martello and an old hunchback who claims to be Aristotle himself, preserved over the centuries through the use of a secret elixir, Martello lashes out at Gravina while examining what he takes to be the differences between tragedy in the early eighteenth century and in ancient Greece.[161] By labelling his pseudo-Aristotle an impostor and by prefacing the six dialogues with the remark that the author venerates the teachings of the true Aristotle spoken by the "impostor" while ridiculing his deceit,[162] Martello covers himself against any Gravina counterattack. However, at the same time he makes it impossible for the modern reader to distinguish between those ideas which Martello would have wanted to defend and those which the "impostor" may well have uttered only to annoy Gravina. No matter. In the course of the six encounters with the "impostor," which are said to have taken place during Martello's 1713 stay in Paris, Martello offers interesting and original views on contemporary theater in France and Italy, including a longer and more thoughtful consideration of the dramatic problems associated with Italian opera than had ever previously appeared in print.

Martello begins by disputing with the "impostor" on Gravina's implication that all modern art is inferior to the art of ancient Greece. Greece, says Martello, is not the seat of the beautiful but only an important part of the artistic world, and he asserts that Italy of recent times has produced paintings superior to those of the Greeks. The "impostor" defends the superiority of ancient Greece in the plastic arts, but he admits that there is no reason why modern theater should necessarily imitate Greek models. His own *Poetics* has been seriously misinterpreted too often. He had intended, says the "impostor," not to lay down eternal dramatic principles but to suggest some general ground-rules for the theater of his "own day." Modern authors who insist on following the letter rather than the spirit of the *Poetics* are lacking in judgment and, therefore, laughable. Gravina's preface to his *Tragedie cinque* is lampooned, but the "impostor" praises the simplicity of plot observed by Gravina, among other modern poets. He stresses the need for serious writers to avoid those events which are ". . . suitable for comedy but inappropriate for tragedy in any era: confusion of identity resulting from similarity of clothing; the confiding to a servant of letters which fall by misfortune into the hands of persons who ought not to see them; leaving home at all hours and overhearing the secret conversations of others; and the use of disguises, especially popular among the Spanish, whose women go about as though masked and concealed by their silk shawls, allowing themselves to be recognized only through special signs that give rise to all sorts of misunderstandings."[163] The "impostor" identifies such dramaturgical tricks as the ordinary sources of plot complication in Spanish comedy. Although neither he nor Martello refers to the opera libretto in this connection, it is significant that these and similar tricks are, as we shall see later, typical of the Italian libretto during the closing decades of the seventeenth century, but much less common in the more serious libretti which characterized the first half of the eighteenth century.

In the second dialogue Martello and the "impostor" discuss Aristotle's famous three unities of action, time, and place, agreeing that the strictness with which those unities had been recently observed by overzealous tragedians had reached a point never intended by Aristotle. The subordination of episodes to a central dramatic idea should remain an important concept, says the "impostor," but the traditions that limited Greek tragedies to a span of 24 hours and to a single stage set were conventions necessitated by the primitive state of scenography. Since, because of the length of time required by the Greeks to reconstruct a stage set, the use of several sets within a single work would have distracted the audience from the drama, Greek writers limited the time spans of their works. But since, in modern time, scenographers like Ercole Rivani, Francesco Manzini, Ferdinando and Francesco Bibiena had furthered the development of scenography to the point that handsome stage sets could be changed very quickly without annoying the audience, neither Martello nor his "impostor" sees any reason for placing strict limits on the number of sets or on the dramatic time span of a single work, so long as the availability of additional means helped, not injured, the dramatic verisimilitude of the work.[164]

During the third dialogue both Martello and the "impostor" give further evidence of the freedom with which they interpret the implications of Greek theory and practice for the modern theater. Greek tragedians used long individual speeches and frequent soliloquies, but the "impostor" sees nothing evil in the system of confidants introduced by seventeenth-century French dramatists, and he approves the modern procedure of alternating shorter speeches that are less tiring for the actors. Gravina disliked asides because it did not seem reasonable to him that an audience should hear what an actor physically closer to the speaker was not supposed to hear, but Martello had no objection so long as the asides, a characteristic of eighteenth- as well as of seventeenth-century libretti, were not improbably long.[165] On the use of love as a central dramatic idea Martello and his "impostor" do not agree, the latter arguing that the aim of drama is the moral enlightenment of the populace, that the overemphasis of non-Platonic love in contemporary drama corrupts character, that the dramatist should represent not what *is* but what *ought* to be. But Martello, one of Italy's most enthusiastic Francophiles of the time, justified his support of love by alleging that the modern public, of which women are said to form a much more important part than in ancient Greece, cannot be treated as though they were contemporaries of Aristotle.[166] The "impostor" recalls that one of the principal goals of Greek tragedy was to remind the public of the importance of freedom by stressing the wickedness of tyrannical kings, but he submits that the political climate in Europe has changed, that although themes on the Greek model might give some pleasure to audiences in independent city-states like Venice and Genoa, they were now for the most part inappropriate: ". . . Where monarchy governs with justice, clemency, and dignity"—as the "impostor" claims is generally the case, especially in Paris and Rome— ". . . it is necessary to seek other political goals for tragedy." Although the kings of ancient times were villains whose tryanny one sought to avoid, the kings of modern times, he asserts, are heroes whose virtues should form the principal theme of contemporary theater for the ethical betterment of the audience.[167] We should point out in this connection that while Italian librettists of the later seventeenth century (even those like Minato, who worked in Vienna for an especially solemn court[168]) often treated the kings and queens in their dramas without special dignity, their successors of the early eighteenth century tended, on the contrary, to draw members of the royalty as lofty characters motivated only by the highest ideals of political virtue and the inevitable *amour*. Zeno's Viennese libretti are probably the most extreme examples of this trend, but the new dignified manner of treating royalty on the stage was by no means limited to the works of librettists employed at court. Martello's concern for stressing the political inappropriateness of too uncompromising an imitation of Greek models is, thus, characteristic of a development which concerned most serious dramatists of the period.

In the fourth dialogue, after a Parisian performance of Racine's *Iphigénie*, Martello and his "impostor" discuss the use of rhyme and non-quantitative meters in modern tragedy, and agree at length that neither is in any way unsuited for Italian tragedy, the opinions of Gravina and Fontanini notwithstanding.[169]

The fifth dialogue, which deals entirely with opera, begins with the "impostor's" assertion that although some writers imagine Greek drama to have been given a complete musical setting, Saint-Evremond was correct when he wrote, "The Greeks used to produce wonderful tragedies in which some parts were sung; the French make wretched tragedies in which they sing everything." The "impostor" claims that he has listened to Italian opera in Venice, Genoa, Milan, Reggio, and Bologna, and that what he has heard is fully as bad as Saint-Evremond found French opera. Martello agrees, but wants to be certain that the "impostor" shares his esteem for the libretti of several of his Italian contemporaries: ". . . the works of severe Moniglia and those of graceful Lemene; *Tolomeo, Achilles*, and the two *Ifigenia*s of Carlo Capece; *Santa Cecilia, Costantino*, and *Ciro* of a very eminent author;[170] all of the works of the most learned Apostolo Zeno; the charming *Dafni* of Eustachio Manfredi; *La caduta de'decimviri* of Silvio Stampiglia; *Onestà negli amori* of Monsignor Bernini, and the greater part of the libretti of Monsignor di Totis, to include the praise one owes to the works of those already dead." The "impostor" concurs in Martello's opinion, but says he is sorry to see so many otherwise worthy poets waste so much of their time on a genre so impermanent as the opera libretto. Martello continues with a remark that is reminiscent of Zeno's above-quoted letter of August 1701 to Muratori:[171] he never resented the time spent on his own libretti more than when the things which pleased him most were ruined through insipid music, or when poetry which would nauseate when read so aroused the enthusiasm of the audience and the singers that even Martello was pleased in spite of himself. The "impostor" replies that mediocre poetry is actually more suitable than the best for musical settings, that in his opinion Italian opera has a beneficial, pacifying effect on the nerves of the Italian public, and that the critics of Italian opera are mistaken when they criticize contemporary libretti as though poetry were on an equal footing in the opera with music: ". . . one has to begin with the postulate that in this charming spectacle music is primary. It is the soul of opera and to it is owed the principal regard of anyone who contributes its poetry or stage machinery."[172] Modern Italian music is, moreover, infinitely superior to that of ancient Greece; French music is not so bad as some would like to claim,[173] but English and German preference for Italian music, the praise awarded Italian music by the French author of the preface to an unidentified collected edition of French arias,[174] and the "impostor's" opinion that the frequency of long vowels in Italian makes it a particularly fortunate language for musical settings,[175] all incline him to prefer Italian music to French. The problem with the critics of Italian libretti, says the "impostor," is that they resent the relative unimportance of poetry's role in opera; and he goes on to propose three novel solutions to the problem: 1) since poetry's role in opera is so minor, perhaps one might drop poetry altogether; 2) since serious poets are offended by the fact that the authors of libretti are also known as poets, perhaps one could avoid hard feelings by calling the latter "versifiers," "mere versifiers," or something even less honorific; 3) since composers know the sort of poetry which they can set best, why not put the composition of both poetry and music into the hands of the same man, as was successfully done in Berlin with the famous castrato, Pistocchi. His text was weak and insipid when read, to be sure, but it was perfectly suited to the music Pistocchi wrote for it and with which it made an impressive effect in performance:[176]

> And so I would wish that the composer wrote the libretto. Although such a text would be mediocre as poetry, an arrangement of this kind would be better for opera as a whole. A composer-librettist could order the whole in his mind and write it all out on paper, the whole musical canvas from the beginning of the drama to the end. Once he had discovered the best location for violence, for tenderness, for the recitatives and arias, for the soprano, the bass, the contralto, and the tenor, he would adapt easy, flowing, and sonorous words and verses in accordance with incidents either taken from the stories of the Greeks or constructed entirely from the inventions of his own imagination. In so doing, he would extract no less applause than money from the mouths and purses of his audience. Since few composers understand verses, much less the manner of their construction, it should not be difficult for our poetaster-versifier to understand enough about music for him to adapt his invention and his verses to musical ideas—just as the painter of the scenery adds colors to the machines, designed by the engineer, which are appropriate to the shape and performance of those machines. A piece of scenery will always be suffered when, not interfering with the intentions of the engineer, it does not hinder the functioning of the ropes and pulleys which are necessary for the balancing and lowering of the machinery. I have not been personally acquainted with any note-loaders—thus one would call them. Seated at their harpsichords, the most versatile men in the universe, they seek out easy words abounding in vowels—just what is needed for the melismas which at times signify little and at others almost nothing. But the performance of such melismas, when put in their proper places, can give pleasure even to a group of litterateurs—and those fellows there are some who feed on criticizing even the most austere and respected poems.

> Our happy dramatists would derive their *argomenti* not from history but from the *favole*. Unlike modern librettists, who introduce whatever is wanted by the composer, the singers, the scenographer, the machinist, the set painter, or even the impresario, these dramatists would consider it too cruel impudently to deform the successive

writings of Livy, Giustino, Salust, and all sorts of venerated authors. When plots are based on *favole*, the situation will still be difficult, but not impossible; for in each case the versifier will have complete authority, as did our forefathers, to make one believe nonsense—to add Italian lies to Greek ones, and, abandoning the ancients, to contrive modern supplements that make a story more suitable for machinery and show. The French do this with great success, and so will the Italians. Although the name of our versifier is not to live on beyond the performance of his works, he shall at any rate have the title of poet, a title which he certainly merits as well as that of virtuoso is merited by the castrati and by the other singers. And what is even more important—he will be able, with authoritative demeanor, to spit out his verdicts on the works of great poets of every language and nation, through the crowds of the philistines. He will have sonorous applause from the musical mouths of the harlots and the actors, and seating himself at sumptuous meals, filling his coffers with necklaces, jewels, and cash, . . . he will feel that all this is a copious reward for the contempt which he will reap after the members of Arcadia and the Crusca have read his libretti.[177] Our versifier, whether he likes it or not, will write bad tragedies for music; but they will have to be tragedies, since otherwise he would not serve the pomp of the royal costumes that gleam in the wardrobes of the impresarios. (One calls such wardrobes *vestiarii* if characters less than kings and demigods are represented.) This indicates why pastoral works appear seldom with music—because they are capable of little richness of costume and of supernumeraries, and because they are not suited to strong scenes and to prominent events, which strengthen a musical spectacle.

You see then with what chains anyone wishing to involve himself with venal libretti will inevitably find himself bound. Somewhat less numerous will be the chains for the man who writes in the service of a prince, who not for gain but for the sake of pomp and munificence wishes to give the nobility, more than the people, an illustrious and gracious drama with music. In that situation even the versifier can be a poet. (But woe to him if he does not retreat from the regular and severe rules of tragedy.) His dramas will be able to be read and praised even outside the theater. This is what happened in Rome to the tragedies of a very eminent author who wished to give more than one performance in his private theater, for his own worthy entertainment and for the pleasure of princes and lords. Thus, the noble Prince of Poland, Alexander, who made the poetry of Capece serve the music of his mother, the Queen, generously opened his theater to the pleasure of the most illustrious persons of the great Roman court. This most agreeable Prince knew how to temper the genius of the poet with that of the composers and of the singers (as those familiar with both arts well know), staging operas which passed before the eyes of Aristotle himself without causing nausea.

Martello is intrigued to hear the "impostor's" view that, at least at some courts, it is possible to write libretti which are not altogether disagreeable to the *letterati*; and he tells the "impostor" that, at Bologna, paying operas have been put on in which certain gentlemen have so restrained the cupidity of the impresarios that the works staged were capable of giving the *letterati* some satisfaction.[178] The "impostor" accedes to Martello's request that he expound on the composition of reasonable libretti, but he points out that what follows is based on observation and experience rather than on reason and philosophy:

> If the absurd madness of agreeing to the composition of a libretto should ever pass through your head, before accepting the assignment you should investigate the capacity of the theater, the reputation of the composer, and the number and quality of the singers under contract to the impressario. Since it is necessary that the poet have some regard for expenses, let him discover how many stage sets the impresario wishes to order from the painter, the nature of the costumes contained in the impresario's wardrobe, and whether he may commission machines from the engineer. If the theater is too small, if the financial supporter of the work is miserly and wishes to offer the public a work of little splendor with a small orchestra and with few set changes, if there is not a good set painter, if the impresario does not wish to speak of an architect and a machinist, if he does not have famous singers for the important roles and a capable orchestra at his disposal, if he is afraid of the pomp of royal and impressive costumes—do not encumber yourself with the task or you will lose your reputation as a poet and, after having served the impresario, will be more his enemy than if, with regret, you had refused to serve him. I have reserved another most important condition for last, that it may remain the more impressed on your memory. Carefully consider the reputation and the discretion of the composer of the music. If, after all this, the impresario is not so stingy (which is not, of course, to say generous), if the theater is sufficiently large, if the composer is one of the more respected and compliant, like the illustrious Bononcini, if some of the singers engaged have a reputation, if the orchestra is large and complete, if you can order a suitable number of sets from an able painter, if the wardrobe is at least adequately well preserved and ostentatious, even if there is no machinist, you may undertake the writing of the libretto with courage—provided that, since you are omitting the use of machines, you persuade the impresario to separate the acts of your work with some graceful ballet. You will be fortunate if you have the use of a French dancer, but there are few touring members of that dancing nation. Under these conditions you would be wise to choose an incredible story using both gods and humans, or a true story whose principal action involves only heroes, suited for such incidents as can be easily represented in the given theater and suited for the singers already hired. Confer with the impresario and the composer, obtain their approval, then follow their ideas, throwing yourself immediately into their execution.
>
> Custom demands that your libretto be divided into three acts since, if you were to divide it into five, you would make people believe that you wished to give them a tragedy, senselessly obligating yourself to rules which you could not observe.[179] In the first act you will take care to prepare the audience for the plot, giving them the necessary notice of the heroes who will appear, of the events that have taken place before the opening of the drama (and on which one's understanding of it depends); and you will manage the first appearance of at least the principal characters who are to take part in the action. In the introduction to your story you should give notice, in order to excite anticipation and astonishment, that the theater has been provided with characters of distinction. Forget the modest principles of tragedy and the epic, and bear in mind that when the curtain rises, the audience will grow cool if it sees two characters who speak together seriously. The public wishes an abundance of people on stage—if not of actual characters in the drama, then of supernumeraries.

A debarcation scene, the dancing of a *moresca*, a fight, or something similar will make your audience raise its eyebrows and bless the money which they have spent at the door to entertain themselves.

In the second act you should look to the development both of the action and of the passions. The frivolous misunderstandings, changes of costume, love letters, and portraits so suspect to tragedians, are held in highest esteem by librettists.[180] Abandoning the severe verisimilitude of Greek, French, and, we assert, also Italian tragedy, openly imitate the ingenious complications used by the Spanish. I do not say that you should omit verisimilitude altogether from your dramatic incidents, but that verisimilitude should not be so important to you as the marvelous. Let improbabilities, then, be the means of your drama, if you like; but given these means, let your incidents appear probable, for thus you will achieve the marvelous and the applause of your audience. The passions are various and contrasting. If you can, oppose hate to love and love to hate. Let anger also play its role, but the amorous passion should triumph over all the others. Let the other passions serve only to highlight the amorous, which, since it is most common to all men, is received with more pleasure. . . .

In the third act heed the loosening or untying of the dramatic knot, and let it take place through the use of a machine. If the impresario will permit this, the work will be better received because of the ostentation, even though the dramatic knot perhaps may not merit inconveniencing a god to descend from heaven to untie it. Let there be recognition scenes and events that show the vicissitudes of human existence. In the identification and recognition scenes the public believes easily in unexpectedly changed costumes; in a combination of circumstances at first concealed; in certain pieces of clothing found in the cradle of a person when he was a baby, and which later, for the purpose of disclosing his identity, appear on the stage or are described.[181] Concerning the vicissitudes of human fortune: it is better that events be actually seen than imagined, since whatever strikes the senses is more pleasing to the public, present in the theater more to see than to think. Let such changes of fortune be always from sad to happy situations in which you may terminate the story through the use of weddings. When this happens, let the poet resolve, for the sake of the republic, that the virtuous be rewarded with happiness and the villains punished with severity. But this latter never goes so far as death, the poet not wishing dead people to sadden the audience in a genre that is staged to delight.

Urged on by the economy of the action equally divided among the acts, you must give some thought to the division of each act into scenes. Here you will have no little sweat. In the first place you will have to inform yourself about the number of the principal singers in order to give them equal opportunities; otherwise you will have insoluble quarrels among those brazen hussies and the corpulent castrati. Then you will give some attention to the voices, intermingling them in such a manner that they support and do not destroy the intentions of the composer. And therefore, I exhort that, before cutting the bread of the acts into scenes, you show it to the composer and ask him which singers, in his opinion, you ought to couple at the beginning, middle, and end of each act. You should agree at this point with the composer. He will give his approval easily if each act includes one of those scenes that are called *scene di forza*, resulting either from some violent and unaccustomed encounter of contrary passions or from some meeting or incident not expected by the audience.

Given this arrangement, I can assure the happy success of your work. And no more will remain for you than the versifying of your drama.

It is necessary that the whole be divided into recitative and arias—or as we call the latter, *canzonette*. Every scene will consist either exclusively of recitative or arias, or as is more often the case, of both recitative and arias. Everything that is narrated, and emotions that are not agitated ought to be expressed in the poetry of recitative; but ideas that have the emotion of passion or indications of anything more violent incline more readily to the *canzonetta*. The recitative should be brief enough not to weary one with its tediousness but long enough not to cause obscurity. The sentences and constructions should be easy, and concise rather than extended. Thus they will be convenient to the composer, the singer, and the listener—to the composer, who will give life to otherwise dead recitative through the frequency of his cadences; to the singer, who will be able to catch a fresh breath in pronouncing the cadences and to take new strength from the pauses; and to the listener who, not accustomed to the music, which changes the ordinary sounds of the words for the ear, will not be obliged to tire himself so much to perceive the sense of the whirling words from a frenzied performance. The recitative, then, ought to limit itself to verses of seven and eleven syllables, alternating and mixed, depending on which falls more suitably and so that, at least with respect to the cadences, there can occur a correspondence of consonances and of rhymes that will be seen more to favor the flowing quality of the music. What I have said about the recitatives bears some limitation in what I have called *scene di forza*, since in these the recitative, the element of greater strength and relevance to the action, ought to prevail over the arias. Here the poet may give vent to a moderate test of his abilities. A prudent composer should allow this. Nor will the singers who are experienced in stage production refuse it. The impresario, too, will have to comply.

The *canzonette* are either simple or compound. We shall call simple those that are sung by a single voice, compound those that are sung by two or more voices. Those for two voices we shall call duets; those for more than two voices are called choruses. Some of the simple arias we shall call "entrances," others "exits," and still others "medial" arias. From their denomination one can infer their use.[182] "Entrances" are appropriate when a person comes on stage, and they are normally used in soliloquies; most often the figure addressed is the soul of the character who is singing. But you should make sparing use of these. It is necessary to employ "medial" arias with the same caution, since the effect is poor when, in the midst of a scene, the actors are obliged to stand silently rigid to hear a colleague sing at his leisure. For that reason it is desirable to have some accompanying action on stage which forces the actors who are not singing to participate in something that does not leave them entirely idle. Then, such arias produce a very fine effect.[183] Only in cases like these is it sometimes permissible to use a question, in all other cases repulsive because it gives no opportunity for a variety of notes in its expression. "Exit" arias should conclude every scene, and a singer ought never leave the stage without exercising his throat on a *canzonetta*. It matters little whether the use of such arias is verisimilar. Be more than certain that your scenes end with spirit and with vigor, and be sure that when you end a scene with an "exit" aria, you do not begin the next with an "entrance" aria, for then there is no contrast in the music.[184] The effects that one has sought for then obstruct one another, and instead of reinforcing, they crush each other. That is the reason why "entrance" arias should appear only at the beginnings of acts. There is no objection to duets that occur in the midst of scenes, for they give reciprocal action to more than one actor; I would even prefer one of them at the end of the second act. A chorus at the close of the last act is inevitable, since the public enjoys listening to the combination of all those voices, each of which it has applauded separately during the opera. The din of the singers and instruments causes the audience to rise to their feet and to depart satisfied and happy with what they have heard, filled with the desire to return.

These arias or *canzonettas* ought to be distributed in such a manner that the singers of greater reputation have an equal number of them, since the rivalries of singers are punctilious and unconquerable, and since it is useful for the performance of the drama if the best voices make an equal display of themselves to the ears of the audience.

After an extended discussion of the metrical schemes most common in operatic arias of the period, the "impostor" turns to a consideration of style in operatic poetry:

I believe that the moderate and graceful is more appropriate to libretti than the serious and magnificent; for music, an art invented for the delight and soothing of souls, ought to be assisted by words and sentiments which clothe the agreeable nature of the pleasures. This is not to say, however, that the magnificent ought not to be used from time to time, if only to form a better contrast with the charming, in the manner that something bitter mixed with sweetness gives the greatest delight to the palate with a bit of spicyness. But if there is too much bitterness one loathes it, and a sensitive young girl would spit it out. I repeat to you, therefore, that the constructions should be graceful, the sentences clear and not long, the words smooth and pretty, the rhymes not insipid, the verses flowing and tenderly sonorous. In the arias I recommend to you comparisons with little butterflies, birds, and brooks. All these are things which guide one's ideas to all sorts of refreshing cheerfulness; and since the ideas are charming, thus too should be the words which depict them. . . . The composer of the music always expands himself in these places with the gracefulness of his notes. You will have observed that even in the worst operas singers earn distinct applause for the performance of pieces in which the diminutives, so hateful to the French taste and language, add charm. Keep in mind that the more general are the ideas put forward in your arias, the more they please the public, since, whether you find them verisimilar or not, they form a repertory which a gentleman can use honorably with his lady, singing them for the occasions of jealousy, of disdain, of reciprocal promises, of absence from one another, and of similar events that befall lovers from day to day. It is, besides, rather easy to succeed in this area, for a poet can write much more comfortably on general subjects, and will sometimes be able, when out walking, to fill his poetic wardrobe with the sort of ideas he can later use for furnishing the recitatives of his libretti. But beware of generalities in your action arias, devoting yourself in that area solely to particular ideas, since, unless you wish the action to turn out coldly, you must look for words that animate it, contributing a spirit especially adapted to that action and to no other. If in the end you are not part of the herd of servile versifiers and would like the person who reads your libretto to recognize you as a poet, honor yourself in the recitatives, and perhaps in one aria per act, genuflecting to the composer, to the singers, and to the impresario himself in order that they may allow the worthwhile parts to remain, for your reputation and for the honor of the sacred muses. Perhaps they will soften those otherwise hardest of hearts to your lamentings; but if you wish for more than that, do not hope for it without strife, hostility, and refusals. It must be enough for you that there are people who do not abhor your works for their purity and spirit; nor ought your spirit of independence end here.

Martello, my friend, the profession of writing libretti is a school of morals which, more than any other, teaches poets how to conquer themselves by renouncing their own wishes. Take heart, and change arias that are not bad into those that are. If a singer would like to nail an aria which has won the public's applause in Milan, Venice, Genoa, or elsewhere at the foot of one of your recitatives, even though the aria in question is far from the sentiment which ought to be expressed at the place where it occurs, what does it matter? Let the singer insert the new aria, otherwise you will see yourself attacked on all sides, your forehead battered with the reproaches of sopranos and contraltos. The best that can befall you will lie in persuading the singers to agree that for the already-composed music you be permitted to write words that are less discordant to your original sentiment; but in this case you entangle yourself in a thorny obligation. That the new verses be equal to the old in the number of both lines and syllables is not a matter that can be neglected; of special importance is the preservation in your new text of those vowels on which the singer can make rapid melismas. An "A" can be changed to an "E" but not to an "I," since this would produce a neighing effect and would bark itself into a "U." In addition, you must preserve the accents, otherwise the short syllables would be produced long and the long short. But tell me, what solution will you find if, in the position of an aria of scorn and disdain, already established in its niche, you have to use another whose text was love but which has now to be reclothed with a scornful text? Unless he was a lout, the composer of the original setting will have adapted his notes to the expression of the original text, so that the music can no longer be successfully adapted to the new text. In such a case I would always deem it better to allow the singers to insinuate their own talents into the arias wherever they wish, rather than make myself an accomplice to their mistakes in overloading the notes. It is enough that the new arias do not clash with the music of those already present, a concern which you should leave entirely to the composer.

What then if the impresario, who is to pay you for your trouble—don't blush, for this is the only sort of poetry destined to serve as merchandise—wants you to load old music with new words? What if, after you have done his bidding, he refuses to pay, because of some temple he claims you have violated or because of some other mistake he asserts you have committed? You wanted to hear Aristotle's *Poetics* applied to the libretto, and now you have heard the whole of it. Aren't you satisfied?[185]

Having heard the "impostor's" description of problems connected with the writing of libretti, Martello asserts that it might be better for morality and artistic taste if one were to put a complete stop to the performance of melodramas. The "impostor" will not retract his judgment that it is easier to write a good tragedy than a libretto, but he feels that although opera *is* a monster, it is a monster whose delights produce a

beneficial effect on Italian society. It is perfectly true, says he, that there
are very few libretti which can be read with pleasure, but the poetry of
a musical drama, like the stage sets and costumes that are used, should
not be considered apart from the music-dominated whole. It is a mistake
to postulate poetry as the first consideration in opera. In the opinion of
the "impostor":

> Poetry is a concern of more importance than the painting of the sets, but of less
> concern than the voices. She is a figure destined to flatter a character in the play
> who is greater than herself—music.

> Music is the essence of opera, of which all the other parts, among which comes
> poetry, are really incidental. If poetry is an essential part, then it is in the sense that
> color, which is only a property of light, accommodated to the surfaces that it serves
> so that it reflects in a variety of manners, appears variously colored. In its true form
> light has no color, but when it humbles itself to the service of solid bodies, it clothes
> its appearance in different manners and gives pleasure even though deformed. Plea-
> sure results because color does not seem to operate through its own capacity but
> through the capacities of other elements.[186] This is the reason why operatic poetry
> gives no greater displeasure than it does, degraded in principle as an accessory ele-
> ment. But however secondary an element poetry may be in the operatic realm, it can
> succeed to the point of actually becoming agreeable. Poetry is only one of those
> gentlemen who have fallen to low esteem and are forced to serve by the necessity of
> material gain. The pride of commanding has not been forgotten, and is badly adapted
> to poetry's present fortune. But when one serves, one is a servant; and in this sense
> poetry performs honorably, giving no commands and obeying only music, who is
> mistress in the theater.[187]

The "impostor" closes his remarks on opera by praising the achievements of contemporary Italian music, which he asserts is in every way
the equal of ancient Greek sculpture. Pasquini, Colonna, "the two Scarlattis," Perti, Bononcini, Albergati, Ariosti, Zanettini, Benati, Pollaroli,
and Pistocchi are all mentioned, but the "impostor" adds that there are
so many worthy masters in Italy that it would take a long time simply to
name them. His final paragraph, accepting music's primacy in early eighteenth-century Italian opera, is distinctly different from anything to be
found in the writings of any previous literary critic of opera:

> The art of music, which has been brought in Italy to so exquisite a perfection,
> deserves that Italy make of it her dearest and most magnificent spectacle, a treasure
> which even her most severe critics ought to trust with laudable joviality. Music de-
> serves that foreign nations agree to take delight from that which so justly gives delight
> to Italians. She deserves besides that voices, instruments, poetry, painting, architec-
> ture, mechanics, the art of miming, and every other art imaginable, woo and obey
> her. And, finally, music deserves that when you publish theatrical works, you do not
> include any libretti, since you would do an injustice to music by stressing what is

merely auxiliary. By separating such poetry from its music, you would bring back the pain of the injustice that comes when operatic poetry is derided by its readers.[188]

In the sixth and last dialogue of *Della tragedia antica e moderna*, Martello and his "impostor" discuss the manners of performance used by the French, the Italians, and the Spanish for the production of tragedy and comedy. Martello suggests that French recitation of prose comedies is similar to that used by Italians, but distinguishes between the manners in which the two countries recite tragedy. French actors, he claims, pay close attention to their audiences' desire to follow the drama and to appreciate stylistic subtlety, but Italians are more concerned with the euphony of end-rhymes whose stress in performance often obscures meaning—a point of some importance for our understanding of the way in which eighteenth-century Italian composers wrote recitative, as will be seen later. When Martello asks the "impostor" to comment on his view that the sing-song recitation of Italian tragedians probably resembles the performance of the ancient Greeks, the "impostor" elaborates at length on the theme that the dialogue of Greek tragedy was declaimed, not sung, that the phenomenon in Greek tragedy which modern singing resembles was limited to the choruses, not always occurring even in them. And he requotes the lines of Saint-Evremond with which he had begun his remarks in the previous dialogue. Martello praises the effectiveness of histrionic restraint among the French, and the "impostor" credits the French for their wisdom in distinguishing, as did the Greeks, between elements appropriate to tragedy and comedy. Long, serious, uninterrupted discourses among serious public figures are appropriate for tragedy but not for comedy, where frequently interrupted, tumultuous, more familiar conversations among persons of lower social rank are more in order. He points out that everything which takes place on the stage must be somewhat exaggerated in order to make an effect on an audience, then begins a comparison between French and Italian use of several conventions of dramatic production. Italian actors are criticized for falling out of character whenever not actually speaking themselves, and for their habit of strolling idly about the stage in front of each other. Martello admits that the French are better actors, but he accuses them of speaking both too loudly and too softly, of turning their backs on the audience, of occasional excesses of gesticulation, of improprieties in costuming, and of allowing actors who have left the stage to reenter it from dramatically improbably directions. He points out that French tragedians carefully avoid an empty stage by devising dramatic webs in which all the actors onstage never exit simultaneously, except during the change of a stage set. But he feels that this precaution is unnecessary if the producer makes certain that entrances

and exits are properly planned and executed. The "impostor" objects
that Martello is too critical of French actors—a line which must have
been especially irritating to Gravina, who derided Martello as the most
extreme of Francophiles.[189] The "impostor" maintains that although there
are some dramatic conventions which are valid at all times and places,
there are others which are not; he amplifies his point by contrasting
French, Italian, and Spanish manners of dancing, reciting, and costuming,
asserting the peculiar appropriateness of each to the area where it is used.
He urges the need for writing more tragedies and for making the public
accustomed to a form of theater that is morally beneficial, concluding
with the prayer that heaven long preserve the life of Scipione Maffei,
"surpassed by none in his love for the truth, a man who pays no heed to
even the most accredited impostors." Complaining of a headache, the
"impostor" bids Martello farewell, and departs for good.[190]

What Martello has to say about Italian opera in the six dialogues,
Della tragedia antica e moderna, is certainly not without humorous exaggeration. But the author's claim to familiarity with the operatic world
of early eighteenth-century Italy is supported by the degree to which so
many librettists of the period seem to have followed the prescriptions he
enumerates. Several of the suggestions on dramaturgical development,
and on the placement of arias and their distribution among the singers,
for example, concern conventions that hardened during the second and
third decades of the century into seemingly immutable laws of procedure.[191] For the generation of impresarios born around the turn of the
eighteenth century these conventions came to mean an indispensable part
of opera, while for critics who yearned for more rational drama they came
to symbolize everything about *opera seria* that was artificial and stilted,
a favorite subject for parody.[192] For Martello they had none of the sanct-
ity of law, but were simply mentioned in passing as practical solutions to
practical problems. Martello writes that one should give each of the principal singers an equal number of arias, in order to avoid quarrels, but
nothing is said about an invariable number of singers or about arranging
the dramaturgical development in such a way that none of the singers
performs a second aria before each of his colleagues has performed a
first. Martello believes that an alternation of recitative and aria should be
observed for the sake of variety, but he tacitly admits the possibility of
scenes consisting exclusively of arias, a decidedly old-fashioned feature
for libretti written at the time Martello published his dialogues. Every
scene, says he, should conclude with an exit aria, and none of the prin-
cipals should exit without an aria, but he does not say that all exit arias
must appear at the ends of scenes. The convention which placed all the
exit arias in the libretti of Metastasio's generation at the ends of scenes
and which made very nearly all of the scene-ending arias exit arias, can

be meaningfully considered the result of two distinct evolutionary processes, each with its own motivating force: the singers' and impresarios' realization towards the end of the seventeenth century that an aria, especially one forming a dramatic climax for the recitative that precedes it, wins more applause when the performer who sings it leaves the stage immediately afterwards;[193] and the growing reluctance of literarily ambitious librettists during the early years of the eighteenth century to see their carefully constructed dialogues spoiled by unwanted interruptions.[194] It is surely to be doubted that singers gave much thought to the location of an aria with respect to the printed divisions of the libretto, or that a singer's failure to exit after one of his arias would have troubled most librettists. (Additional evidence supporting this thesis on the origins of the scene-ending exit aria can be found in the charts on libretto structure that appear below in Chapter III.)

Although Martello considered it impossible to write libretti that could satisfy both the theater and his own aspirations as a poet, it is striking that he by no means condemned opera as had Muratori and Gravina. One can attribute this in part to Martello's respect for the librettists listed towards the beginning of his fifth dialogue, and to his view that some of their libretti, particularly those commissioned by the courts, were not altogether unworthy as works of poetry. But there can be little question that the extraordinary success enjoyed all over Italy by Scipione Maffei's celebrated tragedy, *Merope*, helped convince Martello after its premier in 1713 that the popularity of opera in Italy had not destroyed all taste for more serious things. Concerning the list of librettists for whom Martello professes respect, it is important that Martello speaks of no reform and singles out no individuals from his list to credit as leaders of the others. In Zeno, Stampiglia, Moniglia, Bernardoni, and Capece, he praises librettists who had been similarly honored more than a decade earlier by Crescimbeni. De Totis, Lemene, Pariati, Manfredi, and Bernini are all librettists not so honored by Crescimbeni. The fifth dialogue of Martello's *Della tragedia antica e moderna* was clearly the source for an identical list of exceptional librettists which Quadrio included more than 30 years later in his *Della storia e della region d'ogni poesia*.[195] It seems more than likely that the fifth dialogue of Martello also provided at least part of the inspiration for Benedetto Marcello's famous satire on *opera seria*, *Il teatro alla moda*, which appeared anonymously in 1720, only a few years after Martello's publication.

Mattheson

Our next commentator on the early eighteenth-century history of the Italian libretto is the German singer, composer, historian, and diplomatic official, Johann Mattheson. In the 1722 volume of what is probably the first entirely musical periodical, *Critica musica*, Mattheson reprinted and on facing columns translated into German Raguenet's *Parallèle des Italiens et des Français*, adding occasionally lengthy footnotes of his own which, because of Matteson's earlier involvement in several branches of operatic life, are of special interest. Raguenet is enthusiastic in his praise for Italian music, but praises the dignity of French characterization and the dramatic appropriateness of the French passions, asserting that there are few tragedies or comedies better than the majority of musical texts by Quinault.[196] This is too much for Mattheson, who unburdens himself of the following, characteristically outspoken lines in defense of Italian librettists:

> The author has perhaps seen and read only the most miserable of Italian operas. . . . As we shall see from what follows in this *Parallèle*, Raguenet was in Rome during 1698. Whether at that time he met only rhapsodic libretti of the type he describes is uncertain. We, at any rate, have quite different information and examples not only of recent Italian works, particularly of the outstanding Viennese operas by the incomparable Apostolo Zeno, but also of quite old libretti in which both the intrigues and dramatic expression are beyond criticism. *Croeusus*, a work translated from Italian more than 30 or 40 years ago, can serve as an example of the first. This is a piece in which there are dramatic denouements of a kind that I doubt has ever been shown in a French work. Whoever has the Venetian operas available, let him have a look at the year 1695, where he will find a so-called pastorale-tragedy for music entitled *Il pastor d'Anfriso*, a work which gives the greatest satisfaction in the world. So far as noble sentiments are concerned, I know of no single French opera which in this respect outdoes the libretto which the famous Francesco Silvani prepared and entitled *Il miglior d'ogni amore per il peggiore d'ogni odio*. It was performed in Venice during the year 1703 with music composed by Francesco Gasparini. Whoever wishes to take these and similar works, of which I have seen entire volumes, for rhapsodies, must certainly be crazy. It has been true for several years both here and in England that many libretti are disgracefully torn apart, shredded, and trimmed up with all sorts of rags like a harlequin's costume. But the authors of the works are not guilty on that account; the guilt lies rather on some occasions with the whim of a lady virtuoso, on others with the lack of sense of an impresario who thinks only that whatever is pretty ought to be equally suitable in all places. On still other occasions the guilt lies with the taste of spectators for whom one often cannot make things bizarre enough. Except where this happens, however, Italian poets know how to give their works coherence, consequence, and, most important, a nice intrigue. When the authors themselves are not present, however, the problem which arises reflects sinful deceit rather than lack of knowledge. The impresarios pay more attention to the brilliant than they do to well-regulated order, more attention to the pleasure of the gallant spectator than to the insatiable criticism of a pedant. Let a poet, derided by such a critic, reflect in the manner of Horace:
>
> Caenae fercula nostrae
> Malim convivis, quam placuisse coquis.

Which means: "I would rather have my meal praised by the guests than by the cooks."[197]

Writing no more than four years after Zeno's move to Vienna in 1718, Mattheson indicates the extent to which Zeno's already growing reputation had been furthered by the appearance of his first Viennese works. Corradi, Frigimelica–Roberti, and Silvani, the authors of the three works cited by Mattheson, are a trio of librettists mentioned by no other critic in connection with recent improvement in the Italian libretto. However, because the virtue of dramatic coherence stressed by Mattheson is also Zeno's most articulated goal, and because Matteson, widely experienced in operatic matters, represents a rather different background from that of the Italian litterateurs we have studied thus far, it will be worth our while to include the works of Corradi, Frigimelica–Roberti, and Silvani in our subsequent considerations. Strikingly, none of the three seems ever to have been a member of Arcadia.[198]

Maffei

Scipione Maffei, the Veronese poet, scholar, and critic for whose long life Martello's "impostor" had so earnestly prayed at the end of *Della tragedia antica e moderna*,[199] is the next Arcadian tragedian to comment in print on the dramatic viability of *opera seria*, and the first writer to separate Apostolo Zeno from the assortment of poets we have already seen variously credited for improving the quality of the contemporary libretto. In the introduction to *Teatro ilaliano*, a three-volume anthology of Italy's greatest tragedies, published by Maffei in 1723 as a stimulus to reawakening Italian interest in the performance of tragedy and as a defence against French criticisms of Italian poetry, Maffei sketches the history of theater in Italian, attributing a large share of the blame for its decadence during the seventeenth century to the popularity and influence of opera. Like several of the other critics we have studied, Maffei is willing to admit that contemporary libretti are more reasonable than those he had known in his youth, but he emphatically rejects Martello's idea that the Italian theater has any room for a dramatic type in which poetry acts as music's servant:

It is true that in most recent times several poets of talent have managed the genre with much honor. Among these writers I would name one man, if I did not fear displeasing him, who has written more than forty libretti, who has often taken scarcely a week to compose one of them, and who has known how to merit the approval of an emperor who, with marvelous penetration, immediately distinguishes the strong from the weak, an emperor who no less for his knowledge and wisdom than for his

virtue and victories, will be immortal in every era. But at any rate, until the present
variety of music is moderated, it will never be possible to construct operas so that
they do not always appear like one form of art distorted for the sake of another—a
situation in which the superior miserably serves the inferior, where the poet occupies
the same position as a violinst who plays for dancing.[200]

Later in his preface Maffei expresses two further objections to opera, the
first of them as basic as his refusal to cast poetry in an inferior role, the
second echoing a complaint that had been common to operatic critics for
several decades. It is impossible, says Maffei, to sing about the customs
and passions of modern society in a verisimilar manner and to reduce the
number of arias to the point where they would no longer interfere with
dramatic effect.[201]

Maffei never names the writer of the 40 libretti to whom he alludes
in the paragraph quoted above, but his identification is so precise that
there can be no doubt whatever that he is referring to Apostolo Zeno.
There was only one emperor in Europe and only one poet in his service
who had written as many as 40 libretti. But the reluctance to mention
Zeno's name probably stems from deeper roots than Maffei's apparent
respect for Zeno's modesty. Zeno, Maffei, and Muratori, three of Italy's
most respected scholars of the time, had in 1710 been the founders of
Italy's first enduring literary journal, *Il Giornale dei letterati d'Italia*.[202]
Published in Venice and edited by Zeno himself before his departure for
Vienna, the *Giornale* was modelled on similar periodicals in France and
Germany. Like so much of what took place in the literary circles of early
eighteenth-century Italy, it was intended in part as a forum for the rebuttal
of French attacks on Italian poetry and theater. The introduction to the
first volume of the *Giornale*, probably written by Zeno himself, expresses
guarded resentment towards French criticism:

> One thing only seems desirable for the entire perfection [of French literary criticism]:
> namely, that some of those most worthy critics agree to take the time to instruct
> themselves thoroughly in Italian literature and its history, because their judgments
> on Italian taste in eloquence and poetry, formed as they are from familiarity with
> works of no value and on the opinions of a few men who had not even the slightest
> knowledge of our best authors, accord badly with their other judgments.[203]

Maffei had actually written a libretto during his youth, but after he had
come to feel that the composition of such works was an inappropriate
activity for anyone interested in the reinvigoration of Italian poetry, he
wrote no more libretti.[204] As a defender of Italian honor against French
reproaches it must have been humiliating for him to admit that the former
editor of Italy's leading literary journal was also the author of her best
known libretti.

In *De' teatri antichi e moderni*, a long essay published by Maffei in 1753 to defend his *Teatro italiano* (and the very existence of the theater in society) from the attacks of a reactionary Dominican priest named Concina, Maffei once more refuses to hold any brief for opera:[205]

> How little the mass of the public knows about poetry these days can be perceived by observing that many people actually read libretti that were written for music. Several worthy gentlemen (whose names must be unknown to a foreigner [Concina] who could write with such ignorance about Italian operas) have accomplished wonders in this genre and have even banished the effeminacies of the past century. But they have not been able to bring it about that operas are ever anything but works in which one form of art is distorted for the sake of another, spurious works that are neither tragedies nor comedies. Whenever music is involved, its charm makes everything suffer. One pays no attention to the passage, in a single evening, of dramatic actions which should require months. The beauty of the scenery results in applause for the frequent changing, without any magical art, of the location. For the sake now of one art, now of another, one is not supposed to feel bored, although dramatic accidents lacking in any sort of verisimilitude are represented, as are developments that are very difficult to understand. But when reading a libretto, how can one enjoy a genre whose chief value lies in the arias, words that are unnecessary and often artificially joined, words that are principally concerned with such expressions as "the charming little cloud" or "the pretty little turtledove"?[206]

Although Maffei's condemnation of opera as drama and the libretto as readable poetry seems to be made without reservation, he returns to the subject in his second chapter (while enumerating the morally edifying works of the Italian theater that he wishes to defend against Concina's attack), this time tacitly retracting part of the condemnation just quoted:

> Of musical dramas that have any moral worth there are only the numerous works by the two most celebrated authors of our day, the greater part of which had the merit to appear in the altogether chaste imperial theater, and which compare well with others of the past century. One of these two writers let himself be overly moved with friendly regard when he wrote: "In my day Marchese Maffei's *Merope* is the only dramatic work I have seen produce the miracle of giving pleasure to everyone without any admixture of amorous interests." Ap. Zeno, *Lettere*, Vol. III, p. 540. But other works without love intrigues have also met with public approval.[207]

Influenced no doubt by the literary and popular enthusiasm of the day for the libretti of Zeno and Metastasio, no longer troubled by mid-century with the need for defending Italy's literary respectability, Maffei in his closing chapters twice more uses the well-known integrity of his late friend, Zeno, as a defense against the charges of Concina. Concina had claimed that, of the people directly involved with the theater, only actors and impresarios really approved of it, but Maffei asserts that even in Zeno's final years, his 50 libretti never lost their author's approval.[208]

Concina states that anyone connected with the theater will be condemned
for his sins in the hereafter, but Maffei counters that, if this is the case,
". . . Apostolo Zeno, that man of impeachable morals, so praised by
Concina with such justice, ought to have been deprived of the sacraments
for the greater part of his life."[209] There is no reason to doubt Maffei's
sincerity, but it is clear from Zeno's correspondence, especially during
the final quarter of his life, that Maffei's remarks in *De' teatri antichi e
moderni* about Zeno's libretti would not have pleased Zeno.

With Scipione Maffei we conclude a chonological survey of Italian operatic criticism between 1675 and 1725, a survey undertaken to investigate
the following three questions:

1) To what extent did the Arcadian reformers of the period accept the
   conventions of contemporary opera? Did they insist that spoken tragedy and comedy were the only acceptable forms of theater or did they
   admit the possibility of a dramatically meaningful role for music?

2) What were the features of contemporary opera which those writers
   found most objectionable and for which features was there special
   clamor for reform?

3) Which librettist or librettists were credited with improving the libretto
   and what were their alleged contributions?

The answers yielded by our investigation can be summarized as follows.
Although the early Arcadians were interested in the return of Greek
drama, thought by some to have been performed in ancient Greece without any music, or with very little, none of the critics was so radical as to
suppose that opera could be altogether eliminated from the contemporary
theater. Several of them suggested that a rebalancing of music and poetry
might produce a more dramatic result. The suggestions for achieving more
serious and dramatic opera were several, and so were the poets variously
honored for having exemplified virtues and avoided vices described by
some of the critics. Apostolo Zeno emerged as the most prominent of
those figures, particularly after his arrival in Vienna.

II

Later Writers and the "Reform"

Almost immediately after Zeno retired from Vienna and was succeeded there in 1729 by Pietro Metastasio, his historical position became that of a prophet who had established the outline and conventions of *opera seria* for the coming of Italy's most illustrious poet of the century. The pages which follow present in summary form the views of historians from the time of Metastasio's arrival in Vienna to the present on the relationship of Zeno and Metastasio to each other and to the librettists contemporary with Zeno. Critical views on *opera seria* libretti put forward throughout the eighteenth century are included whenever they relate to problems inherent to the libretti of Zeno and Metastasio or to the settings of those libretti. In the comparative analyses of chronologically progressing members of libretto families which comprise Chapter III, we shall see to what extent these often rather general views mirror the changes in form and content that took place in the libretto during the end of the seventeenth century and beginning of the eighteenth.

Becelli, Giulio Cesare, *Della novella poesia cioè del vero genere e particolari bellezze della poesia italiana*, 3 vols. (Verona, 1732). The author proposes a new Italian theater with plots, characterization, staging, and costuming derived not from antique tradition but from contemporary society. He praises the artistic combination of music and poetry which he feels existed in Italy during the sixteenth century, but derides the lyric poetry set to music during his own day. There is no special consideration of opera as a separate genre, but no attempt to condemn it or to show the need for any rebalancing of its constituent elements. Individual librettists are not mentioned.

Bettinelli, Giuseppe, ed., *Opere drammatiche del Sig. Abate Pietro Metastasio Romano Poeta Cesareo*, 4 vols. (Venice, 1733). In the preface to the first collected edition of Metastasio's libretti, his publisher, Bettinelli, praises Metastasio for having transformed the libretto from a necessarily imperfect form of drama into real tragedy.[1] Nothing is said of any of Metastasio's predecessors in the field.

Edesimo, Evandro, *Considerazioni sopra Il Demofoonte del Sig. Pietro Metastasio* (Venice, 1735). The names of Metastasio and Zeno are linked in print for the first time in an essay which compares the dramaturgical construction of Metastasio's *Demofoonte* with that of Zeno's *Eumene*, praising the latter but criticizing the former, possibly in reaction to Bettinelli's preface to the edition of Metastasio libretti just cited. Edesimo's publication was summarized in the August 27, 1735 issue of Albrizzi's Venetian periodical, *Novelli della repubblica delle lettere*, by a writer who refused to choose between Zeno and Metastasio, asserting that ". . . any comparison between these two great men is only odious." Both poets were annoyed to see themselves compared in print, both of them suspecting that an unknown third party was maliciously trying to stir up animosity between them.[2]

Zeno, Apostolo, *Poesie sacre drammatiche* (Venice, 1735). In the prefatory dedication to the Habsburg Emperor and Empress for the first collected edition of his *azione sacre*, "commonly known as oratorios," Zeno summarizes what he takes to have been his own contribution to the improvement of sacred and secular theater: the selection of dramatic personages best suited to reflect the royal virtues of the Habsburgs; the use in his oratorios of events and dialogue drawn exclusively from the holy scriptures and of a dramaturgical construction increasingly concerned with the unities of action and time, ".and for the most part, also that of place"; the purging of comic and effeminate elements inappropriate to Habsburg dignity, and the elimination of the custom, "introduced through the abuse of art and sustained by the licentiousness of the century," of disfiguring dramatic characters of rank or historical fame so as to make them appear ludicrous. Although Zeno's preface is directly concerned only with his oratorio texts, he begins by attributing the superiority of his Vienna works to the inspiration of Charles VI and Elizabeth Christine, a remark which, because Zeno never wrote any oratorio texts before his arrival in Vienna, can only concern his secular texts. The preface mentions no other poets.

An anonymous review of the *Poesie sacre drammatiche* in *Novelle della repubblica delle lettere* represents a contemporary view on the contents of the preface and on Zeno's place in the history of the libretto:

> After having indicated with brief but strong brushstrokes the condition of the Italian theater during his own career, particularly with respect to oratorios, the author explains the manner he employed to compose in both the sacred and the secular genres, and the obligation under which he found himself to avoid wherever possible the rocks on which, through the fault of their time, the overly heated imaginations of earlier poets had stumbled. Zeno, however, gradually removed the abuses and, according to sound precepts, reduced not only his secular but also his sacred work to the unities of action and time, and for the most part also of place, succeeding in arranging and extending them in such a way that they could not only be sung but staged as well.

Urging Zeno to follow the collected edition of his oratorios with one of his secular libretti, the reviewer closes with a list of original editions of those secular libretti which Zeno was then willing to recognize as his own works.[3]

Serie cronologica dei drammi recitati su le pubblici teatri di Bologna dall'anno di nostra salute 1600 sino al corrente 1737; opera de' Sig. Soccii Filopatrii di Bologna. In a preface which defends the idea of publishing a catalogue of all the operas performed in Bologna despite the editors' condemnation of opera as unedifying and ruleless immorality, there is no reference whatever to any recent improvement in the nature of the libretto.

Riccoboni, Luigi, *Réflexions historiques et critiques sur les différents théâtres de l'Europe* (Paris, 1738). "Lélio," one-time disciple of Marchese Orsi, prime-mover in the early eighteenth-century reformation of the Italian spoken theater, possibly Italy's most important actor during the first half of the century, issues one in his series of laments on the decadence of contemporary Italian theater, this time including some rather unorthodox views on the state of the Italian libretto. Some of the Italian poets who have written libretti:

> . . . have distinguished themselves by a noble and chaste versification, and others by a poetical and elevated imagination; but the greatest part of them do not deserve mention. Formerly the opera comprehended all subjects, but since the Machinery has been laid aside it deals no longer in Fables, Divinities, Music Pastoral, and the like, but confines itself entirely to History. The old operas that have come into our hands are proofs of the Italian genius in treating historical subjects. But at present a barrenness of imagination seems to have succeeded this fertility, the French tra-

gedies being commonly pillaged to furnish out their plans, their scenes, and even their thoughts.[4]

It is impossible precisely to identify the historical periods that Riccoboni has in mind, but given his earlier admiration for Zeno and his participation early in the century in the reforming movement of which Zeno was also a member, it seems likely that his complaint about barrenness of imagination in the most recent libretti was intended as a slap at Metastasio, perhaps a part of the unofficial campaign waged against Metastasio by admirers of Zeno during the 1730s and 1740s.

Quadrio, Francesco Saverio, *Della storia e della ragione d'ogni poesia*, 7 vols. (Bologna, 1739–52). Drawing his opinions and in some cases even unacknowledged paragraphs from the material on opera by Crescimbeni, Martello, Marcello, and Maffei, this encyclopedic compiler of the history of western literature indicates that recent poets have with much difficulty succeeded in purging the Italian libretto of some of its innumerable defects, thus rendering opera ". . . if not perfect, at least sufferable." Quadrio derives his list of reforming librettists from Martello's *Dialogo*, then links Martello's remarks on the advantages to librettists employed at court with Zeno's dedicatory paean of 1735 to the virtues of the Habsburgs, crediting Zeno as a man ". . . to whom this manner of drama is truly in debt for much reform." Quadrio shows his lack of contact with contemporary opera by failing to mention Metastasio, the author of Italy's most sought after libretti as much as a decade before the publication of Quadrio's discussion of opera.[5]

Gozzi, Gasparo, ed., *Poesie drammatiche di Apostolo Zeno*, 10 vols, (Venice, 1744). The first collected edition of Zeno's sacred and secular libretti appeared during the closing years of their author's life under circumstances entirely consistent with Zeno's persistently mixed feelings concerning his secular libretti. Urged by Gozzi to bring out all of his dramatic works in versions unimpaired by the tampering of impresarios, singers, and composers, Zeno at first refused, quoting to Gozzi his letter of 1701 to Muratori. But he agreed at last (insisting that he play no role in the preparation of the edition), after Gozzi had indicated that, were Zeno to refuse the offer of an authorized edition, a less satisfactory, unauthorized edition was bound to appear.[6] Gozzi's preface to the series, delayed until the appearance of the fourth volume, blames the seventeenth-century decay of Italian opera on the opening of public opera

houses. And he specifies the evils which impresarios catering to an une-
ducated public were quick to introduce: a confused and unregulated
movement of the singers on and off the stage, the use of incomprehensible
intrigues of great complexity, the mixture of serious and comic figures,
and the use of serious figures in inappropriate situations—all leading to
a subjugation of the librettist to every one of his colleagues in the opera
house. Gozzi admits that to a great extent this situation still obtained in
1744, but he credits Zeno with having eliminated improbable incidents
and comic characters, praising him for the strength and constancy of his
characterization and for his "retention of the laws." Although Gozzi concedes that Zeno was not alone among the librettists interested in such
things, he asserts that no librettist, either past or present, can be said to
surpass Zeno. The only allusion to Metastasio in the entire preface occurs
in the statement just cited. It is impossible to distinguish in the preface
between ideas that may stem from Zeno himself and opinions which Gozzi
derived from his own reading and experience.

Carli, Gian Rinaldo, *Indole del teatro tragico* (Venice, 1744). Apostolo
Zeno:

> . . . was truly the first to liberate the theater from the impossibilities which had been
> introduced there and from the depravities that had corrupted it. He accomplished
> this deed by displaying on the stage actions that had been reduced to a serious,
> heroic, and edifying verisimilitude, worked out with regularity and with skill. His
> libretti were nothing other than little tragedies adapted to music. Anyone who has
> a grain of sense ought to admit that nothing is lacking to keep such works from being
> complete tragedies except perhaps for a little greater length. If Zeno himself did not
> write *real* tragedies, he did, however, provide examples to which others can apply
> themselves, as has in fact happened. It is for this reason that one can state with
> sincerity that from the drama which was once defunct, a new drama has arisen.[7]

Using information drawn from the prefaces to Zeno's collected editions
of 1735 and 1744, Carli has apparently stated his own conclusions.

Groppo, A., ed., *Catalogo di tutti i drammi per musica recitati ne' teatri
di Venezia dall'anno 1637 . . . all'anno presente 1745* (Venice, 1745). The
quotation that follows appears under the listing for Zeno's first libretto,
"Gl'inganni felici," performed in the Teatro Sant'Angelo during the winter of 1695–96. "The author of this drama, now highly celebrated for so
many others, was certainly the first to elevate our theater. He was the
first to remove the ridiculous and foolish abuse of those characters called

buffoons, introduced into libretti during years gone by. Moreover, he selected actions to stage which are the most illustrious and famous in ancient Greek and Roman history; and finally he gave the libretto an orderly arrangement."[8] Groppo appears to have been the first to credit Zeno with the markedly more regular (later criticized as stereotyped) structure which distinguishes the visual appearance of most libretti of the first half of the eighteenth century from those of the second half of the seventeenth. This is an innovation which Zeno himself never claimed and which, as we shall see later, was actually shared by several of his contemporaries. The lines from Groppo just quoted do not appear in the original edition of the same catalogue brought out anonymously in 1730 by C. M. Bonlini under the title, *Le glorie della poesia e della musica contennte nell'esatta notitia de'teatri della Città di Venezia*. The only other catalogue listing Venetian operas to appear during the eighteenth century, the 1755 edition of Allacci's *Drammaturgia*, was edited by G. C. Viniziano, P. F. Giovanni, and Zeno himself; it interpolates no comments on the history of the libretto.

Calsabigi, Ranieri de', "Dissertazione . . . su le poesie drammatiche del Signore Abate Pietro Metastasio," *Poesie del Signor Abate Metastasio* (Paris, 1755). It is not so ironic as it may at first seem that Ranieri de'Calsabigi, the librettist of Gluck's Viennese reform operas during the 1760s and thereafter the staunch opponent of everything Metastasio's libretti stood for, devoted himself in Paris during the early 1750s to a complete edition of Metastasio's works, to whose completion Metastasio himself looked forward with great eagerness.[9] Calsabigi introduced the edition with a 200-page essay on Metastasio's libretti in particular and on operatic aesthetics in general. His flowery praise for a variety of specific beauties in Metastasio's libretti was enough to secure their author's commendation and to help establish Metastasio's reputation in France. But Calsabigi's frequent failure to defend Metastasio from criticisms he did not hesitate to discuss have suggested to some subsequent writers that Calsabigi's essay of 1755 really indicated a rather different attitude towards Metastasio than appeared on the surface.[10] Urged on by Metastasio, Calsabigi was doubtless pleased enough at his share of the profits from the sale of the edition. His artistic conscience was satisfied through the results of his collaboration with Gluck and Durazzo, and through the publication late in his life of an essay that attacked Metastasio, defended his own work, and briefly explained his involvement in the Metastasio edition of 1755.[11]

Although Calsabigi may not have been sincere in the ideas he stated in his essay of 1755, their influence on later writers was important enough to warrant a quotation of his remarks on Metastasio's predecessors:

> . . . Our operas, after they had been reduced by the illustrious Zeno and later by our own poet (Metastasio) to the regular form in which they are seen today, can be called a perfect imitation of Greek and Latin tragedy, since all the regulations of these are strictly observed—except for the unity of place, for which the perfection attained during our time in the art of scene changing and the necessary correction of the inevitable defects brought about in ancient tragedies by too restrained a unity, have rendered a praiseworthy change."[12]

And, after crediting Zeno as reformer of the secular libretto:

> . . . Before Zeno applied his expert hands (to the oratorio libretto), it had been abandoned to the unskilled and subjected to no rules, wherefore it did not deserve the name of drama but could instead be called a capricious miscellany of verses often put into the mouths of characters ideal for pleasing the versifier and the composer of the music. To that most learned poet is reserved the glory for having subjugated it to strict precepts, for having restricted it to the unities of place, time, and action, for having prescribed its management, appropriateness of dialogue, and spectacle, and for having assigned the sources from which it had to provide itself with maxims, aphorisms, and sentiments in the psalms, threnodies, and prophecies. . . .[13]

Calsabigi is the first of the writers under consideration here whose experience did not include the period during which the changes in the libretto were actually taking place. His essay on Metastasio was intended as an analysis of Metastasio's strengths and weaknesses, not as a history of the libretto. Calsabigi was perfectly right to credit Zeno as an important predecessor of Metastasio and probably correct in assigning him so important a role in the design of a new style in oratorio texts, but by singling out Zeno from a number of other similar predecessors, he did a certain violence to Zeno's role in operatic history, and in so doing established a precedent for the writers who followed him.

Algarotti, Francesco, *Saggio sopra l'opera in musica* (Livorno, 1755). For Algarotti opera will achieve its potential only when its constituent elements are made to cooperate towards common dramatic goals. Like several of the writers studied earlier, he feels that those goals will be achieved when the poet has been liberated from the domination of his colleagues in the operatic workshop, becoming himself the dominating force. After stressing this theme in his introduction, Algarotti devotes a chapter each to the discussion of improvements he feels are necessary in the libretto, in the musical score, in the singing and the acting of the performers, in the ballets, in the scenery, and in the designing of the theater itself.[14] He is less critical of contemporary poets than he is of composers and singers, and at one point he even says that poetry has already returned to the correct path.[15] But elsewhere he criticizes the historical subjects which constituted the principal plot sources for the libretti of his day as not suitable for music, too austere, and monotonous. Lully–Quinault and Vinci–Metastasio are designated the outstanding examples in operatic history of fruitful collaboration between composer and librettist; Metastasio's *Didone* and *Achille in Sciro* are put forward as suitable examples of the simple but impressive libretti that Algarotti has in mind for his opera of the future. Zeno and the other members of his generation are not mentioned, nor is anything said of a libretto reform during the early years of the century, at least not in the manner in which we have become accustomed to seeing it described. Instead of referring to the patriotic search for decorum and regularity with which so many writers associated Zeno, Algarotti understands operatic history in more economic terms. With the opening of public opera houses, asserts Algarotti, singers became more powerful and, because of their exorbitant demands for money, forced the debt-ridden impresarios to abandon mythological libretti whose effect depended heavily on the use of expensive machinery and scenic displays. The impresarios turned to historical libretti that created less expense, continues Algarotti, and in order to fill the void thus created, ". . . introduced a chaster regularity into their drama, seconded by the auxiliary charms of a more poetical diction as well as by the concurring powers of a more exquisite musical composition. . . . That these representations might not appear too naked and uniform, interludes and ballets to amuse the audience were introduced between the acts; and thus, by degrees, the opera took that form which is now practiced in our theaters."[16]

A study of seventeenth-century Venetian libretti suggests that Algarotti's analysis is not a sound one. Mythological libretti, to be sure, were not popular during the latter part of the seventeenth-century, but there is no evidence that the equally spectacular historical libretti were any less expensive than their mythological predecessors. Algarotti is not alone in his complaints about the exorbitant salaries paid to some singers, but one gathers from the accounts of those more closely connected with the situation than he that the most notable rise in the economic fortune of the singers took place not through the opening of public opera houses during the middle of the seventeenth century but (as a result of changes in the musical composition of arias?) towards the very end of the century.[17]

Riflessioni sopra i drammi per musica, aggiuntavi una nuova azione drammatica (Venice, 1757). This anonymous essay, printed as an introduction to a short, two-act, amorous intrigue for four singers entitled *Calisso spergiura*, expresses several views on contemporary opera by no means common to the mainstream of mid-century operatic criticism. Different varieties of theater, says the author, are appropriate to different nations at different times in their histories. The Italians and the English, unlike the French and the Germans, prefer dramas that are more expressive and involve more effective dialogue and more use of comic elements. If their plots and their characters have a striking effect on the imagination, one does not care if they are complicated and self-contradictory or not particularly verisimilar, for one pays more attention to the effect of individual scenes than to the logical development of the entire drama. Because of this, Italian poets perform in the service of their actors, and Italian librettists and composers in the service of their singers—not conversely, as is the case in France. Italian drama, therefore, should not be intended as reading matter, and it makes an accordingly weak impression when one so uses it—a statement directly counter to the literary aspirations that concerned both Zeno and Metastasio in the composition of their libretti. Opera is popular in Italy, continues our anonymous author, because it utilizes four art forms (poetry, music, dancing, and painting), each of which when well executed is capable of giving pleasure by itself. It is possible for opera to please even when all four art forms achieve their effects independently or when one or more of the arts is poorly executed, as is alleged to be the case in mid eighteenth-century Italy.

Imagine the effect, continues our author, if the arts were to cooperate towards a common dramatic goal, if composers were to write arias suited only to specific texts of individual libretti, if singers were to reserve their ornaments for moments of dramatic emphasis, and if dancers were to execute dramatically meaningful choreography. But although our anonymous author begins to sound like Algarotti or like Gluck's preface to the 1769 publication of *Alceste*, he names a series of old-fashioned models whose imitation Algarotti and Calsabigi would never have considered desirable. Pollaroli's 1703 setting of the aria "Da te parto" in Zeno's *Venceslao*[18] is praised for the strength of its expression, and Francesco Silvani's libretto of 1707, *L'Armida abbandonata*, for the reasonableness of its dramatic construction. The nobility in general and foreign courts in particular are taken to task for their ignorance in artistic matters and for a concern with self-indulgent entertainment that has kept opera an ornamental pastime instead of furthering its potentiality as expressive drama—a completely different approach to the subject from that taken earlier by writers like Martello and Maffei.[19] The essay closes with the statement of assorted views on operatic construction in support of special features to be found in *Calisso spergiura*. No opera, including the ballets that ought to be used in the middle and at the end of each act, should last more than three hours. The principal dramatic action should involve a love intrigue, as is the case with *Calisso*:

> . . . it being the experience of more than a century that although music has the duty to express every sentiment of poetry and to add expressive power to every kind of verse, only those libretti have found expressive musical settings that were written with the sentiment of love and with easy and harmonious verses. This was the case first of all with Appolloni's *La Dori*, then with some libretti of Morselli, later with some by Silvani, by Zeno in collaboration with Pariati, with some by Silvio Stampiglia, by Salvi, by Piovene, and with almost all the works of Metastasio. And on the other hand, other works that were better contrived, more bizarre in their invention, more reasonable and better adjusted in their sentiments—as is the case with several works by Frigimelica, by Noris, and especially with those written by Zeno in Vienna, the best regulated and most noble of all, but less amorous and versified with roughness—have not met with equal fortune. This stems from the fact that among both actors and audiences, for every person who feels the goads of ambition, of glory, of selfishness, or of honor, there are ten others who in this age at least will feel the stimulus of love.[20]

The anonymous author, who seems to express the views of a literate opera-goer rather than those of the patriotic litterateurs who dominated operatic criticism earlier in the century, is the first to my knowledge to accuse Zeno in print of stiff and awkward versification, an issue which has been raised often since then, particularly in comparisons between Zeno and Metastasio. He distinguishes between Zeno's Venetian and Viennese libretti, but unlike Zeno himself and other critics of the time, he prefers the former. A study of both the Groppo catalogue and the 1755 edition of the Allacci catalogue reveals that this was a preference shared during the first half of the eighteenth century by impresarios all over Italy. While Zeno went to considerable trouble to have copies of the libretti he wrote in Vienna sent around Italy to his Arcadian colleagues, the opera houses of Italy continued to stage their continually rearranged versions of Zeno's Venetian libretti and turned with enthusiasm to the works of Metastasio; but there were relatively few Italian settings of the works Zeno had written for Vienna. Both Zeno and Frigimelica, who appears from the prefaces of his libretti to have considered himself the very reincarnation of Greek dignity, would have been shocked to see themselves listed together with Matteo Noris, Venice's most popular proponent of seventeenth-century caprice 50 years earlier.

Oeuvres dramatiques d'Apostolo Zeno traduites de l'Italien (Paris 1758). This two-volume French translation of six of Zeno's secular and two of his sacred libretti is introduced by a preface which quotes Martello's list of worthy Italian librettists around the turn of the eighteenth century, but which asserts that Zeno had long been honored as Italy's greatest living poet when Metastasio appeared, first to share the applause, then to overshadow the reputation of his predecessor. Now that Metastasio's works have made so impressive a success in France, the translator of the present edition feels it is time to reclaim Zeno's rightful place with respect to Metastasio, a place which is compared here for the first time to that of Corneille with respect to Racine. Zeno is praised for the variety of his plots, for the liveliness of his dialogue, and for having thrown off the yoke of seventeenth-century bad taste; Metastasio for the tenderness of his thoughts and for the euphonius qualities of his versification. This is the only instance I know in the collected editions of either Zeno or Metastasio where a step is made towards an ideal cherished by both poets: the elimination of at least some of the arias.[21]

Martinelli, V., *Lettere familiari e critiche* (London, 1758). The author recognizes Zeno as the most important of libretto reformers and Metastasio as his illustrious successor. He praises Metastasio for his morality, for the beauty and wit of his imagery, and for the ease with which his poetry can be understood and memorized by an Englishman learning Italian.[22]

On December 7, 1767, asked by Angelo Fabroni to contribute an opinion on Zeno's place in the history of the libretto for Fabroni's forthcoming Latin biography of Zeno, Metastasio wrote a letter acknowledging both his lifelong sensitivity to being charged as Zeno's imitator and his gratitude to the man whose recommendation had introduced Metastasio to Vienna:

> . . . So little sure of myself in knowing how to preserve the due mean between jealousy and affection, I avoid a detailed examination of [Zeno's] works. But I cannot conceal that even were Apostolo Zeno to lack every other poetic merit, that of having demonstrated with happy success that reason and our opera are not incompatible beings (as with the forebearance, nay even with the applause of the public those poets whom Zeno found in possession of the theater when he began to write seem to have believed); that of having shown that opera need not be exempted from the laws of verisimilitude or protected from the contagion of the idiotic and turgid style so dominant at that time; and finally that of having liberated the serious from the ludicrous licentiousness of the comic with which opera was so miserably muddled in those days, are certainly sufficient merits to require our esteem and respect.[23]

Metastasio does not refer specifically to the poetic facility for which contemporary writers usually preferred his own works to Zeno's, but his hint that Zeno's libretti might leave some room for criticism was probably calculated to remind Fabroni of Metastasio's superiority. If so, Metastasio may have tried to soothe his conscience for alluding to Zeno's weakness in versification by giving him more credit than Metastasio must have known Zeno actually deserved for the changes that had taken place around the turn of the eighteenth century in the form and content of the libretto. If there was a specific Zeno contribution which Metastasio could well have made use of, it was the lessening of the role played by amorous intrigue of which Zeno had been so proud in his Viennese libretti. But although Metastasio had written libretti in Italy in which such intrigues were subordinated to some extent to more somber dramatic ideas,[24] he had already returned to a concentration on amorous intrigue by the time he replaced Zeno in Vienna.

Rousseau, Jean-Jacques, "Opera," *Dictionnaire de musique* (Paris, 1768). Rousseau may have been a great admirer of Italian opera, but his dictionary article on the subject gives a peculiar picture of its history. He posits two stages in a process of reform, during the first of which mythological subjects and machines were abandoned in favor of more regular, noble, and sensible plots. This change is alleged as the cause of the second reform, ". . . no less important than the first," in which cerebral elements (political deliberations, conspiracies, and sententious maxims are mentioned specifically) that do not speak to the heart, and *gallant* elements that weaken the tragic tone of the drama, were eliminated.[25] The times and places where these two ostensible reforms took place are left unidentified, but Zeno and Metastasio, compared as in the Parisian Zeno edition of 1758 to Corneille and Racine, are named as the poets who introduced and improved the new variety of opera.[26]

Planelli, Antonio, *Dell'opera in musica* (Naples, 1772). In an essay whose organizational plan and content were admittedly derived from Algarotti, we find a paragraph on the history of opera during the first half of the century which names Zeno as the principal figure in a movement that led to Metastasio, but which interposes the names of several poets who, although once involved with the writing of libretti, exerted little if any influence through their own libretti.

> . . . Among the libretto's first restorers one should certainly number Apostolo Zeno, whose first libretti saw the light of day during the closing years of the last century.

Pier-Jacopo Martello, Abate Frugoni, Marchese Maffei, Paolo Rolli, and others of our worthy poets have followed the same course. But the poet to whom opera is indebted more than to any other man is Abate Metastasio, who . . . with skillful but restrained use of visual decoration has restored to poetry that which she lost during the last century, and has brought opera to a point attained by no one before him[27]

Having stated his slightly unconventional contribution to the by this time increasingly traditional outline of libretto history during the first half of the century, Planelli, like Algarotti, asserts his view that the art forms which constitute opera are too independent of each other to create any unified dramatic effect. He praises the unified effect that is achieved in Calsabigi's *Alceste*, quotes Gluck's preface to the edition of 1769, and states that if Gluck had not used so many textual repeats and had been somewhat more economical in his use of the orchestra, ". . . he would have written music totally in accord with my own taste."[28] In addition to many ideas about the libretto put forward by Algarotti, Planelli puts forward several of his own. Opera is not simply sung tragedy, but an independent genre with conventions and requirements of its own. Unity of place in Greek tragedy is said to have been caused by the primitive state of scene-changing machinery during ancient times. There is no reason on the modern stage to observe this unity strictly, but one should be careful, asserts Planelli, not to change scene at improbable moments, and to keep the scenes used in geographical proximity to each other. It should be allowed, for example, to represent an outer courtyard of a palace in one scene and an inner chamber of the same palace in another, but the use of a scene in Egypt followed by another in Spain is branded as licentious.[29] Happy endings are approved because they are indicative of human progress. Altogether virtuous or vicious characters are preferred because eighteenth-century audiences are said to be fond of decisively drawn characterizations. Since five acts make an opera long and boring, three are approved, as is the recent idea of limiting the number of acts to two. All of the arias should be simple in their language and each aria should concern itself with a single passion that is dramatically appropriate.[30] Aria texts that are maxims or that use comparisons are decried, as is the inevitably undramatic form of the *da capo* aria. In order to ensure the collaboration of all the arts for the most effective dramatic result, Planelli recommends the establishment of a position whose justification we accept without question, but which seems not to have been known in operatic circles during most of the eighteenth century: a dramatic director whose opinions were to carry weight with even the impresario.

Fabroni, Angelo, "Apostolus Zenus," *Vitae Italorum* V (Florence, 1775). In Zeno's first published biography he is designated the predecessor of

Metastasio and ". . . the first among Italian poets to bring extraordinary understanding, discretion, perspicacity, and the elegance of Tuscan dialect to the writing of libretti."[31] Zeno is praised for his choice of plots, ideas, and language, and for his wisdom in excluding dramatic improprieties and scurrilous jokes, but as Metastasio suggested, Zeno is said to be his successor's inferior with regard both to poetical charm and to his power to move an audience's emotions.[32] No other librettists are mentioned. The relevant section from Metastasio's letter of 1767 to Fabroni is quoted in full as a footnote.[33]

Napoli-Signorelli, Pietro, *Storia critica de'teatri antichi e moderni* (Naples, 1777).[34] An imperturable admirer who regarded the period from 1720 to 1760 as the golden age of opera, who condemned Calsabigi's collaboration in Vienna with Gluck and his attacks on Metastasio, and who despised the ballets and pantomime scenes that had begun to encroach during the latter part of the eighteenth century upon the rights of Metastasian dialogue, Napoli-Signorelli mentions Zeno frequently, but only by way of introduction to his idol, Metastasio. Signorelli adds information about the change in operatic ideals around the turn of the century which, if not absolutely unbiased, particularly with regard to the city of Naples, Signorelli's home, gives further support to our theory that the change in question was a many-faceted one with which Zeno was by no means the only librettist concerned:

> . . . Heroic opera, which can be equated with the operas using historical plots that began to be used during the 17th century, when it had a long childhood, then passed during the 18th century through a happy adolescence and a period of much commended virility. One can observe the first stage in Eustachio Manfredi's *Dafni*, in Antonio Salvi's *Arsace*, in Paolo Rolli's *Polifemo*, in *Farnace, Faraemane*, and other works by Biancardi or by Lalli, the Neapolitan, and especially in *Eraclea, Tito Sempronio Gracco, Decimviri, Turno Aricino*, and other works by the Roman librettist, later poet of Emperor Charles VI, Silvio Stampiglia. . . . Signor Zeno, the imperial poet and historian who succeeded Stampiglia, was more regular than Stampiglia, more natural, more majestic, and more lively. He had more imagination, more knowledge of the theater, more truth and more force in the management of his passions, more grandeur in his heroes. His language is pure, his style rich, appropriate both to the plots he selects and to the dramatic situation. He lacks nothing, except perhaps that warmth, that precision, that proportion, and that quality which constitute the merit of the great poet who succeeded him. The libretti of Apostolo Zeno are notable for the variety of their characters and of their plots, enriched as they are through Greek and Roman history and through the history of the barbarians, with which he was familiar. . . . An aspect of Zeno's libretti that gives a good idea of their nature lies in Zeno's ability to prepare in each act of his stories a popular, interesting, and visually impressive scene that will hold the attention of the spectators. . . . And now

we have reached the happier days of the virility of heroic opera, days that are brightened by the passage of the greatest star in the poetry of musical drama, Pietro Trapassi.[35]

After 30 pages of the most effusive praise for Metastasio, characteristic of nearly all the prose written about *opera seria* by Italians during most of the second half of the eighteenth century,[36] Napoli–Signorelli makes an admission equally typical of the essays that appeared on the subject during the final quarter of the century: Metastasio's libretti, alleged so often as Italy's greatest poetry of the century, were not without certain defects! These were, of course, not the fault of Metastasio but ". . . of the system already introduced, of the genre itself, of earlier operas, and, above all, of musical abuses—for example: the large number of lyrical comparisons (excellent in themselves), certain subordinate amorous intrigues, and the use of expression more affected than is proper for the stage." Despite these reservations, the author carries the familiar comparison of Italian librettists to playwrights of the past a step further than we have seen it taken before. He asserts that Metastasio is not only Italy's Euripides, but also her Corneille *and* Racine.[37]

LaBorde, Jean Benjamin de, *Essai sur la musique ancienne et moderne* (Paris, 1780). In a chapter devoted to alphabetically ordered biographical sketches on Italian librettists of both seventeenth and eighteenth centuries, LaBorde includes several of the poets who had been praised with Zeno and Metastasio in the works of earlier writers, but as had become customary by 1780, he reserves terms like "reformer of the Italian theater" for Zeno himself. Zeno, who LaBorde says would have been considered the paragon of librettists had he not been succeeded by Metastasio, is credited with a *revolution* carried out *gradually* in order to avoid antagonizing the innumerable vested interests connected with the production of opera.

Tiraboschi, Girolamo, *Storia della letteratura italiana* (Modena, 1772–81). In a rather miscellaneous list of typically decadent seventeenth-century librettists Tiraboschi includes Giulio Cesare Corradi and Francesco Silvani, two poets credited by earlier writers as participants in the reform movement often associated with Zeno. Although Tiraboschi asserts that ". . . all the glory for bringing opera back to a suitable majesty and decorum is reserved for Zeno," and that ". . . the so much greater glory of uniting in the libretto all the merits that are capable of making dramatic poetry attractive and beautiful belong to the great Metastasio," he gives credit to three poets who are said to have been involved in the same matters that concerned Zeno: Gianandrea Moniglia and Zeno's two immediate predecessors in Vienna, Pietro Bernardoni and Silvio Stampiglia.[38]

Arteaga, Stefano, *Le rivoluzioni del teatro musicale italiano dalla sua origine fino al presente*, 3 vols. (Bologna, 1783–85). The first critical history of Italian opera, written by a former Spanish Jesuit at the urging of Padre Martini, is reasonable in the general precepts of its introductory chapters on operatic aesthetics, but confused in its subsequent chapters on operatic history. Arteaga begins his preface by differentiating among five varieties of opera-lover—the man of the world, the politician, the scholar, the man of taste, and the philosopher—pointing out those facets of contemporary opera which he believes appeal to each of the five. Arteaga himself prefers the judgment of the man of taste for his thorough understanding of each libretto and its place in dramatic history[39]—another instance of a person who considers the reading and studying of libretti the most important activity connected with the musical theater. The preface ends with the eighteenth century's first critical summary of the views of previous Italian operatic critics.

The first two chapters of *Le rivoluzioni* comprise a discussion of operatic aesthetics and an essay on the special appropriateness of the Italian language for musical settings. Arteaga begins his historical survey of musical drama by proceeding chronologically from early medieval times. Our concern is with his tenth chapter, "On the Improvement of lyrical-dramatic Poetry," which he opens by asserting that the improvement noticeable in Italian libretti around the turn of the eighteenth century resulted primarily from the influence of changes introduced earlier in French opera by Philippe Quinault: a new regularity of form, a measure of control over the disordered elements of mythology, an elegance and clarity of style, and a delicacy of sentiment. As soon as Italian poets began to understand that:

> . . . the true, the grand, and the unaffected were the only paths to reach the heart, the apparatus of mythology, the whole development of accidents and of marvels invented solely to surprise the imagination in the absence of nature, disappeared directly. Gods and devils were banished from the theater. At the moment that one learned how to make men speak in a dignified manner, madrigals, antitheses, amorous subtleties, and similar hypocrisies of sentiment were sent their ways, together with fugues, counter-fugues, augmentations, retrogrades, and other such musical stuffings. Noble figures, strong passions, and great characters drawn from Greek and Roman history (almost the only two nations that provide plots for the theater, since they

were almost the only nations where those virtues that can be received from legislation and philosophy were known) were substituted on the stage for the abomination of good taste which had previously dominated everywhere. One perceived that the rapidity, the concision, and the interest which gave birth to emotion were the very soul of musical poetry, and that the slowness, monotony, academic dissertations, and long episodes restricted the effect of an art whose aim is to arouse excitement in the souls of its audience and the disorder of all their emotions. For this reason libretti were much shortened and the number of acts was reduced from five, to which they had become accustomed, to three. Useless prologues that involved preliminary actions separate from the main action were removed. Recitatives were shortened and arias pushed to the ends of scenes, whereas previously they had interfered with every upright thought. An intimate knowledge of the theater makes it clear that since arias are a kind of peroration or epilogue of a passion, they ought not to be placed at the beginning or in the middle of a scene. Because nature does not proceed by leaps but rather through a well-ordered gradation in its movements, it is not verisimilar if, at the beginning of a dialogue, one already sees at the summit of passion a person who then immediately reenters the placid style demanded by recitative.[40]

Other elements of reform mentioned by Arteaga include a more orderly succession of stage sets, a stricter attention to the Aristotelian unities, and the abandonment of the custom of closing every act with a chorus.

It is difficult to understand how Arteaga managed to concoct this strange combination of half truths. Although, for example, translations of Corneille and Racine had become very popular in Italy by the turn of the century, there is but one known instance of an Italian translation of any of the works of Quinault,[41] who figures neither in the polemics of the French critics of Italian literature nor in the often revealing prefaces of Italian libretti. Italian libretti of the Zeno generation were, like Quinault's, more dignified, more serious than their predecessors, but it is hard to imagine anything more remote from most early eighteenth-century Italian libretti than those of Quinault, particularly with respect to form.[42] Mythological libretti had ceased to be popular in Italy some time before the appearance of the new, more dignified libretti of the Zeno generation, but in several German courts, particularly in Vienna, they continued to exist side by side with the historical libretti through the duration of Zeno's stay there. Arteaga is correct when he says that most of Zeno's libretti were based on Greek and Roman history, but incorrect when he states that an important part of the new direction in Italian libretti concerned the dropping of mythological plots. "Fugues, retrogrades, and the like" had never been a notable feature of operatic music. The change from five acts to three took place during the middle of the seventeenth century; an important feature of the new directions taken by Zeno's generation involved an occasional return to the five-act division, but these works represent less than 25 percent of Zeno's secular output. Prologues involving separate preliminary actions appear very infrequently by the final quarter of the

seventeenth century. The recitatives of both Zeno and Metastasio were
often cut to shreds by impresarios making rearrangements in Italy of
works already premiered in Vienna, but the recitatives in all the original
texts of both poets were considerably longer, not shorter, than those of
their seventeenth-century predecessors. Nor did the libretti of poets like
Noris, Aureli, Corradi, Minato, Neri, and Giannini conclude every act
with a chorus.

On the problem of identifying those Italian poets who carried out
the reform, Arteaga frankly admits to confusion:

> . . . Carlo Maggi and Francesco Lemene wrote several dramas in which, although
> both participate in the excessive vices of bad taste and in affected characterizations,
> they nonetheless achieve some regularity and taste. Capece composed several wherein
> one perceives a more fluid and musical poetry with quickness of intrigue. Silvio
> Stampiglia of Rome, an imperial poet, wrote many libretti, almost all on historical
> subjects. Some writers contend that this author was perhaps the first to turn the
> endings of his libretti from sadness to happiness, but the truth is that the custom of
> ending dramas happily is as old in Italy as the drama itself. . . . Stampiglia deserves
> credit not for this but for having been one of the first to purge the libretto of the
> ridiculous mixture of serious and comic elements, of very complicated dramatic ac-
> cidents, and of the sated pomp of the machines. But, on the other hand, his style is
> dry and lacking in warmth. He does not know the art of making his recitative beau-
> tiful, and more important, that of making his arias musical. *La caduta dei decimviri*
> is the most passable of his works. Bernardoni, another imperial poet, and the Flor-
> entine, Antonio Salvi, followed the example of Stampiglia at the same time and with
> some credit, but their names and works have not received any reward from posterity
> other than that of appearing in the voluminous tomes of Quadrio. Marchese Scipione
> Maffei in his *Ninfa fida* lets one see that the talents for tragic poetry are different
> from those for musical poetry, since no one would believe that the author of that
> pastorale, written without interest, without sweetness of style, and without theatrical
> spirit was the same who had written the most beautiful *Merope*. The style of the
> libretti by the Bolognese poet, Jacopo Martello, is erratic, affected, and florid, but
> this author designs his characters adequately and writes some of his arias with good
> taste. Eustachio Manfredi in *Aci* and in *Dafni*, both attributed to him, shows himself
> to be far from the astonishing cultivation of intrigue that sparkles in his lyric poetry,
> especially in the canzona *Donna negli occhi vostri*, which in my opinion is the richest
> jewel on the modern Italian Parnassus.

> The poet who made himself more worthy and who acquired greater celebrity is
> the Candian, Apostolo Zeno, poet and historian of the Emperor, Charles VI. This
> man . . . can rightly call himself the Pierre Corneille of the lyric theater. Among the
> enterprises to which he applied himself to the great advantage of his nation, one was
> the improvement of the libretto. He undertook to correct the corrupt, even vulgar
> customs through which it had been stained, and wherever in the vastness of history,
> in which he was deeply versed, he found bright examples of patriotism, of the virtuous
> desire for glory, of generous constancy in friendship, of gentleness with fidelity in
> love, of compassion towards one's peers, of greatness of soul in adverse circum-
> stances, of prudence, fortitude, and other such virtues, he took them all to adorn

the theater. . . . His style is correct and reserved, his invention diverse, his dramatic events better prepared than those of his predecessors, and the whole proceeds with regularity. . . . Even with such merits this poet is, nevertheless, rather far from having reached perfection. He can be called rather a man of talent than a man of genius. Between his works and those of Metastasio there appears about the same difference as would appear between a pleasant and leafy valley seen by the languid light of the moon, and the same valley brightened by the rays of the sun on the brightest morning of May.[43]

Arteaga was obviously familiar both with the lists of reform librettists that had appeared in earlier essays on the subject and with the tradition of a movement begun by Zeno and completed by Metastasio. In trying to reapportion the proper credit owed to each poet Arteaga awarded Zeno his traditional place as the immediate predecessor of Metastasio, but in so doing he was probably more accurate than previous writers in distinguishing those features of the Zeno libretti that were really unique to Zeno: a deepening seriousness of subject and tone, a diversity of subject matter, and the development of a more regular dramaturgical structure. (This is a thesis that will be supported in detail in Chapter III.)

Arteaga closes his remarks on the history of the Italian libretto with some reflections on the works of Metastasio; in refusing to take a consistent position, Arteaga typifies many of his contemporaries. Metastasio is described on the one hand as a poet of genius, and effusively praised for the excellence of his philosophy and for the musicality of his style. But on the other he is labelled the enemy of realistic drama and harshly criticized for the narrowness of his vocabulary and for the unoriginality of his plots.[44]

Mattei, Saverio, *Elogio dello Jommelli o sia il progresso della poesia e della musica teatrale* (Rome, 1785). This Neapolitan professor of oriental languages, translator of the *Bible* into Italian verses in the style of Metastasio, and biographer of both Jommelli and Metastasio seems to have been the first to suggest an hypothesis on the origins of the libretto reform that was to become very popular with several German historians during the nineteenth century. Maffei implies that the well-known seriousness of the Habsburg Court in Vienna was the real underlying force behind the "reform," while the view of Zeno and Metastasio as the principal poets in the movement is broadened to include Zeno's predecessor in Vienna, Silvio Stampiglia.[45]

A noticeable change in the conception of libretto reform around the turn of the eighteenth century is evident in two publications of Carlo Goldoni

that appeared a third of a century apart. In the original dedication to
Metastasio of his 1754 comedy, *Terenzio*, Goldoni sketches an outline of
libretto history:

> . . . Opera is a variety of composition that is irregular by nature, known neither by
> Aristotle nor by Horace, nor by the other ancient preceptors of authority on drama.
> The singing used in the choruses of the tragedies awakened the desire among lovers
> of novelty to subject all drama to music; and in order to divert the public with melody,
> drama had to be disassociated from that tragic gravity which excited in the audience
> terror and shock rather than pleasure. The first works in this genre were so imperfect
> that they could be designated farces. Several authors during the past century reduced
> them to a better form, and your worthy predecessor, Signor Apostolo Zeno, distin-
> guished himself among all the others in his conduct of the drama, in the truth of his
> characterizations, and in the strength of his sentiments. But the perfection of this
> work remained for you. . . .[46]

However this miscontrues the origins of opera, it does place Zeno
in a context where his contemporaries would have had no trouble rec-
ognizing him: the most famous of several poets working in the direction
of more serious, more coherent libretti. This is not the case in the paragraphs on Zeno and Metastasio which Goldoni included in the section
covering the later 1730s that he dictated during the 1780s for his *Mémoires*:

> . . . Zeno and Metastasio effected the reformation of the Italian opera. Before
> them, nothing but gods, devils, machines, and wonders were to be found in these
> harmonious entertainments. Zeno was the first who conceived the possibility of rep-
> resenting tragedy in lyrical verse without degradation, and of singing it without pro-
> ducing weakness. He executed the project in a manner most satisfactory to the
> public, and reflecting the greatest glory on himself and his nation.
>
> In his opera we see heroes as they actually were, or at least as they have been
> handed down to us by historians; his characters are vigorously supported, his plots
> always well conducted; his episodes are naturally connected with the main action;
> and his style is masculine and vigorous, the words of the airs adapted to the music
> of his day.
>
> Metastasio, who succeeded him, brought lyrical tragedy to the utmost perfection
> of which it was susceptible. . . .[47]

Ending with the traditional comparison of Zeno and Metastasio to Corneille and Racine, Goldoni goes on to describe Zeno's deprecatory remarks on *Gustavus*, a Goldoni libretto submitted for Zeno's criticism
during its author's youth.

In contrast with Goldoni's earlier remarks on Zeno, his comments in the *Mémoires* separate Zeno from his natural context and attribute a position in operatic history to him which he did not have and never claimed. Zeno was not the first to consider the composition of serious libretti. His attention was directed, as we have seen, towards the publication of readable texts, not to a musical performance that supported dramatic action. Judging from Zeno's extant correspondence, he knew nothing about music and had no interest whatever in the adaptability of his aria texts to music. The inferiority of Zeno's texts to Metastasio's for musical settings is, in fact, one of the points most often stressed by the later eighteenth-century Metastasio enthusiasts in the inevitable comparisons of the two poets which, ironically, did so much to establish Zeno's reputation as the reformer of the libretto.[48]

Burney, Charles, *A General History of Music*, IV (London, 1789). Of the half-dozen instances in which Burney juxtaposes the names of Zeno and Metastasio in the final volume of his general history, three occur with reference to those poets' ostensible banishing of comic figures from serious opera, two with reference to their successive roles as "purifiers" and "sublimers" of the opera.[49] The names of Bernardoni, Bernini, Capece, David, deTotis, Frigimelica, Gigli, Lemene, Maffei, Manfredi, Martello, Moniglia, Silvani, Sinibaldi, and Stampiglia are nowhere to be found. Those of Pariati and Cardinal Ottoboni appear only incidentally, without reference to a reform of the libretto around the turn of the century.

In the final volume of Burney's *Memoirs of the Life and Writings of the Abate Pietro Metastasio*, he contributes a comparison of Zeno and Metastasio to dramatists previously unmentioned in this connection, but the idea that Zeno and Metastasio, like Corneille and Racine, were lone pioneers in an uncharted wasteland, remains the same: ". . . Apostolo Zeno seems to have been the Aeschylus, and Metastasio the Sophocles and Euripides of the modern melodrama. What preceded and is subsequent to them appears equally to partake of the wildness and weakness of their predecessors and successors in Greece and Italy."[50]

"Drammi scelti di Apostolo Zeno," *Parnasso italiano ovvero raccolta de' poeti classici italiani* XLVI (Venice, 1790). In his critical notes to this edition of four of Zeno's secular libretti, Andrea Rubbi writes that Zeno was ". . . one of the first reformers of good taste" but states besides that it was Zeno to whom Italy owed that ". . . illustrious province of poetry which Metastasio has adorned to perfection."[51]

Negri, Francesco, *Vita di Apostolo Zeno* (Venice, 1816). Zeno's only full-scale biography is of particular interest because its author had access to two important sources unused by other writers: more than a thousand unpublished Zeno letters and a series of notes transcribed from interviews undertaken during the final years of Zeno's life by Marco Forcellini. Negri's familiarity with many eighteenth-century writings on operatic history and his reluctance to overburden his text with footnotes make it impossible to treat his views on Zeno's role as an operatic reformer as though they all came from Zeno himself; but because one can recognize at least some of the comments that stem from Crescimbeni and his successors, the value of Negri's biography as a reflection of Zeno's own ideas is not altogether destroyed. Negri's remarks on Zeno as a reformer are not limited to his activities as a librettist but include information on Zeno's secretive efforts during the 1680s towards the stylistic purification of his lyric poetry,[52] his share in the reformation of the literary academy that about 1691 became the Animosi of Venice,[53] his leadership in the founding, early in the eighteenth century, of Italy's first durable literary periodical,[54] and his role in concentrating the attention of literary historians on the critical evaluation of primary source material.[55] Clearly Zeno's interest in more serious libretti was not a particular one in a special area but part of a general concern that included every branch of Italian literary and cultural life.

According to Negri, the trouble with most of the libretti from the end of the seventeenth century was partly a matter of bad taste and partly a domination of poetry by music. Nicolo Beregani, Camillo Contarini, and especially Matteo Noris are mentioned as librettists of the old-fashioned, depraved manner, while Domenico David, ". . . whose libretti were perhaps less bad than those of the poets first named because David was a person of much intellect," is the only person other than Zeno designated responsible for the new, more serious libretti. Zeno's contribution is described as a reduction in the number of arias, the banishment of ridiculous and despicable characters and incidents, the concentration on a "decorous and tragic severity," the observation of Aristotle's unity of action, the construction of dramaturgical developments "in accordance with reason," and an attention to consistent characterizations and naturalness of style. Negri states that Zeno undertook all this to rescue melodramatic poetry from its debasement and that he did not accomplish all of his goals in one stroke.[56] Working from Zeno's correspondence Negri indicates that, as early as 1705, Zeno had lost interest in operatic reform and had come to view libretto writing as an easy means to a quick profit.[57] One infers from Negri that the Viennese works of which Zeno was most proud during the later part of his life were the products of a period that began more than a decade after Zeno had given up trying to write libretti which satisfied both dramatic reason and Italian impresarios.

Raccolta di melodrammi serii scritti nel secolo XVIII, ed. Giovanni Gherardini, 2 vols. (Milan, 1822). In the foreward to an edition of eighteenth-century libretti two-thirds of whose contents comprise works by Zeno, Giovanni Gherardini considers the merits of Guidi, Testi, Chiabrera, Maggi, Lemene, and Stampiglia, only to decide that while several librettists around the turn of the eighteenth century made notable achievements as lyric poets, it is Zeno to whom Italy is indebted ". . . for the first true reform of her operatic texts." So great is Gherardini's enthusiasm for Zeno that he compares the relationship of Zeno and Metastasio to that of Galileo and Newton, asserting that the achievements of the latter would have been impossible without the accomplishments of the former.[58]

Klein, J. L. *Geschichte des Dramas*, VI/1 (Leipzig, 1868). This whimsical history of European drama, whose meandering remarks on the career and works of Zeno include extensive digressions on the masculine qualities of the German language and on Burney's and Hawkins's inadequacies as music historians, bases its comments about the birth of *opera seria* on the works of Crescimbeni, Quadrio, and Negri. It praises Zeno for having rid the libretto of Spanish influences and for having brought it back to ". . . classical-French, Greco-Gallic soil." Zeno is credited with having carried out a transformation of the Italian musical theater which he is said to have had in mind from the earliest days of his career. Its principal features, according to Klein, include a reduction in the number of arias, a banishment of comic characters, a more verisimilar dramaturgy, and a more didactic tone and serious style—a series of assets that Metastasio is said to have completed, refined, beautified, and softened. Cicognini and Matteo Noris appear as representatives of seventeenth-century bizarreness, but none of the librettists who participated with Zeno in the "reform" is mentioned. Three libretti from the beginning, middle, and end of Zeno's career are described in detail, quoted at length, ridiculed for their poetic awkwardness, and mocked as dramatic imbecilities.[59]

DeSanctis, Francesco, *Storia della letteratura italiana* (Naples, 1870). The libretti of Metastasio are discussed at length. The generation that preceded him, however, is represented only by Zeno, who is commended as the architect of a formal design into which Metastasio is said to have breathed dramatic life.[60]

Tirinelli, Gastavo, "Silvio Stampiglia," *La scuola romana* (Rome, 1882). At the conclusion of a short biography of Stampiglia, Tirinelli calls him the first reformer of the Italian libretto, but does not specify the nature of his reform.[61]

Landau, Marcus, *Die italienische Literatur am Österreichischen Hofe* (Vienna, 1879). Landau takes as his thesis Crescimbeni's statement that while the Italian language was invented by Italians, its pinnacle of greatness was achieved under the aegis of the Habsburgs.[62] Landau credits Stampiglia and Bernardoni, Zeno's immediate predecessors in Vienna, with having tried to keep their libretti free from the tastelessness and monstrosities of the seventeenth century, and praises both for the simplicity of their lyric poetry. But he criticizes Bernardoni as boring and Stampiglia as dry and colorless, a poet whose recitatives are without harmony and whose arias are unmusical.[63] Zeno's colleague and assistant, Pietro Pariati, is first described in the terms applied earlier to Bernardoni and Stampiglia, than paired with Zeno as responsible for carrying out a "salutary reform."[64]

The degree to which Austria's Arcadian colony represented a polite society of litterateurs rather than an organization of active literary reformers is illustrated by the membership therein of two of Vienna's most bizarre and unreformed librettists, Nicolo Minato and Donato Cupeda—and by Charles VI's never-fulfilled desire for a reform and reorganization of that colony.[65]

Cugnoni, Giuseppe, *Lettere di Apostolo Zeno e Pietro Metastasio* (Rome, 1891). The degree to which the names of Zeno and Metastasio had become indissolubly linked is shown here by the publication, "in honor of the bicentennial of the founding of Arcadia," of three otherwise published letters of Metastasio together with one of Zeno's, none of which is even peripherally related to opera.

Carini, Isidoro, *L'Arcadia dal 1690 al 1890* (Rome, 1891). In another publication marking the Arcadian bicentennial, Isidoro Carini traces the history of the Academy, stressing the varied backgrounds, professions, and reforming interests of the first-generation Arcadians. Carini's catalogue of Arcadian librettists includes nearly all the poets listed earlier by Martello as well as more than a dozen obscure poets whose activity as librettists mostly antedated the founding of Arcadia. All these are said to have begun a reform later completed by Zeno and Metastasio.[66]

Pistorelli, Luigi, *I melodrammi di Apostolo Zeno* (Padua, 1894). Writing the first Zeno biography to include a critical examination of Zeno's libretti, Pistorelli begins by stating that the honor for having gradually lifted opera from the abject position into which it had fallen belonged to the imperial poets of Vienna.[67] Stampiglia and Bernardoni are both praised for having tried to correct the excesses of their predecessors and Stampiglia alone for having expanded the use of historical plots, though Pistorelli takes exception to what he considers the inappropriately inelegant dialogue Stampiglia is said to have put into the mouths of his antique heroes. Zeno, who is alleged to have "girded himself for a reform of the libretto in which, guided by erudition and by reason, he succeeded in preparing the way for the masterpieces of Metastasio," is given a more heroic role in operatic history than ever before. He is said to have brought the libretto closer to classical tragedy, to have given greater attention to the Aristotelian unities, and to have written more expressive and dignified libretti while using fewer arias and unnecessary characters. Metastasio is praised not only for the superior qualities of his poetry and dramaturgy but also for having simplified the inevitable prefatory prose explanations of events that are supposed to have preceded the opening of each drama.[68]

Campanini, Naborre, *Un precursore del Metastasio* (Florence, 1905); Biblioteca critica della letteratura italiana XLIII. In the only critical biography of Pietro Pariati, the Modenese librettist with whom Zeno collaborated in both Venice and Vienna between 1703 and 1721, Campanini carefully marks Pariati's subordinate position with respect to Zeno but, nonetheless, attributes to Pariati an important share in what he calls Zeno's struggle for reform.[69] Campanini's notion of Zeno's reform includes the dropping of mythological, pastoral, and fantastic subjects in favor of concentration on the histories of Greece, Rome, "and other southern peoples"; the reduction of the libretto to a more regular form; the use of simpler plots, more logical dramatic development, more probable action, and a nobler style.[70] He considers the works of both Zeno and Pariati superior to those of Guidi, Testi, Chiabrera, Maggi, and Lemene, but despite what he calls their gradual approach towards the virtues just indicated and towards more musical versification, he ranks them as inferior to the works of Metastasio, whose libretti Zeno is alleged to have envied. Stampiglia is admitted as a librettist who shared Zeno's ideals, but he is said to have had a minimal effect on the content of opera in Vienna during his tenure there.

Campanini's conception of the Zeno–Pariati "reform" includes only aspects of content and tone. In his view, such formal matters as the number of the actors, the nature of the characters, the number of the arias, and the positioning of entrances and exits had already become established conventions with which Zeno was wise enough not to tamper at the time when, early in his career, he undertook the reform.[71] Campanini defends *Ambleto* by Zeno and Pariati from attacks by Guerzoni and Landau on the grounds that its plot is not so confused nor its characters so vague as in the works of many other librettists of the period. And he defends the use of both comic and serious elements in *Alessandro in Sidone* (the last libretto of the Zeno–Pariati collaboration) on the ground that the comic parts are kept distinct from the serious, whose progress they are said to help impel.[72] Led by his notion of Zeno's dynamic struggle against the forces of corruption, Campanini comes here to the defense of works for which Zeno himself would have offered no defense. Zeno was interested in the composition of more serious and more regular libretti, but one gathers from his correspondence that he never allowed artistic scruple to stand in the way of material gain. If conditions were imposed which Zeno felt might harm one of his works, he protested, but almost always in a very restrained fashion.[73] One discovers no instances in which he gave up a theatrical commission to another librettist rather than comply with the changes asked of him. Similarly, Zeno made a reputation early in the century with serious libretti that had no place for comic characters. But there was an old tradition in Vienna of performing a comic or tragi-comic work during every carnival season. Normally Zeno was excused from participating in these productions, but he is known to have assisted Pariati with more than one such libretto.[74]

Fehr, Max, *Apostolo Zeno und seine Reform des Operntextes* (Zurich, 1912). Fehr briefly reviews the comments on opera of several of the writers discussed in Chapter I, concluding therefrom that opera's literary critics during the first half of the eighteenth century mistakenly condemned opera for its lack of resemblance to classical tragedy. Fehr's study of Zeno is based on a thorough knowledge of Zeno's libretti and correspondence, but, apparently unfamiliar with the non-operatic concerns of Zeno's Arcadian colleagues and with the libretti of his immediate predecessors and contemporaries, Fehr divorces Zeno from his environment, making him solely responsible for a libretto reform whose ultimate failure is alleged as the reason for Zeno's later-life distaste for his own libretti.[75] In Fehr's view the reform is primarily a matter of form, of Zeno's evolution of a scheme that placed the already familiar exit aria at the ends of scenes, thus making the scene-ending exit aria the cornerstone of an orderly movement of singers on and off stage. It was an arrangement that, by always retaining one character onstage between successive scenes that share the same set, ensured against the vacant-stage situations about which Perrucci had worried—and, as Fehr points out, simultaneously satisfied both Zeno's desire to keep the arias from interrupting his dramatic action and the singers' wish to exit at the most effective moments. When, in the fifth dialogue of Martello's *Dialogo della tragedia antica e moderna*, the "impostor" speaks of the modern preponderance of scene-ending exit arias, he speaks, to use the words of Fehr, ". . . not to proclaim a new form but simply to confirm what the fashion of the time required. This fashion was Zeno."[76] Fehr admits that if one studies the libretti of Zeno's immediate predecessors in Venice one can detect the same trend towards the dominance of scene-ending exit arias, but, noting that this is a feature not shared by the Viennese works of Bernardoni and Stampiglia, he asserts that earlier historians had given too much credit to Vienna, concluding that Zeno must have completed his reform in Venice before moving to Vienna.[77]

Fehr realizes that Zeno did not invent the historical libretto, but credits him with having devoted greater attention in his dramatic works to plots of historical authenticity. He believes that Zeno's achievement represents a compromise between the ideals of classical tragedy and the necessities of a text for music, two genres which he distinguishes only with respect to the absence of marvelous, pastoral, erotic, and comic elements as well as happy endings in the former. Since Zeno retained all of these except for comedy in his libretti, Fehr rejects the idea that Zeno's "reform" could have had much to do with any change in content.[78]

Fehr's views on the implications of Zeno's reform for music are inconsistent. Early in his book he states that Zeno was able to carry through his "reform" without the opposition of composers and singers because his reform did not challenge music's prerogatives.[79] But later Fehr reverses himself, claiming that the reform was not opposed by musicians because at the time Zeno "subjugated composers to the rule of poetry" there were no composers in Venice vigorous enough to object.[80] More probably, composers did not object because no one at the time, least of all Zeno and his Arcadian colleagues, had any notion of opera as drama. The Arcadian litterateurs whose enjoyment from Zeno's libretti came from reading them were glad to see the longer, more logically worked out dialogues, and were willing to overlook the lyric irrelevance of the aria texts. The composers, singers, and, apparently, the theater audiences, on the other hand, found ways of overlooking the long, arid stretches of "secco" recitative, deriving their musical pleasure almost exclusively from the arias, whose relative share in the whole Zeno and his contemporaries did not alter. Zeno, as we shall try to show, did not personally evolve a new formal arrangement of the libretto, but his efforts towards more serious and consistent plots and characterizations were certainly responsible for increasingly longer recitatives that led to a heightened appreciation of opera as memorable poetry and, indirectly, to the evolution of opera as a recital by musical virtuosi, while delaying its consideration as a possible realm for meaningful drama.

Kretzschmar, Hermann, *Geschichte der Oper* (Leipzig, 1919). Although Fehr's book on Zeno appears in the first footnote of Kretzschmar's chapter on "Italian Opera under the Neapolitans," Kretzschmar ignores Fehr's ideas, attributing the reform to Stampiglia, who is called the foremost of Italian librettists during the closing decades of the seventeenth century and credited with having banished farcical elements, constructed his plots with attention to logical continuity, and chosen subjects of a simplicity and depth previously unknown. Zeno is said to have strengthened and furthered the reforms initiated by Stampiglia, limiting himself to plots pedantically close to the details of his historical sources, and turning the libretto into a school for virtue. Kretzschmar acknowledges that eighteenth-century Italy greatly preferred Metastasio to all of his predecessors, but refuses to compare the works of Zeno and Metastasio, for his opinion of them both is an unfavorable one. He criticizes Zeno for resorting too often to denouements that depend, like those of the later seventeenth century, on the use of disguises and mistaken identities. Kretzschmar does not indicate whether he believes the reform of Stampiglia, Zeno, and Metastasio to have originated in Vienna or in Italy, but the illustrative examples that he cites from the works of all three poets are drawn from their pre-Vienna libretti as well as from those they wrote in Vienna.[81]

Haas, Robert, "Die Oper in Deutschland bis 1750," *Handbuch der Musikgeschichte*, ed. Guido Adler (Frankfurt/Main, 1924). Haas's idea of the seat of libretto reform is clear from the position in which he treats it, in the final paragraph of his chapter on early eighteenth-century opera in

Germany. Consistently, he considers Stampiglia and Zeno of equal importance, crediting them with having introduced more logical continuity of action and with having rid the libretto of irrelevant episodes and comic ornamentation. He points out the derivation of Zeno's dramaturgy from French tragedy. In the opinion of Haas, the one-time director of the music library possessing the world's largest collection of original settings of libretti by Zeno and Metastasio, the strict compartmentalization into recitative and aria which characterized the new libretti resulted in a drying up of dramatic responsibility in the composers who set them.[82]

Belloni, Antonio, *Il seicento* (Milan, 1929). Belloni compares Moniglia's original version of *Ercole in Tebe* (1661) with Aureli's 1679 revision of the work for Venice, then lists a series of trends discernible from his study of *Ercole* that are said to be typical of late seventeenth-century libretti, preparing the way for the later reforms of Zeno and Metastasio: a curtailing and bowdlerizing of comic scenes, a gradual decrease in the importance of the chorus, the disappearance of prologues, a marked cut in the number and variety of the characters, a gradual shifting of most arias to the ends of scenes, and increasingly frequent references in libretto prefaces to Aristotelian maxims.[83] Belloni considers Arcadia a pan-Italian reaction to seventeenth-century taste, but he has several specific suggestions as to the source of libretto reform. The earliest works of Francesco Sbarra, written for performance in Lucca during the middle of the seventeenth century, are said to have been composed ". . . to put the libretto back on the proper path." Elsewhere Belloni asserts that ". . . the first impulses towards the literary reform of the libretto came from Naples," but adds that although the reform was carried out by Italian artists, its cradle was Vienna.[84]

Salzer, E. C., "Teatro italiano in Vienna barocca," *Rivista italiana del dramma* II (1938). In dealing with the Viennese libretti written during the reign of Leopold I (1658–1705), Miss Salzer credits Nicolo Minato with having limited the antics of his comic characters to completely separate scenes,[85] but criticizes his dramaturgy as illogical and unmotivated. Minato's successors in Vienna, Donato Cupeda, Stampiglia, and especially Zeno, are said to be more complicated in this regard.[86]

Calcaterra, Carlo, *Il Parnasso in rivolta* (Milan, 1940). In a useful general discussion of the motive forces behind Arcadia, its reforms, and ideals,

Calcaterra describes Zeno's contribution to opera as the result of a desire to return sense to the libretto, ". . . to give its action an inner logic while disciplining its dramatic development,"—an idea which Calcaterra very properly juxtaposes with the word that Zeno himself was fond of using with reference to the preparation of his dramatic texts, "studio."[87] It is Calcaterra's thesis that Arcadian yearning for "good taste" produced a turning away from marinism and from seventeenth-century bizarreness in libretti, creating poetry of regularized structure and rational dignity but nothing of depth or beauty. Under this heading Calcaterra lists the libretti of Zeno and those of "the other reformed spirits," among whom he includes Stampiglia, Pariati, Bernardoni, Moniglia, and Gigli. In Calcaterra's opinion, the real reform of the libretto came not with Arcadian dignity and regularity around the turn of the century but with Metastasio's infusion of genuine poetic warmth during the 1720s.[88] If one views the libretto only as poetry, this is perhaps the case, but it is impossible to sustain this view with respect to the effect of Arcadian regularization on music and musical drama. In this area it is obvious that it was the events around 1700 which determined the shape and content of nearly all serious opera for almost a century.

Abert, A. A., "Zum metastasianischen Reformdrama," *Kongressbericht der Gesellschaft für Musikforschung, Tagung: Lüneburg, 1950*. Miss Abert takes a position with respect to the changes in the libretto around 1700 that is quite different from any of those summarized thus far. She establishes a line of continuity between the seventeenth and eighteenth centuries by comparing the libretti of Zeno and Metastasio with those of their predecessors, concluding that the "reforms" did not do much to deepen the content of the libretto or to rid it of dramatically artificial denouements. As examples of the latter she cites both centuries' recourse to solutions through the recognition of children previously thought dead, through the identification of men disguised as women and of women disguised as men, through revelation by oracle, and through the accidental interception of important letters entrusted by both heroes and villains to irresponsible messengers.[89] Miss Abert is right to mention the impression of stereotyped stylization experienced by modern readers of the libretti of Zeno and Metastasio, but both poets would have objected that the conflicts (almost always involving some aspect of the subject "inclination versus duty") in the souls of their characters represent an essential distinguishing feature between their own works and those of their predecessors. An early eighteenth-century libretto's sequence of contrasting but non-dynamic states of mind consists of a chain of unrelated arias, but there is an important difference between dramatic criticism and historical analysis.

Rolandi, Ulderico, *Il libertto per musica attraverso i tempi* (Rome, 1951). In the only general history of the libretto ever published, one of the world's foremost collectors of libretti adds several thoughts on the libretti of Zeno not encountered elsewhere. Rolandi ends his consideration of the seventeenth century with a chapter entitled "Reaction against the Decadence of the Italian Libretto," under which he mentions the names of Gigli, Stampiglia, and Bernardoni. The section which follows, on the eighteenth century, begins with a chapter on Apostolo Zeno, who is credited with ". . . a substantial improvement, nay even a true reform of the libretto," but Rolandi's only indication of a specific contribution from Zeno comes with his assertion that Zeno tried to lessen the poetic gap between recitative and aria by rhyming the last lines of his recitatives with the first lines of his arias. Otherwise, his discussion of Zeno's libretti is limited to deprecatory remarks about the unmusical qualities of Zeno's versification and of the names of several of his characters, about his misuse of unemotional maxims, sayings, and aphorisms at moments when more dramatic heat is required, and about the monotony of Zeno's dramaturgical construction.[90]

Giazotto, Remo, *Poesia melodrammatica e pensiero critico nel settecento* (Milan, 1952). In a volume that purports to cover Italian critical commentary on Italian libretti throughout the eighteenth century but which concentrates instead on the writings about Zeno and Metastasio that appeared during the second half of the century, Giazotto attributes the changes before Metastasio's time to Stampiglia, Bernardoni, and Zeno, the succession of poets who wrote libretti for Habsburgs before Metastasio reached Vienna in 1729. The second half of the seventeenth century in general and its closing decades in particular are said to have marked the worst phase of melodramatic corruption. Stampiglia, "towards 1680," is credited with having begun a reform during which the libretto ". . . came to be somewhat relieved and simplified through the exclusion of characters, actions, and scenes, and by means of more dramatic language, if one can so designate the style of Stampiglia and Bernardoni." Stampiglia, who is alleged to have preserved "so many defects" in the musical theater, is praised in the manner once used by Metastasio for Zeno: ". . . he deserves, if no other, the merit of having stripped the libretto, at least in part, of lyrical deformities and of the degeneration that came from Chiabrera and Marino." Zeno is given his customary advantage over his predecessors, this time with the remark that he was the first ". . . who in a definitive manner succeeded in removing critical torpor and, in the meanwhile, in correcting the opinion of those who, shortly beforehand, neither wished nor knew how to accept . . . opera in the name of Aristotle."[91]

A chapter later, Giazotto cites Martello's long list of libretto reformers, and without going into details calls it an "incomprehensible mixture," but excuses Martello on the ground that ". . . in 1715 he did not yet realize the nature of Zeno's reform—or, if one prefers, the Zeno–Pariati reform."[92] Having previously credited Stampiglia as the earliest of the reformers, Giazotto then proceeds to call Stampiglia's *La caduta dei decimviri* (1697), a libretto which Martello, Quadrio, Napoli-Signorelli, and Arteaga had all called one of Stampiglia's best works, ". . . a throbbing example of the perversion that at that time still dominated operatic taste."[93] Giazotto represents as striking an example as one could ask for of the confusion that results from trying to understand the reform in question without recourse to primary sources, the libretti themselves.

Moncallero, G. L., *Teorica d'Arcadia* (Florence, 1953). Moncallero examines a mass of material by first- and second-generation Arcadians on the then recent recovery of Italy's poetic taste, and concludes, unlike Lee, Calcaterra, and Rolla,[94] that Arcadia was not a symptom of change but an important force behind it, that Italian poetry of the eighteenth century represented not a subtle continuation of the seventeenth century but a decisive break with earlier ideals. The principal change in poetry, according to Moncallero, was not so much a matter of content as of style,[95] and numerous illustrations are given of Arcadian poets who, though fascinated with Marino in their youths, later rejected his influence. Quotations from several early eighteenth-century authors on the stylistic contributions to lyric poetry of several of the librettists whom Giazotto was so surprised to find included in Martello's list of improved librettists, suggest that stylistic considerations were probably important for Martello, too. Zeno, who receives due credit for his patriotic contributions to Italian scholarship and literary criticism, is put forward alone for having ". . . brought classical regularity to the Italian libretto."[96]

Burt, Nathaniel, "Opera in Arcadia," *MQ* 1955. Examining what he calls the origins of the Metastasian reform, Nathaniel Burt uses a combination of quotations from Crescimbeni, Zeno, and Bonlini to draw attention to a libretto by Domenico David that is put forward as the first Arcadian opera: *La forza della virtù*, first produced at the Teatro San Giovanni Grisostomo in Venice during 1693. Comparing *La forza* on the one hand with Apolloni's *La Dori* of 1663 and on the other with Metastasio's 1726 revision of *La forza*, Burt points out the decreasing number of arias, the disappearance of comic characters, and the emerging use of exit arias to mark the ends of scenes. But he concentrates on the serious if exaggeratedly pathetic content that distinguishes *La forza* from *La Dori*, and the rationality of characterization and dramaturgy that distinguishes Metastasio's revision of *La forza* from David's original. In Burt's view the conventions that governed eighteenth-century *opera seria*, said here to have been established by the time David and Zeno undertook their reforming activities during the 1690s, represent a limitation that restricted the reformers.[97] He points out that although there are fewer arias in *La forza* than in *La Dori*, the arias of early eighteenth-century operas are notably longer than those of their late seventeenth-century predecessors, but he refuses to take a position as to whether librettists restricted the number of their arias because composers had begun to write longer ones, whether composers seized the opportunity of writing more extended arias once the librettists had reduced their number, or whether both of the developments took place at different times and in different places. David, Zeno, and Metastasio are the only "reform" librettists mentioned.

Powers, Harold, "Il Serse trasformato," *MQ* 1961–62. In that part of his article on three versions of *Serse* that compares Stampiglia's 1694 revision of Minato's 1654 *Serse* with Minato's original, Powers discusses three important differences between the *Serse*s of 1654 and 1694 which he considers characteristic of Italian operatic history during that period: an increasing seriousness of moral tone, the gradual elimination of entrance and especially of medial arias in favor of scene-ending exit arias, and a drift from an external structure in which the entrances and exits of the singers often leave the stage momentarily empty towards a continuity on stage produced by the retention of at least one character between successive scenes that share the same stage set.[98] This *liaison des scènes*, which Powers believes was not established in its ultimate strictness until shortly before Metastasio, the gradual separation of comic and serious elements, and the concomitant seriousness of tone are all attributed to the classicistic influence of French tragedy, and shown to have been trends under way 20 years before the first meeting of the Arcadians or the earliest libretti of either David of Zeno. The formal construction of Zeno's works, which Fehr claimed as Zeno's personal invention, is here indicated to have been not the result of a reform but of the developing experience of singers, impresarios, and librettists with the solution of musico-dramatic problems, an experience that affected the libretti of such "non-reform" poets as Minato and Aureli as well as those of some of the Arcadians referred to in this study previously. In one important respect Stampiglia's 1694 revision of Minato does not represent a change in the direction of the libretti of Zeno and Metastasio. Although it will be remembered that Stampiglia has been mentioned on several occasions as one of Zeno's important predecessors in the reform movement, his revision of *Serse* contains 60 arias, 75 percent more than were included in Minato's original version 40 years earlier. If Stampiglia was in any sense a reformer, clearly he was not involved with any reduction in the number of arias, at least at this stage in his career.

VanderMeer, J. H., *Johann Josef Fux als Opernkomponist* 3 vols. (Bilthoven, 1961). In an introductory chapter on the 20 secular libretti set in Vienna by Fux between 1700 and 1731, VanderMeer presents detailed lists of line lengths, aria forms, and rhyme schemes used by Fux's librettists, and arrives at several interesting observations. Although recitative lines of 7 and 11 syllables appear with approximately equal frequency in the libretti of Cupeda, Bernardoni, and Stampiglia, those of 11 syllables predominate in the recitatives of Pariati and Zeno[99]—a reflection perhaps of an effort to maximize that part of the libretto sometimes alleged to represent the poet's interests.[100] The recitative rhymes of Bernardoni and Stampiglia are shown to occur irregularly in time and position, but those of Pariati and Zeno are said to occur with regularity at the ends of recitative passages, a phenomenon that VanderMeer interprets as a means of emphasizing, not of obscuring, the break between recitative and aria.[101] Aria schemes involving successive lines of dissimilar length and/or successive strophes involving varying numbers of lines are shown to have been used by all of Fux's librettists, but more frequently by Pariati and Zeno than by any of the others. Two-strophe aria texts in which the strophes are of equal length and identical metric structure are the most frequently used by all of Fux's librettists, but a drift from individual strophes of two lines each in the works of Cupeda, Bernardoni, and Stampiglia to three-line strophes in the libretti of Pariati and Zeno, and to four-line strophes in those of Metastasio, is discernible.[102]

VanderMeer points out that Fux's libretti by Cupeda, Bernardoni, and Stampiglia all omit comic scenes and characters,[103] but he incorrectly implies that this is an indication of participation in the early stages of a reform. Fux was never a regular composer of operas in Vienna, but, concentrating on church music, was apparently called upon to provide the usually mythological *feste teatrale* whenever his colleagues normally responsible for those pieces were sick or overworked. This was particularly the case after Fux was appointed *Kapellmeister* in 1715, when his operatic activities became limited for the most part to setting allegorical texts for very special occasions.[104] The works performed in Vienna at such times had a tradition all their own going back well into the seventeenth century. Based on mythological allegories in honor of one member or another of the Habsburg family, they were meant to be impressively serious, making every use of elaborate scenery and spectacular machinery but shunning comic scenes. During the early years of the eighteenth century in Vienna three branches of secular musical theater that had been distinct during the second part of the seventeenth century continued independent of one another. Comic works, often with serious overtones, were performed every year during the carnival season. Historically based libretti of increasingly serious moral tone and decreasing recourse to comic episodes were performed on the birth- and namedays of the reigning emperor and empresses. Mythologically based libretti of the kind described above were reserved for occasions of unusual importance: the celebration of military victories, the birth of male heirs, and the annexation of additional territory. Minato had written the texts for all three branches before his death in 1698, but later each of the three developed its own team of specialists: Pariati (later G. B. Pasquini) and Francesco Conti for the comical, Zeno (later Metastasio) and Caldara for the historical, Bernardoni (later Pariati) and Fux for the mythological. Fux's decreasing activity as an opera composer after his appointment as *Kapellmeister* in 1715 is partly due to his declining health but also partly to the declining popularity of allegorical libretti in Vienna after Zeno's arrival in 1718.[105]

With VanderMeer's work on the operas of Fux we conclude our survey of the principal writings on the change which took place in the Italian libretto during the half century between 1675 and 1725, a change described even in *MGG* X as ". . . a transformation of the operatic genre carried out in connection with the textual reform begun by Zeno and carried to victory by Metastasio."[106] This is a concept which, as we have seen, does not accurately reflect the motivations of poets like Zeno, more interested in the publication of consistently serious and regular texts than in the transformation of opera itself. There *was* a gradual change in the form and content of the libretto around the turn of the eighteenth century, but little apparent change in the traditional prerogatives of the impresario and his employees. The new and more serious libretti seemed more dignified than their motley predecessors when read at home, but the comic intermezzi which appeared between the acts in performance were no less real for either the audience or the comedians simply because they were not printed with the opera proper. The new libretti generally involved fewer secondary characters than their predecessors and in their prefaces little is said about the stage machinery of which the seventeenth century was so fond, but the number of extras who appeared on stage and the amount of energy devoted to visual display did not change. The number of arias was reduced and their placement with regard to the entrance and exit of the singers was regularized, but, since the composers were writing longer arias, the relative shares of recitative and aria were not altered. The increasingly regular position of the arias, although an important memory aid for the singers, could not have made much difference for an audience whose attention wandered easily. More serious dialogue, more consistent characterization, and more logical plot development remained theoretical beauties for admiration by those who read their libretti at home, so long as singers took no pains with the clarity of their pronunciation or with the verisimilitude of their acting, so long as opera was thought not to require the direction of a person thoroughly acquainted with its constituent art forms, a person anxious to represent meaningful drama. It is doubtful whether many impresarios cared whether their librettists prefaced their works with lengthy explanations about their careful observance of the Aristotelian unities, for little change was allowed with respect to the number of stage sets required.

The degree to which the changes instituted by Zeno and his contemporaries were allowed to affect what the public considered essential operatic elements is reflected in the quick passing of at least two unpopular innovations. The division into five acts, which so reminded the Zeno generation of Greek tragedy, was used in some of Zeno's Venetian and in some of his Viennese libretti, in all of the libretti of Frigimelica, in several by Piovene, and in occasional works by other librettists active early in the century, but the five-act division was generally considered to make an opera too long, and it seems to have died out altogether after 1730. The full-length libretti of Metastasio are all in three acts. So long as love intrigues were given their expected due, there were few who objected to plots that stressed more serious ideas. But in Metastasio's generation the considerations of political virtue of which Zeno had been so proud were replaced by a reconcentration of interest in the love intrigue.

We have dealt at some length with the writings which appeared before 1725 on recent change in the Italian libretto, because their authors were men who had known the libretti of the Aureli–Minato generation during their youths and those of the Stampiglia–Zeno generation later in life. We have presented the relevant writings that appeared after the change had taken place in order to show the diversity of opinion regarding its constituent elements, the time and place of its origins and completion, and the relative shares of the various poets alleged to have contributed to it, and to indicate how the tradition of "Zeno's reform" became established.

III

Formal Elements of the Change

In his 1961–62 article on revisions of Minato's libretto, *Serse,* Harold Powers describes the change so far under consideration as gradual and piecemeal.[1] This view of the change, together with my own thesis that the formal aspect of the "Zeno reform" was but a gathering together of elements already existing separately in the libretti of Zeno's predecessors and contemporaries, helps explain both Zeno's lack of personal involvement as a librettist, so evident in his correspondence, and the absence of collaboration between poet and composer that strikes one in studying the Caldara composing scores which are original settings of Zeno libretti. The following study of some formal elements undergoing change in the Italian libretto between 1675 and 1725 is offered in support of these two hypotheses.

Having observed earlier that the number of arias included by Zeno in those of his libretti completed by 1698 was no lower than in the libretti of several other poets active in Venice towards the end of the seventeenth century, let us turn now to a study of the number, placement, and distribution of arias and to the development of the *liaison des scènes* discussed by Fehr and Powers in a representative series of libretti by several of the poets mentioned by the critics discussed in Chapters I and II. In view of what has been said earlier, we shall consider a low number of arias, a preponderance of scene-ending exit arias, an aria distribution scheme that seldom gives the same singer successive arias, a low number of set changes, and a relative absence of interruptions in the *liaison des scènes* to be tendencies towards modernity, the opposite to be indications of more old-fashioned attitudes. The chart on the next page is a key to the symbols and type styles used in this chapter.[2]

Key to Symbols and Type Styles In Charts

Roman numerals: act numbers
Arabic numerals: scene numbers
lower case letters: individual arias in the order in which they occur
Times Roman Italic: entrance aria
Times Roman Bold: medial (non-exit) aria
Times Extra Bold Italic: medial aria followed by the exit of the character who sings it
[ ]: aria concludes the scene in which it appears but the character who sings it does not exit
NB—All combinations of Arabic numeral plus lower case letter (e.g., 2b, 9k, etc.) that do not occur within any of the above, indicate scene-ending exit arias.
*: duet
→: distribution sequences in which the same character sings two or more arias in succession
" ": enclosed in *virgolette*

Liaison des scènes

upper case letters: the characters of the drama
/: new scene
//: set change
—: interruption, between set changes, of the *liaison des scènes*
+: character enters after scene has begun
( ): character on stage but hidden from view of some or all of the other characters
Helvetica Bold Outline: character exits in mid-scene without an aria
Kaufmann Bold: character exits at end of scene but without an aria
DAVIDA ROMAN: only indication of character's exit is his failure to reappear in the next scene
{ }: character exits after scene-ending exit aria

We shall begin by comparing the original of Minato's libretto, *Muzio Scevola,* written for a setting by Cavalli that appeared in Venice during 1665, with two of its subsequent revisions[3] for musical settings produced in Naples during 1698 and in Vienna during 1710.[4] (Although there is some question whether Alessandro Scarlatti or Giovanni Battista Bononcini was the composer responsible for the Naples revision,[5] there is no doubt about Bononcini's responsibility for the Vienna revision.[6])

That part of the plot common to all three libretti can be summarized as follows:

Tarquinio Superbo, a tyrannical king of Rome recently deposed by the Roman populace, has allied himself with Porsenna, the king of the Etruscans, for the purpose of regaining his throne. In the opening scene of all three libretti, Oratio Cocle successfully defends Rome from the invading Etruscans by destroying the Sublician bridge and leaping into the Tiber, but the enemy encamp in Trastevere, holding Elisa and Vitellia (Oratio's wife and daughter) and Valeria (the daughter of Roman Consul, Publicola) among their prisoners. Porsenna falls in love with Valeria, and Ismeno, one of Porsenna's captains, sets his lecherous snares for Elisa. Meanwhile, at a Roman strategy conference, Muzio Scevola, a Roman hero betrothed to Valeria, resolves to enter the enemy's camp by stealth and to kill Porsenna, an expedition in which Oratio decides to participate, too. In Trastevere Porsenna and Ismeno are unsuccessful in their attempts to win the affection of Valeria and Elisa, but while Porsenna is simply disappointed, Ismeno becomes violent, eventually threatening even to kill Vitellia. Once Muzio has crossed the river, he is recognized by Tarquinio, but is able to persuade the latter that he has deserted Rome and wishes to join the Etruscans. Led by Tarquinio to Porsenna's private camp, Muzio throws his spear, but misses Porsenna and kills one of his lieutenants instead. Muzio tries to escape but is apprehended and returned to Porsenna, whom he threatens with death at the hands of one of the other 299 Romans alleged to have sworn Porsenna's assassination. Porsenna, deciding this too great a risk for the dubious benefit of Tarquinio's friendship, offers to free Muzio and to cease hostilities against Rome in return for Valeria, an offer which, despite Valeria's pleadings, Muzio accepts. He returns to Rome to announce Porsenna's offer to the Senate, but Valeria, escaping after Muzio's departure, swims the Tiber on a horse and appears before the Senate just as Muzio is finishing his speech. Greeted coldly by her father, Publicola, and by Muzio, Valeria is told that it is her patriotic duty to sacrifice her own feelings for Rome's safety, and is sent back to Porsenna in the precautionary custody of Muzio. Meanwhile, in an episodic action common to all three libretti, Elisa, whose apparently irresolute conduct towards Ismeno has aroused the jealousy of her unaccountably timorous husband, decides that the only means for preserving her virtue and the life of her daughter is the murder of Ismeno.

In a fashion typical of the libretti of the period, Rome's and Valeria's future are subordinated to what one would normally suppose the episodic sub-plot of Elisa and Oratio, all three libretti reserving the Elisa-Oratio denouement for their final scene. Back in Rome, Porsenna renounces Valeria, his only condition to peace with Rome, when he discovers what should have been transparent to him for more than two acts: Valeria and Muzio are lovers. Only then does Oratio enter, calling for the death of

Porsenna because of Elisa's failure to return to Rome with the other prisoners. Just as Porsenna explains that he cannot be held responsible if Elisa prefers Ismeno to Oratio, Elisa creates a demonstration of feminine virtue and a dramatic climax of sorts by entering with the bloody head of her would-be seducer. The couples pair off happily and Porsenna returns to Tuscany.

Both the 1698 revision and that of 1710 preserve this much of Minato's original, but as is seen in Table B, both revisions involve substantial changes in episodic content, cuts and rearrangements with regard to number and variety of characters, of stage sets, of machines, of ballets, and the like.[7] Minato's original involves all the characters included in the revisions and as many others besides: Clodio and Floro, two inseparable Roman cavaliers whose competition for Valeria's love provides seven musical numbers and six separate scenes but not the slightest contribution to dramatic development; Melvio, a Roman citizen who appears in every scene where the interests of Rome are discussed or prayed for, but who has no meaning as an independent character; Pallas and Venus, two goddesses who appear in a machine at the end of the second act to predict Rome's ultimate victory over the Etruscans, thereby satisfying the enthusiasts for mechanical effects; a statue of Janus whose speech in recognition of a Supreme Being at the end of the first act adds a touch of mystery to the production, while placating the Church's objections to Publicola's invocations of the pagan deities; and two vestal virgins, whose inclusion was doubtless meant to satisfy the needs of two deserving singers of less than outstanding ability. A pair of comic characters (Milo, a male servant of Elisa and Oratio, and Porfiria, Valeria's aged nurse[8]) appear in Minato's original and in the 1698 revision, functioning in both cases in comic dialogues with ostensibly serious characters. But, except for a single instance in the Minato original, they appear only in the 1698 revision in scenes of their own, and then only in connection with dramatic ideas derived from other events in the same libretto. (In writing of the comic intermedii whose popularity in Venice seems to stem from the first decade of the eighteenth century, Bonlini specified separately printed episodes lacking any connection whatever with the events of the libretto proper.[9]) No comic characters of any kind appear in the revision of 1710. A machine-driven lady named Flora is added, however, in a typical Viennese *licenza,* announcing that the anniversary of the peace treaty between Rome and Tuscany falls on the birthday of the person in whose honor the opera has been staged, the Dowager Empress Amalia.

Although the dropping of superfluous characters and scenes in the 1698 and 1710 revisions was doubtless motivated, at least in part, by the desire for tighter, more effective drama, the dramaturgical weaknesses of

Minato's original were not really eliminated. Porsenna spends five separate scenes in the 1665 original and only one scene fewer in each of the
two revisions under consideration here, repeating the same arguments in
support of his claim to Valeria. Muzio spends six scenes in the 1665 and
1698 versions and five in the 1710 production trying without success to
persuade Valeria of her duty to Rome. Similar effects of dramatic inertia
are created by Ismeno's repeated but unfulfilled threats on Elisa's virtue,
Oratio's repeated questionings of Elisa's fidelity, and Tarquinio's repeated
assertions of Porsenna's pusillanimity. All of these scenes provide the
requisite number of arias, but they do so without contributing any forward
motion whatever to the drama. The denouements of Zeno and Metastasio
are every bit as arbitrary as those of the librettists who preceded them,
but it seems to have been Zeno who was first to reconcile the musicians'
demand for several dozen arias with the dramaturgical goal of successive
scenes developing changing reactions to changing situations. Surely this
is the quality to which Zeno was referring when he praised Luisa Bergalli
for the "easy and natural development" of her libretto, *Agide*,[10] the quality to which the Groppo *Catalogo* of 1745 was alluding when it praised
Zeno for the orderly arrangement of his libretti.[11] Zeno's contribution in
this regard will become clearer later, when we compare the dramaturgical
development of a Zeno libretto with that of a libretto by one of Zeno's
predecessors which treats the same subject.

  Continuing our study of changes in the formal design of *Muzio Scevola*, we note a progressive reduction in the number of arias as well as in
the number of scenes (from 65 arias in 60 scenes in 1665, to 64 arias in
49 scenes in 1698, to 51 arias in 43 scenes in 1710), but a variation in the
ratio of arias to scenes from 1.1 in 1665, to 1.3 in 1698, to 1.2 in 1710.
The number of arias may have decreased, but the share of arias with
regard to the whole seems, if anything, to have increased, particularly
when one considers that the average Bononcini aria of 1710 was a much
longer piece than the average Cavalli aria of 1665. The tendency observed
here is in striking contrast to the tendency observed earlier in Venetian
libretti between 1688 and 1698 where, at least in terms of the printed
libretto, though not necessarily in terms of performance time, the ratio
of arias to scenes seems to have decreased. (This was a tendency which
became more marked in the libretti of Zeno that appeared after 1698, as
we shall see later.) Although for the moment there are insufficient data
to prove that it was Venice which led the way with respect to the decrease
in the ratio of aria texts to printed scenes (and hence to overall poetic
length),[12] we may accept this notion as a working hypothesis, at least
with regard to Venice, Vienna, and Naples.

  The following table, showing the numbers and percentages of the various positions of the musical numbers in our three versions of *Muzio Scevola,* indicates a sharp drop between 1665 and 1698 in the number of entrance arias, a falling off after 1698 in the number of medial arias, and a gradual rise in the percentages for both medial and scene-ending exit arias, a phenomenon fully consonant with our hypothesis on the origins of the scene-ending exit aria outlined earlier.

	Entrance arias	Per-cent	Medial arias	Per-cent	Medial exit arias	Per-cent	Scene-ending arias	Per-cent	Scene-ending exit arias	Per-cent
1665	32	49	11	17	0	0	3	5	19	29
1698	6	9	14	25	7	10	6	9	31	48
1710	7	13	6	12	8	15	3	6	28	54

That both the 1698 and 1710 versions represent only way stations on the route to the near monopoly ultimately achieved by the scene-ending exit aria is further demonstrated by the variety of functions assigned those arias that were used in both of the revisions in positions where no arias had previously appeared. Three of 11 scene-ending arias that in 1698 replaced arias of the entrance and medial varieties in the 1665 original, were not exit arias; and only one of those three was transformed into an exit aria in 1710. Of the 30 arias inserted in the 1698 revision in scenes in which no comparable arias of any kind had appeared in 1665, two were entrance arias, four were medial, seven were medial exit arias, and three were scene-ending arias. Of the 10 arias inserted in the 1710 revision in scenes where no comparable arias had appeared in 1698, only half were scene-ending exit arias. Only in the four serious scenes entirely new to the 1698 revision did the librettist restrict himself to nothing but scene-ending exit arias (no new arias were added to any of those four scenes in the 1710 libretto.)

The aria texts in the 1665 original comprise two, three, and even four stanzas each, often with as many as seven or eight lines per stanza. Normally set strophically, they are to be distinguished by the regularity of their line-lengths and by their content from the frequently rhyming lines of 7 and 11 syllables which, although apparently intended by their authors as recitative, according to Salvadori were sometimes set by late seventeenth-century composers as "arie cavate."[13] The aria texts of the 1698 and 1710 revisions are, on the other hand, almost wholly limited to poems of eight lines or less.[14] As in other Italian libretti from the end of the seventeenth century and later, these arias are easy to distinguish visually from the recitative that surrounds them, because of libretto printers' increasing propensity towards the end of the seventeenth century to indent arias markedly with respect to recitative, because of the regular appearance of "reprise" and "tag" lines[15] that follow the arias, and because of librettists' tendency to do away with rhymes in their recitative verses. Although by the turn of the century both Alessandro Scarlatti and Giovanni Battista Bononcini had eliminated almost all aria types other than that variety of *da capo* in which the first part of a two-part text and its *da capo* repetition constitute at least two-thirds of the musical setting,[16] there are isolated examples in both of the *Muzio Scevola* revisions both of the old-fashioned one-line *da capos* (in which not the first section of the poetic text but the second constitutes the body of the musical setting) and of arias (mostly in entrance and medial positions) without any *da capo* whatever. Although none of the "tag-line" *da capo* texts in the 1698 revision includes any internal punctuation more final than commas, all texts are devised so that their two (sometimes three) clauses comprise a series of complete sentences arranged in such a manner that the musical *da capo* involves no logical absurdities of the kind that appear so frequently in other libretti around the turn of the century. The number of instances in which a single singer takes part in two consecutive musical numbers falls from 12 in 1665, to 8 in 1698, and finally to 2 in 1710; and the number of stage sets, an especially meaningful subject for Aristotelian critics, falls from 12 to 9, and then to 8.[17] The number of breaks in the *liaison des scènes* varies from 13 in Minato's original, to 15 and 12 in the two revisions. This element of dramaturgical coherence, of concern during the end of the seventeenth century to impresarios and to Aristotelians alike,[18] was clearly of little relevance to those responsible for either the 1698 or the 1710 revision of *Muzio Scevola*. But the drop in unidentified exits (indicated with the typeface **DAVIDA ROMAN** in the table on pp. 102–104) from 41 in 1665 to 4 and 0 in 1698 and 1710, respectively, suggests that Minato's successors were not totally insensitive to matters of dramatic continuity.

In comparing three versions of *Muzio Scevola* we have noted a sharp decrease in the number of characters, scenes, and, after 1698, arias, the gradual ascendancy of the scene-ending exit aria, the relatively early dominance of *da capo* aria texts comprising two complete sentences of equal or nearly equal length, a striking drop after 1698 in the number of instances wherein the same singer takes part in two or more successive numbers, a falling off in the number of stage sets, and the disappearance of unidentified exits. But these tendencies, none of which is peculiar during this period to *Muzio Scevola*, are offset by less progressive features: a lack of concern for breaks in the *liaison des scènes,* and the use, even in the 1710 revision, of so simple a main plot that the requisite number of aria-contributing scenes has to be achieved through recourse to repetitive episodes.

The charts that follow present a summary view of the position of other librettists around the turn of the century with respect to the tendencies just enumerated.[19]

Table B

Muzio Scevola / *Arias*	*1665*	*I* 1698	*1710*	*1665*	*II* 1698	*1710*	*1665*	*III* 1698	*1710*
A Muzio Scevola	18r	2b 4d* 9k	2b 4d* 8i	7i	4f 7i 15t	**8i** *14q*	→12l *12m*	5h* **9n** / *17t q*	5f* 7j
B Oratio Cocle	**3d** *11j*	[3c] →4d* *10l*	[3c] 4d* *9j* *10l*	→**6g** 6h *11n*	**2b 8k**	2b 4f / 9k*→	6f *13u* 20t	3f *17t q*	3d
C Porsenna	19s	7h 15t	6g 15s	**8k 9l**	5g 6h 11p	6g 7h	1a *15o*	1a 4g 13r	1a 4e 10l
D Publicola	20t*	1a	1a						
E Melvio	20t*			16n			18r		
F Tarquinio			**5e**		8l	9l		1b	1b
G Valeria	5e* 7f* 16o →	[6g] ***8i*** / 13q [13r] ***14s***	7h *13p* [13q] / ***14r***	1a →8j 10m	7j →*14r* **15s**	8j ***14p***→	**9h** 18s	5h* **9m** / *17t q*	5f* 7i
H Elisa	5e* 7f* 12k → / *13l*	5f 11m ***12o***	5f 10k 11n	→3d →5e 5f	[1a] **3d** 3e / **9m**	[1a] (3d) 3e / 9k*→ ***10m***	→10j 11k	2e [6i] [7k] / 11o *17t q*	6h 9k
I Vitellia			12o	2b *trio*	*10m*	***10m***	17q	*11m*	*11m*
J Ismeno		***5e 12n***	***11m***		**3c** 9n	**3c** 10o	→**3c** *16p*	→**2c 2d** 7j	**2c 6g** 11n
K Clodio	2b* 10i			2b *trio* **14r**			2b*		
L Floro	2b* **14n**			2b *trio* 14s			2b*		
M Porfiria	9g [9h] *14m* / 17q	8j **16v**		→2c *13o* [13p] / **14q** 15t	[10o] 16v		→5d 5e 9g / *9i*	→***12p 12q****	
N Milo	*17p*	12p **16u**			12q **16u**			8l 8m *12q** / 14s	

Muzio Scevola Arias	I			II			III		
	1665	1698	1710	1665	1698	1710	1665	1698	1710
O Publio									
P Statue of Janus									
Q Two vestals				[16v]*					
R Pallas				20w 20y*					
S Venus in a machine				→ 20x 20y*					
Chorus 3c									14p
Aria unidentifiable as to character performing it 1a							FLORIA: **14o**		

q = quartet

Liaison des Scènes

Act I

1665   **E** ᵇ **D** **E** **F** // **K** **L** / E D B K L / **A** **B** ᴅ **ᴇ** **K** **L** // **H** I ꝺ̲ C F / C F G H I J   / C G   / M G E   / [K] ʟ ᴳ **M** ⊥   B N

1698   ᴮ [D] **ᴇ** // / [A] ⊥ D B   / [A] [B] ᴅ //   C F G [H] I **J**   / C G   / M G [C] / *G* {M}   ⊥ [A]   ⊥ B N

1710   ᴮ [D] ᶜ ⊥ [A] ⊥ D B   / [A] [B] ᴅ //   C F +G [H] I J / {C] G / {G]   ⊥   [A]   ⊥ B

1665 / H I N **B** / **J** N I {H} ⊥ M G + K L / C G **K L** M / **C** {G} M / {M} **N** ⊥ A F G / **C** O A **9** // D E ρ

1698 / H I N B / **J** {N} I **H** G + C / A F **G** / [C] ○ A F **L M N** +ballo

1710 / H I {B} / **J** I {H} ⊥ G + C / A F **G** / [C] ○ A F

<hr>

Muzio Scevola
Liaison des scènes
Act II

1665 G M / **K L** G {M} ⊥ H I / H I N B / **J** {H} I **N** (B) ⊥ {B} // **A** + C **9** / G C / A C G / **A** {G} ⊥ B + H / B H **J** F // M G

1698 H I / H I N + B / **J** {H} I N (B) // **A** + C **9** / G C / A [C] G / A [G] ⊥ H I B + J [F] / H I [J] // M G

1710 H I / H I B / {H} I J / ⁷ {B} // **A** C **9** / G C / A [C] G / A [G] // H B + J [F] / H [J] + **I** + **I** **9**

1665 / **K** G M + [L] / **C** {M} // D E Q / A D E Q / G A **S E Q** / **9 A** ⊥ **B E** [R S]

1698 / [C] M / {M} {N} // A D / G A **S** / **G** [A] ⊥ {M} **N** +ballo

1710 / // A D / G A **S** / **G** [A]

<hr>

Act III

1665 C F / [K L] **C** F **L** / J N / H J N / {M} **N** ⊥ + {B} // A G / C A G / {M} **G C A** ⊥ **H I N** / J {H} ⊤ [A] //

1698 **C** + [F] ⊤ **J N** + **H** ⊤ [C] A G / [G A] // H + N I / **J H** / H {N} {A} **9** / ⊤ [A] **9** ⊤

1710 **C** + [F] ⊤ **J H** ⊤ [C] A G / [G A] // {H} I + **J** / / {H} I + **J** ⊤ [A] ⊤

Muzio Scevola
Liaison des scènes
Act III

	1665	I 1698	1710	1665	II 1698	1710	1665	III 1698	1710
1665	B+HN/CB⧸	N	/F[C]⊥♪♩⊥♪N+⧸	//EGA/CKLDEAG/BCMNDEAGILK+H					
1698	/CB[H]⊥[M+N]⊥F[C]	/CB[H]⊥[M+N]⊥F[C]	⊥♪[N]+H//GA	/CDAG	/CMN DEAGI+B+H				
1710	/CB[H]	/F[C]⊥	I+H[J]//GA	/GA /CDAG	/C	DAGI+B+H+*Licenza*			

Francesco Silvani

Involved with several Venetian theaters around the turn of the century, Silvani[20] evidently abandoned the traditional mixture of serious and comic elements at least as early as Zeno. The number of his arias is relatively low and, despite his occasional recourse to introductory and medial arias, the scene-ending exit aria dominates. The continuity of his *liaison des scènes* is almost uninterrupted. His plots involve ideas more substantial than the inevitable love intrigues. A comparison of the arias in *L'arte in gara con l'arte* with those in *L'ingratitudine castigata,* two libretti in the same format by the same author for the same printer for use in the same theater during the same season, suggests that, at least around the turn of the century, the printing in libretti of aria "tag" lines and of aria punctuation need not have reflected the wishes of either the poet or the composer, but could depend, as in this instance, on so insignificant a matter as the differing habits of two typesetters.

La costanza in trionfo[a]

The fifth of Silvani's libretti; music by M. A. Ziani; produced in Venice, Teatro Sant'Angelo, winter of 1696–97.

		I	*II*	*III*
A	Gustavo	4c 14n	8i	*11g*
B	Leonilde	*1a*→ 3b 12k 17q	*7g* →7h 11l	5c 10f* 14k
C	Sveno	*7f* 11j 16p	6f 10k	[3a]→ **4b** [8e] 10f* *14j*
D	Marianne	*6e* 10i *13l* [13m] 15o	**3c** →4d 12m*	**11h 12i**
E	Lotario	[7g]→ **9h**	[2b] 12m*	7d
F	Flavio	5d	5e 9j	
G	Riccardo, servant		1a	
	Totals	17/17	12/13	14/11

43 scenes/41 arias   Ratio: .95

I. G B / A B *G* / A {B} / {A} +F / {F} // *D* / C E / C E G / C D *E* G / B C {D} **G** / B {C} / {B} // D F / A D F / *A* C {D} *G* / {C} B / {B}

II. F {G} / F / F D / C F {D} / C {F} / {C} // {B} +A / {A} +F / {F} // E B {C} / E {B} D / {E D}

III. B / A F B / C E A *G* B / C E A *G* B / *A* {B} E / E *G* / {E} // C / B G C / {B C} *G* F / *A* +D +G / E D G / E D G A F / B C E D G A F

a. I-Vnm Dramm. 1186.2.

La pace generosa[a]

Music by M. A. Ziani; produced in Venice, Teatro San Salvatore, 1700. In his foreword to the reader, Silvani draws attention to the force of his style and to his handling of the passions, attributing both to the influence of Seneca.

		I	*II*	*III*
A	Arminio, a German prince	1a 6h	7$\overrightarrow{f}$ [8g] 17m*	1a 10g [12i*]
B	Ismena, his wife	2b **7i** 8j 12o	11h *17l* 17m*	9f [12i*]⃗ **13j**
C	Cilene, Arminio's sister	**4d** 5g 9$\overrightarrow{k}$ 9 1	*1a* 5d 13i	2b 11h
D	Germanico, the Emperor	11n	4c 15j 13i	5d
E	Floro, a Roman captain	*3c** **4e**	6e	3c
F	Cecina, a Roman captain	*3c** **4f** 10m	2b 16k	6e
G	Segeste, Ismena's father			
				13k: general ensemble
	Totals	12/15	17/13	13/11

42 scenes/39 arias   Ratio: .93

I. {A} B / {B} // D E F G / C ⅅ ***E F G*** / {C} ⌿ {A} // B / {B} **G** ⌿ {C} +F / {F} ⌿ {D} +B ***G*** / {B}

II. C / C D E {F} / C D ***E*** / C {D} / {C} E / {E} // A / B +A / (A) B ***G*** / ***A*** B / {B} // C F / {C} F D ⅁ / ***E*** F D / F {D} / {F} ⌿ {B A}

III. {A} ⌿ {C} E / {E} (A) / (***E A***) D / 𝔸 {D} F / {F} // A G / A B ***G*** / A {B} / {A} ⌿ {C} 𝔽 // A B / D F G A B +C

a. I-Vnm Dramm. 1192.2.

L'ingratitudine castigata[a]

Music by Albinoni; produced in Venice, Teatro San Cassiano, 1702, a reworking of a libretto originally produced in Venice in 1698, also with music by Albinoni. In an ironic foreword to the reader, Silvani apologizes that "...the shortness of time available for the staging of this work has not allowed us to beautify it with new scenes and similar things that contribute so much to the universal satisfaction, if indeed one can call something universal which concerns only those who pay more attention to brevity than to the essence of the matter."

		I	*II*	*III*
A	Alarico, king of the Vandals	5e 12n		[4d]
B	Raimondo, aristocratic supporter of Alarico	[1a] 4d* *10j* 10l	4g 9k	3b *8j*
C	Enrico, his son	3c 8h **10k** 13o	**2b** 3d	[2a] *4c* 8i
D	Ginevia, Raimondo's wife	4d*	*4e* [5h]	5e [9k]
E	Brunechilde, widowed queen of Ernesto	2b *6f* 9i	2c *7i* 8j	**6f** $\overrightarrow{6g}$
F	Astorfo, prince, secret supporter of the interests of Brunechilde	7g 11m	1a *4f*	7h 10l
	Totals	13/15	9/11	10/12
		32 scenes/38 arias		Ratio: 1.2

I. B F C / B F C {E} / A B F {C} / A {B D} / {A} // E / E {F} / E +{C} / {E} // A {B} C F / A {F} / {A} +C / {C}

II. E {F} / {E} +C / {C} // D {B} +*F* / D / *A 4* (*2*) // E / {E} B / {B}

III. A / A C / (A) {B} C +F / A *C* / A {D} // E / E {F} // C *B* D / C B D F (E) / C B D {F} E A

---

a. I-Vnm Dramm. 1194.1.

L'arte in gara con l'arte[a]

Music by Albinoni; produced in Venice, Teatro San Cassiano, 1702. In his foreword to the reader, Silvani apologizes this time for using stage sets borrowed from another opera.

		I	II	III
A	Manfredi	[5e] $\overset{\rightarrow}{6f}$ 14n	2b	4c 9i
B	Roggiero	3c $\overset{\rightarrow}{4d}$ 8i $\overset{\rightarrow}{9j}$*	3d 7j	10j* 12l
C	Irene	7g	1a 11l	**8h** 10j*
D	Costanza	2b *8h* 9j* 16p	*3c* **4f 6h**	1a 7g
E	Guglielmo	1a	**4e** 5g	*5d* **6e**
F	Carlo	"12m"		
G	Roberto	[10k] $\overset{\rightarrow}{}$ 11l 15o	6i 8k	**3b** 6f [11k]
	Totals	16/16	11/12	12/12

39 scenes/40 arias   Ratio: 1.

I. D {E} / {D} B / {B} // A {B} **F** / A / {A} C / {C} // D +B / {(B) D} G / G / F {G} / {"F"} ⊥ A G / {A} G F / {G} **F** ⊥ ℂ {D}

II. {C} 𝔽 +A / {A} ⊥ D +{B} / D +E / B D {E} +G / B **D** {G} / {B} // A {G} / A / *A* C / {C}

III. {D} F G / *G* G / *G* +A / {A} // E +D / {G} **E** D / {D} // C A / 𝔼 B **F** C {A} / {C B} //D G +C / D G C {B} A E F

a. I-Vnm Dramm. 1194.2.

Domenico David

David includes a servant role in each of the libretti under consideration here, but while Padiglio and Vafrino are given lines that must have elicited laughter from a Venetian audience, both roles involve important sinister and malevolent aspects as well as the customarily caustic criticism of the servants' social superiors and environments. David is at pains to build his libretti on motive forces deeper than those of the conventional love intrigue, but although he succeeds in drawing several memorable characters (in *Amor e Dover* Matilda and Gofredo impress one as characters of some depth while Roberto, Germando, and Silvio appear to be figures of at least greater than normal individuality), his characters undergo no inner growth or development. Matilda, for example, is as torn between her love for Gofredo and her filial loyalty for Beatrice towards the end of the third act as she is at the beginning of the first. The conflict of mother and daughter in their love for the same man is resolved only when in the tenth scene of the third act, Beatrice, hiding behind a screen, is given the opportunity to overhear Matilda state her views on the primacy of a daughter's duty towards her mother, a speech which persuades Beatrice in an instant that it is Matilda who deserves Gofredo. The unfolding of David's plots is less continuous than that of several of Zeno's later works. The number of his arias is relatively low and the continuity of his *liaison des scènes* generally unbroken, but the placement and distribution of his arias and his relatively high number of set changes are more old-fashioned characteristics. It will be noted when one compares *La forza della virtù* with *Amor e Dover* (two libretti set by the same composer for production in the same theater), that there is a decrease in the number of arias, in the ratio of arias to scenes, in the number of introductory, medial, and scene-ending non-exit arias, in the number of instances in which the same singer takes part in two successive numbers, in the number of characters, and in the number of set changes. Only with respect to the *liaison des scènes* does the later of the two libretti appear less modern than the former.

La forza della virtù[a]

Music by C. F. Pollarolo; produced in Venice, Teatro San Giovanni Grisostomo, 1693. In an unusual prefatory chapter entitled "Allegoria della dramma," David goes out of his way to describe the abstractions of characterization represented by each of the figures in his libretto. For example: "Clotilde…is the image of virtue….Alfonso and Padiglio are representations of those influences within us which, when they are functionaries subjected to the commands of evil desires, behave indecently." In the usual prefatory remarks to the reader, David speaks disarmingly of the operatic delights to which Venetian audiences had become accustomed, but adds a good deal about tragedy's purgation of human conduct, the decorum of a serious composition, and his own "desire to obey the nobility of those precepts determined by writers who know much" which apparently antagonized at least one of David's colleagues more devoted than he to traditional Venetian bizarreness.[b]

	I	II	III
A Fernando, king of Castile, husband of Clotilde, lover of Anagilda	3d 6h 17s	5f 6h	9f* 14k
B Clotilde, wife of Fernando	[1b]→ 2c [9k]→ [11l]→ 12m 15q	*1a* 2c 10k	[2a] 5b [9f*] 11h→ 11i 13j
C Anagilda, in love with Fernando	*5f* [5g]→ [7i] 8j **15p** 16r	6g 7i **12m**→ 14n	[6c] 8e 15l*
D Rodrigo, in love with Clotilde	*1a* * 13n	[1b] 3d 11l	10g
E Alfonso, Captain of the Royal Guards, in love with Anagilda	4e	4e 8j	7d 15l*
F Sancio, Anagilda's father	*1a* * 14o		
G Padiglio, Fernando's facetious servant			
H Virtù, in a machine			**16m** *
I Il Tago, a Castilian river			**16m** *
Totals	17/19	14/14	16/13
	47 scenes/46 arias		Ratio: 1

	I	*II*	*III*

I. B D F / {B} D F E / {A} E / {E} // C / {A} C / C / {C} *ℰ* // B F / B *ǫ* G / B / {B} D A / {D} // C {F} / {B} C / {C} (A G) / {A} G

II. B +D / **E** {B} D / {D} // *ℭ* {E}⊥ {A} *ǫ* / C {A} (E **ɢ**) / {C} E / {E} // *A* B D F **ɢ** / {B} D / {D} // C +*ℰ* / C *ǫ* / {C}

III. B +*ǫ* / B / B A / B A ↕ / {B} *A* // C / C F {E} G / {C} // {A} B / B {D} / B *ℰ* / B C (E) / A B C E / {A} **B** C **D** E **ɢ** / {C E} // A B C E F H I

a. I-Vnm Dramm. 1182.1.
b. Zeno, *Lettere*, no. 566.

Amor e Dover[a]

Music by C. F. Pollarolo; produced in Venice, Teatro San Giovanni Grisostomo, 1697.

		I	II	III
A	Matilda, in love with Rinaldo (disguised as Gofredo)	7h [11k] $\overrightarrow{12l}$	[5d] "14k" 17n	6e 10h* 13j
B	Beatrice, Matilda's mother, in love with Gofredo	3c [9j]	2b *16m*	[8g] $\overrightarrow{10h^*}$
C	Gofredo (Rinaldo), in love with Matilda	$\overrightarrow{5e}$ [$\overrightarrow{5f}$] 6g [13m] 15o	1a 8f 13j	[$\overrightarrow{1a}$] 3b 14k
D	Roberto, Prince of Puglia, impressed with his own appearance, in love with Matilda	[1a] 8i [14n]	6e [10h] 12i	["4c"] $\overrightarrow{5d}$
E	Gernando, German cavalier, fierce and furious	2b	4c "9g"	7f
F	Silvio, flattering councillor of Beatrice	4d	"15l"	["11i"]
G	Vafrino, servant and clever spy of Beatrice			
	Totals	15/15	17/14	14/11
			46 scenes/40 arias	Ratio: .87

I. A B F D C / *A* B G {E} F *Σ* *C* / {B} F (G) / {F} **G** // C / {C} A / {A} D / {D} // B *F* / *B* A / A / {A} **G** // C +D / C D E / E D {C} A B

II. B {C} F / {B} F / *G* E / {E}⊥ A **G** / A {D} / *A* C / {C} // {"E"}⊥ C D / *A* *C* D / {D}⊥ A {C} / {"A"} // B {"F"} / *B* A / {A}

III. C / *B* (C) / {C} // D / {D} A / {A} **G**⊥ {E} // B *F* / B *C* A / {B A} // F / B *G* / B G / B G A {C} D

a. I-Vnm Dramm. 1187.2.

Girolamo Frigimelica Roberti

Count Girolamo Frigimelica Roberti, whose 11 libretti for the Teatro San Giovanni Grisostomo were produced between 1694 and 1708, never called any of his libretti by the traditional name of *dramma per musica,* but limited himself instead to such novel generic subtitles as *tragedia per musica, tragedia pastorale per musica, tragicomedia per musica, tragedia satirica per musica,* and *tragicomedia eroicopastorale per musica.* Nor was this departure from the custom of Venetian librettists without significance for the format, form, and content of Frigimelica's libretti, as different as his subtitles from those of most of his contemporaries. His libretti are all in five acts, a distinction which, despite a scattering of five-act Italian libretti by several poets around the turn of the eighteenth century, is peculiar to Frigimelica. At least the last of Frigimelica's five acts always ends with a chorus. His libretti are always prefaced by a number of expository essays concerning his own perspicacity in dealing with genres unexplored by other mortals and touching on points he claims to have extracted personally from the writings of Aristotle and Horace. He claims to be deeply concerned with the three Aristotelian unities, and in every libretto explains in a separate article how each of the three unities is carried out in the body of the libretto;[21] the most obvious effect of this interest on the libretti themselves lies in the limits placed on the number of set changes. Other prefatory articles include an account of Frigimelica's (ineffectual) attempts to give dramatic coherence to the characters of his libretti, long lists of historical sources from which he claims to derive his plots (though he insists, too, that it is a poet's duty to alter those sources substantially), and occasional, untranslated quotations from Latin and Greek. Frigimelica gives the impression of a pedant in love with the disputable beauties of his own prose. On the one hand he pays homage to Aristotle and asserts that all good libretti should be worthy as readable literature as well as stageable drama, but on the other he praises Venice for "...that glory which merits perfect justice with respect to will power and the most refined taste with respect to intellect."[22] Frigimelica is alone among the Italian librettists of the period in using the prefaces to his libretti as a pulpit for his views on the glories of Greek and Roman drama. Zeno's lack of interest in Frigimelica's libretti is reflected in the silence with which those libretti are treated in Zeno's correspondence. Italy's lack of interest is reflected in the failure of Frigimelica's work to be adapted for production on any of Italy's operatic stages outside Venice, a fate normally shared by "reform" and non-reform librettists alike.

It will be noted that despite Frigimelica's career-long campaign for the Aristotelian unities, his earlier works appear exceptionally old-fashioned in terms of the formal elements discussed earlier. But this old-fashioned quality is not a constant in the libretti of Frigimelica. The decreasing number of arias, the growing dominance of the scene-ending exit aria, and the gradual emergence of a dramaturgical technique that keeps the arias more evenly distributed among the several singers than previously suggests that at least the impresario of the Teatro San Giovanni Grisostomo did not really care what libretto prefaces his audiences read at home so long as his librettists did not try to interfere with the dramaturgical techniques whose use was becoming generally accepted in the theater itself.

Ottone[a,b]

Music by C. F. Pollarolo; produced in Venice, Teatro San Giovanni Grisostomo, 1694; first known work of the eccentric count who taught medicine at the University of Padua and wrote libretti for the Teatro San Giovanni Grisostomo, introducing the external paraphernalia of Greek tragedy to late seventeenth-century Venetian opera but paying little attention to the inner essence of the genre he sought to imitate: *tragedia per musica*.

	I	II	III	IV	V
A Ottone III	2d 2e →	"5*l*" 5n ✓		5f 6h	1a 1b* ["1c"] [2d] 4e → → → → "5h" "6i" 6j 6k [6l*] 7m → → → → →
B Ottone (Fausto)	3f [3i] 6o	2c 2d "2e" 2f* 2g → →	1c 10g 10h* →	[8n]	
C Eleonora	5k 5l [5m] 6n 6p → → →	3i 3j [3k] → →	1a 1b 1d 3e → →	[3c] 4d →	
D Metilde		1a 2f* 2h	8f 10h* 10j	["1a"] 2b 6g 5g [6l*] 9o 6i 10m	
E Lucrezia	4j	5m 5o	7j 9k 10l →	1b* 4f	
F Enrico	"1a" 1b 2c → →				
G Ugone	3g "3h"				
H Adolfo (servant)		[1b]	10i		
Chorus				5e	
Totals	6/16	5/15	10/10	10/13	9/15

40 scenes/69 arias   Ratio: 1.7

✓: Aria begins the scene in which it appears but character who sings it is already present on stage before the beginning of the scene in question.

I. B F / B F A G / B G / B G {E} C / B {C}

II. D H / {D} B H C / C B E A / A {E}

III. B C / A C F / A {C} F B D H / B D A F / B F D G H / D H / D H B A / {D} B H

IV. D H / {D} H G C / {C} G / A G B / A G B D H / D E H / D E H G / {E} / C G

V. A E / A E D / A E D G / A E / A D F / A D H / A B D A H / B D / B {D} G

---

a. In his introduction to a two-volume anthology entitled *Drammi per musica dal Rinuccini allo Zeno* (Turin, 1958), Andrea Della Corte indicates Frigimelica among a group of librettists to whom previous studies had already been devoted, but I have been unable to discover the whereabouts of any Frigimelica study.

b. I-Vnm Dramm. 1183.1.

Il pastore d'Anfriso[a]

Music by C. F. Pollarolo; produced in Venice, Teatro San Giovanni Grisostomo, 1695; *tragedia pastorale per musica*; a work mentioned by Mattheson as giving "the greatest satisfaction in the world."[b]

	I	II	III	IV	V
A Apollo, in love with Dafne	*6h* **7k**	**5j**	1b **7k**	5e	**5h 6j**
B Dafne	1a 2c *7j* 8l	**6l**	5g* [6j] 7l→ **7m**	**2b** 4d	5i
C Clizia, nymph in love with Apollo	3d **5f→** 5g*	1a 2c* 2e	1a 2d **5g*→** 5h	7g	3e→ 3f
D Licisco, shepherd in love with Clizia	4e 5g*	4i	2c 4f	[1a] 3c **9i→ 9j→** 9k	**1b→** 1c
E Erasto, Arcadian shepherd, friend of Apollo	*6i*	2c*→ **2d 3f→ 3g**		[6f] 8h	*4g*
F Arete, head of shepherds for king Admelus, friend of Licisco		**4h**			**1a**
G Corebbo, shepherd, Clizia's guardian		1b			**2d** Clizia sings the same aria in V/3
H Crispide — nymphs in the retinue		**6k***	**6i***		
I Tespi — of Dafne					
J Peneo, Thessalian river, Dafne's father	1b				
K Diana					
L Aurora					
N Night		Chorus: *4e*			*7k*
Totals	8/12	6/12	7/13	9/11	7/11

37 scenes/59 arias   Ratio: 1.6

I. B C G {J} / {B} C G / {C} **G** // *G* D / {D C}⊥ A E / B {A} **E** / {B}

II. C {G} / {C} E / {E} +D / {D} F / A E⫽ B H I A E

III. C {A} / {C} D G / D *G* / {D} *G* ⊥ {C} B H I / B H I / A B H I

IV. D *G* / B D +*C* A / B A {D} / {B} A / {A} / C E / {C} E D / {E} D / {D}

V. {D} **F** ⊥ C G / {C} **G** A E / A *E* / A {B} / *A* // Coro in reggia // Ultima apparenza.
                 d'Apollo   La Notte

---

a. I-Vnm Dramm. 1184.2.

b. See pp. 50–51.

Il Mitridate Eupatore[a]

Music by Alessandro Scarlatti; produced in Venice, Teatro San Giovanni Grisostomo, 1707; *tragedia per musica*.

		I	II	III	IV	V
A	Mitridate (Eupatore)	5e	[1a] 4e 9j*	**2b** 7h	[1a] [3c*]	[1a]→ **2b** 6f **8i**
B	Issicratea (Antigono)	4d	**2b** [3d] 9j*		[7g]	4d 8j*q*
C	Stratonica	**6f**	2c	3d	6f	[5e]
D	Farnace	[7h]	5f	[1a]		
E	Laodice	[1a]→ 2b [6g]	8i	*5f* 8i*	**2b**→ [3c*]→ 4d 8h	[7h] 8j*q*
F	Nicomede	3c 8i	7h	2c 5g 8i*	5e	[3c] **7g** 8j*q*
G	Pelopida		"6g"	4e		8j*q*

Mitridate Evergete ⎤
Tolomeo ⎟ mute roles   Chorus: 8k
Cleopatra ⎦

Totals	8/9	9/10	8/9	8/8	8/11

41 scenes/47 arias   Ratio: 1.15

q: quartet

I. E / {E} F / {F}⌿ A {B} / {A} // C E / D C E / D C E {F} G

II. A B / A B {C} / A B / {A} **B** D G / {D} G / {G} // **B** {F}⌿ A {E} / {A B}

III. D G / D G C {F} A **B** / D {C} G / **B** {G} // E +{F} / E A B / E {A} B F / B {E F}

IV. A (E) G / A E *G* / A E / A {E} **B** F / **A** {F} // B {C} E / B E / D {E} B

V. A G / {A} **B** // **C** E / A {B} E / A C E / {A} C / E **B** / E F / A {B E F G}

a. I-Vnm Dramm. 1201.8.

Il selvaggio eroe[a]

Music by Antonio Caldara; produced in Venice, Teatro San Giovanni Grisostomo, 1707; *tragicomedia eroicopastorale per musica.*

		I	II	III	IV	V
A	Gargore	[3e]	1a→ 1b 8l✓	5i	[3b]	["5e"] 6fq→
B	Gelinda	2c→ 2d 6h	4i [7k]	1a→ 1b* 3g 6j	5d	[3c] 6fq
C	Ramiro		4h	3f		6fq
D	Alarda	1a→ 1b 6g	[1c] 2e	1b* 4h	[1a*] 6e	[4d] 6fq
E	Abide	5f	2d 6j	6i	[1a*] 4c	1b 6fq
F	Serrana	7i*	3g	2e		7g 7i*
G	Bilbili	7i*	3f	2c→ 2d		"1a" 9h→ 7i*

Chorus: 8j

| Totals | 7/9 | 8/12 | 6/10 | 6/5 | 8/10 |

35 scenes/46 arias   Ratio: 1.3

✓: joined by chorus   q: quintet

I. B {D} / {B} **C** ⌐ D A / D A B C / D A B C {E} / {B} **D** ⌐ {F G}

II. D E / F G {D} **E** / **F G** ⌐ {B} **C** ⌐ A D / A D {E} / A B / {A} B D E C

III. {B +D} ⌐ {F} **G** ⌐ {B} **C** ⌐ {D} F ⌐ {A} B E / {B} **E**

IV. D E / D E A / E A C / {E} A C B / {B} C ⌐ A {D}

V. {E} F G / G G ⌐ B C / B C D / B C D A E / {B C D A E} F G / {F G} // A B C D E F G

a. I-Vnm Dramm. 1201.5.

As an added indication that the trends observed in our study of *Muzio Scevola* and in the libretti of Silvani, David, and Frigimelica were not specifically related to a "reform" movement, but were rather the natural results of developing experience with a still new genre whose individual constituent elements were themselves in a state of rapid evolution, it is to be noted that several of the formal elements which characterize the libretti of Zeno and Metastasio appear strikingly early in the works of poets who, usually associated with Venetian bizarreness, were generally opposed to the more serious libretti that had begun to appear in Italy by the turn of the century. Matteo Noris's *Flavio Cuniberto,* for example, produced in Venice's Teatro San Giovanni Grisostomo during 1682,[23] uses a cast that, in addition to eight members of the nobility and their councillors, includes a faint-hearted servant named Bleso; however, Bleso's role is a very limited one and he contributes little to the almost inevitable comic byplay. Noris's character development is non-existent, his dramaturgy is static, and his dialogue is of the most primitive sort, but his *liaison des scènes,* in this particular instance, is as continuous as anything we have seen thus far.

I. F *H* / {F} // I / C *J* / C D G F / C D E F G *J* / {E} // B / B **B** {F} / {B} A C / A C H / ⅮA *C* H / {A} H / {H} // *C* D / D / Ⅾ G / G / *G* E I / {E} I

II. B A / B A F / D *B* **A** F / Ⅾ F / {F} // E I / *C* I *C* / I *G* / {I}⊥ A / A *H* / A / A B / B F / {F H} // I C / I C *G* / I C +E / *J* E / {E}

III. A / A **B** {E} / A / A F H / *A* B *G* H / {B} H / {H} // I G / E I (G) / *C* I G / I {G} // D B / D B A F / G D B A F / H E G D B A F

An exceptional note to the reader which appears at the very end of Giulio Pancieri's libretto, *Il gran Macedone* (Venice, Teatro San Cassiano, 1690), indicates that the practicality of an uninterrupted *liaison des scènes* was not unknown to Italian librettists of the 1670s and 1680s, but that some librettists, though aware of its desirability, simply did not think it worth the effort to bring the development of their plots into correlation with the required number of set changes in a way that preserved that *liaison*:

> If in this opera you perceive that in one and the same set (as for instance in that of the precipitous balconies) characters appear on stage more than once, bear with me, for it has not been convenient to increase the number of set changes.[24]

Aurelio Aureli

Aurelio Aureli, another supporter of the axiom that the best works of art
are those which bring in the greatest profits, did not always pay very
special attention to the *liaison des scènes,* but he was capable when the
need arose of arranging the number, positioning, and distribution of his
arias in the "modern" manner, as is shown by the first of the examples
which follow. One notes from Aureli's positioning and distribution of arias
in the second example, however, that his commitment to the "modern"
manner does not appear to have been very deep.

Circe abbandonata da Ulisse[a]

Music by C. F. Pollarolo; produced in Venice, Teatro S. S. Giovanni e Paolo, 1698; *dramma per musica*.

		I	II	III
A	Circe	1a* 5f $\overset{\rightarrow}{5g}$ 10k	3c 7g 11j*	5d [9h] 10i 16n
B	Ulisse	1a* 6h	4d 8h 11j* 16m	7e *16m*
C	Polidoro	9j 11l	6f 13k	4c *9g** 12k
D	Climene	1c 4e 12m	5e 10i	2a *9g** 11j
E	Evandro	*1b* 7i	1a	3b 13l
F	Bleso	3d 13n	[2b] 17n	8f
G	Mercurio		15l	
	Totals	13/14	17/14	16/14
			46 scenes/42 arias	Ratio: .9

I. A B {D} *E* / *A B* ⌐ {F} // C {D} / C B {A} / C {B} / {E} F C / *G* C / {C} // {A} ⌐ {C} D / {D} / {F}

II. {E} (F) / F B / {A} B **F** / {B} ⌐ C {D} / {C} // {A} ⌐ B / B C / {D} B Ⓒ / {A B} // *G* +C / {C} ⌐ B / B {G} / {B} ⌐ {F}

III. D C / {D} C E / C {E} / {C} // B {A} / B / {B} F / {F} ⌐ C D +A / C D {A} E / C {D} E / {C} E / {E} // A // B F / {A} Ⓑ Ⓕ

a. I-Vnm Dramm. 1188.1.

Rosane, imperatrice degli Assirii[a]

Music by several anonymous composers; produced in Venice, Teatro Sant'Angelo, 1700; *dramma per musica.*

	I	II	III
A Rosane	[1a] *3c* 9j 14n	*3e* 5g *9j* 12n$\rightarrow$ 12o	3c 14j
B Argene	2b 3d *8h*	4f 9k	4d **14h**
C Artabano	5f 13m	**7h** 8i	[8f]$\rightarrow$ 11g
D Dalisa	**6g**	1a 1c	7e
E Feraspe	[4e] **10k**$\rightarrow$*10l*	*1b*	
F Arsace	8i	*2d* 10l	1a$\rightarrow$*1b* 14i
G Orgonte			
H Adrasto			
I Tersillo (servant)	16o		
J Venus		*12m*	
Totals	16/15	12/15	14/10
		42 scenes/40 arias	Ratio: .95

a. I-Vnm Dramm. 1192.6. Among the bizarre aspects of *Rosane* is the appearance, at the libretto's conclusion, of "Allegrezza" in a machine, singing an aria in quasi-French:

> Mon coeur soupire
> Pour les jeux si doux.
> Que son martire
> Fait ben des jaloux.
> En leur absence
> Je meurs de desir;
> En leur presence
> Je meurs de plasir.

Giulio Cesare Corradi

The schematic outlines which follow are based on the last two libretti of Giulio Cesare Corradi, a contemporary of Noris and Aureli whose career as a librettist goes back, like theirs, into the 1670s. Never mentioned, except by Mattheson,[25] among "reform" librettists, he seems towards the end of his career to have nonetheless adopted as "modern" a format for his libretti as that used by any of his younger colleagues.

L'Aristeo[a]

Music by Antonio Pollarolo; produced in Venice, Teatro San Cassiano, 1700; *dramma per musica.*

		I	II	III
A	Aristeo	2$\overrightarrow{a}$ 2b 10j	[1a]$\overrightarrow{}$ 2b [10i*]$\overrightarrow{}$ 11j	[1a] [2c] 9h 12l*
B	Doride	5f 8h [15n]$\overrightarrow{}$ 16o	4d [10i*] [12k*q*]$\overrightarrow{}$ [13l]	**2b** *12k*$\overrightarrow{}$ 12l*
C	Gilde	*4d* 9i 17p	8h 16m	5d 10i
D	Sitalce	[4e] [13k] 14m	5e 7g 12k*q*	11j
E	Evandro	7g	3c 12k*q*	6e
F	Pallamede	3c **14l**	6f 12k*q*	7f
G	Clito, a pirate			8g
				Tutti: 15m
	Totals	17/16	16/13	15/13
		48 scenes/42 arias		Ratio: .88
				q: quartet

I. A *q̸* *G̸* / {A} // {F} G̸ // C D / C D B / C *2̸* B E / C B {E} / C {B} / {C} // {A} D / D +F G / D F G E / B D F G E̸ / F B {D} G̸ / B / {B} C / {C}

II. A / {A} B E / B {E} / {B} // D F / D {F} C / {D} C / {C} // B *G̸* / B A / E F B {A} / {D E} B {F} / B / *B̸* C / C +*q̸* / {C}

III. A / A B̸ / *A̸* B / *B̸* C / {C} // E F / E̸ {F} G +C / {G} C / C D̸ {A} / {C} +D / {D} // B +A / E F B A / D E F B A / C G D E F B A

All of the arias in this libretto are evenly divided *da capo* texts with tag lines.

a. I-Vnm Dramm. 1192.4.

La pastorella al soglio[a]

Music by several anonymous composers; produced in Venice, Teatro San Cassiano, 1702; described on the title page as *opera postuma*, but no further designation is indicated.

		I	II	III
A	Adoardo	**3d** →4e 9i* 15n	2c→ [2d*]→ 3e 8j	5e 11j
B	Sigiberto	6g 11k 16o*	14o	2b
C	Matilde	[7h] →9i* 16o*	[5g] 6h **14n** 15p	6f 12k
D	Valasco	10j	13m	4d
E	Egina	[2c] 5f 12l	**1a** 4f 12l	3c [7g] 10i* [13l]
F	Arideo	**1a**→ 1b 13m	*2b* 2d* [7i] 10k	1a **8h** →10i*
G	Ombra di Alvida			
				Chorus: 15m
	Totals	16/15	15/16	15/13
			46 scenes/44 arias	Ratio: .96

An isolated example of old-fashioned format in this libretto is the complete absence of recitative in Scene 7 of Act II.

I. E {F} / E / E A / E {A} B / {E} B / {B} // C / C D / {C A} D / {D} // {B} E / {E} +F / {F} ⌐ A C D / {A} B C D / {B C} ⊃

II. A E / A E **F** / {A} E +C / {E} C / C / {C} **B** // F / {A} F / F +E (A) / {F} E A / *A* E +(D C) / {E} D C / {D} C / C +{B} / {C}

III. {F} E / E +{B} / {E} +A / A +{D} C / {A} C / {C} // (E) ⒢ / E F / B E F / A B {E F} / {A} B +C / **B** {C} // A E / A E **F** / A E B C D

a. I-Vnm Dramm. 1194.3.

The logical conclusion of our demonstration that the standardized format to be found in the libretti of Zeno and Metastasio was not the invention of Zeno, as has been claimed by Fehr, but the result of trends in which a whole generation of librettists was involved, entails an overview of libretto format in the works of Zeno himself. To put this overview into the proper perspective with respect to Vienna as well as Venice, we shall precede it with a similar overview of the history of libretto format in Vienna during the quarter century immediately before Zeno's arrival there in 1718.

The operatic scene in Vienna was dominated during the final 30 years of the seventeenth century by three Italians holding regular appointments to the court of Leopold I: Nicolo Minato, the librettist; Antonio Draghi, the composer; and Lodovico Burnacini, the scenographer.[26] The extant libretti for the more than three dozen secular three-act works on which these three craftsmen collaborated between 1670 and 1698, the date of Minato's death, show a consistently old-fashioned approach to problems of operatic form: high numbers of characters, arias, set changes, and instances in which the same character sings consecutive arias; low numbers of scenes; a notable deficiency in scene-ending exit arias; a lack of concern for any *liaison des scènes*; and an almost exclusive reliance on multi-stanza arias of the refrain type. In the ostensibly serious works the servants and buffoons make fun of the kings and queens, and in the openly comic works the philosophers of antiquity mock their own inadequacies and the futile senselessness of court intrigue. Plot development and characterization are primitive, the final scene of each act usually serving, for example, not to advance the drama but to introduce the appearance of an otherwise totally unrelated machine or ballet. The dramatically useless lyricism of the arias dominates the shorter connecting passages of expository recitative.

Donato Cupeda

Minato's ultimate successor, Donato Cupeda, who had begun to assist Minato on a regular basis as early as 1694, filled his prefaces with remarks about the artful simplicity of his style and the elegant conduct of his comic characters, but he did nothing to alter the old-fashioned format employed by Minato, as is illustrated in the examples which follow.

La fede publica[a]

Music by Giovanni Battista Bononcini; produced in Vienna at the Imperial Court Theater for the birthday of the Empress, January 18, 1699; *dramma per musica.*

	I	II	III
A Ifigenia	1a 6j 7l 8n **9p**	*1a* 3f* **7n 11t**	*1a* **6g*** *8l* [8n*] **10p** $\overset{\rightarrow}{\textbf{10q}}$ 10r 13w*
B Lisandro	**2c 3e** [7m] 12t	*3d* 3f* *12v* 13x	*7i** **7j*** **8a** *12u*
C Ninfeo	5i **9o** [9q] $\overset{\rightarrow}{[\text{10r*}]}$	[2c] **3e** *9q* [9u]	[2c] *7i** **7j*** [8n*] 9o $\overset{\rightarrow}{13v}$ 13w*
D Dione	[6k] *13u* $\overset{\rightarrow}{\textbf{\textit{13v}}}$	**1b 4h** 8p **9r**	1b 7k
E Rosalba	**4g*** $\overset{\rightarrow}{\text{4h}}$ *12a* 13w	*4g* [5j] $\overset{\rightarrow}{6k^t}$ 6m^t *8o*	*6f* **6g*** 6h *11s*
F Oreste	[3f] $\overset{\rightarrow}{\textbf{4g}}$*	5i 6k^t 6m^t 11u	4e **11t**
G Cleodora	*2b* 2d [10r*]	$\overset{\rightarrow}{6k^t}$ **6l** $\overset{\rightarrow}{6m^t}$ 12w	*4d*
Totals	13/23	13/23	13/23

Another characteristic of innumerable Minato libretti: the number of scenes, at least in Acts I and III, is always the same.

                39 scenes/69 arias   Ratio: 1.78

                                                     ^{t}: trio

I. *A* B *D* *C* *G* G / B {G} / *B* F / {E} F / {C} F // A D / A D B / A *B* C / *A* C / C G / C G B F / {B} E / *D* {E}

II. A *D* / A C / {A B} *C* // *D* E / E F / {E F G} // *A* D / E D / C *D* / A *B* C / *A* {F} *L* B {G} / {B}

III. A {D} / A C / *A B C L* {F} G // A D / *A* D {E} / C B {D} / A *B* C / F A {C} / {A} // E F / E F A B G / {A} B C {D} E F G

In a licenza honoring Emperor Leopold, two allegorical figures named "La fede publica" and "La ragione di stato" receive one aria each.

---

a. A-Wn 407. 371-AM (also A-Wgm Opere Leopoldinae. VI.1).

Il Gordiano Pio[a]

Music by M. A. Ziani; produced in Wiener-Neustadt in honor of the birthday of Archduke Joseph, August 26, 1700; *dramma per musica.* The unusually high number of arias in this libretto apparently resulted here in a text of such length that the poet was forced to adopt a practice often used in Venice but hardly ever in Vienna: the use of *virgolette* in the printed libretto to indicate those passages that are to be cut in actual performance.

	I	II	III	
A Gordiano Pio	*1a* 5g *11m* 15s	→4e 4f *10l* [10mᵗ] ***11o***	"6g"→ 6h *13t* ***16x***	[19ddq]
B Sabina	7i* 7j* **15r**	1b 5g [10mᵗ] 11n 15w	2b*→ 2c *9m* "9n" *11p*	[19ddq]
C Virginia	7i*→ 7j* ***10l*** 14q	*1a 7i* 14u*→ 14v	5f 7i ***7j*** "12r" *17z* 17aa	[19ddq]
D Ottavio	4e	*3d* 6h ***12p*** *14u**	7k "12s" 15w	[19ddq]
E Misiteo	3d **5f**	*9k* 10mᵗ	***11q***	
F Sapore	**3c** *16t* 18w	*13r* 13t *18z*	8l 16y	
G Oronta	12o 17v	2c 12q 18aa	*1a* 2b*→ "4e" 9o ["13u"] 18cc*	
H Megabise	2b *12n* 13p 16u	*8j* **13s** 19bb	3d ***14v*** "18bb"	18cc*
I Feraspe	"6h" 9k 19x	["16x"]→ 17y		
			Tutti: 20ee	
Totals	19/24	20/28	20/31	
		59 scenes/83 arias	Ratio: 1.4	

ᵗ: trio   q: quartet

I. A D / A D{H} / A {F} E D / A E {D} / {A} *E* // I *⅃ B C / B C I / Ⓑ C {I} G / *C* G (D) / *A* Ⓓ G / {G} H / {H}⅃ A Ⓑ {C} B / {A} Ⓑ // F {H} / F {G} / {F} I / {I} Ⓔ

II. {B} C G / *C* {G}⅃ D / D{A} C B / D C {B} / {D} C / {C} // *A G* ⅃ E B / A (*E* B) / *A B* ⅃{G} H ***"D"*** / ***H*** {F} // D {C} (B) / {B} Ⓓ (A) / A E I / *A E I* {D} // Ⓕ {G} H / {H}⅃ A E D

III. G *J* / G {B} / G {H} / {G}⅃ B C / {A} Ⓑ C D / *C* {D} // {F} G / {G} B / B E / Ⓑ *E* (D) / Ⓒ {D}⅃ A G / A *G H* / {D} A / *A* {F} // Ⓑ {C}⅃{H G} // A E B C D / A B C D E F G H I

The break in the *liaison des scènes* (indicated by * in Act I above), like the majority of those that are admitted to the Italian libretto after about 1710, occurs during a garden scene of the kind with which we are familiar through the fourth act of DaPonte's libretto for Mozart's *Marriage of Figaro.* In cases like these, breakings of the *liaison des scènes,* with concomitant gaps in the action on stage, seem to have been regarded as dramatic virtues.

Pietro Antonio Bernardoni

The situation was notably modernized with the appointment during 1701 of Pietro Antonio Bernardoni, a poet who accepted a post that had been turned down by Zeno. On close personal terms with Zeno,[27] Bernardoni is the only poet of his generation consistently to use his Arcadian pseudonymn[28] in connection with his work as a librettist.

L'amore vuol somiglianza[a]

Music by C. A. Badia; produced in Vienna at the Imperial Court Theater for the birthday of the Empress, January 18, 1702; *dramma per musica*; Bernardoni's first full three-act opera produced in Vienna.

		I	II	III
A	Servio Tullo	**3d** 4g **10o** 11q	*6h* 8k	2c 7i
B	Ocrisia	*5h* 6j*→ 7k	*1a*→ [1b] 2d	**1a 3d** 4f* 8k 12n*q*
C	Tullia	8l 9n	*5f*→ 5g*	1b 11m 12n*q*
D	L. Tarquinio	**1a** 3e 8m	**4e** 5g* 10m	*4e*→ 4f* *9l* 12n*q*
E	Aronte	*6i*→ 6j* **11p**	2c	8j 12n*q*
F	Lucrezio	1b **4f**	8j	7h
G	Valerio, Roman cavalier, friend and confidant of Tarquinio	2c	7i 9l	5g
				q: quartet
	Totals	11/17	10/13	12/14

33 scenes/44 arias   Ratio: 1.3

I. D F / D F G / A {D} F G / {A} **F** G // B / B **E** / {B} D / {D} +C / {C} / A F G / {A} F G E

II. B / {B} E / E / **E** D / {D C} // A / A G / {A} **F** G / {G} D / {D}

III. A B {C} / {A} B / B / {B D} // G / G A / **F** {A} **G** {B} E // D / C D / A F G C D / B E A F G C D

a. A-Wn 407.363 AM (also A-Wgm Opere Leopoldine VI.8).

Tigrane, re d'Arminia[a]

Music by Giovanni Battista Bononcini; produced in Vienna at the Favorita Palace for the birthday of Emperor Joseph I, July 25, 1710; *dramma per musica*; Bernardoni's last full three-act opera produced in Vienna.

		I	*II*	*III*
A	Tigrane	4c **12l** $\overset{\rightarrow}{}$ 13m*	3c **9i*** **12l**	[8h] $\overset{\rightarrow}{}$ 9i
B	Mitridate	3b 10j 15n	8h 14m	3c **13l**
C	Cleopatra	*6e* $\overset{\rightarrow}{}$ 7f [13m*] 16o	6f *11k*	[6f] $\overset{\rightarrow}{}$ 7g
D	Aparnia	1a **10i** 11k	*4d* 7g 10j	4d *11k*
E	Oronte	5d 9h	**5e**	*1a* $\overset{\rightarrow}{}$ 2b
F	Idaspe, army lieutenant	8g	$\overset{\rightarrow}{}$ **1a** 2b **9i***	5e 10j

Chorus: 15m

Totals	16/15	14/13	15/13

45 scenes/41 arias   Ratio: .9

I. B {D} E / B E / {B} E A 𝔽 / {A} E / {E} // C / {C} F / {F}⏌ B {E} / {B} D / {D} // A / {A} C / C +E / {B} C E / {C} E

II. F / A {F} / {A} // D / D 𝓔 / {C} D / {D} +B / {B} // 𝓐 𝓺 ⏌ {D} 𝓔 ⏌ C / 𝓮 A 𝓺 / 𝓐 B / {B}

III. E / {E} B / {B} +D / {D} // C {F} / C / {C} A / A / {A} F / {F} // E / D E / B C D E / A B C D E / A B C D E F

---

a. A-Wn 407.382 AM (also I-Vnm Dramm. 842.4).

Silvio Stampiglia

Brought forward by many writers as the librettist who laid the foundation in Vienna for the dramatic edifices completed by Zeno, Silvio Stampiglia was no special friend of Zeno's. One of the 14 founding members of Arcadia, Stampiglia seems, nonetheless, to have been viewed with scorn by Zeno, who wrote that Stampiglia was "...fuller of himself than of intelligence," that although his libretti enjoyed a certain reputation, "...they are more ingenious than learned, ...and are written with more spirit than care."[29] Stampiglia went further than Bernardoni in the elimination of medial non-exit arias, but seems to have paid no special attention to the *liaison des scènes* and to have had no objection to the occasional use of raucously old-fashioned comic scenes with plots which are by no means unrelated to the principal dramatic motives of his dramas.[30] Praised by some writers for having rid his poetic style of marinistic influences,[31] he has been criticized by others as having a style of naive artlessness.[32] Hired by Joseph I, Stampiglia apparently made no impression whatever on Joseph's successor, Charles VI,[33] and left Vienna in 1718 shortly after Zeno's arrival there. The formats of Stampiglia's libretti are typical for the time in which those libretti were written, and, at least in the sense we have been studying, represent no remarkable break from those of poets like Silvani and Bernardoni, as is shown in the following examples.

Turno Aricino[a]

Music by Giovanni Battista Bononcini; produced in Vienna at the Favorita Palace for the birthday of Emperor Joseph I, July 26, 1707; *dramma per musica*; Stampiglia's first full three-act opera produced in Vienna.

		I	*II*	*III*
A	Turno Erdonio	2a **15l**		**7h**
B	Egaria	$\overset{\rightarrow}{4c}$ [4d*] 7g 17n*	$\overset{\rightarrow}{5e}$ 5f [12m*]	*1a* 6g 10k *13n**
C	Livia	[4d*] 6f 12i 17n*	$\overset{\rightarrow}{3b}$ 3c 7h 10l	4e *9i* $\overset{\rightarrow}{9j}$ *13n**
D	Lucio Tarquinio	3b	[1a]	2c
E	Geminio	8h 16m	6g 9k [12m*]	1b 11l
F	Ottavio Mamilio	5e 14k	7i	5f 12m
G	Ascanio	13j	8j	3d

Ensemble: **4d**   Chorus: 14o

Totals	17/14	13/13	14/15

44 scenes/42 arias   Ratio: .95

I.   A E F G / D {A} E F G / {D} **E F G** ⊥ B +C / B C E +{F} / B {C} (E) / {B} E / {E} // C
G +F ⊥ D / G F {D} +C / {C} F G / F {G} / {F} ⊥ *A* E / {E} +B / {B +C}

II.   D / ♭ *G* *q* *ℓ* ⊥ {C} // A D F E G +B / E {B} / {E} // C +{F} / C +{G} / C +{E} / {C}
+B // ♭ E F G / B E F G / *A B ℓ*

III.   E +{E} ⊥ {D} C / C +{G} / {C} +F / {F} ⊥ {B} // A E +B / ♭ F G +C / {C} +B / {B} E
/ {E} F / {F} // B C +A F G / B C A F G E +D

Stampiglia is perfectly familiar with the scene-ending exit aria, but the movement of his characters on- and off-stage does not depend upon it.

---

a.   A-Wn 407.368 AM (also I-Vnm Dramm. 841.1).

Alba Cornelia[a]

Music by Francesco Conti; produced in Vienna at the Imperial Court Theater as part of the celebrations for carnival—first performance on the evening of February 5, 1714; *dramma per musica*; Stampiglia's last full three-act opera produced in Vienna.

		I	II	III
A	Silla	6g	5f	7j
B	Elio	2b 11m	1a→ 2b* 11l	[2b] 3c*→ [3d*] 5g
C	Alba Cornelia	[1a] 3c 7h 10l	2b*→ 3c 7i 12m	3c*→ [3d*] [4e] **5f** **7i** **10o**→
D	Tito Scipione	5f 9k	**7h** 9j	6h* **9m**
E	Emilia	4d→ 4e **9j**	**4d** 10k 14o	6h* [9n]
F	Centulo, Silla's confidant	12n	6g	1a
G	Lesbina, Alba Cornelia's maid	8i 13p*	4e **13n*** 15p*	**8k*** 8l*
H	Milo, a servant	13o→ 13p*	**13n*** 15p*	8k*→ 8l*
	Totals	13/16	15/16	10/15
			38 scenes/47 arias	Ratio: 1.24

a. A-Wgm Opere Carolinae I.1.

Pietro Pariati

Pietro Pariati, a librettist hired by Zeno as an assistant for versification sometime after 1700, later contributed several libretti of his own to the Barcelona court of Charles III. When Emperor Joseph I died unexpectedly in 1711, Charles embarked for Austria, and, shortly after landing at Genoa, learned of his election to succeed his brother as Holy Roman Emperor.[34] Two years after Charles had established himself in Vienna as Emperor Charles VI, Pariati was called to Vienna as one of the customary pair of imperial poets, a position he held until his death there in 1733. After Zeno's arrival in Vienna during September 1718, Pariati's sphere of activity was limited to the composition of texts for allegorical and comic works, oratorios, and serenades, but during the period between 1714 and 1718 he was responsible for most of the full-scale three- and five-act mythological and historical libretti—works in which he used formats, of which examples follow, as modern as any of those used by Zeno after his arrival in Vienna. Until the appearance of the medial arias and breaks in the *liaison des scènes* that occur in Acts IV and V, the format of *Teseo in Creta* has been marked by characteristics that are strikingly "modern": the use of five acts and of a serious plot implicitly limited to a dramatic action 24 hours long, the limited number of characters, set changes, and arias, and the lack of any comic or auxiliary figures. What is old-fashioned about *Teseo* is Pariati's failure to solve the problem to which we referred earlier with respect to the three versions of *Muzio Scevola*: a lack of dramaturgical development, a repetition of situations in which motives and contexts remain unchanged. Tauride continually demands Carilda's love but never receives it, while Arianna repeatedly expresses doubts that are not resolved until the final scene about the honor of Teseo's intentions towards her.

Ciro[a]

Music by Francesco Conti; produced in Vienna at the Imperial Court Theater as part of the celebrations for carnival—first performance on the evening of February 9, 1715; *dramma per musica;* Pariati's first full three-act historical opera produced in Vienna. It is the first Vienna libretto in which comic intermezzi are printed in a separate section at the end of the libretto.

		I	II	III
A	Astiage	2b	6f	11g
B	Ciro	3c 7e^t $\overset{\rightarrow}{9f}$ 18m	5e 12i*	1a 4c 13i **15k***
C	Bardane	10g 16k	4d *8h* 12i*	3b 12h **15k***
D	Emirena	11h [14j] 17l	14k	5d 14j*
E	Idaspe	$\overset{\rightarrow}{4d}$ 7e^t 12i	2c 13j	6e 14j*
F	Sibari, Persian general	1a 7e^t	7g	10f
			Chorus: *1a* 1b	17l
	Totals	18/13	14/11	17/12

49 scenes/36 arias   Ratio: .74

t: trio

I. A B E {F} +C / {A} B C E / {B} C E / C {E} / *e* ⏌ B F / {B F E}⏌ C D / {B} C D / {C}
   D / {D} E / {E} // *A* Ⓑ / D ⏌*A* C Ⓔ D B / B {C} D / {D} B / {B}

II. *A* C B E / B C {E} / C *B* / {C} // F +{B} / F +{A} / {F} +Ⓔ / C +A / A C D / A C D
   E / *A* B C D E / {B} {C} D E / D {E} / {D}

III. C {B} / C +D / B {C} D / {B} D / {D} E / {E} // A B / A B C / A B C Ⓓ / A B C {F} /
   {A} B C / B {C} / {B}⏌ {D E} // A B C F / A B C D E Ⓕ / A B C D E F

a. A-Wgm Opere Carolinae I.4.

Teseo in Creta[a]

Music by Francesco Conti; produced in Vienna in the great hall of the Favorita Palace in honor of the birthday of the Empress, Elisabeth Christine, August 28, 1715; *dramma per musica*; the first musical drama in five acts ever staged in Vienna.

		I	II	III	IV	V
A	Minosse	2c	***2a***	3c		
B	Arianna	5f	5d	7e	$\overrightarrow{\text{5e}}$ 6f	$\overrightarrow{\text{1a}}\,\overrightarrow{\text{1b}}\,[\overrightarrow{\text{1c}}]$ 2d*
C	Carilda	4e	3b*	5d	**3c**	$[\overrightarrow{\text{3e*}}]$ [4f]
D	Teseo	6g	6e	1a	2b **5d**	2d*
E	Piritoo	7h	3b*	2b	1a	[3e*]
F	Tauride, Cretian army general	3d	4c		7g	5g
	Chorus 1	1b				
	Chorus 2	*1a* 1b				
	Totals	7/8	6/5	7/5	7/7	5/7

32 scenes/32 arias   Ratio: 1.

I. A B F +D C / D C {A} B F / D B C {F} / D B {C} / {B} D / {D} +E / {E}

II. F C +E / F C E *A* B D / {C} {E} F / A B D {F} / {B} D / {D}

III. {D} E / B {E} / B +{A} F / F C (B) / B {C} / B +D / {B}

IV. {E} +D / {D}⊥ C F / E C⊥ B +D / F {B} D +A / A D {F}

V. B / {B D} // C E / A C E F / A B C D E {F}

The libretto concludes with an acrostic *licenza* in honor of Elisabeth Christine, followed by two comic intermezzi that were performed after Acts I and III. The intervals following Acts II and IV were given over to ballets, a division of the time between the acts which was characteristic in Vienna after the introduction of comic intermezzi in 1714.

a. A-Wn 4632 AM (also A-Wgm Opere Carolinae I.5).

That the formats of Zeno's own libretti evolved in the same way and at about the same time as those of many of his contemporaries is shown by the review of the Zeno formats which follows.

The disproportionately large number of arias allotted to the role of Berenice, the large number of introductory and medial arias involved in that role, and the interruption after Act III Scene 13 of Zeno's strict *liaison des scènes* to provide an extra scene for the role, all suggest that the singer who performed the part of Berenice in the original production was powerful enough to impose her own wishes on Zeno's otherwise modern format.

The singer who played the role of Atenaide in Barcelona appears to have made the same kinds of demands on Zeno as the one who played Berenice in *Artaserse*; but only minor changes were made in the libretto when it was restaged in Vienna during 1714, perhaps because Zeno does not seem to have been consulted for that production.

Gl'inganni felici[a]

Music by C. F. Pollarolo; produced in Venice, Teatro Sant'Angelo, 1696; *dramma per musica*; Zeno's first libretto. Information for the Zeno libretti charted is based, except in the case of *Odoardo*, on the first collected edition of Zeno's secular and sacred dramatic poetry, *Poesie drammatiche,* 10 vols. (Venice, 1744).

		I	II	III
A	Clistene	3b 6f	**1a** 6f	9h 16o
B	Agarista	[5e] 7g [14n] **16q**→ 17r*	**5e** 8h 12m **16o** 16p	2c [6g] **12k**→ 12l 18p **19q**→*q*
C	Oronta	*4c*→ [4d] 8h 13m 17r*	**12l** 13o	*1a* 1b 10i 15n* 19q*q*
D	Demetrio	***3a*** 12l	*4d* 7g 17r	3d [11j] 19q*q*
E	Orgonte	[10j] ***11k***→ 16o 16p→	[10j] 11k 15n→	4e 15n* 19q*q*
F	Arbante (confidant of Orgonte)	[9i]	3c 9i	*14m*
G	Brenno, court servant		2b	**5f**
	Totals	17/18	17/18	19/17

                            53 scenes/53 arias   Ratio: 1.

                                                                q: quartet

I.   A / A D +E / {A} ***D*** // C / C G +B / {A} C G B / {B} C G / {C} G // F / F E / C ***E*** / C
     {D} / {C} // B G / **A** E B / ***E*** B / {B C}

II. A G / **A** {G} F / {F} // D / (B) D / {A} B (D) / B {D} / {B} // {F} E / E / {E} C / C +{B}
     / {C} // D E / D {E} B G / D {B} / {D}

III. C / ***C*** ***B*** ⊥ {D} // {E} ⊥ G / B C G / **B** C G ***E*** / A ***q*** **G** C / {A} **G** C / {C} // D / E {B} (**B**)
     / E / F E / {C E} **F** // A / A G / A G D B / C E F A G D B

Il Narciso

Music by Francesco Antonio Pistocchi, who sang the title role; Zeno's first libretto written to fulfill a foreign commission. In his 1735 notice in the *Novelle della repubblica letteraria* Zeno complains that the Ansbach edition, used by Gozzi for the 1744 edition of Zeno's dramatic works and the basis of the chart which follows, was "...extremely marred and distorted."

		I	II	III	IV	V
A	Narciso	1a* 3e	[5dᵗ] →6e	**3b** 4d	→1a 2b	→2b **2c** 7iq
B	Eco	4f	[5dᵗ] 7f	3c	3c	→3d 3e 7iq
C	Cidippe	1a* →1b	[2a] 3b	5e	4d*	7iq
D	Uranio	5g	4c	2a 6f **8h***	4d*	7iq
E	Lesbino	6h	5dᵗ	**8h***		1a 4f
F	Tirreno	7j				
G	Chorus	→2c [2d] 7i		7g 8i		→5g 5h 7j
	Totals	7/10	7/6	8/9	4/4	7/10

33 scenes/39 arias   Ratio: 1.3

ᵗ: trio   q: quartet

I. A {C} / A G / {A} B Ⓖ / {B}⊥{D} E / {E} // {F} G

II. C 𝑞 / C / {C} D / {D} +A E B / A 𝓵 B / {A} B / {B}

III. D 𝑞 / {D}⊥ (A {B}) / {A} C / {C} D / {D} // F E G / D E F {G}

IV. A / {A} B / {B} // {D C}

V. E / Ⓐ E / E {B} / {E} // D C G / D C Ġ F / A B C D F G

Odoardo[a]

Music by M. A. Ziani; produced in Venice, Teatro Sant'Angelo, 1698; *dramma per musica*; Zeno's first *dramma per musica* omitted from Gozzi's 1744 publication of Zeno's dramatic works.

		I	II	III
A	Edvino	*4c* 8g 14l	17m	*1a* 10f
B	Odoardo	6e 12k	3b 10g	12h
C	Metilde	[2b] 5d *10i* $\rightarrow$ 11j 17n	8f 12i 15k	9f *11g** $\rightarrow$ 13i*
D	Gismonda	7f 18o	2a **7e** 11h *13j*	5c *11g** 13i*
E	Riccardo	9h 16m	5d 16l	6d
F	Enrico	1a	4c	3b 7e
G	Adolfo, servant			
				Chorus: 17j
	Totals	18/15	17/13	17/10
		52 scenes/38 arias		Ratio: .73

I. C {F} **G** / C / C Ⓖ / C A / {C} A G // {B} D E / {D} E / E +{A} / {E} // C / C A / {B} A (C) / A C / {A} C E / C E / {E} C D / {C} D / {D}

II. B / B {D} / {B} // E +{F} / {E} +C / C / CD / B {C} D / B D / {B} C D / C {D} / {C} +**G** // D / **D** C **G** / {C} +E / {E}

III. A / A F / A E {F} / **A** E / E +{D} / {E} C G / C G +{F} / C G / A {C} G / {A} Ⓖ // C D / {B} C D / {C D} ⦧ B E F / B Ⓔ F C D / B E F C D **A** / B C D E F

a. I-Vnm Dramm. 1190.1.

Faramondo

Music by C. F. Pollarolo; produced in Venice, Teatro San Giovanni Grisostomo, 1699; *dramma per musica*. This is the libretto whose characters and dramaturgical construction were praised in Muratori's letter to Zeno of May 20, 1699.

		I	II	III
A	Gustavo			*11f*
B	Sveno			
C	Adolfo	11g 20n	15i 17j	5b*
D	Rosimonda	2a *12h* 16k	3a 14h 23n 25o*	1a 16g
E	Faramondo	[4c] 5d 15j **19m** 21o	7e 12f 25o*	10e 17h
F	Clotilde	10f *18l*	*7d* 13g 18k	5b* 18i
G	Gernando	6e 14i	4b 20l	8d
H	Teobaldo, Gustavo's captain			
I	Childerico, Rosimondo's confidant, son of Teobaldo	3b	6c 22m	6c
				Tutti: 22j
	Totals	21/15	25/15	22/10

68 scenes/40 arias   Ratio: .6

I. 𝔹 D / ({D}) I E / {I} E / E / {E} G / {G} // A C / H A C / F 𝓐 A C / C {F} / {C} // D / D G / E D {G} / {E} D / {D} // A F / H A F +𝓒 / E +A C / {C} E / {E}

II. A D I / H +G 𝓐 D I / {D} G H I / {G} H I / 𝓗 I / {I} // F +{E} / F D / F D E / H F D E / I 𝓗 F D E I / {E} D I F / D {F} / {D} // A +{C} / F 𝓐 / F {C} / {F} // G H / {G} H I / 𝓗 I / {I} D / D / I +D E / {D E}

III. A {D} / A / A C F / 𝓗 I 𝓐 C F / {C F} I / {I} // E / {G} H (E) / 𝓗 E / {E} // A / A H / A H 𝓒 / A H / A H E C / A H E C {D} F G / 𝓐 {E} F C 𝓖 H / {F} 𝓒 // A E G / A E G I / A E G I H F C / A E G I H F C D

Lucio Vero

Music by C. F. Pollarolo; produced in Venice, Teatro San Giovanni Grisostomo, 1700; *dramma per musica*. This is the libretto from whose first production Zeno dated his own fame as a librettist.

		I	II	III	
A	Lucio Vero	4c 8f*	4c 13k 16n	[10f] 11g*$^{\rightarrow}$ 16lq
B	Vologeso	**2b** 12i [16l*]	8e 12j *19p* 21r*	**16k** $^{\rightarrow}$ 16lq
C	Berenice	6d *10h* 13j [16l*]	[5d] **14l**$^{\rightarrow}$ 15m 21r*	**4b 6c 8e**$^{\rightarrow}$ 13i 16lq
D	Lucilla	**7e**$^{\rightarrow}$ 8f* 18m	*9f* 11i 18o	1a* 11g* [14j] 16lq
E	Aniceto	*2a* 14k	3b 9g 20q	1a* **7d**
F	Claudio	9g	1a 10h	12h
G	Niso, Lucio's servant			
	Totals	18/13	21/18	16/12

55 scenes/43 arias   Ratio: .78

q: quartet

I. A C / A C E +*B* / A C E / {A} C E G / C *G* / {C} // D F / {A D} F / {F} // C +*G* B / C
    B / C {B} **G** / {C} E / {E} // A D C F / A D C F B / *A* D *E E B* F / {D} F

II. A {F} / A E / A {E} G / {A} C / C / C B / C B *A* G / {C B} G // D +{E} / D {F} / A {D}
    / A +{B} / {A} // C E G / A {C} **E** G / {A} G / *G* D / {D} // B / B C {E} / {B C}

III. {D F} // A G / A *E* C / A C / A C *G* / A C / A C *E* / A C / A *E G* / A / {A D} F / {F}
    ⊥{C} // D A F G / C D A F G / {B C D A} F G

Artaserse

Music by Antonio Zanettini; produced in Venice, Teatro Sant'Angelo 1705; *dramma per musica*. Zeno's first collaboration with Pietro Pariati.

	I	II	III
A Artaserse	→ **2a** 2b 6f **14n**	→ [1a] 5d *15m* 15n	14j
B Agamira	[5e] 7g 16p	→ *4b* 4c 14l 17q	*1a* 9g **18n**
C Idaspe	3c* 11k	7g* 11i ***16o***	[2b] 6d
D Spiridate	3c* 12l	→ 7g* 10h 16p	5c* **11i**
E Aspasia	→ [9i] 10j 15o	*6e* 12j ***20r***	7e 16l
F Berenice	4d 13m	6f 20s	5c* 15k
G Dario	8h 17q	13k	8f 17m
H Lido, court servant			
		Ensemble "tutti": 21o	
Totals	17/17	20/19	21/15
		58 scenes/51 arias	Ratio: .88

I. A C D / {A} C D **G** / {C D}∟{F} // B H / {A} G B / G {B} / {G} +E / E / C D {E} / {C}
   D / {D} +F / {F} // A E F C D G (B) / 𝔸 {E} 𝔽 ℂ 𝔻 G B H / G {B} / {G}

II. A B / 𝔸 B 𝒜 / B +𝒢 / {B} +A / {A} // E +{F} / E +D C / H E D C / 𝒜 E D C / E {D}
    C / E {C} / {E} // B {G} / {B}∟{A} +C D / ***C*** {D} // {B} E / E F / 𝒜 E F / ***E*** {F}

III. 𝑩 +A G H / A C H (G) / D 𝒜 C H **G** / C D / E C {F D} / E {C} / {E} G B / {G} B / {B}
     // A H / D A H / C D A 𝒜 / E F 𝒞 𝔇 A / {A} E F +H / E {F} / {E} // B {G} / B +A
     / H B A / C D E F H B A / G C D E F H B A

Atenaide

Produced in Barcelona during 1709 with music by Andrea Fiore, Antonio Caldara, and
Francesco Gasparini; precisely the same text was produced in Vienna during 1714 with
music by M. A. Ziani, Antonio Negri, and Antonio Caldara; *dramma per musica*; Zeno's
first full-length libretto commissioned by the man who was eventually to become Zeno's
employer and patron, Emperor Charles VI.

		I	*II*	*III*
A	Teodosio II	7f 13k	**1a** 6d 11i	6e 14m
B	Pulcheria	4c 14l	7e	5d 8j* 15n
C	Varane	*8g* 11i	2b [10h] 12j	**2b** $\overset{\rightarrow}{}$3c [10k]
D	Atenaide	2b	3c 14l	$\overset{\rightarrow}{7f}$ $\overset{\rightarrow}{7g}$ 7h ***III*** **19o**
E	Leontino	1a 10h	9g	
F	Marziano	5d 12j	8f	$\overset{\rightarrow}{8i}$ [8j*]
G	Probo, the prefect's praetor	6e	13k	[1a]

Chorus: 20p

Totals	14/12	14/12	20/16

48 scenes/40 arias   Ratio: .83

I. D {E} / {D} +B +F / B F / G {B} F / G {F} / {G} +A / {A} // C +G / E C *G* / {E} C /
   {C} +A B F **G** / A B {F} / {A} B / {B}

II. A C G / D G A {C} / A {D} G / A *G* / A / {A} B / {B} F / {F} // A {E} / A C / D G {A}
    C / D G {C} / D {G} / {D} E

III. G / C G / {C} G A B / **G** *A* B / {B} +D / D +{A} / {D} // F +B / F +C *G* / C (F) / (*C*)
     E ***D*** ⊥ G +A B / E *G* A B / B **E** {A} / {B} // A E / F *G* A E / F A E D / B F A E D /
     C B F A E D

The variety of slapstick humor put into the mouths of servants, nurses, and shepherds by librettists like Noris, Aureli, and Minato had, of course, almost completely disappeared by 1710 from the libretti of the genre which came to be known as *opera seria*.[35] One should note, however, that the libretti of Zeno and Metastasio continued to use minor characters like *Atenaide*'s Probo, a type into which those comic servants of the previous generation who did not migrate to the comic intermezzo had been ultimately transformed.[36] Praetors, tribunes, captains, confidants, and councillors whose names appear at the bottom of every cast of characters, they sing two or three arias in each of the later libretti of Zeno and in those of Metastasio, entering and leaving the stage in mid-scene much more frequently than the other characters of the cast. Performed by singers of lesser importance, these roles seem to have existed outside the conventions which grew up with regard to scene-ending exit arias and the like, and were of considerable dramaturgical convenience to the librettists who used them, as we shall see later.

With *Ifigenia in Aulide* we have reached a point towards which the Italian libretto had been evolving for nearly half a century, a point at which its external format was to remain stabilized—some critics would prefer a term like ossified—for more than half a century after Zeno's arrival in Vienna. The number of arias had reached a level which was to remain relatively constant through the rest of Zeno's career. The scene-ending exit aria, having achieved a position of dominance by the turn of the century, had in the works of Zeno achieved a virtual monopoly by the close of the century's second decade. The practicality of an unbroken *liaison des scènes* had been recognized in principle at least since Perrucci's time. But it became a reality only when librettists, partly no doubt under pressure from singers and impresarios, learned how to organize their works in a way that, while minimizing the total number of entrances and exits in their operas, limited those movements on- and offstage to the beginnings and ends of scenes. With this degree of formal stylization there seem also to have come demands from the singers that imposed an additional burden on the librettists' dramaturgical imagination: the welter of restricting conventions about which men like Marcello and even Metastasio wrote with such sardonic humor.[37] It will be noted in *Ifigenia,* for example, that a different character sings the first aria in each act and that in the second and third acts no individual character sings a second aria until each of his colleagues has had one—a principle that is broken only in cases of special concessions to the principal singers: Achille and Teucro, the only two roles in the libretto performed by castrati, are the only two singers allowed more than one aria each in the first act. Ifigenia, the principal soprano in the company, is allowed the privilege of singing the final arias in both the first two acts, a privilege for which Clitemnestra, the second soprano, is compensated with an apparently extra aria in the third act.

The extent to which the format that characterized *Ifigenia* remained unchanged during Zeno's career in Vienna is illustrated by the schematic diagrams which follow for two representative three-act works from among those he wrote during the 1720s. The format in *Nitrocri* is as "modern" as that in *Ifigenia,* except that the scene-ending exit aria slightly loosens its monopoly and that some use is made, both at the middle and at the end of scenes, of exits by principal characters who occasionally do not sing exit arias. Since roughly the same degree of deviation from the *Ifigenia* format can be observed in the dozen other libretti completed by Zeno during his 10-year stay in Vienna, it would appear that the construction of libretti in observance of the letter of regularity to be found in the *Ifigenia* format was not an important issue with Zeno. Nor does it seem to have been an important issue with Metastasio, as is demonstrated by Table C.[38]

Ifigenia in Aulide

Music by Antonio Caldara; produced in Vienna at the "Gran Teatro di Palazzo Imperiale," November 5, 1718; *dramma per musica*. The first libretto written by Zeno for the Habsburg Court in Vienna after his arrival there in the autumn of 1718, *Ifigenia in Aulide* was so pattern-establishing a success that Gozzi used it to open the first volume of his "complete" edition of Zeno's dramatic works.

	I	*II*	*III*	
A Agamennone	11i	9g	7e	
C Clitennestra	12j	2a 14i	5d 15i	
C Ifigenia	13k	4b 17k	4c 13g	20l* with Chorus
D Achille	$\overrightarrow{2a}$ 2b 6f	5c 16j	12f	20l* with Chorus
E Elisena	4d	6d	2b 16j	
F Ulisse	10h	8f	14h	
G Teucro	3e 9g	7e	1a	
H Arcade, Agamennone's confidant	5e	13h		A *licenza* follows in honor of
		Chorus:	*20k* 20l	Emperor Charles VI
Totals	13/11	17/11	20/12	
	50 scenes/34 arias		Ratio: .68	

I. G / {D} G / {G} E / {E} // A {H} / A {D} / A +*H* F / A F / A F {G} / A {F} / {A} B C / {B} C / {C}

II. C E / {B} C E / C E / {C} E D / E {D} / {E} +G / {G} / A {F} / B {A} / B / B C / B C D / B C D {H} / {B} C D / C D / B C {D} / B {C}

III. {G} E / {E} / A B / A B {C} / A {B} / A / {A} H // G / G H B C / G *H* B C E / B C E F / B C E F {D} / B {C} F / B {F} / {B} // {E} G / B G / H B G / F H B G / A B D F H B G

Nitocri

Music by Antonio Caldara; produced at Vienna in the garden of the Favorita Palace for the birthday of the Empress, Elisabeth Christine, August 30, 1722; *dramma per musica.*

		I	*II*	*III*	
A	Nitocri	[7f] 10h	[7d] 15j	4c **18j**	
B	Emirena	[13i] 15k	5c 17l	7e* 9f	
C	Micerino	2a 14j	10f 16k	6d	
D	Mirteo	3b 16l	8e 14i	7e* 17i	
E	Ratese	4c 8g	13h	1a 12h	
F	Manete, Ratese's confidant	5d	[2a]	2b	
G	Imofi, Nitocri's confidant	6e	[11g]	10g	A *licenza* follows in honor of the Empress
			Chorus: *3b*	21k	
	Totals	16/12	17/12	21/11	
			54 scenes/35 arias	Ratio: .65	

I.	D / D {C} / {D} E F / {E} F / {F} // A {G} / A / A {E} / A B / C D {A} B / C ⅅ B / B 𝒢 / B / B {C} / {B} D / {D}

II.	𝓔 F / F / 𝖥 𝖠 B D 𝖢 𝖦 / B D / {B} D C / D C / A D 𝖢 / A {D} 𝒢 +E 𝖥 C / 𝓐 𝓔 C / {C} // A G / A 𝖦 C / A {E} C / A C +{D} / {A} C / B {C} / {B}

III.	{E} F / {F} +A / A C / {A} C 𝖦 / C D / {C} D B / D B / ⅅ B G / {B} G / {G} // E 𝓠 / {E} +A G / A 𝒢 +𝖡 / A / A B C / A B C D / A B C {D} G / A 𝖡 𝖢 G / A B G / A B G C / A B G C D F

Cajo Fabbricio

Music by Antonio Caldara; produced in Vienna at the Imperial Court Theater on November 13, 1729, for the nameday of the Emperor, Charles VI; *dramma per musica*; the last libretto completed by Zeno for production in Vienna under his own supervision. A ballet with chorus featuring "Joy, in a machine" intervenes between Acts I and II, and a *licenza* in honor of Charles VI follows Act III.

		I	II	III
A	Pirro	3c 8h	4c	7e
B	C. Fabbrizio	4d	8f	4c
C	Sestia	5e 11i	[6e] 14i	*8f* 13h
D	Biranna	6f	2b **11h**	2b
E	Volusio	**7g**	[9g]	6d 15i
F	Turio	**1a**	1a	1a
G	Cinea, Pirro's confidant and councillor	[2b]	5d	9g
			Chorus: before scene 1	18j
	Totals	11/9	14/10	18/10
		43 scenes/29 arias		Ratio: .67

I. A F / A G (F) / B {A{ *G G* / {B} C / {C} +D F / {D} F // *E* / {A} B / *B* +C / C +*E* / {E}

II. D {F} / {D} +A B G / A *B* G / {A} G / {G} // C / B C +*G* / {B} +C / C +E / A C E / A C *E* D F / *A* C / C E / F {C} E

III. D {F} / A {D} / A +G / {B} C A G / A G C / G A C +{E} / {A} C *G* / *C B* // {G} A / *A* +B / B / B C / B {C} E / *B* E / {E} // A G / B A G +F / C E B A G F +D

Table C

Title	Date and place of first production; composer	No. of scenes	No. of musical numbers	Ratio	Entrance aria	Non-scene-ending exit arias	
						Medial aria non-exit	Medial aria exit
Didone	Naples, 1724, D. Sarro	52	26	.50	1	1	
Siroe	Venice, 1726, L. Vinci	48	28	.58			1
Catone	Rome, 1728, L. Vinci	44	27	.61		—	
Ezio	Rome, 1728, Auletta	44	30	.70			1 [ ]
Semiramide	Rome, 1729, L. Vinci	34	26	.76	2		
Alessandro	Rome, 1729, L. Vinci	40	22	.55	1		
Artaserse	Rome, 1730, L. Vinci	41	31	.76	1		
Demetrio	Vienna, 1731, Caldara	45	31	.70	1		1 [ ]
Issipile	Vienna, 1732, F. Conti	37	26	.70	1	1	1 [ ]
Adriano	Vienna, 1732, Caldara	36	25	.70	2	1	1 [ ]
Olimpiade	Vienna, 1733, Caldara	35	25	.71	3	1	1 [ ]

Duets	Choruses	Exits without aria	Exits mid-scene, no aria	No appearance next scene	Enters mid-scene	Interruption	Stage sets by act	Licenza
—	—	14	3	—	7	1	3 3 3	✓
—	1	6	—	—	7	—	2 2 3	—
—	1 ensemble	3	2	—	10	—	3 2 3	—
—	1	3	2	—	12	1	2 2 2	—
1	3	6	4	—	10	—	2 2 3	✓
1	2	8	7	—	12	—	3 3 2	—
1	1	2	1	—	12	2	2 2 3	—
1	1	3	5	—	13	—	3 2 3	✓
—	1	2	3	1	8	—	3 2 2	—
1	3	7	3	—	9	1	3 2 2	✓
1	5	5	2	2	7	2	2 ? 2	✓

Title	Date and place of first production; composer	No. of scenes	No. of musical numbers	Ratio	Entrance aria	Non-scene-ending exit arias		
						Medial aria non-exit	Medial aria exit	
Demofoonte	Vienna, 1733, Caldara	36	26	.72		1		
La clemenza di Tito	Vienna, 1734, Caldara	42	29	.71	2	1		
Achille	Vienna, 1736, Caldara	35	26	.74	2	2	1	1 [ ]
Ciro	Vienna, 1736, Caldara	39	26	.66	1	1		
Temistocle	Vienna, 1736, Caldara	37	27	.73		—		
Zenobia	Vienna, 1740, Predieri	29	21	.72		3		
Attilio	Dresden,* 1750, Hasse *Composed in 1740	33	26	.82		—		
Ipermestra	Dresden, 1744, Hasse	30	22	.73		1		
Antigono	Dresden, 1744, Hasse	35	26	.74		1	1	
Il re pastore	Vienna, 1751, G. Bonno	25	19	.76	2			1 [ ]
L'eroe cinesi	Vienna, 1752, G. Bonno	26	20	.78	1			1 [ ]

Duets	Choruses	Exits without aria	Exits mid-scene, no aria	No appearance next scene	Enters mid-scene	Interruption	Stage sets by act	Licenza
1	1	4	5	—	11	1	2 3 2	✓
—	4	5	5	3	13	1	3 2 2	✓
—	4	12	3	—	10	—	3 2 2	✓
1	2	4	—	1	16	—	2 1 2	✓
—	1	5	3	—	15	2	2 2 2	✓
1	1	4	3	—	6	2	2 ? 2	✓
—	1	4	1	—	10	—	2 2 2	—
1	1	4	1	1	9	—	2 2 2	✓
1	1 ensemble	4	3	—	17	—	2 2 3	✓
1	1 ensemble 1 chorus	1	—	—	7	1	1 1 2	—
1	1	2	—	—	10	—	1 1 2	—

Title	Date and place of first production; composer	No. of scenes	No. of musical numbers	Ratio	Entrance aria	Non-scene-ending exit arias		
						Medial aria non-exit	Medial aria exit	
Nitteti	Vienna, 1756, Conforti	32	23	.72	2			1 [ ]
Il trionfo di Clelia	Vienna, 1762, Hasse	35	20	.57	1	1		
Romolo	Vienna, 1765, Hasse	27	20	.74	3			
Ruggiero	Milan, 1771, Hasse	29	18	.62		—		

Duets	Choruses	Exits without aria	Exits mid-scene, no aria	No appearance next scene	Enters mid-scene	Interruption	Stage sets by act	Licenza
1	1 ensemble 3	7	5		15	—	2 2 3	—
1	1	6	4	—	6	2	2 3 3	—
1	4	3	1	—	10	—	2 2 2	—
—	1	5	1	—	11	—	3 1 2	✓

By studying the formats of Zeno's libretti in relation to those of his immediate predecessors and contemporaries, we have seen that, for the period in which the libretti were written, there is nothing remarkable about Zeno's formats. Certainly there is no justification for assigning the credit for Zeno's eighteenth-century reputation to his use of the scene-ending exit aria and the *liaison des scènes*. It will have already become clear to the reader that my own explanation for Zeno's reputation with contemporary critics and his popularity among certain opera lovers of the time derives largely from his ability to fabricate plots that satisfied both the evolving requirements of the operatic stage and the rationalistic wishes of patriotic litterateurs. The following comparison of Minato's *Seleuco* (1666)[39] with Zeno's 1705 treatment of the same subject, *Antioco*,[40] will further clarify the nature of Zeno's contribution. Both works were written for production in Venice. Scene-by-scene summaries of the dramatic action are preceded by the casts of characters.

Seleuco

Seleuco, King of Syria
Stratonica, Queen of Asia, his bride-to-be
Antioco, Seleuco's son
Lucinda, Antioco's bride-to-be
Arbante, a prince, in love with Lucinda
Ersistrato, a royal physician
Eurindo, a page
Rubia, an old woman
Silo, a servant

Antioco

Seleuco, King of Syria
Stratonica, Macedonian princess, destined
   bride of Seleuco but in love with
   Seleuco's son
Antioco
Argene, Lydian princess
Tolomeo, Egyptian prince in love with
   Argene
Arsace, a Phoenician nobleman

Seleuco

Act I   / 1. Antioco, upset over his impending marriage to Lucinda, is seen at the seashore awaiting Stratonica's arrival from Asia. // 2. Stratonica arrives and, when it begins to rain, takes shelter with Antioco in a cave. / 3. While Rubia and Silo cackle at each other about getting wet, Antioco tells Stratonica the strange story of his secret love affair. He is betrothed to Lucinda, but is in love with a girl whom he knows only through a portrait. Antioco asks Stratonica to use her influence with Seleuco to free him from the obligation to marry Lucinda. Stratonica promises to help, but advises Antioco to forget his strange infatuation with the portrait. / 4. Just as Antioco gives Stratonica the portrait for safe keeping, Lucinda arrives with a lantern, whose light shows Stratonica that she herself is the subject of Antioco's portrait, and Antioco that through the portrait he has fallen in love with his father's intended bride. Rubia and Silo make full use of their opportunity to add sardonic asides on the startled reactions of Stratonica and Antioco, who asserts that he has given Stratonica the wrong portrait. She replies that she knows better, claiming that she intends to give the portrait to Seleuco. // 5. Lucinda, alone, spends the whole scene singing an aria on her own unhappiness at the thought of her impending marriage to Antioco. / 6. Arbante pursues Lucinda, but his love is unrequited. Lucinda tells him that she loves Antioco, though she admits that she has previously sworn eternal devotion to Arbante. / 7. Seleuco is shown awaiting the arrival of Stratonica. / 8. He asks Ersistrato whether the latter can discover the cause of Antioco's puzzling behavior, and Ersistrato admits that he has not yet discovered a way. / 9. Eurindo and Silo argue in front of Seleuco about which of the two is to have the privilege of telling Seleuco "the good news." Seleuco inquires anxiously about Antioco, and learns that the latter is in a state of emotional collapse. / 10. When Lucinda asks Seleuco about the cause of Antioco's behavior, Seleuco asserts that it can have nothing to do with Antioco's planned marriage to Lucinda. / 11. Arbante renews his pressure on Lucinda, but is turned away a second time, though Lucinda's asides inform the audience that her refusal of Arbante is a somewhat unwilling one. // 12. Ersistrato, alone, comments on the futility of human existence; since Antioco has all the material goods he could wish for, Ersistrato is at a loss to explain why he is so unhappy. / 13. Seleuco welcomes Stratonica to Syria and after sending her off to rest, expresses his concern to Antioco about the latter's low spirits. / 14. In a scene of amorous dalliance between Stratonica and Antioco that is overheard by Rubia and Silo, Stratonica admits that she loves Antioco, but then determines that she will do her best to drive the feeling from her heart. / 15. In as lascivious a scene as bizarre taste could require, Rubia trips Silo, then sings an aria on the advantages of love affairs with older women. / 16. In an interview with Antioco, Lucinda tries to learn the cause of his unhappiness. She offers to commit suicide, but Antioco tells her that his own death is the only means to a solution. / 17. He refuses to tell Lucinda that he does not love her, but dwells in asides on the subject of his own possible suicide, until Stratonica arrives. / 18. Lucinda kisses Stratonica's hand, and Antioco announces his resolution to kill himself, alleging a hostile destiny as the justification for his plan. / 19. Ersistrato announces that Antioco is suffering from a serious illness; Seleuco orders Antioco put to bed, and the festivities postponed until a more propitious occasion. Antioco and Stratonica exit together after a duet, overheard by Rubia and Silo, about the painfulness of unrequited love. / 20. Rubia is attacked by a baboon, but is saved by Arbante, who seizes the animal by the tail and flings it into the air. This gives rise to a conversation about baboons and to a ballet of baboons and courtiers with which the act concludes.

Antioco

Act I   / 1. Antioco agrees to try to persuade Seleuco of the justice of Arsace's reasons for having led the subjugated Phoenicians against the tyrannical generals Seleuco had placed over them. Arsace commiserates with Antioco on the latter's hopeless love for Stratonica, and Antioco comments on the desperation of a situation so bad that he depends on the likes of Arsace for sympathy. / 2. In a man-to-man talk between Antioco and Seleuco, the King tries to discover the cause of Antioco's unhappiness, but since Antioco does not wish to spoil his father's wedding day, he asks only for the postponement of his own marriage to Argene, a proposal which Seleuco goodnaturedly refuses to accept. / 3. Alone with Argene, Antioco says he does not love her. / 4. In a soliloquy characterized by short, incomplete sentences, Argene speaks of her love for Antioco, her wounded pride, and her desire for revenge. / 5. She promises her love to Tolomeo for the pledge that he will avenge her treatment by Antioco. / 6. Tolomeo is haunted by what turn out to be well-founded doubts about Argene's sincerity. He is troubled by feelings of friendship for Antioco, but decides that Antioco has forfeited that friendship by committing treason against the state (Antioco's friendship with Arsace.) In Tolomeo's view, Antioco deserves to be reported to Seleuco, particularly since such a report will serve Tolomeo's own interests concerning Argene. // 7. Stratonica works herself into a frenzy thinking about Antioco's impending marriage to Argene. / 8. Seleuco tells Stratonica that Antioco does not wish to marry Argene and that she, Stratonica, must persuade him to do it. / 9. In the conversation between Stratonica and Antioco that results from this order, Antioco decides that Stratonica's principal motivation is her ambition to become queen, and in a fit of jealousy, agrees to Stratonica's unwilling order that he marry Argene. / 10. Unfortunately, Seleuco overhears the end of the conversation, and announces his intention to go ahead with the double wedding immediately. / 11. Left alone, Antioco and Stratonica argue about the responsibility for this latest misfortune. After Stratonica's exit aria, (/ 12.) Argene enters to heap jealous scorn upon Antioco, while Seleuco vainly tries to soothe the feelings of both Antioco and Argene. / 13. When Seleuco asks Antioco to conciliate Argene, Antioco says that his services are needed by Arsace, and exits, giving Tolomeo a perfect opportunity to allege to the already suspicious Seleuco that Arsace and Antioco are plotting together to seize the throne. / 14. When Antioco and Arsace enter to request Seleuco's forgiveness for the Phoenicians, Tolomeo's allegation seems justified, and Seleuco furiously refuses the request. / 15. With everyone apparently sided against him, Antioco decides to join Arsace's forces, sending Arsace to inform Stratonica that Antioco is departing to die for his honor, and that he will come presently to announce his decision to Stratonica in person. / 16. In a soliloquy Antioco takes an affectionate farewell from Syria. // 17. Informed by Arsace of Antioco's decision, Stratonica laments her ill-starred love. / 18. In the act's final scene, Antioco insists on the finality of his decision, while Stratonica begs him not to sacrifice his life.

Seleuco

Act II   / 1. Seleuco sings an aria on his discovery that the absolute power of kings does not free them from all emotional problems. / 2. Ersistrato admits to Seleuco that he still has not discovered the reason for Antioco's unhappiness. / 3. Ersistrato and Eurindo examine Antioco at length but learn nothing; Eurindo suggests that the therapeutic powers of music may help disclose the problem (a transparent excuse for / 4. in which a group of musicians arrives to serenade Antioco with a potpourri of arias). Ersistrato begins to suspect the truth when Stratonica arrives

to try to soothe Antioco. / 5. Lucinda spends the better part of the scene threatening to leave. / 6. After Lucinda's departure Stratonica threatens to do the same, finally doing so only after having spent the better part of the scene discussing the possibility with Antioco. / 7. Ersistrato and Seleuco continue their cross-examination of Antioco. // 8. Rubia and Eurindo argue about the advantages and disadvantages of being an old woman. / 9. Arbante tries his luck with Lucinda a third time and is once more repulsed. // 10. Silo advises Ersistrato in particular and the medical profession in general that they contribute nothing to society. / 11. A love scene between Antioco and Stratonica. / 12. Lucinda soliloquizes about her unhappiness in love. / 13. Arbante pursues Lucinda for the fourth time with his usual lack of success. / 14. Stratonica wisely refuses to tell Rubia why she seems so unhappy. / 15. Silo announces a dance in celebration of Stratonica's safe arrival, and Stratonica complains alone of her hopeless love for Antioco. / 16. Lucinda admits to herself that the more indignant Arbante becomes, the more she loves him. / 17. Foiled in his previous attempts, Arbante tries a new approach: he threatens Lucinda with the public disclosure of a series of love letters he alleges she once wrote him, but Lucinda only becomes angrier. /
18. Seleuco tells Antioco of the feasts and dances that have been planned for his amusement. / 19. At the ball itself, Ersistrato spies on Antioco and Stratonica, and discovering their affection for each other, correctly assumes it to be the cause of Antioco's moodiness. / 20. Ersistrato, alone in a corner of the ballroom, considers what he should do about his discovery. The second act, like the first, ends with a ballet, this time involving the ladies and gentlemen of Seleuco's court.

Antioco

Act II / 1. Antioco and Arsace discuss their imminent departure from Syria. / 2. Seleuco discovers them together and curses them bitterly. Antioco offers Seleuco the opportunity to kill him, but Seleuco refuses and leaves the stage. / 3. Antioco laments the fate that has made him not only miserable but also, in the eyes of Seleuco, guilty of treason. He toys with the idea of making love to Stratonica, but decides that *virtù* is more important. / 4. Tolomeo reports to Stratonica that Seleuco has been angered by Antioco's flight from Syria. He steps aside to eavesdrop when Antioco appears for another interview with Stratonica, and decides, when Antioco swoons as soon as Stratonica addresses him, that Argene has been right: there is a clandestine love affair between Antioco and Stratonica. / 5. Seleuco orders Tolomeo to spy on Antioco. / 6. When Seleuco refuses to explain to Stratonica why he is so angry with Antioco, Stratonica incorrectly assumes that it is because the King has discovered the clandestine love affair. She is relieved to hear that Seleuco will pardon Antioco if Antioco will renounce his alliance with Arsace and beg Seleuco's pardon. / 7. Tolomeo hints to Stratonica that he knows of her affair with Antioco. When she replies that she is attempting to have Antioco pardoned and to rekindle love between Antioco and Argene, Tolomeo sees his own interests threatened. / 8. Tolomeo demands that Argene reward him for his intrigues against Antioco. Argene refuses, and a long argument ensues about the tenuous nature of Argene's promises. / 9. Tolomeo privately admits that he has no reason to rely on Argene's word, but asserts that his love gives him no choice in the matter. // 10. Stratonica asks Antioco to go on living but to give up his love for her. Antioco claims that his own virtue keeps him from asking the King for pardon for one crime, when he is actually guilty of another: his affair with Stratonica. / 11. Antioco tries to balance love and virtue, only to decide once more that the only solution lies in suicide. / 12. Overhearing the end of Antioco's soliloquy, Arsace imagines a threat on Antioco and offers to defend him. Antioco refuses the offer, and tells Arsace to leave. / 13. Seleuco accuses Antioco of conspiring with Arsace to seize political control of Syria. Antioco admits that he is guilty but claims that he has been incorrectly charged. Seleuco is naturally eager to learn the nature of Antioco's "real" guilt, but, protecting Stratonica, Antioco refuses to tell. / 14. Arsace rushes out from behind a screen with his sword bared. Seleuco and Tolomeo, who appears on stage at an opportune moment, assume that Arsace was about to attack Seleuco as a part of the conspiracy to which Antioco has just finished pleading his innocence. Arsace is arrested, but insists on Antioco's innocence of any plot. / 15. Seleuco now reasons that Antioco's silence in Scene 13 was only a ruse to help conceal Arsace's attack. Tolomeo persuades the King that Antioco will have to be executed. / 16. Still refusing to reward Tolomeo for his intrigue against Antioco, Argene urges him to tell Seleuco of Antioco's love affair with Stratonica. / 17. Once more Tolomeo is able to stifle his qualms of conscience by reflecting that the end (Argene's affection) justifies the means (his rejection of personal virtue).

Seleuco

Act III   / 1. Lucinda, alone, still seems very much annoyed at Arbante; then she admits to the audience that, still secretly in love with Arbante, she enjoys seeing him suffer. / 2. But when Arbante comes on stage to plead his cause again, Lucinda dismisses him a fifth time. / 3. Ersistrato prepares Seleuco for the revelation of the affair between Antioco and Stratonica by telling him that Antioco is involved with Ersistrato's wife. When Seleuco begins to rage about his son's alleged perfidy, Ersistrato puts the King into a complete frenzy with the news that it is not Ersistrato's wife but Stratonica herself with whom Antioco is involved. Seleuco cannot decide whether to murder his only son or to commit suicide. // 4. Rubia tries but is unable to discover the cause for Stratonica's sadness. / 5. Silo announces that Ersistrato has told Seleuco that Antioco is in love with Rubia. / 6. Alone, Seleuco is still unable to decide on a course of action. / 7. He asks for Stratonica's advice, informing her that he has been considering having Antioco executed. / 8. Seleuco accuses Antioco in person, but when Antioco threatens suicide for the second time, Seleuco suddenly offers him the opportunity to marry Stratonica. Antioco angrily turns down his father's offer, asserting that he does not love Stratonica. Seleuco is, of course, immensely pleased, but / 9. Antioco goes off to brood about the streak of stubbornness that has just cost him Stratonica. // 10. After Silo and Rubia tease Antioco for his witless failure to win Stratonica, Eurindo sings an aria about his physical deformity: since he has had the misfortune to have been born a hunchback, he does not have to worry about troubles that arise from having someone fall in love with him. / 11. Arbante appears before Lucinda for a sixth time, but although she informs the audience in brief asides that she feels drawn to Arbante, she sends him away again. / 12. Stratonica anxiously awaits word of Seleuco's decision about Antioco's future. // 13. In the midst of another emotional crisis, Antioco receives a letter from Eurindo that has been written by Seleuco for transmission to Lucinda. / 14. Antioco reports to Stratonica about his loss of her to Seleuco in Scene 8. /

15. In view of the fact that he is still planning on suicide, Antioco passes on to Arbante the chore of delivering Seleuco's letter to Lucinda. / 16. Arbante delivers the letter, and is, with Lucinda herself, delighted to discover that it orders the letter's deliverer to marry Lucinda. / 17. Silo comments alone on the irony of human affairs. / 18. Seleuco's wedding preparations with a secretly unwillingly Stratonica are interrupted by the totally unexpected appearance of Lucinda with Arbante. / 19. Ersistrato rushes in to tell the King that Antioco has finally carried out his threat of suicide, that Antioco at that very moment lies in the throes of death, all because of his love for Stratonica. / 20. Despite the gravity of his condition, Antioco enters for a last farewell, but informed by the conscience-stricken Seleuco that he is welcome to Stratonica, Antioco announces that he feels much better—well enough, in fact, to join in a final ensemble whose text anticipates his impending marriage to Stratonica.

Antioco

Act III / 1. Freed by the Phoenicians from prison, Arsace considers the best means for him to assist Antioco. / 2. Stratonica tries to persuade Seleuco to spare Antioco, but the King insists on the enormity of his son's guilt, threatening execution for a person whom Seleuco describes only as Antioco's accomplice. Stratonica believes that her affair with Antioco has been discovered and offers herself for execution, but obtuse old Seleuco, who was, of course, referring only to Arsace, tells Stratonica that it will be her task to inform Antioco of the death sentence that has been passed against him. Heartbroken Stratonica's repeated efforts to avoid this assignment are all in vain. / 3. Tolomeo informs Seleuco of Arsace's escape from prison, and then, after defending Antioco's relationship with Arsace, tells Seleuco of Antioco's affair with Stratonica in a scene that ends with Seleuco's exit after a vengeance aria. / 4. Tolomeo proudly tells Argene of his success in convincing Seleuco of the need for Antioco's execution, but instead of the reward he has been anticipating from Argene, Tolomeo receives only curses and a confession of Argene's continuing affection for Antioco. / 5. Tolomeo calls on his valor to carry the day. / 6. Stratonica, in despair, distractedly considers how she is to tell Antioco the news of his impending execution. / 7. Although Antioco had himself decided upon suicide in Act II, he is crushed in Act III to hear the news of Seleuco's decision against him. Stratonica expresses a desire to die with Antioco, but he urges her to live on in order to prove the chastity of their love. Stratonica decides to try once more to win a pardon for Antioco. / 8. Thoroughly remorseful for his deeds against Antioco, Tolomeo informs Antioco that he has just informed Seleuco of the affair between Stratonica and Antioco. Although Tolomeo offers to let Antioco kill him, his full confession puts him in a position for a full pardon; Antioco grants him that pardon without delay. / 9. When Arsace enters in order to free Antioco from prison, Antioco reproaches him for his attack of Act II Scene 14 on Seleuco. Arsace claims that his intentions have been misunderstood, offering to commit suicide himself if Antioco does not believe him. Arsace tries to persuade Antioco to leave prison, but when persuasion fails, Arsace draws his sword and threatens to free Antioco against the latter's will. When Antioco draws a concealed sword in order to protect himself from being freed, / 10. Seleuco enters, bitter in his criticism of Antioco but apparently once more undecided about his earlier decision to execute Antioco. / 11. Although Seleuco was not upset in Scenes 2 and 3 about his plan to execute Antioco, he is now, spending an entire scene weighing his reasons for and against such a decision. // 12. Stratonica confesses her love for Antioco to Argene, who decides because of her own admitted devotion to Antioco to try herself to win a pardon from Seleuco. Both ladies generously offer to concede Antioco to the other if such pardon is granted. / 13. Antioco has by now reconvinced himself of the necessity of his own death. Tolomeo offers to die in his stead, an act of magnanimity that impresses Argene but is of no help to either Antioco or Stratonica. / 14. After a good deal of shouting in accusation of Antioco and Stratonica, Seleuco suddenly decides that his own glory will be best served by yielding Stratonica to Antioco. Argene, impressed by Tolomeo's offer to Antioco in Scene 13, makes no objection to becoming Tolomeo's bride; and Seleuco, just before the final chorus, grants full pardon to all the Phoenicians.

The principal differences between the two versions are best exemplified when one compares the two *main* plots. Minato's version of the story begins with Antioco's seaside reception of Stratonica, and the dramatic, though improbable scene in a darkened cave, while Zeno, preferring to concentrate his attention on the development of character through conflict, opens his version sometime after Stratonica's arrival in Syria, after her liaison with Antioco had already been established. In Minato's version Seleuco spends the whole of the first two acts attempting to discover the cause of Antioco's unhappiness, then offers Stratonica to his son almost as soon as Ersistrato informs him of the affair between Antioco and Stratonica—thus making it necessary that the second half of the final act be elaborated from the improbable intrigue resulting from Antioco's unwitting failure to deliver Seleuco's note to Lucinda. Zeno's version is much more involved, dealing with more complicated characters whose inner conflicts and misunderstandings of each other's motives and actions provide a "natural" basis for the variety of rationalistic plot elaboration that Arcadian critics required. Seleuco is torn between his genuine affection for Antioco on the one hand, and his natural assertiveness and royal responsibility for civil obedience on the other, while Antioco is torn between his sense of filial duty and his love for Stratonica. One does not doubt the depth of Stratonica's love for Antioco, but she is clearly perplexed by the thought that she could conceivably lose both Antioco and the chance to be Queen of Syria, an ambition which once undermines even Antioco's confidence in her. Argene loves a man she knows cannot be hers, but whose loss she finds difficult to accept. Tolomeo is enough of a realist to know that he is probably being misled by Argene, but enough of a dreamer to hope that he may eventually win Argene even so; his sense of personal virtue is weak enough towards the beginning of the libretto to allow him to become convinced that the winning of Argene justifies any means, but it is later strengthened to the point that he begs Antioco's pardon and offers to sacrifice his own life for Antioco's. Although Arsace has ostensibly come to Syria in order to win Seleuco's pardon for the Phoenicians, he allows nothing to stand in the way of his loyalty to Antioco. In the realm of misunderstandings we have Seleuco's misinterpretations of Antioco's friendship with Arsace, Antioco's misinterpretation of Stratonica's advice that he marry Argene, Tolomeo's misinterpretation of Antioco's relationships with both Arsace and Stratonica, Stratonica's misinterpretations of Seleuco's allusions to Antioco's accomplice, and Arsace's misinterpretation of Antioco's soliloquy in Act II. The exposition, development, and solution of these interacting conflicts and misunderstandings are the means that enabled Zeno to create a continuously unfolding drama whose inevitable surrender in the opera house to the requirements of singers, machinists, dancers, and the like would be but minimally reflected to an armchair litterateur of the period.

In Minato's version the sub-plots help extend the length of the libretto and provide the necessary opportunities for the secondary singers, but in Zeno's version they are integrated into the drama, often acting to impel the main plot. Arsace's friendship with Antioco provides a reason for Seleuco to mistrust Antioco before he learns of his son's affair with Stratonica. Argene's feelings for Antioco provide a reason for Stratonica's helpless jealousy concerning Antioco; and Tolomeo's feelings for Argene provide a means for keeping Seleuco disposed against Antioco, delaying until the final act the increased tension that results when Seleuco learns of the Antioco–Stratonica relationship. In what Zeno himself considered his best libretti,[41] every scene, exposing appropriately varying characteristics of the various figures in the drama, reacting to changing circumstances in changing relationships to one another, had a dramatic justification of its own beyond the contribution of an additional scene-ending exit aria. Although there was nothing Zeno could do in his libretti about the embarrassing presence of aria texts, in his best works he was able to avoid reminding his reader, as one certainly is reminded in Scenes 15 through 18 of the first act of *Antioco,* that the poetry in question is not a legitimate tragedy but a text for music. This is an effect which is especially striking in the Viennese works that Zeno considered his masterpieces, where, because Emperor Charles was fond of plots involved with questions of politics and royal ethics, Zeno was able to minimize the tell-tale role of love, concentrating instead on dramatic motives worthy of Scipione Maffei or Antonio Conti.

It is the thesis of this study that Zeno's "reform" involved not a change
in the poetic or musical format of the libretto but an attempt to make its
content more serious and more rationalistic, an attempt to make money
from the only profitable genre of contemporary Italian poetry while creating a kind of literature which, if altogether different from classical tragedy, at least would not expose its author to the charges levelled by
contemporary French writers at the Italian poets who were Zeno's immediate predecessors. This is an end which was served by giving more
care than previously to the construction of a coherent scenario and by
increasing the share of the recitative within the printed text, thereby asserting the libretto's claim to consideration as a species of inherent literary value. There were, to be sure, important musical and musical-
dramatic implications in such a view of the libretto, but Zeno was not
equipped by interest or background to deal with either.[42] So long as the
singers', machinists', and ballet masters' interests were not affected, and
Zeno took every care that they would not be, so long as Italian impresarios
had recourse to the *virgolette* to cut those sections of a libretto that were
felt to be unnecessary in the opera house, the generally increased length
of the recitative was meaningful only for those who read their libretti at
home. In the Vienna of Charles VI, however, where length of performance
time seems to have been regarded as a virtue, the implications for musical
drama were very real, as we shall see in the chapter which follows, a
study of 23 original settings of Zeno and Metastasio libretti completed in
Vienna between 1718 and 1736 by Antonio Caldara.

IV

Caldara and the "Reform" Libretti
by Zeno and Metastasio

Antonio Caldara, the composer responsible for the original settings of all but 2[1] of the 25[2] full-length *opera seria* libretti written for the Habsburg Court by Zeno and Metastasio during the 20-year period between his arrival in Vienna and his death there in 1736, was probably born in Venice about 1670.[3] The known details of his biography before 1716, the date of his appointment as the Habsburgs' *Vizekapellmeister*, assistant to J. J. Fux, are few, but the chronology of his career to that point is relatively clear. Brought up in Venice during the musical ascendancy there of Monferrato, Legrenzi, and Rovettino at St. Mark's and of M. A. Ziani and C. F. Pollarolo in the Venetian opera houses, Caldara had been active at St. Mark's as a singer and string player,[4] had made the musical settings for at least two operas produced in Venice,[5] and had completed arrangements for the publication of two collections of trio sonatas[6] and one of solo cantatas[7] by the time of his appointment on May 31, 1699, as *maestro di cappella*[8] to the opera-loving, pleasure-seeking last duke of Mantua, Ferdinand Carlo Gonzaga.[9] Active in the Gonzaga court through the autumn of 1707, when his name appears in print for the last time as Ferdinand Carlo's *maestro di cappella*,[10] Caldara was probably among those who, in the midst of the War of the Spanish Succession, abandoned the Duke in Venice after Emperor Joseph I's threat in November 1707 to confiscate the property of any Gonzagan courtier who did not do so.[11]

Mentioned in a Florentine oratorio libretto from the early part of 1708 as "di Mantova,"[12] Caldara may have been the composer of *L'ingratitudine castigata*, the first opera staged in Mantua's Teatro Comico under the administration of the Habsburg regent during the spring of 1708.[13] After Lenten activities for Cardinal Pietro Ottoboni in Rome that must have brought Caldara into contact with Händel and Corelli as well as with Alessandro and Domenico Scarlatti,[14] Caldara was called to Barcelona during the summer of 1708 as part of the illustrious musical establishment set up there by Charles III, Habsburg claimant to the contested Spanish throne.[15]

In the fall of 1708 a performance of Silvani's *Sofonisba*, with music by Caldara, was put on in Venice.[16] Either Caldara absented himself from Barcelona for this production or it was staged in his absence, one cannot determine which. That he had returned to Italy at least by the spring of 1709 is indicated not only by the production during May in both Ferrara and Bologna of operas whose libretti bear his name,[17] but also by his appointment during March as *maestro di cappella* to Francesco Maria Ruspoli,[18] host to the Arcadian Academy, financier for the Papal armies, and sponsor of the most lavish musical entertainments of early eighteenth-century Rome.[19] Except for a leave of absence between May 1711 and July 1712, entered upon just after the death of Emperor Joseph I and spent in Italy and Vienna among the appointment seekers to Charles VI (Joseph's younger brother, his successor as Holy Roman Emperor, and Caldara's former patron in Barcelona), Caldara remained in Ruspoli's employ through the spring of 1716,[20] his connection with Vienna preserved through an honorary title[21] and through the performance during 1713–14 of at least three works sent by Caldara from Rome.[22] His ultimate resignation from the service of Ruspoli followed the 1715 publication in Bologna of Caldara's fourth and final opus number, a collection of six two-voiced and six three-voiced motets with figured bass,[23] in whose dedication to Rome's Cardinal Ottoboni the composer praises Ottoboni for his interest in libretti that are "entertaining without being licentious," and speaks of having served him on frequent occasions in the past.[24] The chain of events which ended with Caldara's assumption of duties as Fux's assistant during the summer of 1716[25] began with the death of *Kapellmeister* Ziani on January 22, 1715, and continued with Fux's promotion on March 8 to succeed Ziani,[26] with the arrival from Rome on June 29 of a confusingly worded petition in which Caldara applied for any musical post still available,[27] with Fux's request that the Emperor himself decide on the question of Caldara's appointment,[28] and with the severing of Caldara's connection with Ruspoli on May 24, 1716.[29] The position on which Charles decided was that of Habsburg *Vizekapellmeister* with its unofficial responsibility for the operatic part of the Viennese court's musical life. It was a position which Caldara was to occupy uninterruptedly for the rest of his life and which was to involve him after 1718 in a long-term relationship with the two best-known librettists of the first half of the eighteenth century, Zeno and Metastasio.

After 1718, when Zeno accepted Charles's invitation to succeed Stampiglia as principal imperial poet,[30] Caldara must have become accustomed to setting libretti like *Antioco*, but Table D, summarizing some aspects of libretti set by Caldara before his Vienna appointment, shows the diversity of the libretti with which he had been concerned before 1716. Caldara, one sees, had set texts that were with and without *virgolette*, texts that were with and without comic characters, texts of three acts and of five, texts where there were nearly as many entrance- and medial- as scene-ending arias and those where the latter type dominated, texts which in performance were a long series of arias and those in which recitative and aria had relatively equal shares. Caldara had set the works of poets enchanted with the literary quality of their own libretti as well as the works of those who prefaced their libretti with lengthy apologies and confessions of literary misconduct. He had set the work of poets anxious to make their libretti conform to the precepts of Aristotle and Horace and the works of those who viewed Aristotle and his commentators as the worst of pedants. He had set new libretti written for special occasions and had taken part in the inevitable *rifacimenti* of works already produced elsewhere, sometimes cutting comic scenes, sometimes adding them where none had been present originally. And he had made these settings for a variety of opera houses, public and private, for performances in Italian in at least three different countries. If, before his 1716 arrival in Vienna, Caldara had developed his own aesthetic about the sort of libretto to which his talents as a composer were best suited, the libretti which he set before 1716 do not show it. Taken as a group they suggest rather that Caldara, like many another Italian composer of the period in question, accepted operatic commissions without troubling himself about the form and content of the libretto or about the literary aspirations of the librettist.

The nature of the 25 settings of full-length Zeno and Metastasio texts that he completed in Vienna and the complete absence in the extant Zeno and Metastasio correspondence of any comments about professional contact with Caldara indicates that this aspect of Caldara's activities did not change after 1716. If anything, the bureaucratic channels through which operas came to production in Vienna, the undeveloped state of Zeno's musical interests and abilities, and Zeno's interest in the libretto as a literary genre must have tended to increase Caldara's isolation from Zeno, to destroy the possibility of his participation in any jointly planned musical-dramatic entity. Metastasio, to be sure, was more interested than Zeno in opera as musical drama, but by the time he succeeded Zeno in Vienna during 1729, Caldara had apparently become too accustomed to his own operatic premises and procedures to have been much affected.

Table D

Title [a]	Librettist	City of production	Date	Virgolette	No. of comic characters	No. of acts	No. of scenes	No. of musical numbers	Ratio	No. of entrance and medial numbers
Argene	Badi	Venice	1689	yes	2	3	41	40	1.	14
Il Tirsi	Zeno	Venice	1696	yes	—	5	41	47	1.2	.17
La promessa . . .	?	Venice	1697	yes	1	3	47	47	1.	13
L'oracolo . . .	Silvani	Mantua	1699	yes	2	3	46	49	.9	16
Gli equivoci . . .	?	Casale	1703	yes	—	3	48	52	1.1	17
L'Arminio	Salvi	Genoa	1705		2	3	55	52	.9	12
Partenope	Stampiglia	Venice	1707	no	1	3	34	43	1.3	15
Il selvaggio eroe	Frigimelica	Venice	1707	yes	—	5	35	44	1.3	17
L'inimico generoso	?	Bologna	1709	no	—	3	41	44	1.1	11
L'Anagilda	Gigli	Rome	1711	yes	2	3	34	67	2.	51
L costanza . . .	?	Rome	1711	no	—	3	55	46	.8	12
Atenaide	Zeno	Vienna	1714	no	—	3	49	39	.8	8

a. Library locations for copies of libretti listed above are as follows: *Argene*—I-Vnm Dramm. 1295.1; *Il Tirsi*—I-Vnm Dramm. 1185.5; *La promessa serbata al primo*—I-Vnm Dramm. 1188.5; *L'oracolo in sogno*—I-Bc 730; *Gli equivoci del sembiante*—I-Bc 732; *L'Arminio*—I-Bc 734; *Partenope*—I-Vnm Dramm. 1202.3; *Il selvaggio eroe*—I-Vnm Dramm. 1201.5; *L'inimico generoso*—I-Bc 738; *L'Anagilda*—US-Wc ML 48 S.1491; *La costanza in amore vince l'inganno*—I-Macerata, Biblioteca civica; *Atenaide*—A-Wgn Opere Carolinae I.3.

This view of Caldara's relationships with both Zeno and Metastasio is supported by a study of the musical materials themselves. The operas in question are listed in Table E.

Overtures

Like all but four[31] of the 70 extant Caldara overtures written for secular libretti, the overtures of the 25 scores under study here are three-movement affairs of the so-called Italian variety.[32] Entitled "introduzione" when they bear any title at all,[33] these overtures all begin with allegro movements of 40 or 50 3/4, or (normally) 4/4, measures in which the orchestra is treated in the *concertato* manner, one or two string groups à 4 and continuo pitted against oboes and bassoons and/or one or two groups à 3 of trumpets (with timpani). (As usual in Vienna of the first half of the eighteenth century, those overtures which involve trumpets are always in the key of C.) Based on diatonic, often triadic motivic material which frequently involves syncopated figures, these introductory allegro sections are almost always in major keys and often begin with simple fugal expositions. Constructed so that alternating *ritornelli* and *concertino* sections tonicize a number of local areas after the fashion of a Vivaldi *concerto grosso* allegro, or on the model of a five-part *da capo* aria,[34] these introductory allegros always involve all of the instruments to be used in the overture, and are separated from the sections that follow them by authentic cadences in the tonic of the entire overture. The second section of the inevitable three is always much shorter than the first, sometimes as short as five or six measures marked *largo* or *andante*. Usually in 3/2 or 3/4, in the relative minor, and always involving a reduced instrumentation, the second sections are usually of an improvisatory nature dominated by the first violins, and normally conclude with a half cadence on the dominant, prolonged by a fermata. The overtures for Caldara's 25 Zeno and Metastasio scores normally conclude with bi-partite dance movements in the tonics of the first movements. Often marked "aria," sometimes "stile di minuetto," they usually involve a reduction in the number of real parts from four to three, and comprise a succession of four-bar phrases. There is no evidence that Caldara derived the thematic material of the second and third sections of his overtures from the thematic material of any previous section. The 25 overtures, like the rest of Caldara's overtures for secular texts, are similar but distinct compositions, composed for the works with which they were apparently performed though without any apparent programmatic connection to any of those works. Neither the initial tonic of the opening scene nor the concluding tonic of the first or last act appears to have any relation to that

Table E

Title	Librettist	Date of first performance	Occasion	Place	Autograph score	Libretto[a]
Ifigenia in Aulide	Zeno	Nov. 5, 1718	Emperor's nameday	Vienna Court Theater	A-Wgm Caldara autograph 40	OC II.5
Sirita	Zeno	Aug. 21, 1719	Marriage of Archduchess Maria Josefa	Vienna Favorita	A-Wgm Caldara autograph 42	OC II.7
Lucio Papirio	Zeno	Nov. 4, 1719	Emperor's nameday	Vienna Court Theater	A-Wgm Caldara autograph 44	OC II.9
Ormisda	Zeno	Nov. 4, 1721	Emperor's nameday	Vienna Court Theater	A-Wgm Caldara autograph 46	OC III.3
Nitocri	Zeno	Aug. 30, 1722	Empress's birthday	Vienna Favorita	A-Wgm Caldara autograph 48	OC III.5
Scipione nelle Spagne	Zeno	Nov. 4, 1722	Emperor's nameday	Vienna Court Theater	A-Wgm Caldara autograph 49	OC III.6
Euristeo	Zeno	May 16, 1724		Vienna—specially arranged theater in the palace		OC IV.1
Andromaca	Zeno	Aug. 28, 1724	Empress's birthday	Vienna Favorita	D-Bds Caldara autograph 2	OC IV.3
Gianguir	Zeno	Nov. 4, 1724	Emperor's nameday	Vienna Court Theater	A-Wgm Caldara autograph 51	OC IV.4

Title	Librettist	Date	Occasion	Place	Source	OC
Semiramide in Ascalona	Zeno	Aug. 28, 1725	Empress's birthday	Vienna Favorita	A-Wgm Caldara autograph 54	OC IV.6
Venceslao	Zeno	Nov. 4, 1725	Emperor's nameday	Vienna Court Theater	A-Wgm Caldara autograph 55	OC IV.7
I due dittatori	Zeno	Nov. 4, 1726	Emperor's nameday	Vienna Court Theater	A-Wgm Caldara autograph 95	OC V.3
Imeneo	Zeno	Aug. 28, 1727	Empress's birthday	Vienna Favorita	A-Wgm Caldara autograph 59	OC V.5
Ornospade	Zeno	Nov. 4, 1727	Emperor's nameday	Vienna Court Theater	A-Wgm Caldara autograph 60	OC V.6
Mitridate	Zeno	Nov. 4, 1728	Emperor's nameday	Vienna Court Theater	A-Wgm Caldara autograph 64	OC V.8
Cajo Fabbricio	Zeno	Nov. 13, 1729	Emperor's nameday	Vienna Court Theater	A-Wgm Caldara autograph 66	OC VI.2
Demetrio	Metastasio	Nov. 4, 1731	Emperor's nameday	Vienna Court Theater	A-Wgm Caldara autograph 71	OC VI.5
Adriano	Metastasio	Nov. 9, 1732	Emperor's nameday	Vienna Court Theater	A-Wgm Caldara autograph 72	OC VI.8
L'Olimpiade	Metastasio	Aug. 30, 1733	Empress's birthday	Vienna Favorita	D-Bds Caldara autograph 3	OC VI.10
Demofoonte	Metastasio	Nov. 4, 1733	Emperor's nameday	Vienna Court Theater	A-Wgm Caldara autograph 73	OC VI.11

Title	Librettist	Date of first performance	Occasion	Place	Autograph score	Libretto[a]
Enone	Zeno	Aug. 28, 1734	Empress's birthday	Vienna Favorita	A-Wgm Caldara autograph 67	OC VII.1
La clemenza di Tito	Metastasio	Nov. 4, 1734	Emperor's nameday	Vienna Court Theater	A-Wgm Caldara autograph 74	OC VII.2
Achille in Sciro	Metastasio	Feb. 13, 1736	Marriage of Archduchess Maria Theresa	Vienna Court Theater	D-Bds Caldara autograph 1	OC VII.3
Ciro riconosciuto	Metastasio	Aug. 28, 1736	Empress's birthday	Vienna Favorita	A-Wgm Caldara autograph 62	OC VII.4
Temistocle	Metastasio	Nov. 4, 1736	Emperor's nameday	Vienna Court Theater	A-Wgm Caldara autograph 77	OC VII.5

a. All in the Gesellschaft der Musikfreunde series entitled Opere Carolinae.

of the overture. As in operas by other composers of the period, there are
no overtures for acts other than the first.

Exceptions to the foregoing remarks occur among Caldara's overtures to
secular works as follows:

1) In the overture to *Cajo Marzio Coriolano* (1717), a work beginning with a chorus of Volscians, the opening C major *allegro* is
   followed by an *adagio* of six measures, followed immediately by
   a C major *da capo* chorus whose first part is repeated at the end
   of the scene after intervening recitative.

2) In the overture to *Lucio Papirio dittatore* (1719), an opera which
   opens with a homophonic chorus of Romans singing in joyful
   anticipation of a victory over their enemies, the opening F major
   allegro of the overture is followed by 19 measures of d minor
   largo in 3/4, a bi-partite dance movement in 2/4 for two oboes
   and bassoon, also in d minor, and six measures of 3/2 for strings
   that move from VI^6 of d minor to V of F, the key of the opening
   chorus.

3) In the overture to *Venceslao* (1725), a work opening with an entrance aria for Ernando, Venceslao's general and confidant, an
   initial *allegro* of 90 measures in C major and an *andante* of 8
   measures are followed by the direction to raise the curtain and
   to follow immediately with Ernando's *da capo* aria in C major.

In all three cases the overture is tonally connected with the opera which
it precedes,[35] and hence could not have been easily disassociated in performance from its original context.

4) The 45-measure C major *allegro* which opens *Semiramide in Ascalona* (1725) is followed by a bi-partite c minor *andante*, marked
   "aria, senza oboe," that is followed in turn by a bi-partite 3/8
   movement à 3 marked "stile di minuetto."

5) The overture to *Don Chisciotte in corte della Duchessa* (1727)
   begins with a G major *allegro* in *da capo* form, followed by a
   g minor 2/4 "aria" à 4 in which violins alternate in the upper
   voices with oboes, followed by a repeat of the first part of the
   opening *da capo* movement—as Robert Haas has pointed out, a
   striking expansion of *da capo* form, producing a simple rondo.[36]

6) The overture to *Adriano in Siria* (1732), another work whose first scene opens with a chorus, begins with 56 measures of *allegro* in C major, followed first by a bi-partite *allegretto* in 2/4 marked "aria," and then by two measures of *grave* leading directly to the dominant of a minor, the key of the chorus at the beginning of Scene 1.

Recitative

In the earliest history of opera one of the principal goals had been the discovery of a variety of music capable of setting dramatic dialogue in a manner that would make the text clearly understandable while intensifying its impact. But it did not take long for musicians and their audiences to perceive that, whatever the dramatic qualities of the most carefully made recitative, its effect was not enhanced by length—that the variety resulting from the introduction of instrumental interludes, dancing, and rhythmically regular settings of more lyric texts was usually more than adequate compensation for presumed deviations from the dramatic practices of ancient Greece. As the seventeenth century wore on, Italian librettists restricted the share of lengthy recitatives and increased the number of arias to the point that by the 1670s and 1680s there was often insufficient dialogue to provide any plausible dramatic justification for most of the arias. The movement of which Zeno and Metastasio were the culmination resulted in, among other things, an increasing length of printed dialogue during a period when, for the first time in the history of Italian opera, the musical length of the individual aria had begun to grow perceptibly. The combination of these two tendencies complicated the impresario's problem of keeping performance time within reasonable limits, but it was solved in Italy by the impresarios contemporary with Zeno through the simple resource of the *virgolette*—quotation marks placed around those portions of the printed text which were not to be performed in the theater.[37]

In the Vienna of Caldara's day, however, the Court was not pressed for time. Zeno was permitted to make the recitatives in his printed libretti long enough to effect the depth of characterization and clarity of plot development at which he aimed, and the authorities made no effort to cut any of the recitative in performance. Far from it! A line-by-line comparison of the libretti set by Caldara in Vienna with Caldara's composing scores shows not only that Caldara set all recitative without cuts but that his scores were checked, probably after completion, to guard against the inadvertent omission of a line or two of recitative. Evidence in the composing scores of this procedure is to be found in occasional x's connected with pasted inserts supplying music for the omitted bits of texts,[38] even to fragments whose omission would have affected neither syntax nor sense. There is no evidence in the extant performing parts for the settings in question that the autograph scores do not accurately reflect what was actually performed. That Zeno's secular texts for Vienna average 1300 predominantly 11-syllable lines of recitative will give some indication of the musical length of the recitative involved.[39]

What were Caldara's principles for the composition of recitative and to what extent does his recitative support the dramatic intentions of his poets? Can one support J. H. VanderMeer's recent assertion that, like Fux, Caldara and his contemporaries composed their recitatives painstakingly, with attention to affect, the *partes orationis*, and to a musical line reflecting the rhythmic and pitch characteristics of speech?[40]

Almost all of Caldara's recitative is of the variety which the nineteenth century called "secco,"[41] a single vocal part accompanied in the score by a bass line, in actual performance by harpsichord reinforced by one or possibly two lower string instruments. The isolated examples of *recitativo accompagnato* (a more declamatory style of vocal delivery entailing accompaniment by at least the string instruments of the orchestra) in Caldara's 25 settings under study here are tabulated in Table F.

Representing less than half a percent of the recitative contained in the 25 settings, *recitativo accompagnato* is reserved by Caldara for three kinds of dramatic situations: oaths and prayers to the gods (beginning "Sommi Dei," "Menti eterne e dive," "Numi clementi," etc.) and expressions of deep mental torment. Though Metastasio's correspondence with Hasse and Jommelli shows that by the 1750s and 1760s he considered *accompagnato* a special resource that was easily overused,[42] Caldara's infrequent use of it during a period in which two or three *accompagnati* per opera are the norm,[43] was probably not the result of Metastasio's advice. That the *accompagnati* in both *Demofoonte* and *Temistocle* are resettings of passages which Caldara had first set as *secco*, and that in Metastasio's only extant evaluation of Caldara as an opera composer he is called ". . . a learned contrapuntalist but excessively negligent in expression and in his attention to the delightful,"[44] suggests, if anything, just the contrary. Caldara was a conservative not only in the infrequency of his *accompagnati* but also in the way he composed them. Instead of animating the accompanying parts with an elaboration of short rhythmic motives, in the manner of his more progressive contemporaries, Caldara restricted his *accompagnati* to four-part chords moving at the rate of one or two per measure of 4/4. The *accompagnati* of *Demofoonte* and *Temistocle* involve, in fact, precisely the same outer parts that Caldara composed originally for his *secco* versions of those passages. It

Table F

Title	Date	Act/scene	Character	Singer	Number of lines in printed libretto
Ormisda	1721	II/2	Ormisda	Borosini	16, blank verse
Dramatic situation: An abdicating king prays for assistance.					
Nitocri	1722	II/3	Nitocri	A. Ambrevil	14, blank verse
Dramatic situation: At Ratese's urging Nitocri swears to punish her brother's murderer, whoever he may be.					
Semiramide	1725	V/5	Mennone	Balatri	6, rhymed, metrical poetry
Dramatic situation: Disappointed in love, Mannone raves deliriously.					
Venceslao	1725	III/1	Lucinda	F. Bordoni	11, blank verse
Dramatic situation: Sick at heart because of Casimiro's faithlessness, Lucinda prays to the gods to end her life or her sorrow.					
Ormospade	1727	III/15	Palmide	Conti	9, blank verse
Dramatic situation: Palmide asks the goddess Nemesi for assistance in her plan to kill Anileo.					
Mitridate	1728	III/3	Mitridate	Gaetano	9, blank verse
Dramatic situation: Mitridate swears to honor a mutual defense treaty just signed with the Armenians.					
Cajo Fabbricio	1729	II/beginning	Allegrezza	?	7, blank verse
Dramatic situation: Allegrezza prays for a return of the golden age.					
Demofoonte	1733	III/4	Timante	Domenico	28, blank verse
Dramatic situation: Timante, discovering his true identity, laments his tragic situation.					
Ciro riconosciuto	1736	III/3	Mandane	Reutter	42, blank verse
Dramatic situation: Mandane, discovering that the person whose death she has effectively urged is actually her own long-lost son, despairs.					
Temistocle	1736	III/11	Temistocle	Casati	10, blank verse
Dramatic situation: Caught in a dilemma without a foreseeable solution, Temistocle threatens to poison himself.					

is clear from Table F that Caldara's use of *accompagnato* had nothing to do with special singers particularly skilled in its performance.

The 99.5 percent of Caldara's recitative that is *secco*, often continuing in his secular scores for 100 or more measures at a stretch, gives very little evidence that it was written with care, with much attention to affect, or with a very sophisticated view of the *partes orationis*. Always in 4/4, the invariable meter for recitative in eighteenth-century Italian opera, it provides a musical setting for unrhymed, freely alternating lines of 7 and 11 syllables wherein the musical rhythms, not conflicting with the grammatical accents of the text but doing little to mirror the rhythms of normal speech, are arranged according to the following principles:

1) Except in cases of elision, each syllable of verse receives a single note. (There are no instances in Caldara of the kind one finds in Fux and in earlier Italian composers, where syllables requiring special emphasis are given short melismas.) The normal rate of motion is the eighth note; quarters, sixteenths, and dotted notes are used for variety and to enhance reasonable declamation, but only where it is convenient to do so.

2) All accented text syllables at the ends of lines of poetry as well as those accented syllables immediately before any sort of punctuation in the midst of a line are set so as to fall on the first or third beat of a measure. (From multiple settings of the same text one sees that first and third beats are regarded as equally good for this purpose.) All grammatical accents fall on eighth note subdivisions. When a grammatical accent falls on an even-numbered eighth, it occurs in the midst of a series of sixteenths, as in the following illustrations from *Temistocle* II/5.

3) The endings of all lines of poetry appear in their musical settings as pauses, whether or not there is any punctuation at the end of the line and regardless of any damage that may be done to the sense of the text. (No singer can ever have had a breathing problem in a Caldara recitative.)

The harmonic design of Caldara's *secco* recitative appears to have resulted simply from a matter-of-fact wandering among tonal centers closely related on the circle of fifths rather than from any effort to supply music for specific affects. As will happen frequently in our study of Caldara's operatic works, we refer for the most convincing proof to Caldara's two completely distinct settings of Silvani's *La verità nell'inganno*, a three-act libretto composed by Caldara in 1717 for Vienna and again in 1727 for Salzburg.[45] In the section which follows, a résumé of the first act of *La verità* is presented with charts of the successive cadence points which support the dialogue in Caldara's two settings.

La verità nell'inganno

Argument before the drama: Prussia, King of Bitania, had two sons by two different wives—Nicomede, a prince who was feared by the Romans, and Atalo, a favorite of the Romans. When Prussia decided to allow Atalo, his second-born son, to succeed him, Nicomede left his father's court and was not seen again in Bitania during Prussia's lifetime. Before his death Prussia had planned a marriage between Atalo and Laodicea, daughter of Tiridate, the King of Armenia. But after Prussia's death, before the wedding had taken place, Atalo fell in love with an Assyrian princess named Arsinoe. When Tiridate, in revenge for his daughter's disgrace, captures Arsinoe, Atalo travels to Armenia to rescue her, but is defeated in battle.

The curtain rises on Scene 1: Atalo calls upon an avenging fury to rescue him from the difficult position in which he finds himself.

		V of	V of			
1717	C G a F d g B^{b6} E^b	c	g	g^6 a	‖	aria: F
			V of			
1727	D A b e G^6		a	a d	‖	aria: B^b

/ 2. Nicomede, whose real identity is not known to his brother, enters and describes his own part in the battle. When Atalo, in despair, orders Nicomede to kill him, Nicomede refuses and tells Atalo to flee. Atalo gives Nicomede his crown.

1717 d C a d g F B^{b6} E^b c f^6 c B^b F C a G C^6 F a e b f$^#$ c$^#$ A b D e a G D	‖ aria: G
1727 F C^6 a F^6 d a e^6 D A b f$^#$ E A Db G^6 C e C d F	‖ aria: F

/ 3. Nicomede, who has recognized Atalo, reflects on this strange turn of events, swearing not to divulge his own identity until heaven decides whether or not he is to be King of Bitania.

1717 e a e D b f$^#$ A b D G C	‖
1727 g B^b E^b c g d a C F	‖

/ 4. Wearing the Bitanian crown, Nicomede is taken for Atalo and captured. Just as Laodicea is about to kill him, a long look convinces them both that they are really in love.

When Nicomede says that he would never have refused to marry Laodicea had he seen her first, Laodicea contents herself by ordering Nicomede placed in custody.

```
                                     V of
1717  a F g d F B^b6 E^b   c g B^b    g   c      B^b F  d a  e G    D  a  C F  ‖ aria: B^b

                                                           V of
1727  C a G e b  D       f^#   E^b  A  b^6 D^6  e a^6   C^6  D^6   g  B^b c f  ‖ aria: C
```

/ 5. Farnace, a general of Tiridate in love with Laodicea, tries to begin an amorous conversation with Laodicea, but is told that there are valorous deeds to be done.

```
                V of V of V of
1717  F g    d     g     e  e a  G e  G  ‖ aria: D

             V of
1727  a G    e               e b^6  A^6 D G e  ‖ aria: G
```

/ 6. Laodicea, alone, reflects on the indignity of her newly discovered love for Nicomede, whom she takes for Atalo.

```
1717  A D A E  f^#  b   e     ‖ aria: A

1727  e        b^6  A f^#  c^#  ‖ aria: A
```

// 7. Atalo, dressed as a gardener, laments on his sad plight and hopes to see Arsinoe. When she arrives on the scene, accompanied by Eumene, a son of Tiridate who is in love with Arsinoe, Atalo hides in the shrubbery.

```
1717  e a^6  d C a b      G   C a  ‖ aria: F

1727  e D    b A f^#  E  c^#  B E  ‖ aria: b
```

// 8. When Eumene swears his loyalty to Arsinoe, she effectively urges his speedy exit by warning of the consequences that would ensue if Tiridate were to see them together. Left alone, Arsinoe swears her devotion to Atalo.

```
1717  F B^b  g c  E^b  F g B^b c  d a   G D b A  f^#  c^#  A b D  ‖ Eumene's aria: G  ‖ e G b  ‖

                V of
1727  b    D^6    e  a d^6  C^6 F B^b  E^b6 f c   g   d   F a e   ‖         aria: C  ‖ a G D  ‖
```

/ 9. Tiridate tells Arsinoe of his victory over the Bitinians, then demands her love. Just as Tiridate is about to use violence on Arsinoe, Laodicea arrives.

```
1717 G C a  e  D A D^6 G C^6 F g c^6  B^b6 g  B^b  F G a d^6  C^6 e G   f^#  b^6  a^6  G C  ‖ aria: C

1727 b  A D A    f^#   c^# E^6  b^6 D  e      a G C^6  d^6 g B^b6   c    B^b6 F C  ‖ aria: C
```

/ 10. When Nicomede arrives, Arsinoe recognizes that he is not Atalo and says so. She accuses Nicomede of having killed the King of Bitania but Nicomede asserts he is the King. Because Tiridate believes that Arsinoe is lying, he orders Nicomede killed in order to test her. Although this seems to suit Arsinoe, Laodicea objects, claiming Nicomede as her own prisoner and demanding the right to torture him in private.

1717   C F g Bᵇ Eᵇ c Aᵇ f bᵇ Eᵇ⁶ c Eᵇ   Bᵇ g F C d   a g Bᵇ c g F   d C b G   a e D

1727   C a d⁶   C G e D b A   f♯ c♯ E A   E f♯ b⁶ D e⁶ G D C a e G a F   D⁶

1717	G C	‖	aria: F	‖ d a C d a ‖	aria: C
1727	g	Bᵇ g	‖	aria: Bᵇ	‖ F g d d ‖	aria: F

/ 11. Alone with Laodicea, Nicomede insists that he is the rightful king and that he loves her. Laodicea decides to test him by having Nicomede tell the same story to Arsinoe.

1717   a d   F   Bᵇ⁶ c⁶ Eᵇ Bᵇ F g F d⁶   a   G⁶ D e b f♯ E c♯

<pre>
                                           V of
1727   d g⁶ c⁶ Bᵇ⁶   F   d   a   C G   e   b⁶   A   E c♯
</pre>

/ 12. In the presence of Arsinoe (and of Atalo, who is still hiding behind the shrubbery) Nicomede tells Arsinoe that he does not love her and that she ought to marry Tiridate. When Arsinoe accuses Nicomede once more of having killed Atalo, Atalo can no longer stand the strain and gives up his hiding place, claiming that he is King. Nicomede objects that a gardener cannot be a king and Arsinoe refuses to identify Atalo, hoping to protect him. Laodicea orders both Nicomede and Atalo imprisoned.

<pre>
                                                       V of   V of
1717   b A⁶ D G⁶ C⁶ a⁶ d g   c   F d a C G e   D⁶ G e D⁶ G   a d   d g F Bᵇ
                                   V of
1727   A B E⁶ f♯ D⁶ G e C   a   d⁶ C F⁶ Bᵇ g   c⁶ Eᵇ g c⁶ Eᵇ⁶   Bᵇ   F   C
</pre>

<pre>
       V of   V of V of V of V of
1717   g d   g   c   a   e G b f♯ A E   ‖ aria: A ‖ D G a g ‖ aria: c
1727   G e   E D⁶ G b f♯ A   ‖ aria: a ‖ F d a⁶ e ‖ aria: C
</pre>

/ 13. When Arsinoe expresses her concern at seeing Atalo berefit of his royal garments and insignia, Atalo tells her that the only important values are virtue and love. He maintains that he does not fear death, so long as he can be reunited with Arsinoe after death. The act ends with a duet expressing a typical Habsburg idea: the fates only separate plebeian lovers in the hereafter; members of the nobility have special privileges to compensate for their special responsibilities.

1717   Aᵇ f   bᵇ Aᵇ Eᵇ c Bᵇ g   Eᵇ d G a   g   c Eᵇ Aᵇ ‖ duet: Eᵇ

<pre>
                                          V of
1727   a   d⁶ C F Bᵇ g   Eᵇ Aᵇ   Eᵇ   c g Bᵇ Eᵇ ‖ duet: c
</pre>

Although contemporary German theorists had a great deal to say about the ways in which composers ought to observe the *partes orationis*, systematically following in their recitatives the punctuation of the texts set,[46] it is clear from the foregoing that Caldara followed no system, that his alternation of authentic, deceptive, and Phrygian cadences on root position and first inversion triads was intended only to produce a degree of variety. Root position cadences in which the vocal part doubles the root of the triad are normally reserved for the ends of complete thoughts indicated in the libretti by periods, exclamation marks, and semicolons; questions are usually set by half or by Phrygian cadences, wherein the last note of the vocal part is higher than the penultimate note. But far from demonstrable adherence to any system of musical articulation corresponding to the punctuation of the text, in the haste that is so evident in Caldara's composing scores he used the same cadences for a variety of punctuation, and often mistook periods for semicolons or even question marks.

La verità nell'inganno I/3

1717 version

tu guidi i casi del basso mondo?

1727 version

tu guidi i casi del basso mondo!

The tonal limits of the first-act recitative cadences used in both 1717 and 1727 settings of *La verità* are the tonics of keys from A flat to E, but in Acts II and III, as elsewhere in Caldara's operas, one finds *occasional* cadences on the tonics of keys having as many as five sharps or flats. As one can see from our study of the recitative in the first act of *La verità*, the use of specific keys has as little to do with affect as does the rate of harmonic change, characteristically somewhat slower in Caldara's later recitatives than in those written during his earlier days in Vienna. There is no attempt evident to make a single tonal center last for the duration of a single idea in the libretto. Harmonic sequences, allowed by eighteenth-century theorists in special cases only, occur in Caldara's *secco* with reasonable frequency, usually ascending to support moments of in-

tensifying emotion, but often simply as a means of introducing an element
of musical interest.

Ifigenia in Aulide (1718), II/6

Achille in pena; delusa è Ifigenia.

Ormisda (1721), I/14

Insultarmi?   Accusarmi?

Dafne (1719), I/1

Udio viver tra fonti senza cuore un'petto?   Voi lo vedete o lauri,

voi lo sentite o fiori.

Dafne (1719), II/3

Se bene tutta adorna   ride di liete spoglie questa piaggia.

Augmented and diminished intervals as well as intervals that involve
large leaps sometimes seem to be the result of tone painting or of a striving
for affect. But Caldara's double setting of *La verità* shows how inessential
a part of his makeup such ideas really comprise.

I/I

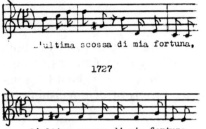

1717

_'ultima scossa di mia fortuna,

1727

L'ultima scossa di mia fortuna,

La verità nell'inganno, II/5

1717

la più forte virtù   il può ben frangere,   non il destin.   On

Dio! lasciami piangere.

1727

la più forte virtù   il può ben frangere,   non il destin.   Oh

Dio! lasciami piangere.

A single cadential formula

beginning on all 12 pitch classes, with the third note drawn from both major and minor scales, and in a variety of rhythmic patterns, occurs with such monotonous frequency in Caldara's *secco* throughout his compositional career that it becomes a reliable means of distinguishing his scores from those of his contemporaries.

Nitocri (1722), I/3

Prence, tanta bontà più mi sorprende, quanto men la sperai. Sinora avversi

l'un fummo all'altro. Odio, livor, sospetto regnò ne'nostri cori.

A further indication of Caldara's inattention to the finer concerns of recitative composition is to be found in some of the corrections that appear in his composing scores. His normal procedure, after discovering at the end of a sentence that he had omitted a number of syllables within that sentence, was not to rewrite the whole passage but to use for the omitted syllables the notes already written, continuing the original melodic line with as many notes as were necessary to provide a new setting for syllables set differently just a moment before.

C. M. Coriolano (1717),[47] I/5

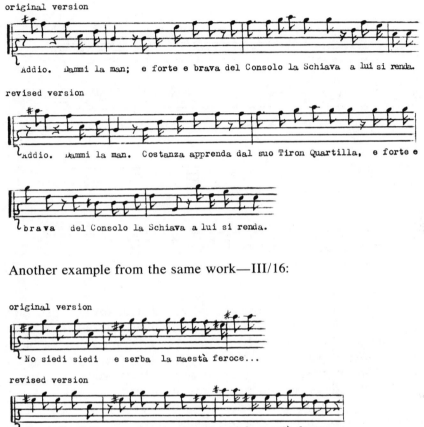

Another example from the same work—III/16:

Similarly, his normal procedure when a librettist wished to make changes in the text after Caldara had finished his setting was not to recompose the scene but only to emend the measures actually involved in the change.

Amalasunta (1726),[48] I/7

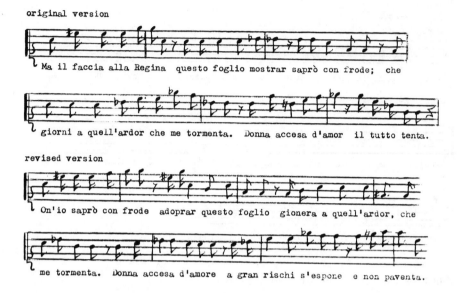

original version

Ma il faccia alla Regina questo foglio mostrar saprò con frode; che

giorni a quell'ardor che me tormenta. Donna accesa d'amor il tutto tenta.

revised version

On'io saprò con frode adoprar questo foglio gionera a quell'ardor, che

me tormenta. Donna accesa d'amore a gran rischi s'espone e non paventa.

Still another procedure indicative of Caldara's attitude towards the composition of *secco* is his revision of the part of Eumene, the only significant change from his 1717 setting of *La verità nell'inganno* for a new Viennese production of that work in 1730.[49] As is clear from the fragment of I/8 shown on the following pages, the change to a lower vocal *tessitura* is accomplished without any change in the accompanying bass part, no doubt in order to avoid the necessity of other changes in the parts of characters who appear in scenes with Eumene.

1717

Mi gira Arsinoe, è vero, entro alle vene di Tiridate il sangue;

1730

la memoria ho del fallo.   Se | prigioniera, espose, ...

Since all the Eumene scenes of the 1730 score, and only those scenes, differ from the score for the original production of 1717, there is no question about the reason for the changes, and no connection whatever with Caldara's completely distinct setting of *La verità* for the Salzburg production of 1727. (That Caldara returned in 1730 to his setting of 1717 only three years after having reset the whole text is an indication supplementing the evidence of the music itself that the 1727 setting was not a response to changing tastes or a part of Caldara's evolution as a composer,[50] but in all probability the result of an understanding with his Habsburg employers. Libretti written for the Habsburg Court were printed before the productions of which they were a part and were thus easily available for the endless *rifacimenti* of impresarios all over Europe. But the musical scores, with only one exception,[51] remained in manuscript.[52] Although none of Caldara's autographs were ever part of the Imperial Library, one can presume that if they remained in Caldara's hands during his lifetime, the music they contained could not be used in performances commissioned by other patrons.[53] Thus, too, we can understand the reason why, after Caldara's appointment in 1716 as Habsburg *Vizekapellmeister*, his operatic scores no longer contain examples of that popular contemporary practice whereby composers used the same aria in more than one opera, sometimes with a text identical or nearly identical to the original text, often with an entirely new text.)

    That Caldara's secco recitative was written unsystematically, hastily, and often carelessly is not to say, of course, that his *secco* does not include some expressive measures in support of dramatic moments in the libretti which he set. In *Ifigenia in Aulide*, for example, when in I/3 Elisena learns that her favorite, Achilles, is betrothed to Ifigenia, Caldara makes use of a repeatedly interrupted, rising vocal line, a chromatic bass, and a diminished seventh chord.

In I/9, when Ifigenia's father, Agamennone, learns from Teucro that, despite his efforts to prevent it, his daughter has already arrived in Aulide, thus sealing her own doom, Caldara uses another diminished seventh, this time followed by a cadence of unusually slow resolution suggesting the possibility of an improvised, affect-heightening melisma on the syllable "pian-."

That all of Caldara's *secco* corrections were not made only with a view towards saving time and effort is shown by his correction of the following passage from II/3, sung by Ifigenia after she has been told that Achille has decided not to marry her.

An example of expressive chromaticism, showing an instance of Caldara's occasional ungrammatic spelling, occurs in II/13 at the moment when Agamennone's confidant, Arcade, tells Ifigenia and her mother that Ifigenia has been unjustly condemned to death by the Oracle of Aulos.

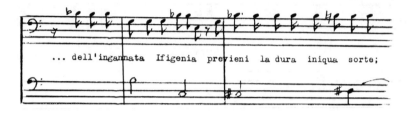

Clitemnestra's II/14 plea to Achille that he protect Ifigenia from those Greeks who, in order to reach Troy, are about to force Ifigenia to submit to the oracle's decree, begins with a number of the expressive means already illustrated but, at what should be the most intense part of Clitemnestra's speech, ends with Caldara's most overused cadence. Caldara seems here, as he does often in his settings of Zeno and Metastasio, to react more to especially affective words than to affective ideas or situations.

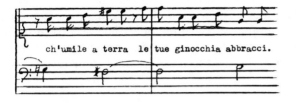

ch'umile a terra le tue ginocchia abbracci.

Where words like "piangere," "morire," "dolere," and the like do not occur, Caldara continues his blissful wandering among closely related keys, no matter what the exigencies of the dramatic situation. When, in *Ifigenia in Aulide* I/3, Elisena complains that she will have to perish in order to learn her own identity and that of her parents, Caldara's response is matter-of-fact.

senza perir, non m'è permesso conoscer genitori, e non me stessa.

When, in I/7 of the same work, Agamennone suddenly notices that his agent, Arcade, has returned, evidently without having been able to prevent Ifigenia's arrival in Aulis, he realizes that there is no stratagem left that will save his daughter's life, but Caldara does not even bother to change his bass.

Ulisse   Agamennone

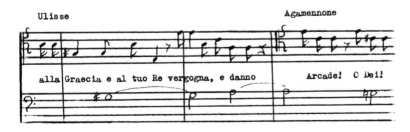

alla Graecia e al tuo Re vergogna, e danno   Arcade! O Dei!

(To be noted as well in this musical example is an instance of the kind of voice-leading carelessness that is characteristic of Caldara—a leap on a strong beat to the doubling of a local leading tone.) The musical result is equally unimpressive when, in I/10, Agamennone reflects on the irony that though Ifigenia has been brought to Aulis in order to marry, she will meet only death there.

...figlia? misere! a liete nozze voi qui guida un mio cemo, e avrete morte.

Secco recitative hardly ever makes very interesting reading, and Caldara's is a good deal less interesting than that of most of his contemporaries. To make matters worse, the extremely long dialogues on which Zeno and Metastasio prided themselves, and the Habsburg regulation that libretti written for Court use be performed without cuts, combined to give the 25 settings under study here at least as much *secco* recitative as any operas ever written. Because the dramatic abilities of individual singers play so important a role in the success or failure of any *secco*, and because the theorists of Caldara's day differ so strikingly in their approbation or condemnation of *secco* as it was actually performed,[55] we cannot say whether Caldara's *secco* was as uninteresting and monotonous in the theater as it appears on paper.[56]

Arias

As we have shown in Chapter III, the gradually decreasing number of arias in the secular libretti of Zeno and Metastasio was part of a general tendency evident in the texts of a variety of contemporary librettists. Partly stemming from early eighteenth-century critics' distaste for arias manifested in such deprecatory labels as "parole non necessarie,"[57] partly the result of pressure from the gradually increasing musical length of the individual aria, this tendency is also evident in the 23 original settings of full-length secular libretti by Zeno and Metastasio made in Vienna by Caldara, as is shown in Table G.

The generally increasing length of Caldara's arias is reflected in Table H, a comparison of data based on the arias in his Vienna (1717) and Salzburg (1727) settings of *La verità nell'inganno*—two settings in which, it will be remembered, Caldara used precisely the same text.

How is one to categorize the more than 600 arias composed by Caldara for his original settings of Zeno and Metastasio libretti, and what are the principles which determined the tempo, meter, motivic design, key, and instrumentation in each of those arias? To what extent in particular do Caldara's arias reflect an affect-oriented approach to the setting of specific types of aria texts?

That Caldara himself very probably did not regard his arias as appropriate material for any of the conventional classification schemes seems apparent for a number of reasons. In the first place, those of Caldara's Italian contemporaries who discuss such schemes have nothing to say about the implications of their schemes for music, and it will be remembered that several of the theorists reviewed in the first part of this book had actually written a number of libretti themselves. Restricting their remarks to recommendations on the kinds of verses appropriate for the expression of certain sentiments, even here the theorists are neither specific nor in agreement with each other. Salvadori maintains that the number of rhymes and of syllables per line is determined by the nature of the sentiment to be expressed, but he gives only general guidelines about the use of specific meters. Long lines are to be used for serious subjects, lines of medium length are to be used for amorous texts, and short lines are to be used for the expression of graceful sentiments.[58] Martello goes to some length in illustrating the variety of verse types available, informing us that arias involving 8-syllable lines are the most frequently used type. Ten-syllable lines, he tells us, are especially good for the expression of fury, while 6-syllable lines work well to express "the amorous languor of a surrendering soul," but all lines shorter than 10 syllables in length are equally appropriate for the expression of any passion less strong than fury.[59] Planelli limits himself to a two-fold classification of sentiments— impetuous sentiments and depressing ones—but admits an impressive variety of line lengths possible for the expression of either of these types. Impetuous sentiments ". . . may give rise to 7-, 8-, 11-, 5-, 10-, 9-, or 6-syllable lines, while depressing sentiments are appropriately clothed in lines of 11, 8, or 6 syllables."[60] Marcello's remarks cannot, of course, be taken at face value, but his comments on the classification of arias do not seem especially exaggerated. The librettist is reminded that the composer will often oblige him to change the meters of his arias, and the composer

Table G

Title	Librettist	Year of production	No. of acts	No. of scenes	No. of musical numbers	Ratio
Ifigenia in Aulide	Zeno	1718	3	50	34	.68
Sirita	Zeno	1719	3	36	33	.92
Lucio Papirio	Zeno	1719	3	34	35	1.03
Ormisda	Zeno	1721	3	50	36	.72
Nitocri	Zeno	1722	3	54	35	.65
Euristeo[a]	Zeno	1724	3	31	25	.81
Andromaca	Zeno	1724	5	37	30	.81
Gianguir	Zeno	1724	5	46	33	.72
Semiramide	Zeno	1725	5	33	30	.91
I due dittatori	Zeno	1726	5	49	39	.80
Imeneo	Zeno	1727	3	32	28	.90
Ornospade	Zeno	1727	3	41	30	.73
Mitridate	Zeno	1728	5	49	35	.70
Cajo Fabbricio	Zeno	1729	3	43	29	.67
Enone[b]	Zeno	1734	5	37	31	.84
Demetrio	Metastasio	1731	3	45	31	.70
Adriano	Metastasio	1732	3	36	25	.70
L'Olimpiade	Metastasio	1733	3	35	24	.71
Demofoonte	Metastasio	1733	3	36	26	.72
La clemenza di Tito	Metastasio	1734	3	42	28	.71
Achille in Sciro	Metastasio	1736	3	35	26	.74

Title	Librettist	Year of production	No. of acts	No. of scenes	No. of musical numbers	Ratio
Ciro riconosciuto	Metastasio	1736	3	39	25	.66
Temistocle	Metastasio	1736	3	37	27	.73

a. Lest the relatively low numbers for *Euristeo* mislead, it should be noted that the work was a very special one, sung and staged by members of the royal family, with Charles VI himself in charge of the orchestra.

b. Although Caldara's setting of Zeno's *Enone* was completed on 30 July 1729 for a performance planned for 28 August 1729, it was replaced at the last minute by a new production of Fux's *Elisa*, first produced in Vienna during August 1719. *Enone* did not receive its first performance until 28 August 1734, nearly five years after Zeno's retirement.

Table H

Text incipit	Character	Act / Scene 1717	Tempo where indicated 1717	1727	Meter 1717	1727	Key 1717	1727	Instrumentation[a] 1717	1727	Length in no. of bars 1717	1727	Verse structure[b] of aria texts
Là di Cerbero	Atalo	I/1 risoluto		allegro	C	C	F	B♭	2	2	71	72	8 7. 8 8 8 7.
Per abbattere	Atalo	I/2 allegro		risoluto	3/4	3/4	G	F	3	3	108	147	8 8. 8 4 8.
Quanto empietà	Nicomede	I/4 —		allegro moderato	3/8	3/8	B♭	C	3	2	105	153	4 5 5 4; 4 5 5 4.
Formidabile	Farnace	I/5 andante		—	C	¢	D	G	1	2	38	149	8 7. 8 8 7.
Ah, se tu fossi	Laodicea	I/6 allegro		allegro e spiritoso	C	3/8	A	A	2	3	115	163	6 6 5. 7 11.
Parto, ma tutto il core	Eumene	I/8 allegro		tempo giusto	3/8	C	G	C	3	2	143	90	7 6. 7 7 6.
Empio, vivi	Tiridate	I/10 allegro		allegro assai	¢	C	F	B♭	1	3	87	80	8 7. 8 7.
Traditor del tuo furor	Arsinoe	I/10 risoluto		presto	C	3/8	C	F	3	3a	55	148	3 4 7. 8 8 7.
Taci, che non sai	Nicomede	I/12 —		larghetto	¢	12/8	A	a	4	4c	105	45	7 5 7 5. 7 4 6 5.
Ti guardo	Laodicea	I/12 andante		allegro	C	¢	c	C	2	2	76	170	3 7 10. 3 7 10.
Ah no, vivi	Arsinoe and Atalo	I/13 largo		largo	3/4	C	E♭	c	3	4a	97	61	4 4. 3. 4. 4 5 4: 5 7 7.

Gran difessa	Eumene	II/2	allegro	andante	C		F	G	4d	2	56	71	88.88.
Scuopri, Signor	Laodicea	II/3	—	allegro	2/4	C	C	Bb	2	3	81	61	87.76.87.76.
Nelle membra	Tiridate	II/4	risoluto	risoluto	3/4		b	A	3	3	84	133	887.887.
Avro più di costanza	Nicomede	II/4	allegro	risoluto	2/4		D	D	4	2	125	104	766.766.
Ah, in questa lagrime	Atalo	II/5	largo	largo	3/4		F	F	3	3	74	71	665. 665.
O Dio, perche	Arsinoe	I/6	—		¢	¢	d	a	4	4	117	139	6666.6666.
No che un cielo	Eumene	II/7	allegretto	—	12/8	C	Bb	D	3c	4a	98	113	10 10. 10 10.
Lo sguardo	Arsinoe	II/10	andante	allegretto	3/8		g	C	2	2	149	186	665.665.
Baccia o ferito cor	Laodicea	II/11	allegro	allegro	C	2/4	a	Bb	1	3	56	128	665.665.
Col tuo nome	Atalo	II/12	largo	largo	12/8		f	g	3	2	53	52	88.888.
Corro, volo	Arsinoe	II/13	presto	presto	C		C	C	3	3	62	75	8.8.4488888448.
Se un volto	Eumene	III/1	—	allegro	2/4		A	A	2	2	154	169	11 11. 11 11.
Mi vuoi re?	Tiridate	III/3	allegro	allegro	C		E	D	1	4a	77	128	8;88.88.
Largo, largo	Arsinoe	III/4	—	presto	C		Bb	F	4a	2	35	39	848.4448.
Non mi giova	Nicomede	III/5	larghetto	andante	3/4		F	Bb	2	4b	177	157	888.888.
Nel fulgor di luci	Farnace	III/6	allegro	—	C		g	F	3	3	76	80	87.87.

Text incipit	Character	Tempo Act / Scene 1717	Tempo where indicated 1727	Meter 1717	Meter 1727	Key 1717	Key 1727	Instrumentation[a] 1717	Instrumentation[a] 1727	Length in no. of bars 1717	Length in no. of bars 1727	Verse structure[b] of aria texts
Golosia di sua grandezza	Atone	III/10 allegro	allegro e risoluto	3/4	C	E^b	C	1	3	122	92	8 8. 8 8.
Alle sue pene	Nicomede	III/10 —	allegretto	2/4	3/8	C	d	3	2	174	160	5 5 4. 5 5 4.
Per la silva	Arsinoe	III/11 larghetto	larghetto	C	C	G	a	1	1	17	21	8 7. 8 7 7.
Quel bel volto	Laodicea	III/12 allegro	allegro moderato	3/8	2/4	D	B^b	1	2	169	148	8 7. 8 7.
Si mie stelle	Tiridate	III/13 andante	allegro	C	C	B^b	c	4	2	72	100	5 7 6 5. 5 7 6 5.
La facella d'amor	tutti	III/14 allegro	allegro	3/8	3/8	C	D	3	2	22	36	6 6 5. 6 6 5.
								Average length:		93	107	

a. The numbers in the "Instrumentation" columns of Table H and in the tables of Appendix E stand for the instrumentation schemes indicated below. G and F clefs indicate the number of parts notated in score in treble and bass clefs. C clefs are used, unless otherwise indicated, to represent alto clefs. Words which occur below in parentheses so occur in the scores here charted.

1) 𝄢 [continuo]; 2) 𝄞 𝄡 𝄢 ; 2a) 2 𝄡 𝄢 ;

3) 2 𝄞 𝄡 𝄢 ; 3a) 2 𝄡 𝄢 (Con Strumti. e Fagott obbligato);

3b) 2 𝄞 𝄡 [2 parts on 1 system] 𝄡 ; 3c) 2 𝄞 𝄡 (Oboe e Fagotti);

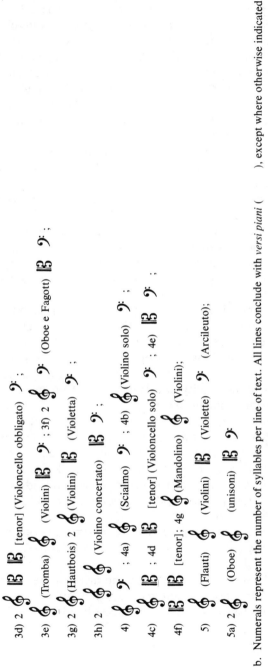

3d) 2 [tenor] (Violoncello obbligato) ;

3e) (Tromba) ; 3f) 2 (Oboe e Fagott) ;

3g) 2 (Hautbois) 2 (Violini) (Violetta) ;

3h) 2 (Violino concertato) ;

4) ; 4a) (Scialmo) ; 4b) (Violino solo) ;

4c) ; 4d [tenor] (Violoncello solo) ; 4e) ;

4f) [tenor]; 4g (Mandolino) (Violini);

5) (Flauti) (Violini) (Violette) (Arcileuto);

5a) 2 (Oboe) (unisoni) ;

b. Numerals represent the number of syllables per line of text. All lines conclude with *versi piani* (   ), except where otherwise indicated.

is admonished to be certain that his arias are alternately lively and pathetic to the end of the opera, regardless of the texts involved.[61] Neither in the extant correspondence of Zeno and Metastasio nor in the prefaces to any of their printed libretti is there mention of any scheme for the classification of arias, with respect either to texts or to music.

Secondly, the aria classification schemes that have been drawn up since Caldara's death do not relate specifically enough to well-defined collections of arias to allow one to judge the appropriateness of classification criteria that often do not seem to be mutually exclusive. That the criteria for the miscellaneous schemes outlined below vary to such an extent weakens the probability that any of them was in general use during Caldara's lifetime:

When Goldoni asks an operatic company in Milan to give its opinion of his libretto, *Amalasonta*, he is told that ". . . the author of the text should provide the composer with the different nuances which form the *chiaroscuro* of the music, and he should take care lest one pathetic aria follow another of the same type. It is necessary to distribute bravura arias, action arias, *arie di mezzo carettere*, minuets and rondos with the same care."[62]

Goldoni's English contemporary, John Brown, distinguishes five varieties of arias: *aria cantabile* (". . . the proper subjects for this air are sentiments of tenderness"), *aria di portamento* (". . . chiefly composed of long notes . . . the subjects proper to this air are sentiments of dignity"), *aria di mezzo caratere* (". . . a species of air, which, though expressive neither of the dignity of this last, nor of the pathos of the former, is, however, serious and pleasing"), *aria parlante* (". . . admits neither of long notes in the composition, nor of many ornaments in the execution. The rapidity of motion of this air is proportioned to the violence of the passion which is expressed by it. This species of air goes sometimes by the name of *aria di nota e parole*, and likewise of *aria agitata*"), *aria di bravura* (". . . chiefly, indeed, too often, merely to indulge the singer in the display of certain powers in the execution, particularly extraordinary agility or compass of voice."[63]

The nineteenth-century Venetian bibliographer of opera, Taddeo Wiel, lists the following five varieties of aria: *mezzo caratere, cantabile, parlante, bravura, col violino*.[64]

Bernard Flögel's 1929 article on the arias of Händel's operas initiated a series of classification schemes in which affect is related to tempo. Flögel's scheme classifies arias under three headings, as follows:[65]

Allegro	*Andante*	*Largo-Adagio*
bravura arias	minuet	recitative-arioso
"volkstümlich" arias	arioso	free cantabile arias
arias influenced by	"mixed affects"	influenced by dance
dance forms, esp.		forms: sarabande,
minuet, gavotte, gigue		siciliano

Rudolf Gerber's *MGG* article, "Arie," uses a scheme that, by marrying Goldoni–Brown to Flögel, results in a three-fold classification which implies that arias of "mezzo carattere" were those of medial tempo.[66]

J. H. VanderMeer's recent study on the operas of Fux uses an affect-oriented classification scheme which refines on and adds to Flögel's as follows:[67]

ALLEGRO

    a) heroic pieces: frequent broken chords and leaps in the melodic writing; anapaestic and dotted rhythms, syncopations frequent; harmony normally diatonic; frequent use of trumpets. Affects: triumph, love of battle, arrogance, cheerfulness, steadfastness, royal dignity

    b) hunting pieces: except for their use of horns instead of trumpets, these share all characteristics of the above. (Viennese arias involving horns are always in F.)

    c) rage or vengeance pieces: almost always in 4/4; harmony somewhat more chromatic than the above, especially through the alternation of major and minor modes and the use of the Neapolitan sixth.

    d) pleasant and tender pieces: diatonic melodic writing in predominantly stepwise motion; phrase structure more periodic than in any of the above; much less use of coloratura writing; rhythm simpler, little use of syncopated figures. Affects: gentle melancholy, graceful pleading, tender consolation, loving warning, gaiety, ridicule.

    e) heroic-tender pieces: arias which share characteristics of categories a) and d) above.

    f) pieces with the character of dance forms: gavottes, bourrées, minuets, passepieds, gigues (both French and Italian varieties), chaconnes.

ANDANTE

    a) minuets: flowing melodic writing, periodic phraseology the norm; harmonic writing usually diatonic; rhythms normally simple, though syncopated figures occur frequently at cadential points; possible influence of folk music. Affects: melancholy, tender love, pastoral atmosphere, naive joy, cheerfulness, steadfastness.

    b) cantabile pieces without dance influence (VanderMeer's idea of the *aria di mezzo carattere*): almost always in 4/4; melodic, harmonic, and rhythmic style like that described under the cantabile adagio pieces, below; phraseology irregular. Affects: amorousness, sadness, parting of lovers, jealousy, steadfastness, energetic happiness, determination.

    c) heroic andantes: pieces of mixed affect.

    d) dances of only partly heroic character.

LARGO-ADAGIO (relatively few in number, reserved for especially emotional situations)

    a) sarabande arias: melodic phrases long and irregular in construction; frequent examples of chromaticism for expressive purposes; accompaniment normally limited to continuo only. Affects: sadness, melancholy, despair.

    b) siciliano arias: tempo indications vary—largo, larghetto, adagio, and andante all occur; stepwise melodic writing, frequent *appoggiature* for expressive purposes. Affects: despair, loneliness, jealousy, sympathy, sadness, tenderness.

POLYPHONIC PIECES—Affect: objective view of one's own emotions.

    a) fugal arias: rapid tempo and use of minor keys are normal here.

    b) pieces in madrigal style: meter normally 2/2; diatonic harmony prevails.

In VanderMeer's favor is the point that, unlike the authors of countless German dissertations on "_____ als Opernkomponist," he does not try to show that specific categories of texts always imply single affects which, in turn, result inevitably in specific keys, meters, tempos, and instrumentation patterns.[68] But if VanderMeer is correct in maintaining that Fux's choice of musical setting was circumscribed by the affects implied in individual aria texts, and that Fux's understanding of affect must generally have corresponded to Mattheson's outline of the subject in *Das neueröffnete Orchester*, he is incorrect in suggesting that the scheme applies in similar measure to Fux's contemporaries—to Caldara and to other Italians of his generation.[69] That Caldara's musical reaction to an aria text was controlled as much by the idea that successive arias should differ as it was by any variety of *Affektenlehre* is shown conclusively through the manner in which his 1727 setting of *La verità nell'inganno* differs from his 1717 setting of that libretto, a third reason for rejecting the idea that, in the corpus of Caldara's arias, specific kinds of texts imply specific varieties of musical setting. That most but not all of the arias in Caldara's two settings of *La verità nell'inganno* differ with respect to tempo, meter, key, and instrumentation indicates that the differences truly reflect Caldara's normal approach to the setting of aria texts and not a special situation in which consistent divergencies[70] in these respects were a necessary concomitant of a second setting commissioned by a non-Habsburg patron.

    Operatic essayists began even during the eighteenth century to criticize Zeno for his insensitivity to the musical aspects of poetry. His use of such unmusical proper names as Asaf and Mahobet, Childerico and Peuceste, Aglatida and Gismondo, and his recourse to aria verse forms involving the juxtaposition of awkwardly combined metrical feet and of stumbling lines of irregularly varying length are the principal charges. To these may be added the complaint that the subject matter and mode of expression, while excellent perhaps for a rationalistic delineation of complicated plot and character development on the *Antioco* model, must often have been anything but inspiring for the composers who set Zeno's libretti.

In *Ifigenia in Aulide* II/6, for example, Teucro spends the scene trying to persuade Elisena to be his. Elisena, who yearns for Achilles and wishes only to use Teucro for her own purposes, ends the scene with an aria which intentionally leaves Teucro in doubt as to Elisena's long-range plans, but may also have troubled Caldara. How is one to write an aria in support of so disingenuous a text?

> Non vo', se deggio piangere,
> Sola piangere, e invendicate.
> Tu consola, e tu difendi
> Il mio sdegno, ed il tuo amore;
> Mostra fede; e poi m'attendi
> Bon spergiura, e non ingrato.

In *Lucio Papirio* I/6, Fabio's wife, Papiria, observes both the populace's enthusiasm for her husband's military victory and her father's angry response to a military action he had explicitly forbidden. If one begins with the premise normal for Caldara and his contemporaries that the setting was not to involve radical changes of tempo, what kind of aria would one compose in support of emotions so mixed as Papiria's?

> Sento applausi; miro allori;
> Roma è lieta; il Tebro esulta:
> E il mio tenero cor languendo stà.
> Dico a lui: Bando a'dolori;
> Ei sospira, e non lo fa.

In *Euristeo* I/5, Cisseo, the King of Macedonia, congratulates Ormonte on the victory just achieved over the hostile Tessaglians, but Cisseo's aria, closing the scene, indicates that his relief at Ormonte's victory is (because Ormonte had been promised Cisseo's daughter as a reward for victory) not unalloyed delight.

> Si è vinto: al mio regno
> Ritorna la calma:
> Ma un certo mi sento
> Affanna nell'alma
> Che solo è per te.
> Nell'arduo cimento
> Del giusto amor mio,
> E forza, che anch'io
> Per esserti grato
> Obblii di essar Re.

Although an armchair reader of libretti would doubtless have appreciated
Zeno's refusal to oversimplify Cisseo's feelings, the composer's task could
have been facilitated had Zeno restricted his probing of Cisseo's personality to the recitative which precedes the aria just quoted.

Similar problems for the composer result in Zeno's libretti from texts
which, owing to their use of conditional constructions or comparisons,
are deficient in affective implication. When Metastasio called Caldara
". . . a worthy master of counterpoint but excessively negligent with respect both to expression and to his attention to the delightful,"[71] he was
referring, whether he realized it or not, to habits of aria composition that
had been forced upon Caldara earlier in his career. In I/3 of Zeno's *Nitocri*, for example, Mirteo disputes Ratese's right to the *prima donna* with
the assertion that virtue has other sources than illustrious ancestors.

> Piace la vita umile
> Al saggio agricoltor,
> Più di cipresso altier, che l'aria imgombra.
> Lieto da quella ei coglie
> Alla stagion miglior frutto gentile,
> Ma da questo non ha, che inutil'ombra.

In Zeno's *Atenaide* I/13, King Teodosio, fearful lest his sister, Pulcheria,
allow her love for Marziano to upset plans for a politically advantageous
marriage between Pulcheria and Varane, orders Marziano into exile, and
then counters Pulcheria's demand for an explanation with a scene-ending
exit aria.

> Qual la sua colpa sia,
> Forse . . . ma dir non voglio,
> Già che Pulcheria il sa.
> Se fosse ver, saria
> In me troppo cordoglio;
> In te troppo viltà.

Nor can it have been easy for Caldara to discover especially appropriate
settings for those Zeno texts which, like the following example from *I due
dittatori* II/3, supply practical advice or ethical maxims.

> Troppo giovane tu sei.
> Son colpevoli trofei
> Quei che lodi, e che difendi.
> D'un Roman sta il primo onore
> Nell'essequio, e non nel brando;
> E dell'arte del comando
> Tu assai parli, e poco intendi.

Operatic theorists of the period warn about the problematic nature of passionless texts, particularly texts featuring involved comparisons of the kind that lead composers to seize upon superficial aspects of the objects compared.[72]

Although there are arias which show that Caldara was not totally insensitive to the musical implications of dramatically suggestive texts, his operatic output abounds in examples of passionless arias. In *La verità nell'inganno* I/10, King Tiridate, bitter because his daughter has been spurned by the King of Bitania, addresses an aria of scorn to the captured Nicomede, whom Tiridate believes to be the King of Bitania:

> Empio, vivi, e per tua pena
> Pensa ogn'or, che fosti Re.
> Peso accresca alla catena
> Il perduto onor del piè.

However, in neither of his two settings does Caldara's music make a notable contribution to the dramatic effect.

1717

In II/3 of the same work, Laodicea, frustrated in her attempts to decide whether Nicomede or Atalo is the real King of Bitania, asks her father to discover the identity of the King who had scorned her;

> Scuopri, Signor, la vittima
> Alla vendetta mia.
> (Scuoprimi, amor, qual sia
> La fiamma del mio cor.)
> Dimmi qual sia quell'anima,
> Che infida oso tradirmi.
> (O se dovro arrossirmi
> Del mal concetto ardor.)

However, the melodic material of Caldara's two settings is as mechanically conceived as before.

Very often Caldara's arias seem actually to contradict the dramatic intention of the poet, as is the case in I/4 of *Ifigenia in Aulide*, where Elisena, immediately after learning that her beloved Achilles has become betrothed to another, threatens to bathe Achilles's nuptial altar in her own blood, closing the scene in an aria of grim determination.

A vista del crudele,
Ma amabile[73] idol mio,
Quest'anima fedele
Con gloria spirerò.
Forse in morir si forte,
Pietà, se non amore,
In lui risveglierò;
O con si nobil sorte
Della rival nel core
Invidia desterò.

Ormisda I/7 is a monologue by the King of Persia himself, a despairing plaint about the heart-rending duties of a monarch whose wife and sons are contending for his own crown. The comparison aria with which Zeno closes the scene is not at all inappropriate to the situation in which it occurs, but by using a poetic format that involves short lines of few feet,

Son da più venti
Legno percosso.
Porto non veggio.
Stella non ho.
Tra le framenti
Torbide brame
Posso, e non deggio.
Voglio, e non posso.
Penso, e non so.

Zeno draws from Caldara a syllabic setting in 3/8 which hardly suggests the violence of a storm at sea.

In Scene 14 of the same act, Cosroe, the rightful heir to Ormisda's throne, asks himself why he suffers the indignity of his stepmother's vile accusations, then, comparing himself to the shepherd of a threatened flock, closes the scene with an aria whose musical setting by Caldara supports neither Cosroe's mood nor the shepherd's.

> Vede quel pastorello
> L'avido lupo ingordo,
> Che nel piu scelto agnello
> Cerca sfamar il denta; a sel difende.
> Tal per difesa anch'io
> Del ben, che solo è mio,
> Senno userò, e valor
> Contra quel rio furor, che mel contende.

Vede quel pas to- re llo   l'avido lupo in gor do,

One has the impression that, especially when pressed for time, Caldara often did not take the trouble to read and to understand the texts he was setting, but that he reacted simply, and often wrongly, to the suggestion of individual words taken out of context.

More than 95 percent of the arias in Caldara's extant operatic output can be categorized as members of that class which Gerber labelled the "5-part *da capo* aria,"[74] the predominant aria form for all composers of *opera seria* between 1720 and 1750.[75] Based on metrical, rhymed texts which normally divide into two sections of similar length,

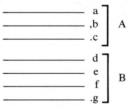

the musical setting of a "5-part *da capo* aria" can be represented in diagram as a large-scale ternary form whose nearly identical bi-partite outer parts[76] come, especially after the century's second decade, to dominate a very much shorter middle section. The principal section of the musical setting frequently begins and ends with an instrumental ritornello, part of which often recurs in the midst of the principal section (hereafter called the A section).

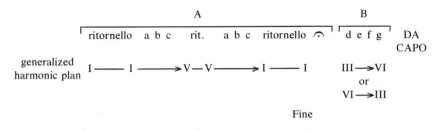

The comments which follow summarize the ways in which Caldara's "5-part *da capo* arias" vary from the generalized scheme just outlined:

1) If the aria is in the minor mode, the principal area of secondary tonicization in the A section is more often the relative major than the dominant.

2) The B section more often involves tonicizations of the mediant and/or sub-mediant than those of any other areas, but there is a great variety of possibilities for arias in both major and minor modes. If the relative major is the principal area of secondary tonicization in the A section of an aria, Caldara avoids it as such in the B section.

3) The A section is most often subdivided into two sections, each of which involves at least one full statement of the text for that section, but one also finds A sections that are subdivided into three or even four parts and, especially during the earlier part of Caldara's career, A sections which do not get subdivided at all. Very often the text is subjected to fragmentation so that, usually after the text section has been stated as a whole, individual words and even syllables are taken from context, repeated, and per-muted to fit the requirements of the vocal line.

4) B sections, too, may be subdivided, though rarely into more than two parts, and never so that the subdivision of the B section affects the subsidiary relationship of that section to the A section.

5) The introductory instrumental ritornello is a very frequent but certainly not inevitable element. The ritornello concluding the A section is similar in proportions to the initial ritornello; very often it is identical to the initial ritornello, enabling Caldara, while composing, to complete work in the section just before the *Fine* without any more effort than a plotting out of the requisite num-ber of measures and the jotting down of the words "come sopra."

Except in arias accompanied by continuo only, a ritornello concluding the A section occurs only in arias which have an introductory ritornello. Almost every continuo aria in Caldara's operas
appears in company with an apparently orchestral ritornello à 4.
Sometimes the orchestral ritornello occurs before the aria, sometimes afterwards. Some ritornelli occur both before and after-
ward, and upon occasion two such ritornelli are somewhat
different from one another. Medial ritornelli in the A section,
usually serving to emphasize tonicizations already effected and
to give the singer a chance to breathe, are very much shorter, as
are the medial ritornelli which may occur in subdivided B sections.

6) The great majority of the *da capo*s in Caldara's operatic arias are
complete *da capo*s. An incomplete *da capo* may involve an abbreviation of the introductory ritornello, effected either by ap-
pending a new instrumental section at the end of the B section
or by cutting all or part of the introductory ritornello through the
use of the *dal segno* convention. There are no incomplete *da
capo*s by Caldara wherein an abbreviation of the A section is
effected by recomposing that section.

None of the possible *da capo* formats just enumerated is peculiar to
Caldara, nor were there any important manners of *da capo* aria composition current in Italy during Caldara's lifetime which he did not make use
of.[77]

The *da capo* aria whose A section can be subdivided into at least
two large vocal sections is a phenomenon which became dominant for
Caldara during the second decade of the eighteenth century. Although
one can see from his earliest extant operas that it had already assumed
major importance for him during the century's first decade, an examination of those scores shows a significantly greater number of other *da
capo* formats than appear in Caldara's operatic scores after his move to
Vienna in 1716. This is important, for it sheds light on a problem which
has troubled historians of *opera seria* for some time: how is one to explain
the change during the half century 1675–1725 from a situation in which
aria texts consisted of at least two strophes which, beginning and ending
with refrains, were set strophically, to a situation in which bi-partite texts
formed the basis of ternary musical structures dominated by the first of
the two parts? Or, put differently, how is one to explain the change from
da capo arias with short A sections and sometimes longer B sections to
da capo arias with short B sections and very long A sections.[78] Characteristic examples of the types between which the change takes place will
serve to clarify the discussion:

L'Amazzone (I/1)[79]

Text by G. C. Corradi (?)
Music by Alessandro Scarlatti, c. 1690

Dovresti haver o cara,
Men tirannia nel sen,
Che val leggiardo aspetto
Se in vece di diletto
Mortir da lui s'ottien.
         Dovresti...

Dovresti haver o bella
Men crudelta nel cor,
Che giova esser veggosa
Per dar come a la rosa
Punture di rigor.
         Dovresti ...

L'Atenaide (III/6)[80]

Text by Apostolo Zeno
Music by Antonio Caldara, 1714

Vanne tosto: fuggi: vola,
Disleal, lungi da me.
Teco venga ira, tormento,
Smania, rabbia, e pentimento.
Quanto a me fosti infedele,
Sia crudele altri con te.
         Vanne tosto ...

The musical settings of these texts by Scarlatti and Caldara, which may be found in Appendix F, can be diagramed as follows:[81]

"Dovresti haver"

	ritornello	a a/2 b a a/2 b	c d e c d e	(rit.) a a/2 b a a/2 b b		ritornello à 4
		f f/2 g f f/2 g	h i j h i j	f f/2 g f f/2 g g		
e:	I ——	I —————————	I →V→ III	I ————————→ I		I ——— I
no. of bars	3	7	7	7		4
		A-10	B-7	A-7		

"Vanne tosto"

	ritornello	a b b	rit.	a	rit.	a b a b b/2	rit.	⌒		c d e f e f f/2		DA
D:	I ——	I	I →V	V	I ————————	I — I			I II→III →VI		CAPO
no. of bars	4	8	2	2	2	15	4	Fine		12		
				A-37					B-12		

Two of the most striking stylistic differences between the two arias just diagramed are characteristic of great numbers of arias contemporary with "Dovresti haver" and "Vanne tosto": in the former, a concentration on syllabic settings which mirror the design of the poetry and a hesitancy to elaborate secondary tonal areas over more than the briefest of time-spans; in the latter, a much greater use of melismatic writing, often in the setting of words which do not particularly suggest melismatic writing, a musical phraseology that is much less dependent on the design of the poetry, and, at least in the A section, a greater sophistication in the elaboration of

secondary tonal areas. That some composers of the early eighteenth century still lacked experience and confidence in the elaboration of secondary
areas is an observation one makes repeatedly in studying the B sections
of *da capo* arias written during the period 1700–1720. Caldara's return to
D major early in the B section of "Vanne tosto" represents a good case
in point, an example of tonal aimlessness that is by no means isolated in
Caldara's operatic output.

It is, in my opinion, the tendencies towards melismatic writing and
towards more sophisticated means of establishing secondary tonal areas
which are principally responsible for the drift during the 1680s and 1690s
from arias like "Dovresti haver" to those "5-part *da capo* arias" of the
"Vanne tosto" model. At the point in the evolutionary process where the
growing length of the A section makes the setting of multi-stanza texts
impractical—and "Dovresti haver" represents not the starting point but
a way station along that route—impresarios, librettists, and operatic
theorists react almost simultaneously. When Minato's libretto *La risa di
Democrito* was set by Antonio Pistocchi for production in Vienna during
1700, the libretto differed in several respects from that used for the original
Draghi setting produced in Vienna during 1672.[82] That there were several
arias dropped, several added, and several substituted is a phenomenon
common to a great deal of seventeenth- and eighteenth-century operatic
history. Of special interest here, however, is the treatment of 10 aria texts
which, having comprised two or more strophes each in 1672, were simply
reduced to one strophe each for the Pistocchi setting of 1700, a process
which must have been applied during the period to a variety of libretti.
Librettists, for their part, began writing shorter aria texts whose two
sections, both normally independent clauses, were usually similar in length,
characteristics which the theorists are quick to notice. Salvadori's treatise, published in 1691, distinguishes between canzonetta and aria texts.
In the former, writes Salvadori, one may have as many stanzas as one
likes, but in the latter one should restrict oneself to two sections, each of
which, normally comprising two 6- or 8-syllable lines, must represent a
complete thought, ". . . in order to allow for the *da capo*."[83] C. F.
Hunold and Barthold Feind both stress the necessity of keeping the aria
texts short, Hunold setting a maximum length of 12 lines of text, including
the *da capo*,[84] while Feind insists that no aria text should comprise more
than 8 lines of poetry.[85] Pier-Jacopo Martello refers specifically to music's
role in the temporal expansion of the aria, adding the sensible observation
that texts which involve smaller numbers of syllables per line may comprise greater numbers of lines.[86] That the dominance of the "5-part *da
capo* aria" was established gradually is shown by those works of the
period 1690–1710 which include both "modern" and old-fashioned arias,

and by the existence during the same period of arias which share some but not all characteristics of the "Vanne tosto" scheme outlined on page 215. Formal plans for a variety of such arias composed by Caldara before 1716 are outlined below:

Opera pastorale,[87] completed by Caldara in Mantua during 1701. (The work was put on during 1710 and 1711 in Macerata and in Rome, apparently under the composer's direction, and entitled *La costanza in amore vince l'inganno*. The inevitable revisions made for these productions include the dropping of all but one of the "old-fashioned" arias.)

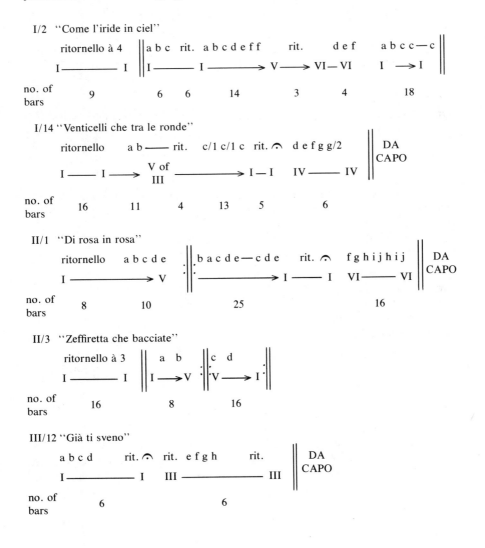

I/2 "Come l'iride in ciel"

II/14 "Venticelli che tra le ronde"

II/1 "Di rosa in rosa"

II/3 "Zeffiretta che bacciate"

III/12 "Già ti sveno"

III/20 "Dove andaste speranze del seno"

ritornello	a b b— rit. ⌒ c d — d/2		DA
I ——————————— I	————————→ IV	‖	CAPO

no. of bars	13	5

Atenaide,[88] whose second act was composed by Caldara for performance in Barcelona during 1709.

II/1 "Qui grazie ancelle"

ritornello * a b c d a b c d d   rit. ⌒   e f g h h   DS

I——— I ——————————— I ——— I   V——— V   *

no. of bars	19	25	19	11

II/14 "Eccelso trono"

ritornello a b c d e ‖: a b c d e c d e——rit. ⌒ ‖ f f/2 rit. g g/2 g ‖ DA

I——— I ——→ V :‖: I ——————— I ——— I :‖ VI ——→ II→ V ‖ CAPO

no. of bars	13	8	23	13	17

Giunio Bruto,[89] whose second act was composed by Caldara, probably during 1711, as a result of a commission from Emperor Joseph I.

II/8 "Gia di Gigli"

a b c d e   rit.   a b c d e ‖: e f g ——— :‖

I ——→ V ——→ I ——→ V :‖·I ——————— I :‖

no. of bars	9	6	9	14

II/11 "Spero morte"

ritornello   a rit. a a/2 a/2   rit. ⌒ b c d d   DA

I——— I ——————————— I ——— I   VI ——— VI → III   ‖ CAPO

no. of bars	6	1	2	6	4	9

Caldara's operatic arias during the first decade of the eighteenth century are as variable in format as are those of his Italian contemporaries. But from his 1716 arrival in Vienna until his death 20 years later his conformity to the "5-part *da capo* aria" scheme outlined above on pages 213–214 is almost unvarying.

For more than 200 years writers on *opera seria* have complained repeatedly about the stereotyped nature of the dramatically unconvincing "grand *da capo* aria" which, between 1720 and 1750, monopolized all musical settings of secular texts by Zeno and Metastasio. Sometimes criticized for the invariability of its construction, sometimes for the repetitious quality which results from the inevitable *da capo*, sometimes for the dramatically unmotivated melismas and cadenzas employed by both composers and performers, and sometimes for the composers' lack of concern for finding appropriate music for each new text, the "grand *da capo* aria" is easily one of the most censured genres in all of musical history. J. H. VanderMeer's three-volume work on the operas of Fux, the most recent and thoroughly documented effort to reevaluate several traditional bases of *opera seria* criticism, compares variants in *da capo* aria construction with variants from A. B. Marx's "sonata allegro" principle, and draws up a catalogue of instances in which Fux's *da capo* aria construction is alleged to result from specific elements in the libretti he was setting, concluding that Fux's arias are no more stereotyped than are the first movements of later eighteenth-century instrumental works, that Fux and his contemporaries were actually a great deal more sensitive to problems of musical dramaturgy than previous critics had ever realized.[90] VanderMeer has, of course, performed an important service in emphasizing the multiplicity of manners in which "grand *da capo* arias" vary from one another. But he errs, it seems to me, on several counts. The "grand *de capo* arias" of Caldara's time differ from later eighteenth-century "sonata allegro" movements in that exposition and recapitulation in the latter differ from each other in harmonic direction, while the *da capos* of the former simply repeat, harmonically, a course already traversed. While I see no musical objection to such a procedure, the musical-dramatic viability of conventions which include an inevitable return to the dramatic starting point and which permit long instrumental ritornelli that leave the singer all too often in embarrassing inactivity are another matter altogether. It is true, no doubt, that some composers of "grand *da capo* arias" must have been more sensitive than others to the dramatic implications of the texts they were setting. But as a comparison of parallel settings of the same libretto by a variety of composers will show, there existed few, if any, rhetoric-oriented conventions entailing the musical laying out of specific kinds of aria texts in specific manners. In view of the fact that Italian theorists of the period have nothing to say about the existence of such conventions, this is not, after all, a surprising situation. The comparisons of formal plans for parallel arias in the first acts of Caldara's two settings of *La verità nell'inganno*, which constitute Appendix G, certainly do not suggest that Caldara's operatic arias were much influenced by German treatises on rhetoric, if he knew those treatises at all.[91] If, in Fux's operas, decisions about the repetition and fragmentation of poetic lines and parts of lines, decisions about the location of melismas, and decisions to divide the A and B section of an aria through the addition of an instrumental ritornello[92] really resulted from considerations of rhetoric, as VanderMeer asserts, it should be clear from Appendix G that this cannot often have been the case with Caldara. Much more apparent in his operatic works are the influences of routine, of musical syntax, and of vocal convenience.

Coloratura

That Italian musicians contemporary with Caldara must often have allowed the display of vocal facility to outweigh considerations of musical and dramatic propriety is indicated by the frequency of contemporary complaints about melismas of excessive length. Uffenbach writes of having timed the performance of a melisma on a single vowel, performed during 1715 in the church of Sant'Apollinare, Rome, at 13 minutes.[93] Martello derisively indicates the importance given, in the writing of texts for substitute arias, to the retention of open vowels for the invariable *fioritura* at the close of every sentence.[94] Marcello expresses contempt for composers who set open vowels melismatically, regardless of whether they occur in ". . . words of passion or of movement like *tormento*, *affanno*, *canto*, *volar*, *cader*, etc." or in adverbs or ". . . substantive nouns like *padre*, *impero*, *amore*, *arena*, *regno*, *belta*, *lena*, *core*."[95] Both Tosi[96] and Riva,[97] writing during the 1720s from London and Vienna, are critical of the increasing popularity of melismatic writing and improvisation, a popularity which continued undiminished in most Italian opera, at least through the end of the eighteenth century.[98]

Later nineteenth-century German writers on Italian opera, working in the shadow of Wagnerian theory and practice, found the melismatic aspect of eighteenth-century Italian opera lifeless and undramatic. Hugo Goldschmidt, in *Die Lehre von der vokalen Ornamentik*, is generally critical of all *opera seria* composers in this regard, but is noteworthy here for the violence of his attack on the *fioriture* of Caldara, who is called ". . . a worthy master of both sacred and instrumental music, but superficial as a composer of dramatic music, and subject to the most insipid taste of fashion."[99] Alice Gmeyner's 1927 dissertation on Caldara views Goldschmidt's charges against Caldara as exaggerated and biased.[100] But VanderMeer, as we have seen in several other instances, seeks fundamentally to revise the traditional critical position on *coloratura* writing as an undramatic sin of eighteenth-century vocal practice. According to

VanderMeer, the use of melismas in the operas of Fux—and, by explicit extension, in the operas of Caldara as well—is carefully reserved for the underlining of important words, for the heightening of affect, and for tone-painting[101]—a rather broad basis of definition for a phenomenon whose connections with rhetoric VanderMeer is seeking to establish.

That a more sensible position on Caldara's use of melismas lies somewhere between those of Goldschmidt and VanderMeer is suggested by Table I, a comparative listing of words set melismatically in the first act of Caldara's parallel settings of *La verità nell'inganno*. (The relationship of each word in the table to its poetic context may be observed by consulting the texts of Appendix G.)

Table I

		1717 setting	*1727 setting*
I/1	Atalo	passerò; accrescerò	
I/2	Atalo	m'avanza; costanza	sorte; avanza; forte; costanza
I/4	Nicomede	rubella; bella	rubella; empietà; crudeltà
I/5	Farnace	battaglia; amore; l'orme	battaglia; valor; l'orme
I/6	Laodicea	troppo; petto	troppo; bolle
I/8	Eumene	mè; consagrà	eletti; consagrà
I/10	Tiridate	fosti; ogn'or; catena	pena; catena; piè
I/10	Arsace	vendicata; diffenderlo	vendicata; diffenderlo
I/12	Nicomede	rai	rai
I/12	Laodicea	stral; piagò; l'ingannò	piagò; l'ingannò
I/13	Arsace–	amore	
	Atalo		

There is clearly no differentiation among aria types with regard to the appropriateness of melismas, nor do anything like all of the melisma-bearing words listed above appear in both 1717 and 1727 columns. Although there are a number of "words of passion or movement" in Table I, Marcello would doubtless have raised his eyebrows at the appearance of melismas with words like "troppo," "mè," "fosti," and "rai." That so few of the melisma-bearing words are monosyllables, that so many of them appear at the ends of lines or rhyme with other melisma-bearing words which do, suggests that Caldara was sensitive to some of the considerations which Martello regarded with such disdain.

It is true that there are a great many dramatically unmotivated melismas in Caldara operas. It would be hard to imagine, for example, how any of the following (taken from the two versions of Eumene's I/8 aria in *La verità nell'inganno*) could be said to support, in any meaningful way, either Eumene's unhappiness at leaving Arsinoe or the words which serve as text for the melismas cited.

Eumene I/8 "Parto, ma tutto il core"

Eumene I/8 "Parto, ma tutto il core"

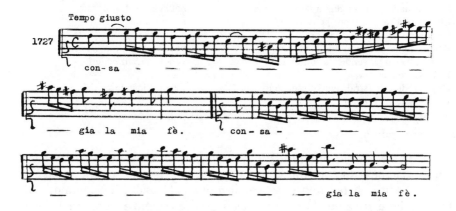

But, although one could easily assemble a long catalogue of apparently meaningless melismas, it would be wrong to insist that *all* of Caldara's operatic melismas are equally unmotivated from a textual point of view. Evidence to the contrary can be seen in the "nouns of passion or motion" contained in Table I.

It is one thing to assert that repeated melismas have no place in Wagner's later music dramas, and quite another to imply that, unless such melismas can be justified on the kind of grounds which Wagner would have thought acceptable, they have no place in the operatic output of an eighteenth-century composer—in a genre which functioned, not as *Gesamtkunstwerk*, but on several independent planes, including sung concert and visual spectacle in the theater, and armchair drama read in one's study. Singers and audiences, it is clear, were fond of vocal display, and librettists were constrained to provide words appropriate for such displays at specified moments in their aria texts. Where a text set by Caldara provided him with the requisite opportunities for melismas, the resulting setting might suggest that one is dealing with a rhetoric-oriented composer. But Caldara's frequent supplying of melismas for texts which suggest none indicates that his attention to rhetoric was, if it existed at all, anything but a primary concern.

Non-Da Capo Arias

The majority of those few post-1716 operatic arias in which Caldara does not conform to the 5-part *da capo* scheme outlined on page 213 are the result of specific poetic or dramatic situations. If, as happens for example in *Enone* I/5, an aria text comprises but a single complete thought and thus contains only a single instance of final punctuation, it is not set as a 5-part *da capo* aria, but, rather,

> Già salvo il germano,
> L'amante già sposo,
> Perchè si angoscioso,
> Mio core, perchè?

in the manner of a bi-partite dance movement or as a *cavatina*—a short self-sufficient A section followed neither by a B section nor by a *da capo*.[102] (Infrequent in occurrence, such arias are found most often at the beginnings of scenes, though Caldara's scene-opening arias also include a number of the "grand *da capo*" variety.) If, on the other hand, an abnormally long aria text comprises several complete thoughts and, thus, involves several instances of final punctuation, as happens in *Sirita* III/3, for example, Caldara chooses

> Langui finora il cor
> Certo di non goder.
> Forte nel suo dolor
> Non ebbe altro piacer,
> Che di penar
> Senza sperar.
> Il labbro non oso
> Dirvi del sen trafitto,

> Pupille vaghe,
> Le piaghe,
> E sospiro.
> Ma debole sospiro
> D'immenso aspro martiro
> Fede non fa.
> Ne mai svegliar pieta
> In te sperai, crudel,
> Ch'io gia sapea fedel
> Penare amante di altra belta.
> Cosi
> Languendo,
> Piangendo,
> Tacendo
> Vissi in amor:
> Se dirsi vita
> Puo di chi muor
> Sempre al dolor.
> Or solo a me traluce
> Di speme il bel seren,
> Se ben di fosca luce
> Forse e balen.
> Ma per chi ognor langui,
> Sempre ascoso a'rai del di,
> Lume torbide, e lontano
> Bello anche appar.
> Per me sperar
> Dolce or sara:
> Che almeno
> Nel mio seno
> Di qualche bene
> Amor godra.
> Si: spera, o cor.
> Si: godi, o amor.

between two manners of *da capo* setting: one in which the greater part of the text is used for the B section, and one in which that part of the text used for the A section is repeated only in the *da capo*. (The tendency towards lengthy aria texts is normally limited, during the period 1700–1750, to intermezzo arias for comic characters, where the customary syllabic style of musical setting and rapid manner of performance kept individual arias from becoming unduly prolonged.) Very rarely is the logical carrying through of a dramatic action considered sufficient cause to interfere with the completion of a "grand *da capo* aria," but this does happen, as in Ciro I/8, where Astiage falls asleep while singing a medial aria.

> Sciolto dal suo timor,
> Par che non senta il cor

L'usato affanno.
Languidi gli occhi miei. . . .

Three unusual instances in Caldara's post-1716 operas of the formally less stereotyped arias, so common around the turn of the century, are outlined below.

Cajo Marzio Coriolano (1717) III/5[103]—Vetturia

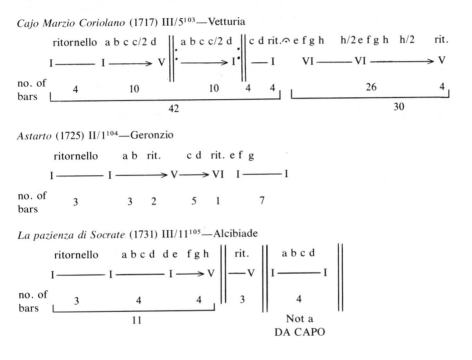

Astarto (1725) II/1[104]—Geronzio

La pazienza di Socrate (1731) III/11[105]—Alcibiade

Instrumentation

More than 90 percent of Caldara's operatic arias are scored in one of three standard manners:

1) as continuo arias, wherein the vocal part is accompanied by a single, normally unfigured continuo part, realized (usually no doubt by the composer) at the harpsichord, and strengthened at times by 'celli (with or without violons), by one or more bassoons, and by Francesco Conti's theorbo. A short orchestral ritornello, almost always à 4 and related thematically to the aria with which it appears, frequently precedes and/or follows the performance of a continuo aria.

2) accompanied by an à 3 ensemble whose three staves are notated in treble, alto, and bass clef, respectively. Many such arias bear the autograph rubrics "U^{ni}," "Un^{ni}," and "V. V. Un^{ni}."

3) accompanied by an ensemble à 4, notated in the manner normal for an eighteenth-century string quartet—two treble clefs, one alto clef, and one bass clef. Almost all such arias bear the autograph rubric "Con Strumenti."

Types 1 and 2 predominated during the early part of Caldara's career, but Caldara, like most of his Italian contemporaries,[106] wrote fewer and fewer continuo arias during the century's second and third decades, especially after his move in 1716 to Vienna. Table J, a representative sampling of the part played by the continuo aria in operas written throughout Caldara's career, illustrates this development.

Table J

Title	Date of completion	No. of musical numbers	No. of continuo arias	Percentage of continuo arias
Opera pastorale	1701	45	18	40
L'inimico generoso	1709	44	18	41
Atenaide, Act II	1709	13	4	31
Giunio Bruto, Act II	1711	18	6	33
Atenaide, Act III	1714	14	3	21
Cajo Marzio Coriolano	1717	42	12	29
La verità nell'inganno	1717	35	7	20
Ifigenia in Aulide	1718	34	7	21
Dafne	1719	29	5	17
Lucio Papirio	1719	35	4	11
Camaide	1722	37	6	16
Nitocri	1722	35	7	20
Scipione nelle Spagne	1722	39	10	24
Euristeo	1724	25	3	12
Astarto	1725	31	2	6
Semiramide in Ascalona	1725	30	1	3
La verità nell'inganno	1727	34	1	3
Imeneo	1727	28	1	3
Ornospade	1727	30	1	3
Enone	1729	31	1	3
Demetrio	1731	31	1	3
Adriano	1732	25	1	4
Demofoonte	1733	26	1	4
La clemenza di Tito	1734	29	0	0
Temistocle	1736	27	0	0

The demise of the continuo aria is not difficult to understand. Always the briefest of the various aria types, often used when a composer was pressed for time or left uninspired by an aria text,[107] frequently assigned to secondary singers, the continuo aria became a second-class citizen early in the century. The increased length and difficulty of the sung portion of so many arias must, moreover, have made the increased length of the ritornelli possible in orchestrally accompanied arias a welcome relief for weary singers—and an important source of contrast for a period which especially valued *chiaroscuro*. That these developments took place at a time when poets like Zeno and Metastasio were trying to limit the number of arias in their libretti, principally by eliminating arias from the roles of secondary characters,[108] makes it clear how a composer like Hasse could have written more than 100 *opere serie* which contain not even a single continuo aria.[109]

Type 3, while relatively infrequent in appearance during the earlier part of Caldara's career, becomes progressively more important until, by the time of Caldara's Metastasio settings during the 1730s, it shares a virtual monopoly with type 2. The gradual elimination of variety in the instrumentation of Caldara's operatic arias is illustrated in Table K.

Table K

	Date of completion	No. of musical numbers	Type 1	Type 2	Type 3	No. of other pieces	No. of other types
Opera pastorale	1701	45	18	14	3	10	8
L'inimico generoso	1709	44	18	14	4	8	7
Cajo Merzio Coriolano	1717	42	12	9	9	12	6
Astarto	1725	31	2	19	6	4	2
Demofoonte	1733	26	1	12	12	1	1

Some examples of the variety of instrumentation schemes characteristic of scores from the earlier part of Caldara's operatic career are tabulated below. The G, C, and F clefs in the list are treble, alto, and bass clefs, unless otherwise indicated; the order of clefs, from left to right, reproduces, with one exception—the staff for the vocal soloist(s), always occurring immediately above that of the continuo part, has been omitted—the vertical order of the parts, from top to bottom, as they occur in Caldara's scores.

Opera pastorale (1701)

I/4 —Atalanta	𝄞	𝄞	𝄢		"Aria con Oboe" (& fagotti)
II/3 —Meleagro	𝄡	𝄢			"Con Violette"
II/11—Silvio	𝄞	𝄢			upper and middle strings in unison
III/12—Meleagro	𝄡	𝄡			"Violette"

Atenaide, Act II (1709)

II/8 —Marziano	𝄞	𝄞	𝄞	𝄡	𝄢	"Oboe" (2 parts, each on its own staff), violins in unison, violette, continuo

L'inimico generoso (1709)

I/1 —Idegardo	𝄞	𝄞	𝄞	𝄡	𝄡 𝄢	"Trombe" (2 staves), "Violini Uniss.[ni]," "Viole" (2 staves), continuo
I/2 —Oronte	𝄞	𝄞	𝄢			upper strings, "Viole con il Basso," continuo
II/9 —Valentiniano	𝄡	𝄢				"Uniss.[ni]," continuo

Giunio Bruto, Act II (1711)

II/10—Bruto	𝄡	𝄢	"Violini e Violette Unisoni," continuo

Atenaide, Act III (1714)

III/1 —Probo	𝄡	𝄢	"Violini e le Viole all'Uniss.," continuo
III/6 —Teodosio	𝄞	𝄢	"Violini all'Unissono," continuo
III/10—Varane	𝄞 𝄞 𝄞 𝄞	𝄡	𝄢	"Hautbois" (2 staves), "Violini" (2 staves), "Violetta," continuo

Another means of orchestral variety, employed almost as infrequently in Caldara's earlier operas as in his later ones, is the use of instrumental soloists performing *obbligato* parts. Some examples, each accompanied by the text which the aria sets and by an indication of the key, meter, and tempo for each setting, are listed in Appendix H, which indicates that Caldara sometimes observed a rationale in connecting specific solo instruments with specific kinds of poetic ideas. Solo violin with running sixteenth or thirty-second notes is frequently used in setting texts that concern storms at sea, the motion of the winds, and similar kinds of movement, physical and psychic. The violoncello seems often to have been used, in similarly rapid motion, in support of texts expressing resolution in the face of frustrated love, while the chalumeau, used exclusively in arias of slow tempo and in minor, supports texts of despondency and despair. Trumpets, always used together with timpani and in the key of C major, are associated in Caldara's scores, as in those of so many other dramatic composers, with martial scenes, while oboes, always used à 2 in an à 3 texture completed by bassoons, appear in connection with pastoral ideas, sometimes even when the pastoral scene represented is not an especially idyllic one, as happens, for example, in *Ormisda* I/14.

But while there are occasional instances in Caldara's operas of an association between instrumental timbre and dramatic situation, the remarkable aspect of those scores in this respect is the uncommonness in them of such associations. To what extent the dearth of arias involving *obbligato* instruments in Caldara's later operatic scores reflects his contemporaries' overriding fondness for vocal virtuosity and to what extent it simply reflects the pressures of Caldara's busy schedule one cannot say; but it is a striking phenomenon in a composer whose mature years were spent in a court which employed one of the largest, ablest, and most varied instrumental ensembles of the period.[110]

That the vast majority of Caldara's operatic instrumentation schemes cannot have resulted from any concern with rhetoric or affect may be inferred from the degree to which the instrumentations for the 34 pieces in Caldara's parallel settings of *La verità nell'inganno* (represented in Table H) differ from one another. Only 12 of the 34 pairs of parallel pieces in those two scores share the same instrumentations, and 11 of those 12 belong to types 2 and 3—by far the most numerous instrumentation schemes in the two scores and certainly the most neutral of them with respect to affect.

Although Caldara's operatic scores suggest that he was as routine in his treatment of the orchestra as we have observed him in other aspects of his activity as an opera composer, our understanding of the conventions understood by the copyists of his orchestral parts and by the players under his direction is, one should bear in mind, less than complete. While original instrumental parts have been preserved in the Austrian National Library for nearly all of the operas composed by Caldara for Vienna, they are preserved only in skeletal sets[111] comprising one part each for the first and second violins, violas, and continuo, which all too often contain *ripieno* parts instead of those used by the principal players. The autograph scores themselves, with their frequent indications for temporary tacets in one or more groups of instruments (most often in order to keep the instruments from covering the voice or to provide an element of contrast, especially in the B section of certain arias) enable one to determine some of the instruments which must have taken part in a given aria, but they seldom enable one to decide with conviction about all elements of the instrumentation, particularly with respect to the role played by oboes and bassoons and concerning the division between solo and tutti strings. "Unisoni" and "strumenti," two critical terms normally associated throughout Caldara's career with instrumentation types 2 and 3, respectively, are of particular importance here. Which instruments, in arias marked "Unisoni" (or some abbreviation for it), are those supposed to play the uppermost lines? Violins 1 and 2, *ripieno* and solo violins, all violins in unison with oboes, or all soprano instruments in the Habsburg ensemble? Are arias marked "Strmti," "Strumenti," or "Con Strumenti" to be played by more or by fewer instruments than those marked "Unisoni" and, as with "unisoni," which are the instruments intended? Since the trumpet parts actually written out on independent staves in Caldara scores all occur in C major pieces, and since there are no indications in any Caldara autograph that trumpets were meant to double parts performed by other instruments, it is reasonable to presume that the words "unisoni" and "con strumenti" cannot be masking the assumed participation of trumpets. Since there were neither flutists nor chalumeau players on contemporary Habsburg payrolls[112] it has been assumed that flutes and chalumeaux were played in Vienna by oboists;[113] hence, it is unlikely that flute and chalumeau took part in pieces marked "Unisoni" and "Con Strumenti." There are, of course, a variety of pieces in which the three staves devoted to the instrumental accompaniment of an aria are divided among two oboe parts and a bass for bassoons, and there are pieces in which two or three quasi-independent parts for oboes and bassoons are written as the top two or three staves of six- or seven-stave scores whose lower staves are marked "Violini" and "Viola," but neither of these facts is of assistance in deciding on the presence or absence of oboes and bassoons in arias marked "Unisoni" and "Con Strumenti." Oboes have, of course, a more limited range than violins, and they are much more limited than violins in the facility with which they can execute rapid passagework and a variety of leaps. But since there are a variety of Caldara arias for which autograph "con oboe" and "senza oboe" indications alternate in material that could not possibly be played as written even on twentieth-century oboes, neither range nor a demand for technical facility impossible on the instrument can be taken as necessarily valid criteria for assuming the intended inclusion or exclusion of oboes. The existence of arias headed "Unisoni senz' Oboe," "Violini Unisoni," and "Con Strumenti senz' Oboe" might lead one to think that Caldara considered oboes normal participants in pieces of instrumentation types 2 and 3, but such rubrics may often have been only precautionary, and even autograph indications about the omission of oboes may frequently have been added after the completion of the arias in which they occur. Finally, the word "strumento" or "istrumento" is listed in Italian dictionaries as a word used to denote any musical instrument. But the existence of Caldara arias surviving in autographs marked "Con Strumenti et Oboe," "Con Strumenti Arpeggiate," and "Con Strumenti Pizzegati" goes a long way towards persuading one that the normal orchestra for the accompaniment of Caldara's operatic arias was composed of strings and continuo, with oboes and bassoons added for special occasions, though perhaps more often than specifically indicated in the autograph scores.

Since it is altogether probable that such matters were not always clear to Caldara's copyists at the time they were preparing the performing materials for his operas, musicians responsible for modern performances of Caldara arias will not sin in using their own good sense to reach *ad hoc* solutions to some problems of instrumentation, at least until the discovery of one or more *complete* sets of original parts. Such solutions should, of course, be based on what the evidence of the autograph scores suggest were considerations meaningful to Caldara himself: the matching of instrumentation to the vocal strength of the individual singer and the creation, wherever possible, of variety between successive arias.

One should mention, in concluding this discussion of Caldara's operatic arias, some modern "Neapolitan" habits of instrumentation in scores written by a Venetian composer (who seems never even to have visited Naples) more than a decade before the popularity of Leo, Vinci, Pergolesi, and company. Besides Caldara's use of fewer and fewer continuo arias, one notes the frequency with which he allows especially the treble instruments of his orchestra to double the voice, the frequency with which the normally inactive violas are directed to double the continuo, and the frequency with which the continuo instruments are dropped in favor of a real bass played by the violas. That, moreover, Caldara's melodic writing frequently involves what Wilhelm Fischer has called the *Liedtypus*,[114] but that the harmonic rhythm of Caldara's later arias is not notably slower than that of his earlier arias, indicates how complex and piecemeal a matter is the development of the style formerly attributed in too large a measure to Naples.

Vocal Ensembles

Vocal ensembles play but a minor role in all *opera seria* from the earlier eighteenth century, and Caldara's settings of secular texts by Zeno and Metastasio are no exception, as shown by Table L.

Representing 4 percent of the set pieces in Caldara's Vienna settings of Zeno libretti and only 2 percent of the set pieces in his original settings of Metastasio libretti, the vocal ensembles consist almost entirely of duets, the great majority of which are set for soprano and alto. Although Zeno's ensembles occur in a variety of dramaturgical positions and concern several sorts of subjects, Metastasio's are notably more stereotyped, with regard both to placement and to subject matter.

Poetic texts for vocal ensembles by Zeno and Metastasio take various forms. Sometimes the text is evenly divided between the singers in longer speeches as in *Venceslao* III/13,

VENCESLAO	Si, si, sodi, che il dolce tuo sposo
	Potrai lieta neì seno abbracciar.
	Quella fede, che diedi pietoso,
	Giusto ancora saprò conservar.
LUCINDA	Si, si, godo, se trovo quel bene,
	Che soave la vita ni fa.
	In me torna la gioja, e la spene,
	Se in te amore ritorna, e pietà.

but elsewhere the singers may exchange shorter speeches, as in *Nitocri* III/7.

EMIRÉNA	Ferma.
MIRTEO	No. Vado a morir.
EMIRENA	Amore ti arresta.
MIRTEO	Onore m'invita.
EMIRENA	Amare partita!
MIRTEO	Pietade funesta!
EMIRENA	Serbar puoi la cara vita.
MIRTEO	Con infamaia, e con martir.
EMIRENA	Ferma.
MIRTEO	No. Vado a morir.

Table L

Title[a]	No. of vocal ensembles	Location	Singers involved		Subject of text
Ifigenia	1	III/20 (part of final number)	Ifigenia	—S	Happiness at solutions of problems
			Achille	—A	
Sirita	0				
Lucio Papirio	3	I/11	Papiria	—S	Love duet
			Q. Fabio	—A	
		I/14	Cominio	—S	Disagreement on an appropriate course of action
			M. Fabio	—A	
			L. Papirio	—T	
		III/10 (just before a set change)	Papiria	—S	Lovers' parting in anticipation of death
			Q. Fabio	—A	
Ormisda	2	I/3	Arsace	—A	Disagreement on an appropriate course of action
			Palmira	—A	
			Ormisda	—T	
		II/6	Palmira	—A	Antagonists revile one another
			Cosroe	—A	
Nitocri	1	III/7	Emirena	—S	Lovers disagree on the male's right to die for honor's sake
			Mirteo	—A	

Opera	No.	Location	Characters		Description
Scipione nelle Spagne	3	I/6 (opens a new set)	Sofonisba Lucejo	—S —A	Lovers' joy at an unexpected reunion
		I/17 (closes act)	Sofonisba Lucejo	—S —A	Love duet
Scipione nelle Spagne		III/14	Sofonisba Scipione Elvira Cardenio	—S —A —A —T	Four characters react differently to the news of Lucejo's banishment.
Euristeo	0				
Andromaca	3	I/1	Astianatte Telemaco	—S —S	Oaths of vengeance for the fall of Troy
		IV/2	Andromaca Ulisse	—S —T	Two natural enemies anticipate each other's future discomfiture.
		IV/6 (concludes an act)	Andromaca Pirro	—S —A	Andromaca and one of her admirers remark on their markedly different reactions to the same situation.
Gianguir	1	V/7 (concludes a set)	Semira Cosrovio	—S —A	Lovers contemplate life after their impending deaths.
Semiramide	1	IV/6 (concludes an act)	Mennone Aliso	—S —S	An army general and a shepherd sing on the weaknesses of character connected with political corruption.
Venceslao	3	III/13	Lucinda Venceslao	—S —A	A father and his future daughter-in-law look foward to a marriage.

Title[a]	No. of vocal ensembles	Location	Singers involved	Subject of text
		IV/2	Lucinda —S Casimiro —A	Love duet
		IV/4	Erenice —S Ernando —T	Ernando is urged to avenge Erenice.
I due dittatori	4	II/5	Minuzio —A F. Massimo —T	Two political leaders heap scorn upon one another.
		III/1 (opens act)	Velia —S Erminio —S	Love duet
		IV/16	Velia —S Q. Fabio —A Minuzio —A	Each of three characters reacts to news of an impending battle.
		V/2	Arisbe —S Osidio —B Valerio —S	An abandoned damsel scorns the claims of two former suitors.
Imeneo	1	III/10	Alisa —S Odrisio —A	Odrisio's offer of love is dismissed derisively.
Ornospade	1	II/9	Palmide —S Mitridate —S Vorrone —B	Each of three characters reacts to Artabano's clemency.
Mitridate	1	IV/5	Aristia —S Farnace —A	Believing she is about to die, Aristia tries to persuade Farnace not to risk his own life in avenging her.

Cajo Fabbricio	0				
Enone	2	I/4	Eurialo Clecne	—S —A	Disagreement on allowing oneself to be guided by love alone
		II/7	Paride Enone	—S —S	Enone appears to promise Paride her love
Demetrio	1	III/13	Alceste Fenicio	—A —T	Love duet
Adriano	1	I/14 (concludes act)	Emirena Farnaspe	—S —A	Lovers' farewell before anticipated death
Olimpiade	1	I/10 (concludes act)	Aristea Megacle	—A —S	Megacle bids his beloved a mysterious farewell.
Demofoonte	1	II/11 (concludes act)	Dircea Timante	—S —S	Lovers' unhappy parting
La clemenza di Tito	0				
Achille in Sciro	0				
Ciro riconosciuto	1	I/13 (concludes act)	Arpalice Ciro	—S —S	Arpalice tries to persuade Ciro to disclose everything.
Temistocle	0				

a. The titles in Tables L and M, like those in Table G, are listed in the chronological order of their production dates. (The production dates for Caldara's settings of *Scipione nello Spagne* and *Venceslao*, two Zeno libretti already produced in Italy before Zeno's 1718 move to Vienna, are 4 November 1722 and 4 November 1725, respectively.)

Combinations of longer and shorter sections, as in *Adriano* I/14, are equally frequent.

FARNASPE	Se non ti moro allato,
	Idolo del cor mio,
	Col tuo bel name amato
	Fra labbri io moriro.
EMIRENA	Se a me t'invola il fato,
	Idolo del cor mio,
	Col tuo bel nome amato
	Fra labbri io moriro.
FARNASPE	Addio, mia vita.
EMIRENA	Addio,
	Luce degli occhi miei.
FARNASPE	Quando fedel mi sei,
	Che piu bramar dovro?
EMIRENA	Quando il mio ben perdei,
	Che piu sperar potro?
FARNASPE	Un tenero contento
	Eguale a qual ch'io sento,
	Numi, chi mai provo!
	⎤ a due
EMIRENA	Un barbaro tormento
	Eguale a qual ch'io sento,
	Numi, chi mari provo?

Duet texts may be marked "a due"—in part, as in the example printed from *Adriano*, or as wholes, which happens, for example, in *Scipione* I/6.

LUCEJO e	Non lo credo agli occhi miei,
SOFONISBA	E pur sei
a due	L'idolo mio.
	Ho timor, che un tanto bene
	Sia lusinga della spene,
	Sia fantasma del desio.

Speeches may be distributed so that each one ends with a completed line of poetry, as in the example printed above from *Venceslao*, or so that some lines of poetry are constituted by a succession of short speeches, as in *Scipione* III/14.

ELVIRA	O timore!
CARDENIO	O destino!
SCIPIONE	O pena!
SOFONISBA	O vita!
SCIPIONE	Piano;
ELVIRA	Temo;
a due	E mi o infedele.etc.

In trios concluding *I due dittatori* IV/16 and *Ornospade* II/9, each of three singers leaves the stage after the completion of his own stanza.

While this variety of poetic forms is mirrored in some of the vocal ensembles written by Caldara for his earlier operatic works, it is not characteristic of the vocal ensembles in his Vienna settings of Zeno and Metastasio texts. In those pieces, as with the solo arias discussed earlier, the 5-part *da capo* format maintains so tight a monopoly that the composer's most important formal consideration is simply the determination of where the A section ends and the B section begins. Working so often under the pressure of time,[115] Caldara often seems, however, to have begun setting a text without having read it carefully enough to make even so simple a decision as this. The duet which concludes Act II of Metastasio's *Demofoonte*, for example, comprises a statement of a particular situation (an outpouring about the lovers' impending separation) followed by a general observation which, according to the singers, is entailed by the situation they have just described.

TIMANTE	La destra ti chiedo,
	Mio dolce sostegno,
	Per ultimo pegno
	D'amore e di fe.
DIRCEA	Ah! questo fu il segno
	Del nostro contento;
	Ma sento che adesso
	L'istesso non e.
TIMANTE	Mia vita, ben mio!
DIRCEA	Addio, sposo amato.
a due	Che barbaro addio!
	Che fato crudel!
(a due)	Che attendeno i re
	Dagli astri funesti,
	Se i premii son questi
	D'un alma fedel?

Caldara's composing score[116] includes a setting of the duet's A section which indicates how much Caldara had written before he perceived Metastasio's intended point of division.

Caldara's first setting of "La destra ti chiedo":

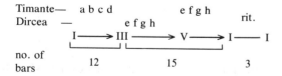

His ultimate solution for the duet makes characteristically economic use of 22 serviceable bars from the beginning of his first setting. (It is examples such as this which help convince one that Caldara's view on structural balance in even small-scale pieces cannot have been very sophisticated.)

Timante —	a b c d		i	k e	rit.	⌢	m n o p	rit.		DA
Dircea —		e f g h		j k e			m n o p			CAPO
	I ——→ III ——→ V —→ I ——————— I ——→ IV ——→ I									

no. of bars	12	10	9	6	8	7

But if the vocal ensembles in Caldara's Zeno and Metastasio settings are similar in format to the solo arias in those works, they often seem more carefully made than many of the solo arias. Generally shorter than the solo arias, the ensembles dispense with those monotonously repetitive diatonic sequences that do so much to make the solo arias dull reading. Although the duets are sometimes nothing more than juxtaposed snippets for one solo voice after another, and although they contain a good deal of vocal writing in parallel thirds and sixths, the presence of more than one part above the continuo does sometimes lead to imitative counterpoint and, thus, to a texture more interesting than that in which one insipid three- or four-bar phrase aimlessly follows a long series of others.

The vocal ensembles in Caldara's settings of Zeno and Metastasio libretti have, of course, nothing whatever to do with any reform. Continuing a seventeenth-century tradition, they represent simply an element of textural variety, not a means towards more effective drama. The scores under study here do contain, to be sure, ensemble texts in which the characters involved disagree strongly with each other, but Caldara does little (if anything at all) to write the sorts of vocal parts which might be said to reflect differences in personality, and the *da capo* convention insures against the possibility of any forward motion, dramatically, within an ensemble. The opening scene in *Don Giovanni* could not have encompassed Donna Anna's confrontation of her seducer, the duel, and the Commendatore's death had Mozart been obliged to conclude his ensemble in the manner that it begins—with Leporello singing "Notte e giorno faticar."

Choruses

Although in 1702 Crescimbeni had enthusiastically welcomed what he took to be a new interest in both Venice and Rome in act-ending choruses—an indication, he hoped, that the Italian libretto might be about to recover some of the dignity of ancient Greek drama[117]—there is no evidence that either Zeno or Metastasio paid much attention to such implied advice. Table M summarizes the use of the chorus in those libretti of Zeno and Metastasio which were set in Vienna by Caldara.

Bulking only slightly larger in our 25 libretti than the 32 vocal ensembles studied earlier, the 49 choruses listed in Table M include 24 that are simply part of a contemporary convention—that serious operas end with normally eulogistic choruses, labelled by Metastasio himself as superfluities.[118] With the possible exception of the chorus which concludes Metastasio's *Demofoonte*, none of the 49 functions in the manner expected of the "coro stabile" by conservative Italian critics: as an omnipresent character, commenting to the audience at regular intervals on the progress of the drama. Choruses in the libretti of both Zeno and Metastasio function rather in creating points of emphasis just before or just after a change of set—particularly on occasions where sumptuous scenery or costumes were to be employed. Such choruses were used, to quote Metastasio once more, ". . . to represent sacrifices, triumphs, celebrations, and other similar occasions . . . with dignity, delight, and verisimilitude."[119]

But if choruses comprise only a minor part in the 25 libretti of Zeno and Metastasio set in Vienna by Caldara, they comprise an even less essential part in Caldara's settings of those libretti. Sometimes written only shortly before the works in which they occur were to be produced, Caldara's operatic choruses are normally short, diatonic, homophonic pieces in major keys. Set almost entirely in syllabic style and employing a minimum of text repetition, they are characteristically scored for an SATB group, with an à 4 orchestra doubling the vocal parts. The great majority of Caldara's operatic choruses are set up, as one would expect, after the fashion of his *da capo* arias, even though such an arrangement sometimes means ending the chorus with the second rather than with the first stanza of the text, as in *Achille in Sciro* III/8:

Table M

Title	No. of choruses	Location	Subject of text	Remarks
Ifigenia	1	III/20 (final scene)	Rejoicing on Ifigenia's marriage and on the apparent removal of obstacles to a Greek victory at Troy	Involves subdivided chorus. Principal part of number recurs at the very end of the scene.
Sirita	5	I/11 (opens scene)	Joys of hunting	B section sung by soloist, Sirita.
		II/8 (choral scene)	In praise of love and the hunt	Chorus subdivided; 4 of the work's 6 soloists are also involved.
		III/11	In praise of love and marriage	Soloists: due del Coro
		III/12	General rejoicing at news of impending royal wedding	Soloists: 2 of the principals; due del Coro
		III/13 (concludes work)	In honor of the newlyweds	
Lucio Papirio	3	I/1 (opens work)	Romans greet the news that auguries for military victory are favorable.	
		III/1 (opens act)	Roman people support the cause of Q. Fabio	Soloist: M. Fabio

Title	Number	Location	Description	Notes
Ormisda	2	III/16 (concludes work)	Roman people applaud Lucio's magnanimity.	Soloists: all 7 of the principals
		II/1 (choral scene)	"Coro di ministri di Mitra, satrapi, popoli, soldati, Persiani ed Armeni." The court of Persia prays to one of its gods.	
		III/18 (concludes work)	In praise of virtue and of Cosroe	
Nitocri	2	II/3	Traditional mourning chorus for Nitocri's murdered father	Half chorus alternates with full chorus.
		III/21 (concludes work)	In praise of Nitocri's selflessness	
Scipione nelle Spagne	1	III/17 (concludes work)	In praise of love and virtue	
Euristeo	1	III/12 (concludes work)	In praise of royal blood	
Andromaca	1	V/7 (concludes work)	Prayer to god of light for a safe voyage from Troy	
Gianguir	2	I/9	Chorus of soldiers celebrate victory over Persia.	Soloists: 3 of the principals

Title	No. of choruses	Location	Subject of text	Remarks
		V/9 (concludes work)	In praise of Gianguir and the Mongols' victory	Same chorus repeated at end of *licenza*, in praise of Elizabeth Christine
Semiramide	1	V/8 (concludes work)	In praise of Semiramide	Same chorus repeated at end of *licenza*, with a few words changed, in honor of Charles VI
Venceslao	1	V/9 (concludes work)	In praise of Cosimiro, the new king of Poland	
I due dittatori	2	V/7	Victory chorus for Massimo's triumph over Carthage	First part repeated, with a few words changed, at end of *licenza*
		V/7 (concludes work)	Chorus of rejoicing	
Imeneo	3	I/7 (opens scene)	Chorus of shepherds and nymphs honors a princess.	*Tutti* chorus alternates with a "Coro di ninfe" and a "Coro di pastori."
		I/7 (closes scene)	Danced chorus of shepherds and nymphs honor the goddess Tedifera.	
		III/14 (concludes work)	In honor of Imeneo	Chorus performs B section of a piece whose A section is taken by two soloists: Imeneo and Alisa.

Ornospade	1	III/16 (concludes work)	In praise of virtue	
Mitridate	2	V/7 (opens scene)	In honor of a couple newly engaged	A "sinfonia di accompagnamento," which does not appear in any of the musical sources for Caldara's setting, is alleged by the libretto to follow both A and B sections of the chorus.
		V/8	In preparation for the wedding ceremony, the chorus asks for the protection of appropriate divinities.	
Cajo Fabbricio	2	II/opening	An allegorical entertainment, presented to the characters of the drama, before the actual opening of the second act	One imagines that, had Zeno himself participated in the editing of *Poesie drammatiche*, this scene would have been cut—as were all other references in that edition to balli, intermedii, etc.
		III/18 (concludes work)	In praise of glory	B section sung by 5 of the principal soloists
Enone	2	III/1 (opens act)	Chorus of nymphs and shepherds wishes King Priam fine weather.	

Title	No. of choruses	Location	Subject of text	Remarks
		V/8 (concludes work)	Happiness of nymphs and shepherds at happy outcome	
Demetrio	2	I/7 (opens set)	The Syrian people invoke the presence of the divinities for the ceremony at which their new king is to be named.	Chorus subdivided into "Primo e Secondo Coro" during middle of the movement
		III/15 (concludes work)	In honor of Demetrio, the newly chosen king, and his queen	
Adriano	2	I/1 (opens work)	Chorus of Roman soldiers sings in honor of the Roman emperor, Adriano.	The first stanza of the chorus is repeated later in the same scene.
		III/10 (concludes work)	In honor of Adriano's opera-ending display of virtue	
Olimpiade	4	II/4 (opens set)	In praise of pastoral peace and innocence	Verses between choral refrain sung by Argene
		II/6 (opens scene)	In praise of the athletic prowess of Licida, who is about to complete in the Olympic games	Chorus subdivided into "Parte del Coro" and "Altro Parte del Coro" during middle of the movement

Work		Scene	Description	Notes
		III/6 (opens set)	Chorus anticipates the horrors of a human sacrifice.	Chorus subdivided during middle of the movement. The choral refrain central to this movement is repeated in the midst of III/7.
Demofoonte	1	III/10 (concludes work)	Hymn of thanksgiving	
La clemenza di Tito	2	III/12 (concludes work)	Reflective chorus on human happiness	
		I/5 (opens set)	In praise of Tito	The first part of the chorus is repeated later in the scene.
		III/13 (concludes work)	In praise of Tito	
Achille in Sciro	4	I/1 (opens work)	In praise of Bacchus	Smaller chorus alternates with *tutti*.
		II/7 (opens set)	Chorus of revellers bids care to withdraw.	
		II/7	Achilles sings strophic love song with choral refrain.	

Title	No. of Choruses	Location	Subject of text	Remarks
		III/8 (concludes work)	In celebration of multiple marriages, sung while cloud machine descends in preparation for the *licenza*	
Ciro riconosciuto	1	III/14 (concludes work)	Ciro, who has lived for some time as a shepherd, is identified as the son of Cambise, and summoned to become King.	The first part of this work-ending chorus is used to introduce the opera's final scene.
Temistocle	1	III/11 (concludes work)	In praise of virtue	

Ecco, felici amanti,
Ecco Imeneo già acende;
Già la sua face accende,
Spiega il purpurso vel.
Ecco a recar sen viene
Le amabili catene
A voi, per man de'numi,
Già fabbricate in Ciel.

a b c d d/1 d/1 d
e f g h h/1 h/1 h rit. ⌢ e f g h h/2   rit.   DA CAPO

I————————I — I   VI——→I

no. of bars   18   4   16   6

or though it means using the same music for the first and last sections of the text, as in *L'Olimpiade* II/6.

Tutto il Coro ⌈Del forte Licida
Nome maggiore
D'Alfeo sul margine
⌊Mai non sono.

Parte del Coro ⌈Sudor pia nobile
Del suo sudore
L'arena olimpica
Mai non bagno.
Altra parte L'arti ha di Pallade
L'ali ha d'amore:
D'Apollo e d'Ercole
⌊L'ardir mostro.

Tutto il Coro ⌈No, tanto merito,
Tanto valore
L'ombra de' secoli
⌊Coprir non puo.

			parte	altra	
ritornello*	*tutti*		rit.	del Coro	parte	DA CAPO
	a b c d	a b c/1 c d d		e f g h	i j k l	sino al segno*
I————	I ——→	III ————————→	I — I ——→	VII——→V		con le seguenti parole:

"No, tanto merito, "
etc.

But the length of some of the choral texts supplied by Caldara's librettists does oblige him, from time to time, to other formal schemes. The reiteration of a refrain often leads to a rondo-like structure, but in such cases there is seldom any transition between successive sections. Where it is possible to avoid such transitions, as in the chorus concluding *Imeneo* I/7, Caldara also saves himself the trouble of writing out repetitions of the refrain.

Coro di pastori e di ninfe
L'alma cantiamo
Madre Frugifera,
Difa Tedifera,
Che queste piagge cotanto amo.

Coro di ninfe
Lei celebriamo
Che globe a fendere
Col ferro adunco
Pria ne insegno.

Coro di pastori
Di ghiande a pascersi,
Di ghiande a pascersi,
De' miti cibi
L'uso addito.

Tutto il Coro
L'alma cantiamo, etc.

Coro di ninfe
La Dea onoriamo,
Che il carro anguifero
Per le sals'onde
Resse, e guido.

Coro di pastori
E con le accese
Faci nell'Etna
La cara figlio
Cercando ando.

Tutto il Coro
L'alma contiamo, etc.

¢	ritornello	*a b c d	rit.	a b c d	rit. ⌒
	I ——— I ——→	V I — I	———	I — I	
no. of bars	12 12	12	12	10	

	Coro di ninfe (SSA)		Coro di pastori (ATB, accompanied by oboes & bassoons)		
¢	e f g h m n o p	𝟛 𝟠	i j k l q r s t	DEL SEGEO	
	VI ——— VI		III ——— III	*	
no. of bars	8		8		

Long choral texts which, like the one opening *Achille in Sciro*, do not involve poetic refrains, are normally composed in the manner of an allegro movement from a contemporary concerto grosso—with successive sections of the text set so as to tonicize a variety of scalar degrees and with some of the vocal sections separated from those that follow them by instrumental ritornelli.

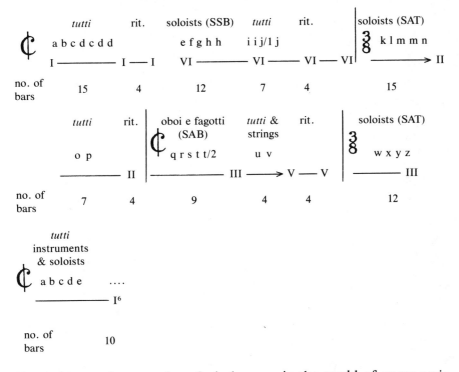

From time to time one does find choruses in the world of *opera seria* which contribute to dramatic pathos, choruses which, like the finale of Metastasio's *Attilio regolo*,[120] remind one of those in the *Orfeo*s of both Gluck and Monteverdi. But *Attilio*, at whose conclusion Rome bids farewell to a leader who would rather sacrifice himself than an iota of Roman principle, was written only after Caldara's death. While there are many such texts in the Caldara oratorios, the opportunities for pathos provided him in the choral movements of secular libretti were very limited, if they can be said to have existed at all.

V

Conclusion

All things considered, it is not surprising that Caldara's *opere serie* on texts by Zeno and Metastasio were hardly known outside of Vienna even at the time they were written,[1] for to at least this writer they seem less interesting, from a musical point of view, than dramatically similar works by either of Caldara's colleagues at the Habsburg Court—the respected contrapuntalist, J. J. Fux, and the daringly unorthodox Francesco Conti.[2] But Caldara, whose church music attracted the attention even of J. S. Bach,[3] cannot have been anything like the eighteenth century's least skilled composer of *opere serie*. The important positions he occupied throughout his career, at whose conclusion he was earning a considerably larger salary as *Vizekapellmeister* than that paid during the same period to *Kapellmeister* Fux,[4] testify to the esteem in which Caldara was held by employers who were themselves musicians of sorts.[5]

One has the impression, in studying Caldara as a composer increasingly involved with *opera seria*, that the routine of working repeatedly with such dramatically unpromising libretti cannot but have had, as Caldara grew older, a deadening effect for whatever enthusiasm he may once have had for the genre. The only composing score which survives for a pre-1717 *opera seria* by Caldara—the *Opera pastorale*, first completed in 1701[6]—shares an important characteristic with Caldara's extant composing scores for comic libretti completed after 1716[7], a characteristic which distinguishes these composing scores from those for the post-1716 Zeno and Metastasio settings. The composing scores for the *Opera pastorale* and the comic works are marked with all sorts of corrections—major changes in voice leading, alternations in the balancing of successive phrases, strengthenings of cadential points, adjustments in vocal range, and the cutting, substituting, and adding of arias. But while the signed and dated autographs in which Caldara set the Zeno and Metastasio libretti are clearly composing scores, Caldara seems to have completed them more rapidly, and to have expended noticeably less effort in readying them for the copyists who produced the orchestral parts and copy scores for the Imperial Library. Although the cleaner appearance of the Zeno and Metastasio scores is partly to be explained by the fact that most of them were never subjected to *rifacimenti*, it seems probable that their appearance would have been more like that of the *Opera pastorale* had Habsburg bureaucracy been less effective in checking the normal prerogatives of Italian singers and composers, had Zeno viewed his libretti more as texts that were to be set to music and staged, rather than as completed art works to be distributed in print to *letterati*.

To assert, as VanderMeer has done, that composers like Caldara produced scores of inestimable strength and variety through scrupulous attention to principles stated or implied in treatises on rhetoric, is a novel development in the criticism of *opera seria*. But I believe that VanderMeer overstresses a long series of individual instances while ignoring the total effect of an *opera seria* and, especially with respect to Italy, the educational backgrounds of the composers responsible for *opera seria* scores. If VanderMeer is correct with regard to Fux, the *opere serie* of Caldara, and his double setting of *La verità nell'inganno* in particular, indicate that there were also composers at work during the period, especially in Italy, who were at least as much concerned with contrast between successive musical numbers and with a variety of opportunities for individual singers as with any species of *Figuren-, Incisionen-,* or *Affektenlehre*.

Since opera is an art form which involves several constituent art forms, it can only suffer, as a whole, if those responsible for the constituent art forms insist on going their own separate ways. The libretti written during the closing decades of the seventeenth century by men like Minato, Aureli, and Noris were dramatically monstrous, but the possibility of dramatically viable Italian opera was not at all improved when poets like Zeno decided that they could both have their cake and eat it by writing libretti that could be read in private, on the one hand, or set to music and staged, on the other. Had Zeno been more sensitive to the demands of musical drama, he would have spent time consulting with the composer who was to realize in music the dramatic implications of the libretto. If pressed during such a consultation, a sensitive composer could have told his librettist, as easily in 1730 as in 1786, that the recitatives were far too long and the arias far too numerous and too distinctly separated from the rest of the text for anything like meaningful musical drama to result. But neither Zeno nor Caldara had ever had the fortune to experience a Monteverdi opera. Both composer and poet were content, like the rest of their contemporaries, to work in isolation from one another, and to blame the dramatically muddled spectacles which resulted on the evils of the system. In so doing, they abandoned opera to the mother of the *prima donna* and to the trainer of the bear, who asserted their own interests in the fashion indicated by Marcello.

To criticize Zeno, Metastasio, and Caldara for not having pondered the means and goals of their craft is not, it seems to me, to criticize a genre according to inapplicable standards or as a result of historical perspective impossible for men who lived more than 200 years ago. While *opera seria* seems ridiculously stilted and stereotyped to many twentieth-century critics, we should remember that there were many to whom it seemed patently absurd during the 1720s and 1730s. Had an opera-oriented composer of ability, insight, and means pressed an open-minded writer of genius for a libretto altogether different from those turned out by Zeno and Metastasio, something remarkable could have happened, even in Habsburg Vienna of Charles VI. To point out that this did not happen in Caldara's case is simply to give Caldara the place he deserves in operatic history, that of an able, well-paid, but altogether unquestioning purveyor of musical settings for dramatically impossible libretti. As we have shown, it is only in a very special sense that Zeno and Metastasio can be said to have participated in any reform of the libretto. The toxic effects of the medicine they helped to administer, especially evident in the Caldara scores studied in this book, were to keep the musical-dramatic aspect of serious Italian opera in a comatose condition for decades.

Notes

Preface

1. Alice Gmeyner, "Die Opern M. A. Caldaras," University of Vienna dissertation, 1927.

2. The possibility of interests shared by Zeno and Caldara was implied by Max Fehr in his 1912 University of Zürich dissertation *Apostolo Zeno und seine Reform des Operntextes*, which urged the need for a thorough study of Caldara's scores. Claude Palisca's contribution to *Musicology* includes a more recent reminder of how little has been known about Caldara's operas.

3. For a study of these forces' effect on a single libretto, see my article, "The Travels of Partenope" in *Studies in Music History; Essays for Oliver Strunk* (Princeton, 1968), pp. 356–85.

4. J. H. VanderMeer, *Johann Josef Fux als Opernkomponist* (Bilthoven, 1961).

Chapter I

1. For a more detailed description of these developments, see D. Grout, *A Short History of Opera*, 2nd ed. (New York, 1965), pp. 78–100; H. Kretzschmar, "Die venetianische Oper," *VfMw* VIII (1892), 1–76; *idem*, "Betiräge zur Geschichte der venetianischen Oper," *JMP* XIV (1907) 71–81; *idem, Geschichte der Oper* (Leipzig, 1919), pp. 81–107; H. Prunières, "I libretti dell'opera veneziana nel secolo XVII," *RassM* (1930) 441–48; U. Rolandi, *Il Libretto per musica attraverso i tempi* (Rome, 1951), pp. 50–64; E. Wellesz, "Cavalli und der Stil der venetianischen Oper," *SzMw* I (1913), 1–103; H. C. Wolff, *Die venezianische Oper in der 2. Hälfte des 17. Jahrhunderts* (Berlin, 1937); S. T. Worthsthorne, *Venetian Opera in the 17th Century* (Oxford, 1954). Although it is clear that Venice dominated the world of Italian opera during the second part of the seventeenth century, scholars dealing with this area during the past decade have generally agreed to discard adjectives like "Venetian" and "Neapolitan" on the ground that the mutually exclusive stylistic distinctions they had come to imply bear no meaningful relationship to historical fact. For the best summary of the issues involved here, see E. O. D. Downes and H. Hucke, "The Neapolitan Tradition in Opera," *Report of the 8th Congress of the International Musicological Society: New York, 1961* (New York, 1961–62), I, 253–84; II, 132–34.

2. Giovanni Maria Crescimbeni, *Comentarii intorno alla sua istoria della volgar poesia* (Rome, 1702) I, 234–35. Crescimbeni concedes here that Cicognini's contemporaries,

Giulio Strossi, Ottavio Transarelli, and Marc'Antonio Tirabosco, may have been equally responsible, but in another publication, *La Bellezza della volgar poesia* (Rome, 1700), he mentions Cicognini alone. Subsequent writers seem to have followed the tradition begun with *La bellezza*. . . .

3. Pier-Jacopo Martello, *Della tragedia antica e moderna* (Rome, 1715), reprinted in *Scrittori d'Italia* CCXXV, 203–4; Luigi Riccoboni, *An Historical and Critical Account of the Theatres in Europe* . . . (London, 1741), pp. 58–59.

4. Gianvincenzo Gravina, *Della tragedia* (Naples, 1715), pp. 18–21.

5. *Ibid.*, p. 29.

6. *Ibid.*, pp. 47–48.

7. Scipione Maffei, *Teatro italiano* (Verona, 1723), I, ix–x.

8. *Ibid.*, p. x.

9. Benedetto Marcello, *Il teatro alla moda* (Venice, 1720), *passim*.

10. Gianvincenzo Gravina, *Della ragion poetica* (Milan, 1819), p. 224. (The original publication of Gravina's treatise appeared in Rome during 1708.) *Riflessioni sopra i drammi per musica* (Venice, 1757), p. 35. The Biblioteca Nazionale Marciana's copy of this anonymously published treatise bears a pencilled attribution to the famous eighteenth-century Venetian architect, Giovanni Maria Ortes, but I can find no substantiating evidence for this ascription.

11. Gabriel Maugain, *Etude sur l'evolution intellectuelle de l'Italie de 1657 à 1750 environ* (Paris, 1909), pp. 238–39.

12. Cicognini himself writes in his 1649 preface to *Giasone*: ". . . I write from mere caprice. My caprice aims simply at delight. To cause delight is in my opinion simply to adapt oneself to the genius and taste of one's listener or reader; if in the reading or recitation of my *Giasone* I am found to have succeeded in this, I shall have realized my intention. If not, I shall have lost many days in writing and you a few hours in reading or listening to it: thus the greater loss will be mine." Quoted from the English translation by Nathaniel Burt in his article, "Opera in Arcadia," *MQ XLI* (1955), 164. Francesco Sbarra's preface to the 1651 Venetian libretto for his *Alessandro vincitor di se stesso* is written in the same tone: ". . . this species of poetry has today no aim other than to delight, whence one is obliged to accommodate oneself to the custom of the times; if the recitative style were not relieved by scherzi . . . it would induce more disgust than delight." Remarks along similar lines are to be found in, among many similar sources, the following libretti: Aureli, *Erginda* (Venice, 1652); Aureli, *Gli amori d'Apollo* (Venice, 1663); Aureli, *Perseo* (Venice, 1665); M. Noris, *Attila* (Venice, 1672); C. Ivanovich, *La costanza trionfante* (Venice, 1673); Acciajuoli, *Il girello* (Venice, 1682); d'Averara, *L'amante fortunato per forza* (Venice, 1684); D. David, *L'amante eroe* (Venice, 1691); A. Zeno, *Il Tirsi* (Venice, 1696).

13. G. B. Marino, *L'Adone* (Venice, 1626), f. b1ᵛ.

14. Francesco Fulvio Frugoni, *L'Epulone, opera melodrammatica esposta, con le prose morali-critiche dal P. Francesco Fulvio Frugoni* (Venice, 1675), p. 196.

15. Crescimbeni, *Comentarii*. . . , I, 250.

16. Frugoni, *op. cit.*, p. 162.

17. *Ibid.*, pp. 172, 191.

18. For a summary of critics who have blamed the ills of Italian tragedy during the seventeenth and eighteenth centuries on the cancerous popularity of Italian opera, see Emilio Bertana, *Il teatro tragico italiano del secolo XVIII prima dell'Alfieri*, Giornale storico della letteratura italiana, supplementary series IV (Turin, 1901), 143 ff.

19. Frugoni, *op. cit.*, pp. 175–76.

20. For a useful discussion of some problems related to the *Poetics*, see Gilbert Murray's preface to the Oxford Press edition first published in 1920.

21. Frugoni, *op. cit.*, p. 171.

22. *Ibid.*, p. 186.

23. *Ibid.*, p. 188.

24. *Ibid.*, pp. 189–90.

25. *L'Epulone* does not appear in any of the three standard contemporary catalogues of musical-dramatic works performed in Venice during the seventeenth century: C. Ivanovich, *Minerva al tavolino* (Venice, 1681), continued in a second edition which appeared in 1688; C. B. Bonlini, *Le glorie della poesia* (Venice, 1730), published anonymously; A. Groppo, *Catalogo di tutti i drammi per musica recitati ne'teatri di Venezia dall 1637 sin all'anno presente* [1745] (Venice, n.d.).

26. Frugoni, *op. cit.*, p. 188.

27. For a detailed discussion of the interactions between French and Italian cultures during the seventeenth and eighteenth centuries, see Maugain, *op. cit.*

28. Dominique Bouhours, *La manière de bien penser dans les ouvrages d'esprit* (Paris, 1715), pp. 356–57; the first edition appeared in 1687.

29. Bouhours, *Entretiens d'Ariste et d'Eugène* (Paris, 1671), quoted in Maugain, *op cit.*, p. 252.

30. Charles de Marguetel de St. Denis, Seigneur de Saint-Evremond, *Mixt-Essays: Tragedies, Comedies, Italian Comedies, English Comedies and Operas* (London, 1685), p. 14.

31. *Ibid.*, pp. 22 ff.; *Oeuvres meslées*, a three-volume edition of Saint-Evremond's writings published in London in 1709, contains the following essays on opera: "Sur les opera," II, 214–22; "Les opera, comedie," II, 223–92; "A Monsieur Lulli," III, 106–7.

32. Saint-Evremond, *Mixt-Essays*, p. 28.

33. *Ibid.*, pp. 14–18.

34. On seventeenth- and eighteenth-century Italian reaction to French philosophy and literature, see Maugain, *op. cit.*; Bedarida and Hazard, *L'influence française en Italie au dix-huitième siècle* (Paris, 1935); G. L. Moncallero, *L'Arcadia* (Florence, 1953) I, especially Chapter 5.

35. Maugain, *op. cit.*, pp. 3–10.

36. *Ibid.*, pp. 11–23.

37. *Ibid.*, pp. 24–38.

38. *Ibid.*, pp. 36–37.

39. *Ibid.*, pp. 287–88.

40. *Ibid.*, pp. 93–110.

41. *Ibid.*, pp. 242 ff.; Antonio Belloni, *Il seicento* (Milan, 1929), pp. 87ff.; Carlo Calcaterra, *Il Parnasso in rivolta* (Milan, 1940), Chapter 5.

42. On Christina's relationship to several Italian composers of her time, see A. Sandberger, "Beziehungen der Königin Christine von Schweden zur italienischen Oper und Musik . . . ," *Bulletin de la Société union musicologique* V, 121–73; A. Cametti, *Cristina di Svezia, l'arte musicale e gli spettacoli teatrali in Roma* (Rome, 1931); *Historia della Sacra Real Maestà di Cristina Allessandra Regina di Svezia* (Modena, 1656), pp. 115–43.

43. Cametti, *op. cit.*, p. 8.

44. R. Russo, "Cristina di Svezia." *Enciclopedia italiana* (Milan, 1939) XI, 972.

45. See Irene Behn, *Der Philosoph und die Königin* (Freiburg, 1957); Ernst Cassirer, *Descartes, Corneille, Christine de Suède* (Paris, 1942); for both sides of Christine's correspondence with Descartes, see S. Chevalier (ed.), *Lettres sur la morale* (Paris, 1935).

46. Russo, *loc. cit.*

47. See, for example, Gianvincenzo Gravina, *Discorso sopra L'Endimione* (Rome, 1692), pp. 67–68; H. Montesi Festa, "Cristina di Svezia," *Atti dell'Accademia degli Arcadi* XI, 5–21.

48. Giulio Meregazzi, *Le tragedie di Pierre Corneille nelle traduzioni e imitazioni italiane del secolo XVIII* (Bergamo, 1906); Vincenzo de Angelis, "Per la fortuna del teatro di

Racine in Italia," *Studi di filologia moderna* VI, 33–48; *idem, Critiche, traduzioni, ed imitazioni italiane del teatro di G. Racine durante il secolo XVIII* (Arpino, 1914); A. de Carli, *Autour de quelques traductions et imitations du théâtre français publiées à Bologne de 1690–1750* (Bologna, 1920); *idem, L'influence du théâtre français à Bologne de la fin du XVII siecle à la grande revolution* (Turin, 1925); L. Ferrari, *Le traduzioni italiane del teatro tragico francese nei secoli XVII–XVIII* (Paris, 1925). The author's interest in these volumes resulted from the already mentioned work of Bedarida and Hazard, where they are all cited.

49. Fausto Torrefranca, "La prima opera francese in Italia," *Festschrift für Johannes Wolf* (Berlin, 1929), pp. 191–97.

50. *Mémoires de M. de Coulanges* (Paris, 1820), pp. 173–74. This contemporary diarist, apparently unknown to Torrefranca, identifies the translator as a French Jesuit named Bertet, and describes the circumstances under which the work was performed for a privately invited audience at Rome's Palazzo Colonna, the residence of Cardinal de Bouillon. Cametti's presumption (*Il Teatro di Tordinona* [Tivoli, 1938], I, 74) that the work was printed but never performed, is thus shown to have been incorrect.

51. Bedarida and Hazard, *op. cit.*, Chapters 2 and 3.

52. G. G. Salvadori, *Poetica toscana* (Naples, 1691), pp. 2–3.

53. *Ibid.*, pp. 50, 54, 61, 82.

54. *Ibid.*, p. 50.

55. *Ibid.*, pp. 52–53, 56–57, 60–61.

56. *Ibid.*, p. 52.

57. *Ibid.*, p. 55.

58. *Ibid.*, pp. 56 ff.

59. *Ibid.*, p. 60.

60. *Ibid.*, pp. 61–62.

61. *Ibid.*, p. 70.

62. On the history and significance of "arie cavate," see N. Pirrotta, "Falsirena e la più antiche delle cavatine," *Collectanea historiae musicae* II, 355–66.

63. Salvadori, *op. cit.*, pp. 71–79.

64. *Ibid.*, pp. 80–88.

65. Andrea Perrucci, *Dell'arte rappresentativa* (Naples, 1699), p. 63.

66. *Ibid.*, p. 137. Similar reactions, of which examples follow, are a common phenomenon in libretto forewords even during the earlier part of the decade. Paolo Emilio Abate Radi, *Argene* (Venice, 1689): "This is not a work of art, not a drama, not one of those deliveries for which mothers require oil or for which mountains impregnate themselves in order to conceive; it is rather an entertainment for pleasure, a disinterested pastime of amiability intended as an amusement to safeguard the matrons of Venice during the warm hours of the day from the abuses of the sun which, indignant to see itself divided in their faces, implants on those serenely blushing faces the clearest signs of impassioned jealousy." Anonymous, *Il Bellerofonte* (Rome, 1690): "This little work, which flew from my writing desk to the harpsichord like a streak of lightning, claims neither the laurels of an epic nor the fame of shorter forms. It is a chivalrous recreation—call it in fact what you like—that came into being to bring light to the theater, not for the ambition of being seen. It was written rapidly, not well; its weakness is in part necessary and in part natural. Kind reader, do not lower yourself to bother with it. . . ." M. Noris, *I regii equivoci* (Venice, 1697): ". . . Here I am once more in the Teatro Sant' Angelo with a bundle of royal misunderstandings (regii equivoci), words, and deeds. My imagination is most recondite and most difficult to handle because it is managed with verisimilitude and naturalness. I have worked up a story that is appropriate to the place, but despite its slightness, you will find the invention new and not insufficient, not taken either from epics, romances, or from comedies recited in the spoken theater. It is original on two accounts: first, because it is my own, and secondly, because the dramatic thread is led with naturalness on a curiously twisted route to an unexpected conclusion. The writers of antiquity clamor about this quality: it is the art of invention. I do not write of either woods or pastures. I do not seek out lively points from the dead or sentiments from cadavers in order to give myself a reputation for the humorous or the serious. Comedy has always been my special predilection, because it gives relief to the stage when relief is needed, and because it is the soul of the destiny that animates it. It is very difficult to use, especially if used with judgment in accordance with whether the subject of the drama with which it is involved is tender, heroic, or of some other genre. That is the reason why it is used by so few . . ." G. B. Neri, *L'Erifile* (Venice, 1697): ". . . Although this new libretto of mine may depart at times from the rules . . . , if it pleases you it will have achieved its goal completely. I consider a poet who knows how to please, to be a great observer of precepts." L. Lotti, *La saggia pazzia di Giunio Bruto* (Venice, 1698): ". . . That, moreover, you will accept the episodes in the present drama with your customary humanity is the prayer of a pious muse, who, desirous only of your loving sympathy, does not yearn for laurels and does not compare himself with those so many individuals who are the spheres of the poetic heaven." A. Marchi, *Radamisto* (Venice, 1698): ". . . I do not write in order to acquire glory but only in order to serve you well and to be regarded with indulgence, since my total application is in the *tessitura* and management of the many accidents, in the imitation of verisimilitude, and in the distribution of the parts for the expression of the music. . . ." M. Noris, *Il ripudio d'Ottavia* (Venice, 1699): "Since the horrors of slaughter and of death, outmoded features of despotic dramatic genres, have been sent to oblivion, making way as usual for precendent-setting novelty, I have written the present drama, whose three acts are characterized by three different qualities: the charming, the passionate, and the heroic. I hope that in its invention you will discover the easy with the novel, which is another way of saying that you will not be affected by affectation nor badgered by fatigue. Perhaps you will perceive the noble, the elevated, and the tender in that section whose quality is passionate (a difficult feat to accomplish well in the moving of souls), to

which my modest inspiration and humble muse have truly devoted their greatest application. From those who have written history and poetic fantasies I have taken nothing but the naked facts of history. I have stolen nothing with which to clothe those facts since, as I have told you often in my other dramas, I have never been desirous of imitation or of translation; nor am I now."

That the prefaces of Lotti, Noris, Neri, and Merchi were not directed solely against the "reform" librettists usually mentioned in general histories of opera is indicated by the response of Francesco Silvani in his foreward to *L'innocenza giustificata* (Venice, 1699): ". . . It is altogether proper that I take this occasion for now and for all time to insure my public reputation with a public protest, solemnized by the authority of print, that all of the dramatic compositions and other works which have already appeared or which are to appear in print under my name, are and will be entirely the labors of my own poor skill. They are mine in their invention, in their arrangement, and in their elocution, except to the extent that I have touched upon some of the better ideas of Tacitus, Juvenal, Seneca, and others, which I have brought together in the drama that I am now presenting to you and also in another which, God willing, I shall present to you during the end of the present carnival. Thus, the composition of these works is entirely my own; and I have neither communicated with nor received the least advice from anyone—except in writing the libretto entitled *Il principe selvaggio*, performed in the Teatro Sant'Angelo during 1696, a work that was composed by me with the assistance of another person who, for that reason, shall remain anonymous. So great is the intensity of my desire not to make myself appear the author of a work that is not entirely my own; and so indeed should run the course of every man of honor."

Silvani seems to have gone out of his way in order to miss the point. Noris and company prided themselves on the fecundity of their unbridled imaginations, challenging the creativity of librettists like Silvani who, sometimes openly but sometimes tacitly, based their works in whole or in part on the works of their classic and neoclassic predecessors. Silvani defends himself from the charge of working with a silent collaborator—a sin which he has apparently committed even so—but he passes over his dependence on authors of the past as a completely natural phenomenon not worthy of discussion.

For the extent to which Zeno and Metastasio based their works on previous models, taking care in so doing to guard themselves against the charge of outright plagiarism, see Willy Pietzsch, *Apostolo Zeno in seiner Abhängigkeit von der französischen Tragödie* (Leipzig, 1907); Evandro Edesimo, *Considerazioni sopra Il Demofoonte del Sig. Pietro Metastasio* (Venice, 1735); Rolland, *Lettres écrites de Suisse, d'Italie, de Sicilie, et de Malthe* (Amsterdam, 1780), V; Charles DeJob, *Etudes sur la tragédie* (Paris, n.d.); Apostolo Zeno, *Lettere* (Venice, 1785), nos. 453–58, 667; Pietro Metastasio, *Tutte le opere* (Verona, 1948–54), III, 128–29, 163–64. That some Italian libretti were derived from French models even before Zeno's time is indicated by Bonlini's comments (*Le glorie della poesia, e della musica*, pp. 115–16) on Adriano Morselli's *L'incoronazione di Xerse*, produced at Venice's Teatro San Giovanni Grisostomo during the winter of 1691.

67. Perrucci, *op. cit.*, pp. 1–3, 27–28.

68. *Ibid.*, pp. 148–52.

69. *Ibid.*, p. 179.

70. *Ibid.*, p. 80.

71. *Ibid.*, pp. 161, 272.

72. *Ibid.*, p. 49.

73. *Ibid.*, pp. 51–52 ff.

74. On the history of Arcadia, see Crescimbeni, *L'Arcadia* (Rome, 1711): the final 54 pages contain a useful catalogue of the early Arcadians, including dates of initiation into the Academy and the pastoral names of the members; Isidoro Carini, *L'Arcadia dal 1690 al 1890* (Rome, 1891); Moncallero, *op. cit.*; Michele Maylender, *Storia delle accademie d'Italia* (Bologna, 1926), I, 232–91.

75. The introduction to the first issue (1710) of the *Giornale dei letterati d'Italia*, Italy's most important literary periodical of the time, concentrates on just this point. After some pointedly ironic remarks of praise for France's avidly anti-Italian periodical, *Le Journal de Trévoux*, the *Giornale*'s anonymous editorialist (probably none other than Apostolo Zeno, its principal editor until 1718) voiced an opinion that was to appear again and again in subsequent issues of the *Giornale*: ". . . Some of these worthy French gentlemen ought to be good enough to take the time to instruct themselves in a thorough-going fashion about Italian literature and its history. They should do this because their judgments on Italian taste in oratory and poetry, based on works of no value and on the opinions of a few men who have the least knowledge of the best works of our writers, correspond badly to the correctness of their other pronouncements."

76. Moncallero, *op. cit.*, pp. 33–34.

77. Crescimbeni's own statement on the motives shared by the original 14 Arcadians reads as follows: ". . . to reawaken in . . . Italy good taste in humane letters, particularly in Italian poetry." (*La bellezza della volgar poesia* [Venice, 1730], pp. 216–17.) It should be noted in this regard that Maylender (*op. cit.*, I, 249) has questioned whether the earliest Arcadians really shared any explicit and specific plan for literary reform. For a summary of various views on the extent to which the existence of Arcadian goals actually affected the standard of eighteenth century Italian literature, see Moncallero, *op. cit.*, pp. 39 ff. For a summary of recent criticism of Arcadian artificiality, see Carlo Calcaterra, *Il Barocco in Arcadia* (Bologna, 1950).

78. Crescimbeni, *L'istoria della volgar poesia* (Rome, 1698), II, 169–74.

79. *Idem, La bellezza* (Venice, 1730), pp. 106–8.

80. Apostolo·Zeno, *Lettere* (Venice, 1785), nos. 12–13.

81. *Gl'inganni felici* (1695); *Odoardo* (1698).

82. *L'amante eroe* (1691); *La forza della virtù* (1693); *Amor e Dover* (1697).

83. G. C. Corradi, *L'amor di Cursio per la patria* (Teatro SS. Giovanni e Paolo, 1690); R. Pignatta, *La costanza vince il destino* (Teatro SS. Giovanni e Paolo, 1695); Frigimelica-Roberti, *Rosimonda* (Teatro San Giovanni Grisostomo, 1695); G. C. Godi, *Eraclea* (Teatro San Salvatore, 1696); Burlini, *La forza d'amore* (Teatro SS. Giovanni e Paolo, 1697).

84. Zeno, *Lettere* (Venice, 1785), no. 75.

85. *Ibid.*, no. 412.

86. *Ibid.*, no. 51.

87. *Lucio Vero* (Venice, 1700); *Artaserse* (Venice, 1705). *Aminta* (Florence, 1703) involves a role for a facetious shepherd named Elpino. It is to be admitted, of course, that the absence of comic characters is a striking characteristic of historically based Italian libretti of the period after 1700. In Venice such libretti appear frequently immediately after the turn of the century and by 1710 they had become the rule there.

Their dominance in other centers of Italian opera seems, however, to have come only later. Additional comic scenes, probably written by Silvio Stampiglia, were inserted in libretti of Venetian origin performed in Rome's Teatro di Tordinona during the early 1690s (Cametti, *Il teatro di Tordinona*, II, 342 ff.) and comic scenes involving characters who participate in the dramas' principal plots appear in Stampiglia's original libretti during the latter part of the decade. But during the first decade of the eighteenth century the situation in Rome, like that in many another Italian city of the period [see, for example, the just-cited Florentine revision of Zeno's *Griselda* or C. Ricci, *I teatri di Bologna nei secoli XVII e XVIII* (Bologna, 1888), p. 146], changed in the manner to which the preface for the 1711 revision of Girolamo Gigli's *Anagilda* (performed in the private theater of Francesco Maria Ruspoli in Rome) alludes: ". . . This work, which has appeared so many times in the various theaters of Italy, now appears in Rome with some minor changes and with the addition of several arias with which the original author himself has decided to animate it, the better to adapt it to modern usage. At the bidding of the generous person at whose expense the work is performed, . . . the author has added two ludicrous roles, completely separate from the knot of the drama, as is now customary on the stages of Venice and elsewhere. With these roles are interwoven the intermezzi, composed for your greater pleasure with charming invention involving ballets and supernumeraries." (Gigli's original version of this libretto, entitled *La fede nei tradimenti*, had been produced in Siena during the carnival of 1689 by students from the Collegio Tolomei. In his preface to that libretto he had actually apologized for the total absence of comic characters.) The degree to which the rest of Italy followed the Venetian example of excluding independent comic episodes from the printed libretto, labelling them "intermezzi," and restricting them to the intervals between the acts, is dealt with by Charles Troy in his study, *The Comic Intermezzo: A Study in Eighteenth-Century Italian Opera* (1979 publication by UMI Research Press). Edward Dent's suspicion about the tradition that *opera buffa* sprang directly from the comic intermezzi (*SIMG* XI–XII) is supported by the fact that comic texts in Neapolitan dialect appeared in operatic settings in the Teatro dei Fiorentini, Naples, as early as 1708–9, while interpolated comic episodes in *opera seria* were finally replaced there by act-separating intermezzi only after the success of Metastasio's *Impresario delle Canarie* in 1724 (see Hucke, *op. cit.*, I, 259).

Early eighteenth-century Viennese libretti were more modern than those of Hamburg in their handling of comic characters, but noticeably behind the example of Venice. In the Viennese libretti of Donato Cupeda (active in Vienna from 1696 until his death in 1704) buffoons are sometimes omitted altogether, but princes and kings are often made to behave like clowns. Comic figures which did not appear in the original of Lemene's *L'Endimione* are added for the Vienna production of 1706. During Stampiglia's career in Vienna (1706–14) comic characters diminish both in number and in importance, and by the time of Pariati's arrival in 1714, their appearance in serious operas had been limited, with minor exceptions, to comic intermezzi, which in Vienna characteristically appeared as printed appendices to the libretti with which they were performed.

In Hamburg, where both Hunold [*Theatralische Galante und Geistliche Gedichte* (Hamburg, 1706), p. 134] and Feind [*Gedancken von der Opera* (Hamburg, 1708), pp. 103–5] complained about the impropriety of scurrilous scenes introduced into serious works from Paris, Venice, and Vienna as well as in libretti written in Hamburg itself, the use of comic episodes involving principal characters began to wane only during the second decade of the century, disappearing there completely only with the ultimate demise of opera itself. See, on this subject, H. C. Wolff, *Die Barockoper in Hamburg* (Wölfenbüttel, 1957), Chapters 5 and 6. Sirvart Poladian, in her Cornell University dissertation, "Handel as an Opera Composer," quotes the preface of the libretto for the 1729 Hamburg production of Handel's *Riccardo*: ". . . The added comic elements will displease our courteous reader the less because variety of this sort is not only in fashion but has almost become even a kind of necessity." Since independent comic intermezzi began to appear in Hamburg after 1718 (Wolff, *Die Barockoper in Hamburg*, p. 116), it is clear that, at least in some areas, familiarity with comic intermezzi did not preclude the use of comic episodes within the body of a work.

88. Crescimbeni, *Comentarii* (Rome, 1702), I, 234 ff.

89. Crescimbeni is not known to have written any texts that were ever set to music, but his comment in the *Comentarii* that the chorus had begun to replace the comic intermezzo in recent Roman and Venetian *favole pastorale* of merit suggests that he may have considered his own *Elvio*, a *favola pastorale* published in Rome during 1695, appropriate for musical setting, even though it had no arias.

90. L. A. Muratori, *Della perfetta poesia italiana* (Modena, 1706), II, 58 ff.

91. Guido Biagi, "Lettere di Lodovico Antonio Muratori," *Rivista delle biblioteche e degli archivi* VII (1896), 40–41; Zeno's libretto, *Faramondo* had been produced, with music by C. F. Pollarolo, at the Teatro San Giovanni Grisostomo, Venice, during the winter of 1698–99.

92. *Il Tirsi* (Venice, 1696) and *Odoardo* (Venice, 1698) are the only two of Zeno's early libretti not to appear in *Poesie drammatiche* (Venice, 1744), the first "complete" edition of his libretti. On Zeno's later disaffection for his dramatic works, especially the

earlier ones, see Zeno, *Lettere* (Venice, 1785), nos. 588, 620, 651, 653, 666, 672, 691, 694, 716, 745, 810.

93. G. A. Moneglia, *Poesie drammatiche*, 3 vols. (Florence, 1689–90).

94. P. A. Bernardoni, *Poemi drammatici*, 3 vols. (Vienna, 1706–7).

95. G. Gigli, *Opere*, 3 vols. (Siena, 1797).

96. F. Silvani, *Poesie drammatiche*, 4 vols. (Venice, 1744).

97. A. Zeno, *Poesie drammatiche*, 10 vols. (Venice, 1744); *Oeuvres dramatiques . . . , traduites de l'Italien*, 2 vols. (Paris, 1758); *Poesie drammatiche*, 11 vols. (Orleans, 1786); *Poesie drammatiche*, 12 vols. (Turin, 1795).

98. P. Metastasio, *Opere drammatiche*, 4 vols. (Venice, 1733–37); *Poesie*, 9 vols. (Paris, 1755); *Opere*, 12 vols. (Paris, 1780–82); *Tragédies-opera, traduites en francais*, 5 vols. (Vienna, 1751). The number of Metastasio editions that have appeared since the poet's death in 1782 is so large that Bruno Brunelli, the editor of the meticulously thorough *Tutte le opere* [5 vols. (Milan, 1943–54)] does not even bother to list them (Brunelli, ed., *op. cit.* I, 1383).

99. A copy of this libretto is to be found in the extensive libretto collection of Apostolo Zeno himself, now among the holdings of the Biblioteca Nazionale Marciana, Venice.

100. A. Zeno, "Al lettore," *Il Tirsi* (Venice, 1696); a copy is to be found among the holdings of the Music Division of the Library of Congress, Washington, D.C. (The call number is Schatz 5728.)

101. Biagi, *op. cit.*, p. 46.

102. *Giornale dei letterati d'Italia* V (1711), 277 ff.; XVIII (1714), 331 makes the same point with respect to Scipione Maffei's *Merope*.

103. Zeno, *Lettere*, no. 565.

104. N. Campanini, *Un precursore del Metastasio* (Florence, 1904), p. 84.

105. Zeno, *Lettere*, no. 448; no. 434 shows that it was customary during Zeno's day in Vienna to distribute the libretti well in advance of the actual performances. In no. 756 Zeno asserts that in reading a good libretto one should be moved in a manner similar to that affected by a fine tragedy. The careful arrangements made by Zeno during his first years in Vienna for the distribution of his latest libretti to learned friends in Italy are further evidence of his interest in the libretto as a literary genre.

106. For a specific instance, see Metastasio's letter of instructions to Giuseppe Bettinelli, the Venetian publisher of Metastasio's first collected edition (*Tutte le opere*, ed. Brunelli, III, 96–97).

107. Francesco Negri [*Vita di Apostolo Zeno* (Venice, 1816), xliv] quotes a Poleni letter in which Zeno's *Euristeo* (Vienna, 1724) is judged to have a potential as great as that of Guarini's *Pastor fide*, if only Zeno were to replace all of the arias with more dialogue.

108. Zeno, *Lettere*, nos. 310, 756, 1249.

109. Metastasio, *Tutte le opere*, ed. Brunelli, IV, 398–99. There is no real conflict between Edward Dent's contention that Metastasio's libretti were written only to be sung (*SIMG* XIV, 503–4) and Metastasio's just-cited assertion, some time after the works had been written, that they were equally effective when performed without music.

110. Zeno, *Letere*, no. 54.

111. See, for example, Zeno, *Lettere*, no. 605, 663.

112. Biagi, *op. cit.*, p. 41.

113. Zeno, *Lettere*, no. 57.

114. *Ibid.*, no. 59.

115. *Ibid.*, no. 62.

116. *Ibid.*, no. 165.

117. For the details of this famous early eighteenth-century polemic, see Adolfo Boeri, *Una contesa franco italiana nel secolo XVIII* (Palermo, 1900).

118. For an overview of Zeno's libretto output, see Appendix A.

119. For Zeno's interests in the libretto as a commercial genre, see the *Lettere*, nos. 43, 432, 469, 1093; for instances of his embarrassment at his growing fame as a librettist, see nos. 91, 92, 165, 180.

120. Negri, *op. cit.*, pp. 113–14.

121. Zeno, *Lettere*, nos. 407, 412, 414, 417, 419.

122. *Ibid.*, no. 432.

123. *Ibid.*, nos. 430, 432, 434, 435.

124. Negri, *op. cit.*, p. 256. Abortive discussions with the very courteous Director and staff of the Haus-, Hof- und Staatsarchiv in Vienna suggest that the documents connected with this bureaucratic procedure are no longer extant.

125. On Zeno's Habsburg patrons, see J. B. Küchelbecker, *Allerneueste Nachricht vom Römisch-Kayserl. Hofe* (Hanover, 1730), pp. 138–51, 250–60; P. A. Lalande, *Histoire de l'Empereur Charles VI* (The Hague, 1743); G. Adler, "Die Kaiser . . . als Tonsetzer," *VfMw* VIII (1892), 252–74.

126. For Charles's reactions to Zeno's libretti, see the *Lettere*, nos. 436, 439, 455, 476, 495, 521, 543, 565, 588, 745, 773.

127. The normal occasions for the production of secular dramatic works with music occurred, during Zeno's stay in Vienna, at the following times of the year: carnival (usually a comic work); the birthday of the Empress, Elizabeth Christine, on or shortly after August 28, usually at the Favorita Palace on the southern outskirts of Vienna, very often in the open air; the nameday of the Emperor, Charles VI, on or shortly after November 4 in the Great Theater of the Hofburg; a less pretentious, shorter work, usually in one act, on or shortly after the Empress's nameday, November 19, in the Great Theater of the Hofburg. The libretti ordered for the Emperor's nameday all bear the line "at the command of the Empress" on their title pages and involve plots that feature male protagonists and predominantly masculine virtues, each ending with a *licenza* in honor of Charles VI. The libretti ordered in honor of the Empress, on the other hand, all bear the line "at the command of the Emperor," involve plots that feature female protagonists and predominantly feminine virtues, and end with *licenze* in honor of Elizabeth Christine. For a chronological catalogue of all musical-dramatic performances produced by the Habsburgs from early in the seventeenth century until the death of Charles VI in 1740, see Franz Hadamowsky, "Barocktheater am Wiener Kaiserhof," *Jahrbuch der Gesellschaft für Wiener Theaterforschung* (1951–52), issued as a separate publication by Sexl Verlag, Vienna, during 1955. Superior to its predecessors in inclusiveness, in accuracy, and in indicating the sources from which information is drawn, it replaces the following: A. Weilen, *Zur Wiener Theatergeschichte* (Vienna, 1901); L. Köchel, "Verzeichnis der Opera, Serenaden, Feste teatrali und Oratorien welche am kaiserlichen Hofe in Wien von 1631 bis 1740 gegeben wurden," *J. J. Fux* (Vienna, 1872). Except for a useful map of Viennese theaters, A. Bauer's *Opern und Operetten in Wien* (Vienna, 1955) was out of date for the period in question when it appeared.

128. Zeno, *Lettere*, no. 543.

129. Perrucci, *op. cit.*, p. 80. The number of late seventeenth- and early eighteenth-century Italian (particularly Venetian) libretto forewords which stress the desirability of brevity is legion.

130. Besides the comments of Zeno in *Lettere*, nos. 445, 455, 536, 542, 600, see the early eighteenth-century anonymous translator's note on the subject at the end of the 1709 English translation of Raguenet's *Parallèle des Italiens et des Français*, quoted in Oliver Strunk's *Source Readings in Music History* (New York, 1950), p. 488.

131. In Cupeda's libretto for the 1700 Viennese production of *Gordiano Pio*, for example, in whose preface the use of *virgolette* is explained and justified.

132. See pp. 178–79 of the text.

133. Zeno, *Lettere*, nos. 436, 588, 749.

134. Negri, *op. cit.*, pp. 240–88.

135. Zeno, *Lettere*, no. 756.

136. The entire preface to the publication of 1735 is quoted by Gasparo Gozzi as a preface to the eighth volume of his Zeno edition of 1744, *Poesie Drammatiche*.

137. Zeno, *Lettere*, nos. 810, 914.

138. Zeno *Poesie drammatiche* X, xii–xiii.

139. Antonio Valsechi, *Orazione in morte di Apostolo Zeno* (Venice, 1750), pp. xlviii ff. Copies of this and of P. F. H. Menegatti's Latin oration on Zeno's death, *In funere Illustrissimi Domini Apostoli Zeni* (Venice, 1750), are to be found in the Biblioteca Querini Stampalia, Venice.

140. E. Reich, *G. V. Gravina als Aesthetiker* (Vienna, 1890); A. Galletti, *Le teorie drammatiche e la tragedia in Italia nel secolo XVIII* (Cremona, 1901), Chapter 4; P. Metastasio, *Tutte le opere*, ed. Brunelli, III-V, *passim* (for specific references see the detailed listing on V, 897).

141. Guidi was one of the earliest Arcadians, initiated into the Academy on June 10, 1691. The 14 founding members were the following: Paolo Coardi, Giuseppe Paolucci, Vincenzio Leonio, Crescimbeni, Gravina, Giovanni Battista Zappi, Carlo di Tournon, Pompeo Figari, Paolo Antonio di Negro, Melchiorre Maggio, Giacomo Vicinelli, Paolo Antonio Viti, Agostin Maria Taia, and Silvio Stampiglia, the original group's only full-time librettist; Crescimbeni, *Arcadia* (Rome, 1711), pp. 329, 336. Other Arcadian librettists, listed in the order of their initiation into the Academy, included: Paolo de'Conti di Campello (October 5, 1690), G. Masselo (October 16, 1690), G. Sinibaldi (February 2, 1691), P. A. Bernardoni (May 13, 1691), Francesco Palmieri (May 13, 1691), Francesco Acciajuoli (June 10, 1691), L. Adimari, Girolamo Gigli, Francesco Lemene, Carlo Maria Maggi, Giovan Casimo Villifranchi (September 18, 1691), Bernardino Moscheni, C. S. Capece (January 3, 1692), G. A. Spinola (April 10, 1692), G. A. Moniglia (June 13, 1692), Cardinal Pietro Ottoboni (May 12, 1695), Domenico David, Scipione Maffei, Eustachio Manfredi, Pier-Jacopo Martello, Apostolo Zeno (April 29, 1698), Donato Cupeda (April 23, 1703). (For bibliographical information on many of the above, see Carini, *op. cit.*, Chapter 5.) It is to be noted that not all Arcadian librettists were equally interested in the resurrection of serious drama (Villifranchi, for example, was the author of *La serva favorita*, whose preface was quoted above on page 34), nor were all of the neo-Aristotelians of the period members of Arcadia (Frigimelica-Roberti, for example, had not joined Arcadia by the time of Crescimbeni's 1711 list of members). For information on the publication and performance of Guidi's pastorale, see Carini, *op. cit.*, pp. 20–23.

142. G. V. Gravina, "Discorso sopra *L'Endimione*," *Prose* (Florence, 1857), pp. 260–64. The question of whether a poet, be he tragedian or librettist, should be allowed to alter mythology or history was a source of concern for many of the librettists with whom this study is concerned. Corneille, in his treatise on tragedy, had viewed history as an established body of unassailable detail and had asserted its inviolability, an idea which subsequent French Aristotelians added to the ammunition with which they attacked Italian librettists. Several of the old-fashioned Italian poets reacted with guffaws; implying in their forewords that their audience's unfamiliarity with history permitted any license in its use [see, for example, Noris's preface to *Catone Uticense* (Venice, 1701)], they continued the familiar practice of dividing their prefatory "ar-

gomenti" into two sections—one for those elements of the plot that are derived from history and another for those that stem only from the poet's imagination. Their more intellectual compatriots worked, however, on theories to justify tampering with history, and tried to distinguish those elements which should remain free from tampering from those which need not. Some asserted that the very distinction between history and poetry lay in the invention of the latter [see, for example, D. David, preface to *Amor e Dover* (Venice, 1697)]; some maintained that the addition of unhistorical detail made their libretti more dramatic and verisimilar [see, for example, D. David, preface to *La forza della virtù* (Venice, 1693)]; others claimed that the avoidance of historical horror was better in accord with contemporary distaste for dramatic unpleasantness [see the anonymous preface to *La promessa serbato al primo* (Venice, 1697) or Bernardoni's preface to *L'amore vuol somiglianza* (Vienna, 1702)]. Aureli [*Circe abbandonata* (Venice, 1697)] and Scipione Maffei [*Osservazioni sopra la rodoguna* (Venice, 1719), pp. 165–75] both distinguished the contradicting of history from the addition to it of verisimilar detail. Crescimbeni (*La bellezza*, dialogue 6) and Zeno (*Lettere*, nos. 495, 796) both distinguish between the permissible contradicting of secular history and the impermissible altering of sacred history, a point on which Zeno took the trouble of checking with the Church itself. The former, says Zeno, would be impossible in real tragedy, but in melodrama, where the only yardstick for achievement is practical success, a librettist has too many obligations to his patrons, to the scenographer, and to the composer to afford the luxury of using nothing but established historical fact. Zeno's interests in literary history certainly increased his familiarity with ancient and medieval political history, but the citing of historical sources in his libretto prefaces seems to have been intended more as a defense against charges of plagiarism than as an effort to meet French criticism by using plots that conform in every detail with historical tradition.

143. Gravina, *op. cit.*, pp. 251–56.

144. *Ibid.*, p. 272.

145. Gravina, "Della ragion poetica," *Prose*, pp. 89–92.

146. *Ibid.*, pp. 85–88, 132–33, 137–38 *et passim*.

147. Gravina, *Della tragedia* (Naples, 1715), pp. 116–17.

148. *Idem*, "Della ragion poetica," *Prose*, pp. 13–15.

149. *Idem, Tragedie cinque* (Naples, 1712).

150. *Idem, Della tragedia*, pp. 1–6, 69–74.

151. *Ibid.*, p. 7.

152. *Ibid.*, pp. 13–18.

153. *Ibid.*, pp. 21–22, 25–26, 37–40.

154. *Ibid.*, pp. 10–15.

155. *Ibid.*, pp. 7–8, 13, 42, 52.

156. *Ibid.*, pp. 22, 102.

157. *Ibid.*, pp. 58–64, 95–97, 101, 106–17.

158. *Ibid.*, p. 65.

159. For biographical information on Martello, see his autobiography, originally published
in the *Raccolta di opuscoli scientifici e filologici del Calogierà* II (1729), reprinted in
Scelta di curiosità letterarie C (Bologna, 1869), iii–xlv; Angelo Fabronio, *Vitarum
Italorum* (Rome, 1746), I, 215–52; Giovanni Fantuzzi, *Notizie degli scrittori bolognesi*
(Bologna, 1781–94), V, 332–41. The most complete catalogue of his works appears as
an appendix to the recent anthology of his works, *Pier-Jacopo Martello, scritti critici
e satirici*, ed. Hannibal S. Noce, Vol. CCXXV (Bari, 1963) in the series, *Scrittori
d'Italia*. Noce's catalogue includes the following libretti: *Il Perseo* (Bologna, 1697); *La
Tisbe* (Bologna, 1697); *L'Apollo geloso* (Bologna, 1698), restaged in Modena during
1708 and again in Bologna during 1720; *Gli amici* (Bologna, 1699), restaged in Bologna
during 1734.

160. Martello, *L'impostore* (Paris, 1714), printed in Italian; reprinted the following year in
Rome as the second volume of Martello's *Teatro italiano* this time under the title *Della
tragedia antica e moderna*; reprinted during 1963 under the latter title as part of Noce's
just-cited Martello anthology. The page references in the notes which follow relate to
Noce's edition.

161. For a detailed discussion of the conflicting views of Gravina and Martello on the merits
of Greek, Latin, French, and Italian tragedy, see A. Galletti, *Le teorie drammatiche
e la tragedia in Italia nel secolo XVIII* (Cremona, 1901), Chapters 2–4.

162. Martello, *Della tragedia antica e moderna*, p. 189.

163. *Ibid.*, p. 204. Although the 1667 Venetian preface to Giovanni Faustini's libretto,
L'Alciade, printed 16 years after its author's death in 1651, congratulates Faustini for
having gotten away from the use of transvestism, so popular in Venetian libretti during
the middle of the century, the appearance of men and women in the normal costumes
of the opposite sexes remained a standard element in Venetian opera through the turn
of the century. Muratori (*Della perfetta poesia italiana*, II, 51–52), Martello (*Della
tragedia, loc. cit.*), and Hunold (*op. cit.*, p. 129) all complain about it after 1700, but
examples of its use in eighteenth-century libretti become much less frequent.

164. Other early eighteenth-century writers on opera who, like Martello, agreed on the
desirability of limiting the number of scene changes in a given work but who recognized
the impossibility of limiting opera, like Aristotelian tragedy, to a single set for an entire
work: Muratori (*Della perfetta poesia italiana*, II, 53, 61), Hunold (*op. cit.*, p. 135),
Feind (*op. cit.*, pp. 86–89), Metastasio (*Tutte le opere*, III, 14–15), Zeno (*Lettere*,
no. 756). One of the reasons for eighteenth-century librettists' continued use of several
stage sets was certainly the impresarios' continued interest in attracting a public easily
impressed by visual elements, but another reason seems to stem from one of those
traditions with which contemporary Italian opera had become enmeshed: the principal

singers' habit of not exiting more than once between any two set changes. How else could one explain the following notice inserted at the end of Giulio Pancieri's libretto, *Il gran Macedone*, performed during the autumn of 1690 in Venice's Teatro San Cassiano? "If in this opera you perceive that during one and the same stage-set . . . the actors appear more than once, have pity on us, for it was not convenient to add to the number of set changes." A reduction in the number of stage-sets did take place in Italian opera during the half-century between 1675 and 1725, but it is not surprising that a reduction from an average of 10–12 sets per work to one of 8–9 was not the sort of change which the most conservative of the Aristotelians had in mind. (For evidence that the tradition to which Pancieri alludes was a real one, see the charts between pages 101–53.)

Most of the prattling about the Aristotelian unities that one finds in Italian libretto prefaces from as early as the middle of the seventeenth century is foolish and irrelevant, but although eighteenth-century librettists could not go as far as Gravina would have liked towards a stricter interpretation of the Aristotelian unities, one sees signs that the new familiarity with those unities was not without practical result. Zeno asserts in his already quoted letter of 1730 to Gravisi that he prefers his oratorios to his secular libretti because in the former he was better able to maintain the three unities. In the dedicatory preface to the 1735 publication of those oratorio texts he stresses their conformity to the unities of action and time, ". . . and for the most part also to that of place." But allusions to the unities in the prefaces to the secular libretti listed below indicate that although contemporary impresarios may have thought Greek tragedy pedantic, Zeno by no means ignored the three unities in his secular works: *I rivali generosi* (Venice, 1697); *Eumene* (Venice, 1698); *Aminta* (Florence, 1703); *Alessandro Severo* (Venice, 1717); *Lucio Papirio dittatore* (Vienna, 1719); *Meride e Selinunte* (Vienna, 1721); *I due dittatori* (Vienna, 1726). Similar allusions in the original prefaces of Metastasio, all of whose works, according to Calsabigi (preface to the 1755 Paris edition of Metastasio's works, p. xxiv), were written in strict accordance with the unities of time and action, appeared in the following libretti: *Semiramide* (Rome, 1729); *Alessandro nell'Indie* (Rome, 1729); *L'Olimpiade* (Vienna, 1733). By 1785 Stefano Arteaga (*Le rivoluzioni*, II, 64) was prepared to assert not only that librettists of the earlier eighteenth century had paid attention to the Aristotelian unities, but even that perhaps they had paid too much attention.

165. Martello, *Della tragedia*, pp. 226–28.

166. *Ibid.*, pp. 230–37. Other Italians of the period who complained about the dominance of amorous intrigue in contemporary Italian theater of all varieties include the following: Frigimelica-Roberti, preface to his libretti, *Rosimonda*, produced during 1696 at the Teatro San Giovanni Grisostomo, Venice; Muratori, *Della perfetta poesia italiana*, II, 62–66; Gravina, *Della tragedia*, pp. 27–28; Zeno, *Lettere*, no. 756 (quoted above in full on pp. 30–31).

167. Martello, *Della tragedia*, pp. 238–40.

168. For a review of court-parodying comic operas produced during carnival seasons in later seventeenth-century Vienna, see E. C. Salzer, "Commediografi italiani a Vienna," *Rivista italiana del dramma* II, 269–96.

169. Martello, *Della tragedia*, pp. 242–69.

170. An apparent allusion to Pietro Pariati, who was Zeno's Venice-based assistant for libretto versification early in the eighteenth century, then court poet in Vienna (and occasional collaborator with Zeno after the latter's arrival there in 1718) from 1714 until his death in 1733. For a biographical study of Pariati and a review of his works, see Naborre Campanini, *Un precursore del Metastasio* (Florence, 1889); reprinted in 1904 as Volume 43 of the series, *Biblioteca critica della letteratura italiana*. It is hard to imagine why Martello's reference to Pariati should have taken so cryptic a form: *Ciro* and *Costantino* were produced in Venice's Teatro San Cassiano during 1710 and 1711, respectively.

171. See page 27.

172. Martello, *Della tragedia*, pp. 274–75.

173. A reference no doubt to Raguenet's *Parallèle des Italiens et des Français* (Paris, 1702). Italians writing on music around the turn of the century had too little contact with and interest in French music to bother with the subject. Although the Italians of the period were troubled by a literary inferiority complex with regard to the French, most of the arguments on the merits of French versus Italian music seem to have taken place on the northern side of the Alps. Martello's discussion of the subject with the "impostor" took place, typically enough, in Paris, and the volume in which that discussion was first published appeared there as well.

174. Martello, *Della tragedia*, p. 276.

175. *loc. cit.*; for a more reasoned eighteenth-century discussion of the musical advantages of Italian over other languages than one finds in the polemics of the French and Italians, see Stefano Arteaga, *Le rivoluzioni del teatro musicale italiano* (Bologna, 1783–85), I, Chapter 2.

176. Martello, *Della tragedia*, pp. 276–77. According to the bibliographical information currently available, there is no identified extant example of a Pistocchi setting of one of his own libretti.

177. One can easily imagine Zeno's inner reaction to this statement—or to a similar remark inserted by Crescimbeni in the mouth of Giovanni Battista Zappi, one of the 14 original Arcadians, on the occasion of the Arcadian induction of Archangelo Corelli, Alessandro Scarlatti, and Bernardo Pasquini on April 26, 1706: ". . . You know quite well that such texts as these, written only for the sake of music, are not very suitable for the refined taste of eminent litterateurs like the shepherds of this Academy." [Crescimbeni, *Arcadia* (Rome, 1711), p. 289]. The Crusca, a literary academy founded in Florence during the second half of the sixteenth century, active in the dissemination of the Tuscan dialect as the purest form of the language for literary Italians, published a dogmatic but influential Italian dictionary that first appeared in 1612. It was in the third edition (1691) of this dictionary that Apostolo Zeno, also interested in the stylistic reform of the Italian language, published his first scholarly work, *Compendio del vocabolario della Crusca* (Venice, 1705). For more information on Zeno's activities as a scholar, see Giovanni Chiuppani, *Apostolo Zeno in relazione all' erudizione del suo*

tempo (Bassano, 1900); and Luigi Menghi, *Lo Zeno e la critica lettararia* (Camerino, 1901). For more information on the Crusca, see Maylender, *op. cit.*, II, 122–46.

178. Since Martello does not specify the works he has in mind, one suspects an allusion to his own libretti or to those of his teacher and mentor, G. G. Orsi, the Bolognese litterateur whose essay, *Considerazioni sopra la maniera di ben pensare* (Bologna, 1703), seems to have been Italy's first articulate reply to the earlier attacks of Bouhours' *La manière de bien penser dans les ouvrages d'espirit* (Paris, 1687). Orsi's libretti were cited with praise by Perrucci (see above, pp. 14–15) but left unmentioned by all of the other critics with whom this study is concerned. They received no special attention from the author of the only catalogue of Bolognese operatic performances drawn up during the eighteenth century, *Serie cronologica dei drammi recitati su le'pubblici teatri* (Bologna, 1737).

179. The following five-act operatic productions were staged in Venice during the period 1680–1720: Frigimelica, *Ottone* (Teatro San Giovanni Grisostomo, 1694); Frigimelica, *Irene* (Teatro San Giovanni Grisostomo, 1695); Frigimelica, *Il pastor d'Anfriso* (Teatro San Giovanni Grisostomo, 1695); Frigimelica, *Rosimonda* (Teatro San Giovanni Grisostomo, 1696); Giulio Cesare Godi, *Eraclea* (Teatro San Salvatore, 1696); Apostolo Zeno, *Il Tirsi* (Teatro San Salvatore, 1696); Apostolo Zeno, *Venceslao* (Teatro San Giovanni Grisostomo, 1703); Zeno, *Pirro* (Teatro Sant'Angelo, 1704); Frigimelica, *La fortuna per dote* (Teatro San Giovanni Grisostomo, 1704); Frigimelica, *Il Dafne* (Teatro San Giovanni Grisostomo, 1705); P. G. Barziza, *Filippo re della Grecia* (Teatro San Giovanni Grisostomo, 1706); Zeno and Pietro Pariati, *Il Sidonio* (Teatro San Cassiano, 1706); Urbano Rizzi, *Taican re della Cina* (Teatro San Cassiano, 1707); Frigimelica, *Mitridate Eupatore* (Teatro San Giovanni Grisostomo, 1707); Frigimelica, *Il trionfo della libertà* (Teatro San Giovanni Grisostomo, 1707); Urbano Rizzi, *Achille placato* (Teatro San Cassiano, 1707); Zeno and Pariati, *Anfitrione* (Teatro San Cassiano, 1707); Frigimelica, *Il selvaggio eroe*(Teatro San Giovanni Grisostromo, 1707); Frigimelica, *Alessandro in Susa* (Teatro San Giovanni Grisostomo, 1708); Zeno and Pariati, *Engelberta* (Teatro San Cassiano, 1709); Domenico Lalli, *L'amor tirannico* (Teatro San Cassiano, 1710); Pariati, *Costantino* (Teatro San Cassiano, 1711); A. G. Piovene, *Publio Cornelio Scipione* (Teatro San Giovanni Grisostomo, 1712); Piovene, *Marsia deluso* (Teatro S S Giovanni e Paolo, 1715); Piovene, *Polidoro* (Teatro S. S. Giovanni e Paolo, 1715); Antonio Salvi, *Ariodante* (Teatro San Giovanni Grisostomo, 1718); Benedetto Pasqualigo, *Ifigenia in Tauride* (Teatro San Giovanni Grisostomo, 1719); Pietro Suarez, *Leucippe e Teonoe* (Teatro San Giovanni Grisostomo, 1719); Francesco Muazzo, *Paride* (Teatro San Giovanni Grisostomo, 1720).

Of the almost 400 distinct musical productions staged in Venice during the period in question, less than 10 percent were in five acts. Of the 29 in five acts, more than a third were the work of Count Frigimelica-Roberti; more than half of them were staged in Venice's most magnificent theater of the period, the Teatro San Giovanni Grisostomo. (For comparisons of the Teatro San Giovanni Grisostomo with other Venetian theaters of the period, see Bonlini, *Le glorie*, pp. 27, 149–50; L. N. Galvani (pseudonymn for Giovanni Salvioli), *I teatri musicali di Venezia nel secolo XVII* (Venice, 1879), p. 121; T. Wiel, *I teatri musicali di Venezia* (Venice, 1897), pp. xlii–xlix.

The following five-act operatic productions were staged in Vienna during the period 1680–1730: Pariati, *Teseo in Creta* (1715); Pariati, *Il Costantino* (1716); Pariati and

Zeno, *Don Chisciotte in Sierra Morena* (1719); Zeno and Pariati, *Alessandro in Sidone* (1721); Zeno, *Meride e Selinunte* (1721); Pariati, *Archelao, re di Cappadozia* (1722); Pariati, *Creso* (1723); Zeno, *Andromaca* (1724); Zeno, *Gianguir* (1724) Zeno, *Semiramide in Ascalona* (1725); Zeno, *Venceslao* (1725); Zeno, *I due dittatori* (1726); Pasquini, *Don Chisciotte in corte della Duchessa* (1727); Zeno, *Mitridate* (1728); Zeno, *Enone* (completed during 1729 but not performed until 1734).

Of the almost 100 distinct multi-act secular musical productions staged in Vienna during the period in question, less than 20 percent were in five acts; equally divided between Pariati and Zeno, they were used at first primarily during the carnival season. Zeno's first five-act libretto for Vienna came only after he had collaborated with Pariati in a five-act comic libretto, and received the Emperor's assurance (*Lettere*, nos. 455, 542) that five-act libretti were not too long to suit the Habsburgs.

180. Muratori (*Della perfetta poesia italiana*, II, 51–53) had objected to just these conventions, which Zeno, who learned how to construct his libretti without them, was generally successful in avoiding.

181. The use of rationalistic denouements is another characteristic which distinguishes Zeno and several of his contemporaries from the majority of their predecessors.

182. Martello and his contemporaries used the terms "entrance" and "exit" to mean just the opposite to what is intended when we use them. For Martello, one "exited" from the wings onto the stage and "entered" the offstage area after one's aria had been completed. The present translation achieves Martello's meaning by substituting "entrances" and "exits" for "escite" and "ingressi."

183. Martello is quite correct when he alludes to the decreasing numbers of entrance and medial arias in the libretti of the period, but it would appear that the reason he cites for their disappearance could not have been what caused their disappearance. One would imagine that the production problem mentioned here by Martello concerned the very presence of arias, not merely their positioning within a scene.

184. The restricting of "entrance" arias to soliloquy scenes beginning immediately after set changes is another convention which distinguishes the Zeno generation of librettists from its predecessors.

185. Martello, *Della tragedia*, pp. 281–91.

186. Martello's view of optics is old-fashioned, but the point of his analogy is clear enough.

187. Martello, *Della tragedia*, pp. 294–95.

188. *Ibid.*, p. 296.

189. A. Galletti, *Le teorie drammatiche*, pp. 134–78.

190. Martello, *Della tragedia*, pp. 297–320.

191. Several pertinent sources of information on the rigidity of middle eighteenth-century *opera seria* conventions have been summarized by Donald Grout, (*Short History of Opera*, pp. 185–86); see also R. Haas, "Josse de Villeneuve's Brief über den Mechanismus der italienischen Oper von 1756," *ZfMw* VII, 129–63.

192. Benedetto Marcello's famous essay of 1720, *Il teatro alla moda*, is, of course, the best known, but it was not without imitators. For a review of these, see U. Rolandi, "Il teatro allamoda di B. Marcello e le sue propaggini," *La scuola veneziana* (Siena, 1941). For a discussion of Marcello's satire itself, see Reinhard G. Pauly, "Benedetto Marcello's 'Il teatro alla moda' " (Columbia University masters thesis, 1947); *idem*, "Benedetto Marcello's Satire on Early Eighteenth-Century Opera," *MQ* XXXIV, 223–33, 371–403; XXXV, 85–105, which includes a complete English translation of Marcello's often translated essay.

193. See p. 44, above.

194. See, for example, notes 107–8.

195. Francesco Quadrio, *Della storia e della ragione d'ogni poesia* (Milan, 1744), III, 434.

196. For an English translation of Raguenet's essay and of Le Cerf de la Vieville's anti-Italian reply of 1704–5, *Comparison de la musique italienne et de la musique française*, see O. Strunk, *Source Readings in Music History* (New York, 1950), pp. 473–507.

197. Johann Mattheson, *Critica musica*, I, 108.

198. None is included at any rate in the list of Arcadians, complete through March 9, 1711, which Crescimbeni appended to his publication, *Arcadia* (Rome, 1711), pp. 329–75.

199. See p. 41, above.

200. Scipione Maffei, *Teatro italiano* (Verona, 1723), I, vii–viii.

201. *Ibid.*, p. xxxviii.

202. For bibliographical information on the *Giornale* and on other Venetian periodicals of the time, see Rosanna Saccardo, *La stampa periodica veneziana fina alla caduta della repubblica* (Padova, 1942).

203. *Giornale dei letterati d'Italia* I, 25–26.

204. Ippolite Pindemonte, "Elogio di Scipione Maffei," *Opere del Maffei* (Venice, 1790), I, 9, 40–41, 127 ff.; the libretto in question, *La fida ninfa*, had been reprinted in an anthology assembled by Antonio Avena, *Scipione Maffei, opere drammatiche e poesie varie* (Bari, 1928), pp. 226–68. Its first appearance in print took place in Maffei's *Teatro italiano* (Verona, 1730); its first performance, with music by Antonio Vivaldi, celebrated the opening of Verona's Teatro Filarmonico in 1732.

205. *Opere del Maffei* (Venice, 1790), I, 86–87.

206. *Ibid.*, I, 128–29.

207. *Ibid.*, I, 149.

208. *Ibid.*, I, 228.

209. *Ibid.*, I, 271–72.

Chapter II

1. An attempt perhaps to answer one of the objections raised by Maffei in his *Teatro italiano* of 1723; see p. 46.

2. Zeno, *Lettere*, no. 894; Metastasio, *Tutte le opere*, III, 305–8.

3. *Novelle della repubblica delle lettere per l'anno MDCCXXXV* (Venice, 1736), pp. 361–64; for a catalogue of Zeno's secular libretti, including those listed on pp. 362–63 of the publication just cited, see Appendix A.

4. Quoted from the original English translation, *An Historical and Critical Account of the Theatres in Europe* (London, 1741), p. 83; for a recent critical biography of Riccoboni and a study of his works, see Xavier de Courville, *Luigi Riccoboni dit Lêlio* (Paris, 1943). See also note 66, above.

5. F. S. Quadrio, *Della storia e della ragione d'ogni poesia* (Milan, 1744), III/2, 425 ff.

6. Zeno, *Lettere*, nos. 810, 914, 1226; Gasparo Gozzi, "A'lettori," *Poesie drammatiche di Apostolo Zeno* (Venice, 1744), IV, xi–xiii.

7. Quoted from Remo Giazotto, *Poesia melodrammatica e pensiero critico nel settecento* (Milan, 1952), p. 94.

8. A. Groppo (ed.), *Catalogo di tutti i drammi* (Venice, 1745), pp. 76–77.

9. Metastasio, *Tutte le opere*, III, 904–7, 947–48, 986–88, 1013, 1068–69.

10. Stefano Arteaga, *Le rivoluzioni*, II, 82; A. Einstein, "Calzabigis 'Erwiderung' von 1790," *Gluck Jahrbuch* II, 68.

11. For information on Calsabigi's *Risposta di Santigliano* (Venice, 1790), see Heinrich Welti, "Gluck und Calzabigi," *VfMw* VII, 26–42; Einstein, *op. cit.*, II, 56–102; III, 25–50; R. Giazotto, *op. cit.*, pp. 103–38.

12. Ranieri de'Calsabigi, "Dissertazione," *Poesie del Signor Abate Metastasio* (Paris, 1755), p. xxiv.

13. *Ibid.*, pp. cxxxi–cxxxii.

14. The text from the original edition of an anonymous English translation of 1768 has been reprinted by O. Strunk (*op. cit.*, pp. 657–72) for the section on the libretto and its musical setting.

15. *Ibid.*, p. 670.

16. *Ibid.*, p. 660.

17. Frugoni (*op.cit.*, pp. 172, 191) complains in 1675 that the audience gives more attention to the singers than to the drama and that the singers are paid more than the librettists, but does not indicate that fees for singers were bankrupting contemporary impresarios. In the chapter of *Annali d'Italia* entitled "Era volg. ann. 1690," while describing the operatic extravagances of the Dukes of Modena and Mantua, Muratori criticizes the practice ". . . which became prevalent during that period, of paying each of the best singers two or three hundred *dopie* or more." (From other financial records of the period it is clear that Muratori must be speaking here of annual salaries.) Bonlini, in a footnote to his listing of the 1720 production of Francesco Muazzo's libretto *Paride* at Venice's Teatro San Giovanni Grisostomo, states that the number of active operatic theaters in Venice had been reduced because of exorbitant demands by the singers, adding that in earlier days the payment of amything more than a hundred *scudi* for a single singer had created a great stir, but that by the 1720s, when his catalogue was in preparation, it was common to pay more than 1,000 *zecchini*. Luigi Riccoboni, in his essay, *Réflexions historiques et critiques sur les differens théâtres de l'Europe* (Paris, 1738), remarks that Italian singers had been overpaid ". . . for something like thirty years."

18. I have been unable to locate any extant copy of this aria.

19. See pp. 40, 51–52.

20. *Riflessioni sopra i drammi per musica* (Venice, 1757), pp. 40–41.

21. A copy of this rare publication is to be found in the Bibliothèque Nationale, Paris. Its contents are as follows: Vol. I—*Merope, Nitocri, Lucio Papirio, Joseph*' Vol. II—*Andromaca, Imeneo, Mitridate, Jonathas*.

22. Giazotto, *op. cit.*, pp. 104–5.

23. Metastasio, *Tutte le opere*, IV, 585.

24. See especially the two pre-Vienna works in which Metastasio did not use a happy ending: *Didone abbandonata* (Naples, 1724) and *Catone in Utica* (Rome, 1728).

25. With regard to the elimination of mythological plots, see pp. 61–62; with regard to the elimination of political deliberations, conspiracies, and the like, see pp. 56–57.

26. Rousseau seems to have relied in this passage on an inaccurate recollection of the 1758 Zeno edition and perhaps on a reading of Algarotti.

27. Planelli, *Dell'opera in musica* (Naples, 1772), pp. 14–15.

28. *Ibid.*, pp. 94, 138–39.

29. Restraint of the variety Planelli recommends here is characteristic of the libretti of the Zeno generation, but not of the works of their immediate predecessors.

30. Planelli is, to my knowledge, the first Italian operatic historian to mention the possibility of a two-act division, and the first Italian since the middle of the seventeenth century to deal at length with the question of the affections.

31. Fabroni, "Apostolus Zenus," *Vitae Italorum* (Florence, 1775), V, 1.

32. *Ibid.*, pp. 4–5, 39–40.

33. *Ibid.*, pp. 67–68.

34. This compilatory history of European theater was written by a Neapolitan essayist, historian, dramatist, and librettist while living in Spain during the first half of the 1770s. Published for the first time in Naples during 1777, it was supplemented by editions of 1787–90 and 1798, appearing in its final form in 1813, two years before its author's death.

35. Napoli-Signorelli, *Storia critica de'teatri antichi e moderni* (Naples, 1813), X, 130–34. "Metastasio" was Trapassi's pen name.

36. For a detailed account of these writers, see Giazotti, *op. cit.*, pp. 139–84.

37. Napoli-Signorelli, *op. cit.*, X, 160–70.

38. Girolamo Tiraboschi, *Storia della letteratura italiana*, vols. XXII–XXV (Milan, 1833) in the series, *Biblioteca enciclopedica italiana*. Tiraboschi's discussion of libretto history is to be found in vol. XXV, 568–70.

39. Stefano Arteaga, *Le rivoluzioni*, 2nd ed. (Venice, 1785), I, xiii–xxv.

40. *Ibid.*, II, 62–63.

41. See Chapter I, notes 48–50.

42. I am reminded by Professor J. M. Knapp that Händel's libretti for both *Teseo* and *Amadigi* exhibit an unusual dependence for the period on the models from which they were derived: Quinault's *Thesée* and Houdar de la Motte's *Amadis de Grèce*.

43. Arteaga, *op. cit.*, II, 67–73.

44. *Ibid.*, II, 78–176.

45. Giazotto, *op. cit.*, pp. 167–68.

46. Carlo Goldoni, *Tutte le opere*, ed. Giuseppe Ortolani (Verona, 1959), V, 685–89.

47. *Ibid.*, I, 187; quoted also in Giazotto, *op. cit.*, pp. 68–69.

48. Giazotto's previously cited *Poesia melodrammatica e pensiero cirtico nel settecento* offers a much more detailed view of later eighteenth-century criticism than is necessary here.

49. Charles Burney, *A General History of Music* (New York, 1957), II, 546, 659, 675, 822, 892, 909.

50. Burney, *Memoirs of the Life and Writings of the Abate Pietro Metastasio* (London, 1796), III, 326.

51. *Parnasso italiano* (Venice, 1790), XLVI, 327–28.

52. Francesco Negri, *Vita di Apostolo Zeno* (Venice, 1816), pp. 36–37, 52–53.

53. *Ibid.*, pp. 53–58.

54. *Ibid.*, pp. 147–59.

55. *Ibid.*, pp. 82–104.

56. *Ibid.*, pp. 64–67.

57. *Ibid.*, pp. 116–17.

58. *Raccolta di melodrammi serii scritti nel secolo XVIII*, ed. Giovanni Gherardini (Milan, 1822), I, vii–xvi. In addition to single works by Giuseppe Parini, Marco Cottellini, Castone della Torre di Rezzonico, Ranieri de'Calsabigi, and F. Saverio de'Rogati (all appearing at the end of Vol. II, this anthology includes the following works by Zeno: Vol. I (secular libretti)—*Temistocle, Andromaca, Merope, Ifigenia in Aulide, Scipione nelle Spagne, Nitocri*; Vol. II (oratorios)—*Sisara, Ezechia, Daniello, Isaia, Naaman, Giuseppe*.

59. J. L. Klein, *Geschichte des Dramas* (Leipzig, 1868), VI/1, 126–87.

60. Francesco De Sanctis, *Storia della letteratura italiana* (Naples, 1870), II, 386.

61. Gustavo Tirinelli, "Silvio Stampiglia," *La scuola romana* (Rome, 1882), pp. 6–10.

62. G. M. Crescimbeni, *Comentarii intorno alla sua storia della volgar poesia* (Venice, 1730), I, 181.

63. M. Landau, *Die italienische Literatur am österreichischen Hofe* (Vienna, 1879), pp. 20–23.

64. *Ibid.*, p. 54.

65. *Ibid.*, pp. 12, 19, 23, 49–50.

66. Isidoro Carini, *L'Arcadia dal 1690 al 1890* (Rome, 1891), pp. 446–93. Arcadian librettists of the seventeenth century listed by Carini but not previously mentioned here, include the following: Giacomo Sinibaldi, Conte Carlo Enrico di San Martino, Pellegrino Masseri, Giacinto Masello, Domenico d'Aguino (Principo di Caramanico), Carmine Niccolo Caracciolo, Nicola Saverio Valletta, Filippo Acciajuoli, Girolamo Bartolommei, Ludovico Adimari, Francesco Palmieri da Pisa, Giovan Cosimo Villifranchi, Bernadino Mescheni, Giovan Andrea Spinola, and Marc'Antonio Rimena.

67. Luigi Pistorelli, *I melodrammi di Apostolo Zeno* (Padua, 1894), p. 10.

68. *Ibid.*, pp. 11–12, 46, 108.

69. Naborre Campanini, *Un precursore del Metastasio* (Florence, 1905), pp. 22, 28.

70. *Ibid.*, pp. 50–51.

71. *Ibid.*, pp. 61–63.

72. *Ibid.*, pp. 65–82.

73. Zeno, *Lettere*, nos. 310, 523, 536, 563, 743, 748, 781, 1119, 1123.

74. *Don Chisciotte nella Sierra Morena* (1719); *Alessandro in Sidone* (1721).

75. Max Fehr, *Apostolo Zeno und seine Reform des Operntextes* (Zurich, 1912), p. 75.

76. *Ibid.*, pp. 78–84.

77. *Ibid.*, p. 85.

78. *Ibid.*, pp. 59–75.

79. *Ibid.*, p. 36.

80. *Ibid.*, p. 58.

81. Hermann Kretzschmar, *Geschichte der Oper* (Leipzig, 1919), pp. 158–62.

82. Robert Haas, "Die Oper in Deutschland bis 1750," *Handbuch der Musikgeschichte*, ed. Guido Adler (Frankfurt/Main, 1924), pp. 681–82.

83. Antonio Belloni, *Il seicento* (Milan, 1929), p. 430.

84. *Ibid.*, pp. 432, 436.

85. Elizabeth C. Salzer, "Teatro italiano in Vienna barocca," *Rivista italiana del dramma* II (1938), 52.

86. *Ibid.*, p. 56.

87. Carlo Calcaterra, *Il Parnasso in rivolta; barocco e antibarocco nella poesia italiana* (Bologna, 1961), p. 229.

88. *Ibid.*, p. 230.

89. Anna A. Abert, "Zum metastasianischen Reformdrama," *Kongressbericht der Gesellschaft für Musikforschung; Lüneburg 1950* (Kassel, n.d.), pp. 138–39.

90. Ulderico Rolandi, *Il libretto per musica attraverso i tempi* (Rome, 1951), pp. 75–78.

91. Remo Giazotto, *Poesia melodrammatica e pensiero critico nel settecento* (Milan, 1952), pp. 11–13.

92. *Ibid.*, pp. 29–30.

93. *Ibid.*, p. 30.

94. Vernon Lee, *Studies of the 18th Century in Italy* (London, 1880); Carlo Calcaterra, *op. cit.*; Alfredo Rolla, *Storia delle idee estetiche in Italia* (Turin, 1905).

95. G. L. Moncallero, *Teorica d'Arcadia* (Florence, 1953), pp. 38–40; 87–90.

96. *Ibid.*, p. 205.

97. Nathaniel Burt, "Opera in Arcadia," *MQ* XLI, 153.

98. Harold Powers, "Il Serse trasformato—I," *MQ* XLVII, 482–84.

99. J. H. VanderMeer, *Johann Josef Fux als Opernkomponist* (Bilthoven, 1961), II, 25.

100. Zeno implies this himself in a letter dated 11 March 1713 and addressed to S. Salvini in Florence. After complaining about the way in which his libretto *Merope* had been distorted for the 1712 premiere in Venice, Zeno concludes, ". . . I confess to you that . . . I am considering revising *Merope* in my own fashion, arranging it as a real tragedy in 11-syllable verses uninterrupted by arais."

101. VanderMeer, *op. cit.*, II, 25.

102. *Ibid.*, II, 29–32.

103. *Ibid.*, II, 8, 10, 11.

104. Fux wrote only two multi-act secular dramatic works after 1715: *Angelica vincitrice di Alcina* (1716), celebrating the birth of Archduke Leopold and Prince Eugene's victory at Peterwardein over the Turks; *Costanza e Fortezza* (1723), in honor of Charles's and Elizabeth's coronation as King and Queen of Bohemia.

105. For bibliographical information on all three groups, see Chapter 1, note 128.

106. Anna A. Abert, "Oper," *MGG* X (Kassel, 1962), col. 9.

Chapter III

1. Powers, *op. cit.*, p. 483.

2. It will be noted that, for reasons of typography, the symbols used in this study are different from similar symbols employed in my article, ''The Travels of Partenope.''

3. The libretti concerned (identified, as are other source materials in this study, according to the RISM code) are the following: Venice (1665)—US-Wc ML 48 S.1739; Naples (1698)—US-Wc ML 48 S.9528; Vienna (1710)—I-Vnm Dramm. 842.6.

4. Since the forewards of other libretti show that Silvio Stampiglia was active in Rome during 1695, in Naples during 1698, and in Vienna during 1710—at about the times that revisions of *Muzio Scevola* were presented in each of those cities—it is quite possible, though by no means certain, that Stampiglia was involved in all three revisions. (That I have not been able to locate a copy of the Roman libretto, listed by Cametti in *Il teatro di Tordinona*, does not affect the present study.)

5. Alfred Lorenz, *Alessandro Scarlattis Jugendoper* (Augsburg, 1927) I, 27.

6. Franz Hadamowsky, *Barocktheater am Wiener Kaiserhof* (Vienna, 1955), p. 100; Kurt Hueber, ''Die Wiener Opern Giovanni Bonocinis von 1697–1710,'' University of Vienna dissertation (1955).

7. Act II scene 3 of the 1710 revision is identical to Act II scene 9 of the 1698 revision.

8. The nurse is named Lesbia in the 1698 revision.

9. [Bonlini,] *Le glorie della poesia, e della musica* (Venice, 1730), pp. 149–50.

10. Zeno, *Lettere*, no. 605.

11. A. Groppo, *Catalogo di tutti i drammi per musica recitati ne'teatri di Venezia dall 1637 sin all'anno presente* (Venice, n.d.), p. 77.

12. That the number of scenes really reflects overall poetic length and not merely a reorganizing of uncut material, may be seen from the following figures:

	1665	1698	1710
Number of pages of printed text in libretto	80	61	69
Largest number of lines per printed page	35	38	39
Approximate number of lines in libretto	2800	2300	2000

13. See p. 8.

14. Martello, who urged librettists never to allow the first sections of their aria texts to exceed four lines in length, ". . . because of intercalation," was not the only contemporary theorist to give such advice. C. F. Hunold (*Theatralische und Geistliche Gedichte*, p. 5) and Barthold Feind (*Deutsche Gedichte*, pp. 97–98) both advise German librettists to limit the length of their *da capo* texts, but indicate the *da capo* itself, rather than "intercalation," as the length-producing element.

15. These two labels may be employed to distinguish the two types of text just outlined from one another. The "reprise," a refrain syntactically separable from its poetic context, is normally used in connection with the older type; the "tag," a word or two which, when detached from context, makes no sense whatever, is normally used in connection with the newer type.

16. Lorenz, *op. cit.*, I, 134 ff.; Hueber, *op. cit.*, I, 220–22.

17. Since the number of stage sets used in the successive productions of a single libretto obviously depended in part upon the facilities afforded by local impresarios, one cannot impute all such reductions to Aristotelian considerations.

18. For Perrucci's views on the subject, see pp. 9–11.

19. The present state of early operatic history makes it impossible, of course, to prove that the libretti charted are all truly representative of the poets who wrote them and of the times and places in which they were written. But in supporting the thesis that Zeno's formats were not extraordinary for the time they were written, it is not necessary to discuss the extent to which libretti from the turn of the eighteenth century, chosen without special bias from the works of Zeno's best known contemporaries, are representative of their authors.

20. For both biographical and bibliographical information on Silvani and the other librettists dealt with in this study, see Umberto Renda and Piero Operti, *Dizionario storico della letteratura italiana*, new ed. by Vittorio Turri (Turin, 1959); *Enciclopedia della spettacolo* (Rome, 1954–62).

21. For an indication that Zeno was not impressed by Frigimelica's pretensions, see the Zeno *Lettere*, nos. 230, 236, 262.

22. From the author's preface to *Mitridate Eupatore* (Venice, 1707), I-Vnm Dramm. 1201.8.

23. I-Vnm Dramm. 1167.5.

24. I-Vnm Dramm. 1178.3.

25. See pp. 49–51, above.

26. For a description of the operatic scene in late seventeenth-century Vienna, see Hadamowsky, *op. cit.*, pp. 7–69; Salzer, *op. cit., passim*; Egon Wellesz, "Die Opern und Oratorien in Wien von 1660–1708," *SzMw* VI, 5–138.

27. Zeno, *Lettere*, nos. 57, 130.

28. Cromiro Dianio.

29. Zeno, *Lettere*, nos. 141–43, 164, 645.

30. See, for example, Stampiglia's *Partenope* (Naples, 1699), one of two Stampiglia libretti mentioned by Zeno (*Lettere*, no. 645) as having brought fame to their author. For an analysis of *Partenope* and 12 of its earliest *rifacimenti*, see my article "The Travels of Partenope."

31. Giazotto, *op. cit.*, p. 11; Hueber, *op. cit.*, pp. 19–20.

32. Pistorelli, *op. cit.*, p. 11; Arteaga, *op. cit.*, II, 68.

33. Only one of Stampiglia's works was produced in Vienna between Charles's succession in 1711 and Stampiglia's departure in 1718. Zeno comments on Charles's coldness towards Stampiglia in a letter dated February 17, 1725, and addressed to his brother, Pier Caterino Zeno, Stampiglia's first biographer.

34. M. Landau, *Geschichte Kaiser Karls VI* (Stuttgart, 1889), pp. 674–76.

35. The term "opera seria," variously applied to all manner of works written between 1650 and the end of the eighteenth century, should be reserved for those works which result from the trends reviewed here. To my knowledge, its first appearance during the eighteenth century was as the title of a work by Calsabigi, produced in Vienna during 1769 with music by Gassmann.

36. One ought not to overlook the possibility that although such roles appear in print to be perfectly harmless, there would have been no obstacle in the theater itself to the coarsest of pantomime and improvisation.

37. See, for example, Metastasio's classic letters to Pasquini, Dieskau, and Hasse (librettist, impresario, and composer)—nos. 273, 275–77 in B. Brunelli's recent edition of Metastasio's works—on stage positions for each of the singers in the Dresden (1748) production of *Demofoonte*. One ought not to forget that Metastasio was himself the author of the satiric intermezzo, *L'impresario delle Canarie*, produced in Naples during 1724 between the acts of Metastasio's own *Didone abbandonata*.

38. The table is based on the most recent edition of Metastasio's works, *Tutte le opere*, ed. Bruno Brunelli (Milan, 1943–54).

39. I-Vgc Sartorio, whose preface indicates that the Venetian text of 1666 represents a somewhat revised version of the (now missing) original, first produced in Naples.

40. I-Vnm Dramm. 1198.4.

41. Zeno himself admitted that earlier works usually tend to be forgotten in the glow of later successes (*Lettere*, no. 749). But he seems, nonetheless, to have been fond of particular works: *Merope* (1712), *Ifigenia in Aulide* (1718), *Nitocri* (1722), *Cajo Fabbricio* (1729); for his comments on these, see the *Lettere*, nos. 310, 435, 588, 749. In a letter dated 30 December 1740 and addressed to the Modenese impresario, Domenico

Vandelli, Zeno recalls that it was with *Lucio Vero* (1700) that he first made his reputation in Italy, but he adds that his Viennese works represent his best achievement in the genre.

42. On Zeno's self-confessed lack of musical background, see the *Lettere*, nos. 207, 434, 505, 1180.

Chapter IV

1. There is no apparent reason why Caldara did not make the original settings for Zeno's *Meride e Selinunte* (Vienna, 1721) and for Metastasio's *Issipile* (Vienna, 1732), composed by Giuseppe Porsile and Francesco Conti, respectively.

2. The 23 such libretti set by Caldara are catalogued on pp. 174–76 in a list which, comprising all of Caldara's Vienna settings of full-length *seria* libretti by Zeno and Metastasio, includes two libretti which Zeno had written before 1718 for productions in Italy and Spain: *Venceslao* (Venice, 1703) and *Scipione nelle Spagne* (Barcelona, 1710). Caldara may conceivably have been the composer of the *Scipione* music performed in Barcelona, but, if so, he must have set the libretto twice, for Caldara's dated autograph for the 1722 production in Vienna (A–Wgm Caldara autograph no. 49) is clearly a composing score.

3. Evidence of Caldara's Venetian origin includes the title page of his first publication (*Suonate a 3* Venice, 1693), where he is described as "Musico di violoncello veneto"; the introduction to the libretto *Anagilda* (Rome, 1711), where he is named as the Marchese Ruspoli's "Veneziano maestro di cappella"; and the use of the qualifying "Venetiano" after every appearance of his name in the 1755 edition of Allacci's *Drammaturgia*. Although the registrations of Caldara's birth and baptism are still to be found, two independent records of his death in Vienna (a burial certificate in the Archive of St. Stephen's and an obituary in the *Wiener Diarium*) agree upon December 28, 1736, as the date of death and upon 66 years as Caldara's age at death.

4. Francesco Caffi, "Storia della musica teatrale in Venezia," four-volume unpublished manuscript in the Biblioteca Marciana, Venice (Marciana MS 10465). Caffi's biography of Caldara is to be found between folios 78 and 81.

5. *L'Argene* (Venice, 1689) and *La promessa serbata al primo* (Venice, 1697)—I-Vnm Dramm. 1295.1 and 1188.5, respectively. According to *Allacci 1755*, Caldara also set the second act of Zeno's *Tirsi* (Venice, 1696); Wotquenne's *Catalogue de la bibliothèque du Conservatoire Royal de Musique de Bruzelles* lists as no. 703 a manuscript anthology of arias alleged to include several by Caldara from the second act of *Tirsi*, but repeated requests for a microfilm have yielded no response. There are no known extant musical remains for either *L'Argene* or *La promessa serbata*.

6. Claudio Sartori, *Bibliografia della musica strumentale stampata in Italia fino al 1700* (Florence, 1952), items 1693j (1700e) and 1699c.

7. *Cantate da camera a voce sola* (Venice, 1699). This publication, of which I know no extant copy, is cited in J. G. Walther's *Musikalisches Lexikon* (Leipzig, 1732), p. 128.

8. A transcript of Caldara's letter of appointment as Mantuan *maestro di cappella*, found by the author in Mantua's Archivio di State, comprises Appendix B.

9. For more information on the last days of Gonzagan rule in Mantua, see Federigo Amadei, *Cronaca universale della citta di Mantova* (Mantua, 1954–55); G. Fochessati, *I Gonzaga di Mantova* (Milan, 1930); for an article on the Mantuan musical scene during Caldara's tenure there, see Ursula Kirkendale, "The War of the Spanish Succession Reflected in Works of Antonio Caldara," *Acta* XXXVI, 221–33.

10. *Il selvaggio eroe* (Venice, 1707)—I–Vnm Dramm. 1202.5.

11. Fochessati, *op. cit.*, p. 249.

12. R. Lustig, "Saggio bibliografico degli oratorii stampati a Firenze dal 1690 al 1725," *Note d'archivio per la storia musicale* XIV, 116.

13. For a list, discovered by the author in Mantua's Archivio di Stato, of operas performed in Mantua between 1708 and 1752, see Appendix C. An eighteenth-century manuscript score, entitled *L'ingratitudine castigata* and bearing an attribution to Caldara in the hand of the scribe who copied the score, survives as part of the Santini Collection in the Library of the Episcopal Seminary, Münster.

14. Kirkendale, *op. cit.*, p. 223.

15. Joseph Rafel Carreras y Bulbena, *Carlos d'Austria y Elisabeth de Brunswick-Wolfenbüttel* (Barcelona, 1902), pp. 120, 124, 150–56; E. I. Luin, "Sulla vita e sulle opere di Antonio Caldara," *La scuola veneziana* (Siena, 1941), pp. 41–42. That Caldara must indeed have spent some time in Charles's Barcelona court is clear from a variety of evidence cited by Carreras and Luin, but their publications abound both in gratuitous assumptions and in inconsistencies with the accounts of chroniclers actually present in early eighteenth-century Barcelona, e.g., D. G. Francesco Gemelli Careri, *Aggiunta a viaggi di Europe* (Naples, 1711).

16. I-Vnm Dramm. 1203.1, p. 12.

17. *La Partenope* (Ferrara, 1709)—I-Bc 737, p. 11; *L'inimico generoso* (Bologna, 1709)—I-Bc 738, p. 5. On the latter's lack of success, see Corrado Ricci, *I teatri di Bologna nei secoli XVII e XVIII* (Bologna, 1888), p. 403. A score (A-Wn 17200) entitled *L'inimico generosa* and attributed to Caldara, agrees in all particulars with the Bologna libretto of 1709. Manferrari (*Dizionario universale delle opere*) and Paumgartner (*Enciclopedia dello spettacolo* article on Caldara) notwithstanding, there is no evidence that *L'inimico generoso* was ever produced in Vienna.

18. Kirkendale, *op. cit.*, p. 223.

19. For a short but useful article on Ruspoli, see H. Hucke, "Ruspoli, Francesco Maria Marchese di," *MGG* XI, 1126–28.

20. Kirkendale, *op. cit.*, p. 223. The publication of Ruspoli's household documents, discovered by Kirkendale in the Ruspoli Archive of the Biblioteca Vaticana among *buste* no longer available to the public, is forthcoming.

21. In the baptismal certificate of his only child, a daughter born in Vienna during early May, 1717, Caldara is called "Magister Capellae Augustissimi Imperatoris" (Protocollem Baptiztor, Cathedral Archive of St. Stephen's, Vienna, 1.4.1711–24.1.1713; the certificate for Sophia Jacobina Maria Caldara is dated May 9, 1712). In the libretto for the new production of Zeno's *Atenaide*, performed in Vienna on November 27, 1714, Caldara (who composed the third act of the new setting) is called "Compositore di camera di S.M.C.C." (A-Wgm Opere Carolinae I.3).

22. In addition to the third act of *Atenaide*, cited above, there were three oratorios: *S. Ferma* (A-Wn 17080); *Maddalena ai piedi di Christo* (A-Wn 17101); *S. Flavia Domitilla* (A-Wn 18142).

23. *Motetti a due, a tre voci*, op. 4 (Bologna, 1715).

24. The dedication has been reprinted in G. Gaspari's *Catalogo della biblioteca del Liceo musicale di Bologna* (Bologna, 1892), II, 389.

25. The Gesellschaft der Musikfreunde's Caldara autograph collection includes a cantata entitled "Non trovo fedeltà," dated August 8, 1716 in Vienna. The first use at Court of operatic music by the newly appointed *Vizekapellmeister* came on November 19, 1716, with the performance of Caldara's intermezzi *Barlafusa e Pipa* after Acts I, II, and IV of Antonio Lotti's *Costantino*.

26. J. H. VanderMeer, *Johann Josef Fux als Opernkomponist* (Bilthoven, 1961), I, 10.

27. Haus-, Hof-, und Staatsarchiv, Vienna: Obersthofmeisteracten (1715), no. 41. A German translation of this document appeared as early as 1886 in La Mara, *Musikerbriefe aus fünf Jahrhunderten*, I, 147–48. A transcript of the Italian original was appended, together with a variety of other documents concerning Caldara's financial dealings after 1716 with the Habsburgs, to the 1894 dissertation of the well-known Wagnerian bass, Felix Kraus—"Biographie des K. K. Vize-Hof-Kapellmeisters, Antonio Caldara."

28. Ludwig von Köchel, *Johann Josef Fux* (Vienna, 1872), Appendix VI, document no. 16. For Fux's reactions to other financial requests made by Caldara and his widow, see documents nos. 174, 179, 246.

29. Kirkendale, *op. cit.*, p. 223.

30. Zeno, *Lettere*, nos. 412–19.

31. The overtures to *Il Tiridate* (1717); *L'inganno tradito dall'amore* (1720); *Amalasunta* (1726); *La verità nell'inganno* (1727): A-Wgm Caldara autographs nos. 39, 45, 56, and 58, respectively. These four pieces, all beginning with slow movements in the French manner, are marked "Overture, largo," "_____," "And^te alla francese," and "Largo e staccato." The overture to *L'inganno tradito dall'amore* concludes with

a bi-partite minuet, as does that for *Il Tiridate*, added only, however, after Caldara had written "Fine dell'Ouverture" after a proceding section in slow tempo.

32. For more information on similar pieces by Caldara's contemporaries and successors, see Herbert Livingston, "The Italian Overture from Alessandro Scarlatti to Mozart," University of North Carolina dissertation, 1952.

33. Except, of course, as indicated above in note 31. That Caldara was not especially careful to distinguish the "French" and "Italian" types through special generic designations is indicated by the fact that the overture to *La verità nell'inganno* (1727), a tri-partite piece in the "French" manner, is followed by the words "Fine dell'Introduzione"—Caldara's normal remark after the conclusion of an overture in the "Italian" manner.

34. This useful term seems to have been coined by Rudolf Gerber in his *MGG* I article, "Arie." It has been adopted in the meantime by E.D.D. Downes in his superlative Harvard dissertation (1958), "The Operas of Johann Christian Bach as a Reflection of the Dominant Trends in Opera Seria, 1750–80," and by Donald Grout in the second edition (New York, 1965) of his *Short History of Opera*. For information on Caldara and the five-part *da capo* aria, see pp. 213–14 ff.

35. The overture to the pastorale *Amor non ha legge* (1726) is of interest in this respect. After a 33-bar *allegro* and a 4-bar *adagio*, the overture concludes with an instrumental "aria alla pastorale" in 12/8, outlined below.

$$I \text{ —— } I \quad \overset{\frown}{:\|} : \quad III \text{ —— } III \quad :\| \quad DC$$
$$\underset{\text{Fine}}{}$$

no. of bars: 4   6

However, the aria is followed by an unusual bit of eighteenth-century aleatoric philosophy: "Se piacesse doppo questa aria si puo ripigliar il primo allegro, e finir con quell l'introduzione."

36. Robert Haas, *Die estensischen Musikalien* (Regensburg, 1927), p. 34.

37. *Virgolette* appear less frequently in Italian libretti from later in the eighteenth century, but when one is dealing, for example, with a 1750 *rifacimento* of a libretto first printed in 1710, the absence of *virgolette* in the 1750 version hardly ever indicates adherence to the recitative of the original libretto. A line-for-line comparison of the recitative in two such libretti consistently shows that the problem of excessive recitative has been solved in the later version simply by cutting a great deal of it, without recourse to *virgolette*.

38. X's not connected with such situations were probably made by the scribes responsible for the copy scores and parts.

39. The following will help put the figure quoted for Zeno recitative in the proper perspective. The complete texts for Rinuccini's *Dafne* and *Euridice* comprise 445 and 790

lines, respectively. Of the 722 lines in the complete text of Alessandro Striggio's *Orfeo*, fewer than 400 are composed of recitative. In Da Ponte's *Nozze di Figaro* and in his *Cosi fan tutte* there are fewer than 900 lines of recitative each.

40. VanderMeer, *op. cit.*, II, 49–68, 241–42.

41. For more on eighteenth-century recitative and on the origin of the term "secco," see E. O. D. Downes, "Secco Recitative in early Classical Opera Seria," *JAMS* XIV.

42. Metastasio, *Tutte le opere*, ed. Brunelli (Milan, 1948–54), III, 431–35; IV, 383–84.

43. Downes, "The Operas of Johann Christian Bach," pp. 359–60. Eighteenth-century Italy's most enthusiastic composer of *accompagnato* was almost certainly Niccolò Jommelli, in whose opera *Pelope* (Stuttgart, 1754) there are 10 complete scenes of instrumentally accompanied recitative. [H. Abert, *Niccolo Jommelli als Opernkomponist* (Halle, 1908), p. 276].

44. Metastasio, *Tutte le opere*, V, 402. That Caldara was a musical conservative in other respects as well is indicated in a letter addressed by Metastasio on May 7, 1770, to Saverio Mattei (*Tutte le opere*, V, 9): ". . . With regard to the Marcello *Psalms*, I must confess . . . that I do not know enough music to judge them properly. I do remember hearing them spoken of rather disparagingly by the most accredited craftsmen. The celebrated Caldara, a worthy contrapuntalist and Emperor Charles VI's favorite *maestro di cappella*, . . . once said of the Marcello *Psalms* in my presence: 'I would not know how to find anything rare except extravagance in these pieces.' " That a letter of Francesco Conti written during 1723 in praise of Marcello's *Psalms* was among those used by their composer as a preface to the second volume of the *Psalms*, suggests that difference in musical outlook which I find reflected in the music of Caldara and Conti.

45. Composing scores are extant for both settings: A-Wgm Caldara autograph nos. 39 and 58.

46. For a summary and bibliography of these theorists, see VanderMeer, *op. cit.*, II, 207–25, 242, 251–53.

47. A-Wgm Caldara autograph no. 38.

48. A-Wgm Caldara autograph no. 56.

49. The setting performed in 1730, including the revised part for Eumene, constitutes A-Wn 18240. The castrato who performed Eumene, named Giovanni in the scores for both productions, was probably the same person on both occasions.

50. For a contemporary revision apparently motivated by considerations such as these, see H. Hucke, "Die beiden Fassungen der Oper 'Didone abbandonata' von Domenico Sarri," *Kongressbericht der Gesellschaft für Musikforschung: Hamburg 1956* (Kassel, 1957), pp. 113–17.

51. The single exception: Fux's setting of Pariati's libretto *Elisa*, first performed in Vienna on August 28, 1719, and published in Amsterdam during the same year by Jeanne Roger.

52. For a comprehensive catalogue of the manuscript collection richest in operatic materials from seventeenth- and eighteenth-century Vienna, the Österreichische National-bibliothek, see J. Mantuani, *Tabulae codicum manusciptorum*, vols. IX–X (Vienna, 1897-99).

53. For a locator list of Caldara's extant autographs for the secular dramatic works, see Appendix D.

54. A-Wgm Caldara autograph no. 40.

55. For a comprehensive survey of those theorists, see Friedrich-Heinrich Neumann, "Die Theorie des Rezitativs im 17. und 18. Jahrhunderts unter besonderer Berücksichtigung des deutschen Musikschriftums des 18. Jahrhunderts," University of Göttingen dissertation, 1955. The first chapter of the dissertation, "Die Aesthetik des Rezitative," was published as a monograph in 1962 by Heitz of Strasbourg.

56. In their studies of eighteenth-century Italy, German scholars should pay at least as much attention to Italian theorists as to German. Tosi will never win a reputation as a speculative theorist, but he knew the early eighteenth-century operatic scene in Italy at least as well as men like Werckmeister and Mattheson. Tosi's complaint that modern composers ". . . neglect with too harmful indifference the teaching of recitative composition to their students" [*Opinioni de' cantori antichi e moderni*, ed. L. Leonesi (Naples, 1904), p. 70], that they ". . . do not wish to spend their precious time in writing recitatives which, according to their dogmas, ought to be let fall from the pen and not from the mind" (*ibid.*, p. 72), finds a readier echo than the German theorists in one who has read through volumes of Caldara's secular recitatives.

57. L. A. Muratori, *Della perfetta poesia italiana* (Modena, 1706) II, 44.

58. Salvadori, *Poetica toscana all'uso* (Naples, 1691), p. 32.

59. Martello, *Della tragedia antica e moderna* (Rome, 1715), reprinted in *Scrittori d'Italia* CCXXV, 286–89.

60. Planelli, *Dell'opera in musica* (Naples, 1772), pp. 47 ff.

61. Benedetto Marcello, *Il teatro alla moda* (Venice, 1720), English translation by R. Pauly in *MQ* XXXIV, 379, 382–83.

62. Goldoni, *Tutte le opere*, ed. Giuseppe Ortolani (Verona, 1959) I, 129.

63. John Brown, *Letters on the Italian Opera*, 2nd ed. (London, 1791), quoted by D. Grout in *A Short History of Opera* (New York, 1947), p. 185. One of the statements most clearly implying that such schemes as Brown's represent compositional thinking of the time, is to be found in W. J. Rockstro's article, "aria," first appearing in the second edition of *Grove's Dictionary* and retained, with additions, since then. Having troped

Brown, Rockstro continues: "Though we sometimes meet with operatic airs of the eighteenth century which seem, at first sight, inconsistent with this rigid system of classification, a little careful scrutiny will generally enable us to refer them, with tolerable ,certainty, to one or other of the universally recognized orders."

64. Taddeo Wiel, *I teatri musicali veneziani del settecento* (Venice, 1897), p. xxxiv.

65. Bernard Flögel, "Studien zur Arientechnik in den Opern Händels," *Händel Jahrbuch* II, 150–56.

66. Rudolf Gerber, "Arie," *MGG* 1, cols. 620–21. Gerber's threefold scheme comprises ". . . die virtuose Bravourarie, . . . die Arien *'di mezzo carattere'*. . . . und die Largo- und Adagiosätze. . . ."

67. J. H. VanderMeer, *op. cit.*, II, 69–97.

68. Schemes in which aria texts are categorized without any implication that specific kinds of texts determine specific varieties of musical setting include the following: Max Fehr, *Apostolo Zeno und seine Reform des Operntextes* (Zurich, 1912): action texts, reflective texts, comparison texts; Alice Gmeyner, "Die Opern M. A. Caldaras," University of Vienna dissertation, 1927: texts suggesting pictorial illustration, texts involving expression of individual reaction, texts of allegiance and homage; Edward Dent, "The Operas," *Handel, A Symposium* (London, 1954): texts in which one character expresses emotion to another character directly; sententious texts, philosophical texts.

69. VanderMeer, *op. cit.*, II, 70–72, 83, 96.

70. For a comparison of Caldara's setting of a Metastasio libretto with subsequent settings of the same text by Hasse, Gluck, Galuppi, and Mozart, see William J. Weichlein, "A Comparative Study of Five Musical Settings of *La Clemenza di Tito*." University of Michigan dissertation, 1956. For more on the degree to which Caldara's musical reaction to a specific text was apt to vary from the reactions of his contemporaries, see Appendix E.

71. Metastasio, *Tutte le opere* (ed. Brunelli) V, 402.

72. See, for example, C. F. Hunold, *Theatralische Galante und Geistliche Gedichte von Menantes*, (Hunold's pseudonym), (Hamburg, 1706), pp. 89–113.

73. *Poesie drammatiche*, the first collected edition of Zeno's sacred and secular dramatic works (Venice, 1744), prints "dolce" in place of "amabile."

74. Rudolf Gerber, "Arie," *MGG* I, cols. 619–21.

75. E. O. D. Downes, "The Operas of Johann Christian Bach," pp. 19–20.

76. In the autograph scores of Caldara's operas the composer never writes out the *da capo*; that the copyists of the scores intended for Charles VI's personal library punctiliously copied out the same *da capos*, without ever adding any clues about the location

or variety of ornamentation to be performed in the *da capo* repeats, suggests that Habsburg copyists of the period were paid by the page.

77. The most comprehensive discussion to date of aria forms in eighteenth-century *opera seria* is to be found in Downes's just-cited dissertation, pp. 386–425.

78. See, for example, Egon Wellesz, "Die Opern und Oratorien in Wien von 1660–1708," *SzMw* VI, 5–138; and, more particularly, Owen Jander, "Alessandro Stradella and his Minor Dramatic Works," Harvard University dissertation, 1962, pp. 225–26.

79. I-Rsc.

80. A-Wn 18091.

81. In this and in other similar diagrams in the pages which follow, "a/1" and "a/2," for example, refer to the first and second halves of textual line "a".

82. Copies of the requisite libretti may be compared in the Archive of the Gesellschaft der Musikfreunde, Vienna: A-Wgm Opere Leopoldinae I.7 and VI.5.

83. G. G. Salvadori, *Poetica toscana* (Naples, 1691), pp. 34, 77–79, 85.

84. C. F. Hunold, *op. cit.*, pp. 5–6.

85. Barthold Feind, "Gedancken von der Opera," *Deutsche Gedichte* (Hamburg, 1708), pp. 97–98.

86. Martello, *op. cit.*, p. 287.

87. The charts that follow are based on Caldara's composing score, A-Wgm Caldara autograph no. 37.

88. The charts that follow are based on A-Wn 17192/2.

89. The charts that follow are based on A-Wn 16692, identified by Robert Haas [Comitato per le onoranze a Filippo Juvarra, *Filippo Juvarra* (Milan, 1937), p. 145] as the score for the opera ordered from Rome by Emperor Joseph I a few months before his sudden death from smallpox on April 17, 1711. There is no evidence that *Giunio Bruto*, whose three acts were composed by Cesarini, Caldara, and Alessandro Scarlatti, and whose stage sets were the invention of Filippo Juvarra, was ever performed in Vienna. The internal evidence of all three acts and the fact that Cesarini, Caldara, Scarlatti, and Juvarra were all in Rome during 1710–11 support Haas's dating of the score against 1694, the date assigned to it by Umberto Manferrari in his often unreliable *Dizionario universale delle opere melodrammatiche* (Florence, 1954).

90. J. H. VanderMeer, *op. cit.*, II, 99–134.

91. For a bibliography of the relevant theorists, see VanderMeer, *op. cit.*, II, 251–53. For a comprehensive survey of the same theorists, see H. H. Unger, *Die Beziebungen zwischen Musik und Rhetorik im 16.–18. Jahrhundert* (Wurzburg, 1941).

92. A comparison of all 33 pairs of closed forms in Caldara's two settings of *La verità* does indicate that Caldara may have allowed the text he was setting to influence his decision to include or to omit an introductory instrumental ritornello. Of the 13 musical numbers that begin in 1717 without an introductory ritornello, all but two begin in the same fashion in the 1727 setting. And there is no aria text which, having been set without an introductory ritornello in 1717, is given one in 1727. Situations for which Caldara seems not to have favored the use of introductory ritornelli are of three kinds: slow movements, wherein the length of time required for the ritornello might have proven dramatically embarrassing to singers unskilled in pantomime; arias like those in *La verità* I/10 and II/3, occuring at moments where a dramatic challenge posed in recitative demands an immediate answer in the aria that follows; and *allegretto* movements in 3/8.

93. Eberhard Preussner, *Die musikalischen Reisen des Herrn von Uffenbach* (Kassel, 1949), p. 82.

94. Martello, *op. cit.*, p. 291.

95. Marcello, *op. cit.*, p. 383.

96. Tosi, *op. cit.*, pp. 82–83.

97. Giuseppe Riva, *Advice to the Composers and Performers of Vocal Music*, translated from Italian (London, 1727), pp. 5–7.

98. Burney, *Memoirs of the Life and Writings of the Abate Pietro Metastasio* (London, 1796), III, 183–84.

99. Hugo Goldschmidt, *Die Lehre von der vokalen Ornamentik* (Berlin, 1907), p. 51.

100. Alice Gmeyner, "Die Opern M. A. Caldaras," University of Vienna dissertation, 1927, pp. 162–64. (The use of an "M" in connection with Caldara's name is evidently the result of misprint or a misunderstanding. I know of no extant documents in which the initial "M" precedes Caldara's name.)

101. VanderMeer, *op. cit.*, II, 222–25.

102. On the history and significance of "arie cavate," see N. Pirrotta, "Falsirena e la più antiche delle cavatine," *Collectanea historiae musichae* II, 356–66.

103. A-Wgm Caldara autograph no. 38.

104. A-Wgm Caldara autograph no. 53.

105. A-Wn 17144.

106. Robert Haas, *Die Musik des Barocks* (Potsdam, 1928), p. 202; E. O. D. Downes, "The Operas of Johann Christian Bach," pp. 289–90.

107. Hunold, *op. cit.*, p. 92.

108. R. Freeman, "The Travels of Partenope," *Studies in Music History, Essays in Honor of Oliver Strunk* (Princeton, 1968), pp. 356–85.

109. Rudolf Gerber, *Der Operntypus Johann Adolf Hasses und seine textlichen Grundlagen* (Leipzig, 1925), p. 29.

110. For a catalogue of instrumentalists employed by the Habsburgs during Caldara's tenure in Vienna, see Ludwig von Köchel, *Die kaiserliche Hofmusikkapelle in Wien, 1543–1867* (Vienna, 1869). For a comparison of the Viennese *Hofmusikkapelle* with other establishments of the period, see A. Carse, *The Orchestra in the 18th Century* (London, 1940), pp. 18–27.

111. Bearing call numbers adjacent to those of the copy scores, these skeletal sets of instrumental parts, labelled "Parti cavate quattro," have been catalogued by J. Mantuani in *Tabulae codicum manuscriptorum* (Vienna, 1897-99), vols. IX–X.

112. Köchel, *Die kaiserliche Hofmusikkapelle*, pp. 72–81.

113. VanderMeer, *op. cit.*, II, 203.

114. W. Fischer, "Zur Entwicklungsgeschichte des Wiener klassischen Stils," *SzMw* III, 24–84.

115. One can tell something about the speed at which Caldara must have worked, not only from the great number of works he turned out in Vienna for several patrons and from the internal evidence of the operatic scores themselves, but also from the dates with which he so carefully furnished those scores. (The composing score for *Demetrio* concludes with the remark, "Fine a 12 7bre all'ore 9 di Mattina.") The majority of the 25 scores under study here were completed less than a month before the date of their first performance. Metastasio told Burney (*The Present State of Music in Germany, the Netherlands, etc.*, ed. P. Scholes under the title, *Dr. Burney's Musical Tours in Europe* (London, 1959), II, 103) that *Achille in Sciro* was conceived and completed in all respects within 18 days. In the cases of *Enone* and *Temistocle*, among others, Caldara's dates upon the completion of successive acts enable us to determine his compositional speed even more precisely. The five acts of *Enone* were completed on the 14th, 19th, 23rd, 27th, and 30th of July 1729; the three acts of *Temistocle*, Caldara's last *opera seria*, were completed on September 20, September 30, and October 5, 1736.

116. A-Wgm Caldara autograph no. 73.

117. G. M. Crescimbeni, *Comentarii intorno alla sua istoria della volgar poesia* (Rome, 1702), I, 239–40. Crescimbeni refers here explicitly to Cardinal Pietro Ottoboni's *Adonia*, but he may well have been thinking of the works of Frigimelica as well.

118. Burney, *Memoirs of the Life and Writings of the Abate Pietro Metastasio* (London, 1796), I, 329; also in Metastasio, *Tutte le opere* (ed. Brunelli), III, 435.

119. Metastasio, "Estratto dell'arte poetica," *Tutte le opere* (ed. Brunelli), II, 1061–62.

120. Metastasio's letter of instructions to Hasse on the setting of *Attilio* (*Tutte le opere*, III, 427–36) is very instructive. One gathers from a number of letters (*Tutte le opere*, III, 488–89, 522–29, 539–40) that Metastasio was especially fond of this work.

Chapter V

1. While the Viennese scores of Conti and Bonocini, for example, were reused elsewhere in Europe, those of Caldara were not. The Zeno and Metastasio libretti set by Caldara were, of course, produced widely throughout the century, but with musical settings by other composers. This situation contrasts with the naturally wider dissemination of Caldara's earlier publications of instrumental and sacred music, some of which had made enough of an impression on Telemann for him to have mentioned Caldara, Steffani, Rosenmüller, and Corelli as the four composers whose works he had used as models. [Johann Mattheson, *Grundlage einer Ehrenpforte*, ed. M. Schneider (Berlin, 1910), p. 357.]

2. For more information on Francesco Conti, the most modern of the three principal Habsburg composers active in Vienna during Caldara's stay there, see, in addition to Paumgartner's article in *MGG* II, Josef Schneider, "Francesco Conti als dramatischer Komponist," University of Vienna dissertation, 1902; Wulf Arlt, "Zur Deutung der Barockoper: 'Il trionfo dell'amicizia e dell'amore' " (a work by Conti), *Musik und Geschichte, Leo Schrade zum sechsigsten Geburtstag* (Cologne, 1963), pp. 96–145. A Columbia University dissertation on Conti's life and operatic works was completed in 1963 by Hermine Williams, but, in accord with its author's wish, a Columbia regulation keeps it from being read before the summer of 1968.

3. A Caldara Magnificat in C, copied in the hand of J. S. Bach, was reported by Philipp Spitta in *Joh. Seb. Bach*, 2nd ed. (Leipzig, 1916), II, 509.

4. For a comparative summary of salaries paid to Habsburg musicians in Vienna, see Köchel, *Die kaiserliche Hofmusikkapelle in Wien, 1543–1867* (Vienna, 1869); the documents relevant to Caldara's financial negotiations with the Habsburgs are transcribed in appendices to Felix Kraus's University of Vienna dissertation, 1894, "Biographie des K. K. Vize-Hof-Kapellmeisters, Antonio Caldara (1670–1736)."

5. For information on Charles VI's activities as composer and performer, see Guido Adler, "Ferdinand III, Leopold I, Joseph I, und Karl VI als Förderer der Musik, *VfMw* VIII, 252–74.

6. A-Wgm Caldara autograph no. 37.

7. Pasquini's *Don Chisciotte in corte della Duchessa* (Vienna, 1727); Pasquini's *I disingannati* (Vienna, 1729); Minato's *La pazienza di Socrate con due moglie* (Vienna, 1731); Pasquini's *Sancio Panza governatore dell'isola Barattaria* (Vienna, 1734). (For the Minato libretto Caldara composed only the overture and the third act.) The composing scores for all four works may be found in the Archive of the Gesellschaft der Musikfreunde: A-Wgm Caldara autographs nos. 57, 63, 69, and 68, respectively.

Appendix A

A List of Zeno's Libretti

Zeno's Libretti

Title	Date of first production	Place	Composer(s)	Poesie drammatiche, volume
Gl'inganni felici	1695/96	Venice	C. F. Pollarolo	7
Il Tirsi	1696 (fall)	Venice	I —A. Lotti II —Caldara III —A. Ariosti IV and V— ?	
Il Narciso	1697	Anspach	F. A. Pistocchi	7
I rivali generosi	1697	Venice	G. Vignati	5
Eumene	1697/98	Venice	M. A. Ziani	5
Odoardo	1698	Venice	M. A. Ziani	
Faramondo	1699	Venice	C. F. Pollarolo	6
Lucio Vero	1700	Venice	C. F. Pollarolo	3
Temistocle	1701	Vienna	M. A. Ziani	1
Griselda	1701	Venice	Ant. Pollarolo	3
Il Venceslao	1703	Venice	C. F. Pollarolo	5
Aminta	1703	Florence	Albinoni	6

Title	Date of first production	Place	Composer(s)	Poesie drammatiche, volume
Pirro	1704	Venice	Aldovrandini	7
Il Teuzzone	1706	Milan	P. Magni & C. Monari	4
L'amor generoso	1707	Venice	Fr. Gasparini	6
La Svanvita	1707	Milan	A. Fiore	7
Engelberta	1708	Milan		4
Atenaide	1709	Barcelona	I —A. Fiore II —Caldara III—Fr. Gasparini	1
Scipione nelle Spagne	1710	Barcelona	? see Chapter IV, note 2	4
Merope	1711/12	Venice	Fr. Gasparini	1
Alessandro Severo	1717	Venice	A. Lotti	6
Ifigenia in Aulide	1718	Vienna	Caldara	1
Sirita	1719	Vienna	Caldara	6
Lucio Papirio	1719	Vienna	Caldara	1
Psiche	1720	Vienna	Fux and Caldara	7
Meride e Selinunte	1721	Vienna	G. Porsile	3
Ormisda	1721	Vienna	Caldara	4
Nitocri	1722	Vienna	Caldara	3
Euristeo	1724	Vienna	Caldara	5
Andromaca	1724	Vienna	Caldara	2
Gianguir	1724	Vienna	Caldara	2
Semiramide in Ascalona	1725	Vienna	Caldara	2
I due dittatori	1726	Vienna	Caldara	2

Title	Date of first production	Place	Composer(s)	Poesie drammatiche, volume
Imeneo	1727	Vienna	Caldara	4
Ornospade	1727	Vienna	Caldara	2
Mitridate	1728	Vienna	Caldara	5
Cajo Fabriccio	1729	Vienna	Caldara	1
Enone	1734	Vienna	Caldara	3

Libretti Written in Collaboration with Pietro Pariati

Title	Date of first production	Place	Composer(s)	Poesie drammatiche, volume
Antioco	1705	Venice	Fr. Gasparini	10
Artaserse	1705	Venice	Ant. Zanettini	10
Ambleto	1706	Venice	Fr. Gasparini	9
Statira	1706	Venice	Fr. Gasparini	10
Flavio Anicio Olibrio	1707/08	Venice	Fr. Gasparini	10
Astarto	1708	Venice	Albinoni	10
Il falso Tiberino	1708/09	Venice	C. F. Pollarolo	
Zenobia	1709	Barcelona	?	
Sesostri	1710	Venice	Fr. Gasparini	9
Costantino	1711	Venice	Fr. Gasparini	9
Don Chisciotte in Sierra Morena	1719	Vienna	Fr. Conti	9
Alessandro in Sidone	1721	Vienna	Fr. Conti	9

Appendix B

Caldara's Patent of Appointment
as Gonzagan *Maestro di Cappella* in Mantua

Archivio di Stato—Mantua
    R. Mandati; Vol. 61—ab anno 1698 usque ad Annum 1704;

Riesse così singolare in n[ost]ro concetto la molta virtù di Ant[oni]o Caldara, nella profess[ion]e del contrapunto, cantar di musica e tasteggiare, oltre il Cembalo, diverse sorti d'Instrum[en]ti della q[ua]lle in diverse prove funzioni di Cam[er]a, di Chiesa, e di Teatro ci a dato con piena sua lode e N[ost]ra sodisf[azion]e e più sperimenti che non potiamo non rigua[rdare] la med[essi]me con particolare agradim[en]te e la persona sua con precisa benignità. Non bastandoci p[er]ciò se non è anche dedota in evidenza e manifesta d'ogni uno col tenore delle p[rese]nti che saran[n]o di n[ost]ra mano firmate, e dal n[ost]ro consueto suggello munite, lo eleggiamo dichiariamo diputiamo n[ost]ro Maestro di Capella da Chiesa e da Teatro in retribuzione ancora del ossequio riverentiss[im]o che ci a semp[r]e professato, sperando che da q[ue]sto si specioso onore, che gli faciamo, negli maggiorm[en]te eccitato il suo spirito a prestarci saggio, più vertuosi serviggi, più meritevoli vogliamo p[er]ò che p[er] tale sia da tutti riconosciuto, trattuto, e rispett[at]o, a goda de q[ue]lli onori, gratie, privilegi, perogative, premi che dagli altri simili Virtuosi e N[ost]ri Ser[vito]ri attuali, legitam[en]te si godono, oltre la provis[ion]e di Sei dopie al mese, spesa mobile ed affito di Casa di sett[ant]a scudi l'an[n]o, già da noi statigli benig[namen]te assegnato quasi che può talvolta occorerli. Cassagli col N[ost]ro sovrano leco. Mant[ov]a 31 Maggio 1699, Ferd[inand]o Carlo.

Jacobus Pirolus Can[cellari]us

Appendix C

Mantuan Opera Under the Habsburgs

Mantua—Archivio di Stato

Archivio Gonzaga—Sezione H (Finanze) Busta VIII (1669–1787), includes a single manuscript page listing the titles of operas performed in Mantua between 1708 and 1752. Titles that appear below in parentheses represent pencilled additions in the manuscript. All titles are in the order in which they appear in the manuscript.

Nel Teatro detto il Comico

1708	*Primavera*	*L'ingratitudine castigata, o sia l'Alavico*
1710	*Carnovale*	*L'Aretusa; (Opera pastorale)*
1711	*Primavera*	*Arenione*
1711	*Carnovale*	*Armide abbandonata; Armida al campo*
1712	*Primavera*	*Alciade*
1713	*Primavera*	*L'amor politico e generoso*
1714	*Primavera*	*Il tradimento premiato*
1715	*Carnovale*	*Il Demetrio; Il Tolomeo*
1716	*Carnovale*	*Ercole sub Tremondonte; L'Antioco*
1717	*Carnovale*	*La pastorella al soglio; La Griselda*
1718	*Carnovale*	*La Cunegonda; Lucio Papirio*
1719	*Primavera*	*La Merope*
1719	*Carnovale*	*Il Teusone; Tito Manglio*
1720	*Carnovale*	*Alessandro Severo; La Candace*
1722	*Primavera*	*Il Climene*
1723	*Carnovale*	*Orlando furioso; L'Artabano*
1726	*Autunno*	*Il Filindo pastorale*
1726	*Carnovale*	*Lucio Vero; La Zenobia*
1727	*Carnovale*	*Siroe, re di Persia; La Didone*
1728	*Carnovale*	*Venceslao; L'Engelberta (o sia La forza dell'innocenza)*
1729	*Carnovale*	*Il Tamerlano; La Partenope*
1731	*Carnovale*	*Il Costantino; L'Adelaide*
1732	*Carnovale*	*Semiramide; Il Farnace*

Nel Nuovo Teatro

1733	*Carnovale*	*Il Caio Fabricio; Il Demetrio*
1737	*Carnovale*	*La Zoe imperadrice dell'Oriente; Adriano in Siria*
1738	*Carnovale*	*Il Temistocle; Alessandro nell'Indie*
1742	*Carnovale*	*L'Arsace; Artaserse*
1743	*Carnovale*	*Il Catone in Utica; La Semiramide*
1744	*Primavera*	*furono rappresentate quattro opere bernesche, cioè: Li gelosi; L'Origille; Il Don Bertoldo; (?)*
1745	*Carnovale*	*Il Sisace; La Zenobia*
1747	*Primavera*	*opere bernesche, cioè: La finta cameriera; La comedia in comedia*
1750	*Carnovale*	*opere bernesche, cioè: Amore tutto puo; Il Filandro*

Nel Regio Ducal Teatro Vecchio

1752	*Carnovale*	*L'Ippermestra; Antigono*
1752	*Primavera*	*Il re pastore; Alessandro nell'Indie*

Appendix D

Autograph Scores for Caldara's Larger Secular Dramatic Works

Title	Librettist	Date and place of first performance	Library call number
Opera pastorale	?	Mantua, 1701	A-Wgm CA[a] no. 37
C. M. Coriolano	Pariati	Vienna, 1717	A-Wgm CA no. 38
La verità nell'inganno	Silvani	Vienna, 1717	A-Wgm CA no. 39
Ifigenia in Aulide	Zeno	Vienna, 1718	A-Wgm CA no. 40
Zaira	?	?	A-Wgm CA no. 41
Sirita	Zeno	Vienna, 1719	A-Wgm CA no. 42
Dafne	Biavi	Salzburg, 1719	A-Wgm CA no. 43
Lucio Papirio	Zeno	Vienna, 1719	A-Wgm CA no. 44
L'inganno tradito dall'amore	Lucchini	Salzburg, 1720	A-Wgm CA no. 45
Il Germanico morte	?	Salzburg, 1721	A-Wgm CA no. 47
Ormisda	Zeno	Vienna, 1721	A-Wgm CA no. 46
Nitocri	Zeno	Vienna, 1722	A-Wgm CA no. 48
Camaide	Lalli	Salzburg, 1722	A-Wgm CA no. 50

Title	Librettist	Date and place of first performance	Library call number
Scipione nelle Spagne	Zeno	Vienna, 1722	A-Wgm CA no. 49
Andromaca	Zeno	Vienna, 1724	D-Bds CA no. 2
Il finto Policare	Pariati	Salzburg, 1724	A-Wgm CA no. 52
Gianguir	Zeno	Vienna, 1724	A-Wgm CA no. 51
Semiramide in Ascalona	Zeno	Vienna, 1725	A-Wgm CA no. 54
Astarto	Zeno–Pariati	Salzburg, 1725	A-Wgm CA no. 53
Il Venceslao	Zeno	Vienna, 1725	A-Wgm CA no. 55
Amalasunta	Bonlini	Vienna, 1726	A-Wgm CA no. 56
Etearco	Stampiglia	Salzburg, 1726	S-St
I due dittatori	Zeno	Vienna, 1726	A-Wgm CA no. 95
Don Chisciotte in corte della Duchessa	Pasquini	Vienna, 1727	A-Wgm CA no. 57
La verità nell'inganno	Silvani	Salzburg, 1727	A-Wgm CA no. 58
Imeneo	Zeno	Vienna, 1727	A-Wgm CA no. 59
Ornospade	Zeno	Vienna, 1727	A-Wgm CA no. 60
Amor non ha legge	?	Graz, 1728	A-Wgm CA no. 61
La forza dell'amicizia	Pasquini	Vienna, 1728	A-Wgm CA no. 65
Mitridate	Zeno	Vienna, 1728	A-Wgm CA no. 64
I disingannati	Pasquini	Vienna, 1729	A-Wgm CA no. 63
Cajo Fabbricio	Zeno	Vienna, 1729	A-Wgm CA no. 66
La pazienza di Socrate	Minato	Vienna, 1731	A-Wgm CA no. 69
Il Demetrio	Metastasio	Vienna, 1731	A-Wgm CA no. 71
L'asilo d'amore	Metastasio	Linz, 1732	A-Wgm CA no. 70
L'Adriano	Metastasio	Vienna, 1732	A-Wgm CA no. 72

Title	Librettist	Date and place of first performance	Library call number
Sancio governatore	Pasquini	Vienna, 1733	A-Wgm CA no. 68
L'Olimpiade	Metastasio	Vienna, 1733	D-Bds CA no. 3
Demofoonte	Metastasio	Vienna, 1733	A-Wgm CA no. 73
Enone	Zeno	Vienna, 1734	A-Wgm CA no. 67
La clemenza di Tito	Metastasio	Vienna, 1734	A-Wgm CA no. 74
Scipione africano	Metastasio	Vienna, 1735	A-Wgm CA no. 75
Il natale di Minerva tritonia	Metastasio	Vienna, 1735	A-Wgm CA no. 76
Achille in Sciro	Metastasio	Vienna, 1736	D-Bds CA no. 1
Ciro riconosciuto	Metastasio	Vienna, 1736	A-Wgm CA no. 62
Temistocle	Metastasio	Vienna, 1736	A-Wgm CA no. 77

a. In Appendix D, "CA" stands for "Caldara autograph." The Caldara autograph collection of the Gesellschaft der Musikfreunde, acquired with the estate of the Archduke Rudolf, bulks in the Gesellschaft's autograph holdings only behind the Gesellschaft's collection of Beethoven autographs.

Appendix E

Comparisons of Caldara's Settings of *Atenaide*, *Psiche*, and *Astarto* with Contemporary Settings

Apostolo Zeno's libretto, *Atenaide*, was written for production in 1709 at the Barcelona court of the Habsburg claimant to the Spanish throne, Charles III. The music for each of the three acts survives under call number 18091 of the Österreichische Nationalbibliothek in separately bound volumes bearing the names of three different composers: Andrea Fiore, Caldara, and Francesco Gasparini. When the same libretto was produced five years later in Vienna, the text was set once more and by another trio of composers: M. A. Ziani, Antonio Negri, and Caldara. Their names appear on the title pages of 17192, another three-volume set among the holdings of the Nationalbibliothek. Table X is based on a comparison of MSS 18091 and 17192.

Zeno's serenade *Psiche* was written for production on November 11, 1720, the nameday of Habsburg Empress Elizabeth Christine. National-bibliothek 17264 preserves the music that was written for that occasion, mostly by Fux but with the last third of the score completed by Caldara, apparently after Fux had fallen ill or had become preoccupied with another assignment. Zeno's text was used once more to celebrate Emperor Charles's birthday in October of 1722, giving Fux a chance to complete the score that Caldara had finished for the 1720 production, and giving us the opportunity to compare, in Table Y, the Fux and Caldara versions for the final third of Zeno's text. Nationalbibliothek 17230 contains the music performed for the 1722 *Psiche*.

Astarto, a libretto completed by Zeno and Pariati for production in Venice during 1708 with music by Albinoni, was reset for the Viennese carnival of 1718 by one of Caldara's colleagues on the Habsburg payroll,

Francesco Conti. Table Z compares the arias of Conti's setting with those of another setting of the same text made by Caldara for production at the archiepiscopal court of Salzburg during the autumn of 1725.

Table X

Text incipit	Character	Act/ Scene	Tempo where indicated 1709	1714	Meter 1709	1714	Key 1709	1714	Instrumentation 1709	1714
Ti stringo	Leontino	I/1	adagio	andante	C	C	B♭	C	3b	1
Della rubella	Eudossa	I/2	—	allegro	2/4	3/8	G	A	2a	3
Puo voler	Pulchearia	I/4	vivace	allegro	12/8	C	A	C	1	1
Vedro se pareggi	Marziano	I/5	andante	andante	3/8	3/4	g	g	2a	3
Imeneo più chiare	Probo	I/6	andante	—	3/4	C	d	F	4	1
Trovo negli occhi	Teodosio	I/7	affetuoso	affetuoso	C	C	F	E♭	4b	1
Reggia amica	Varane	I/8	andante	andante	3/4	3/8	C	c	3	3
Più non sono	Leontino	I/11	—	giusto tempo	¢	12/8	G	b	1	1
Per darmi la vita	Varane	I/12	—	vivace	3/8	C	g	G	5	1
Di novi allori	Marziano	I/13	presto	allegro	2/4	C	A	C	2a	3e
Qual la sua colpa	Teodosio	I/14	aria d'attione	—	12/8	3/8	B♭	d	1	2
Quanto posso	Pulcheria	I/15	—	—	¢	C	G	a	2a	1
Qui grazie ancelle	Teodosio	II/1	allegro	vivace	2/4	3/8	A	G	2	3

Text incipit	Character	Act/ Scene	Tempo where indicated		Meter		Key		Instrumentation	
			1709	1714	1709	1714	1709	1714	1709	1714
Tu non m'intendi	Varane	II/2	allegro	spiritoso; andante	C	C	C	B♭	1	3
Son colpevole	Eudosse	II/3	larghetto	largo	C	C	F	g	4d	3
Vorresti, il so	Teodosio	II/6	allegro	vivace	2/4	2/4	B♭	F	4	3
Ricordati di me	Pulcheria	II/7	allegro	largo	3/4	3/4	F	A	1	3
Bel piacer	Marziano	II/8	allegro	andante	C	3/8	d	D	5a	1
Se cieco affetto	Leontino	II/9	allegro	vivace	3/8	¢	c	A	2	3
Parli quella	Varane	II/10	allegro	—	¢	C	D	F	1	1
Al tribunal d'amor	Teodosio	II/11	allegro	vivace	C	3/8	g	D	4	2
Il mio amore	Varane	II/12	presto	presto assai	C	C	C	G	3	2
Vado a recar	Probo	II/13	andante	andante	3/8	C	F	e	1	3
Eccelso trono	Eudossa	II/14	allegro	presto	3/4	C	A	C	4	3
Al me perfide	Probo	III/1	—	non tanto stretta	C	¢	F	E♭	2	4e
Parto, che so	Varane	III/3	—	allegro	C	C	D	A	3	1

Piu non voi	Pulcheria	III/5	—	allegro	3/4	2/4	B♭	B♭	3	3
Vanne tosto	Teodosio	III/6	presto	risoluto	3/8	C	A	D	2	4
Vanne tosto	Eudossa	III/7	—	largo	3/4	C	b	a	1	3
In bosco romito	Eudossa	III/7	—	larghetto	12/8	12/8	F	c	3f	3
Cor mio, che prigion sei	Marziano	III/8	—	andante	3/4	C	d	F	1	1
Gia vieni	Varane	III/10	—	allegro	12/8	C	F	C	2	3g
Infausta reggia	Eudossa	III/11	—	larghetto	3/4	C	G	G	1	3
M'accende amor	Teodosio	III/14	—	allegro assai	C	C	D	F	3e	3
Te solo	Pulcheria	III/16	—	allegretto	12/8	3/8	G	g	4	3
Si, son tua	Eudossa	III/19	—	allegro	2/4	2/4	A	a	4	1
Bel goder	Chorus	III/21	—	allegro	4/2	3/4	G	D	3	2

Table Y

Text incipit	Character	Tempo where indicated		Meter		Key		Instrumentation	
		1720	1722	1720	1722	1720	1722	1720	1722
Perche vivere	Psiche	—	allegro assai	3/4	3/8	A	F	3	3d
Pur sei giunta	Venere	allegro	molto allegro	C	C	a	F	4	3
Nulla pavento	Psiche	—	allegro assai	2/4	3/4	G	E♭	2	2
Fier guardo	Mercurio	allegro	vivace	3/8	2/4	e	g	1	3
Figlio audace	Venere	risoluto	—	3/8	C	E♭	D	3	1
Dal suo ciel	Chorus	largo	un poco allegro	C	C	g	C	3	3
Lascia la spoglia	Giove	allegro	su'l stile di madrigale	¢	¢	D	B♭	3	3
Tuoi saranno	Chorus	—	—	2/4	6/8	B♭	F	3	3
Grande Elisa	Chorus	—	—	2/4	6/8	B♭	F	3	3

Table Z

Text incipit	Character	Act/ scene	Tempo where indicated		Meter		Key		Instru- mentation	
			1718	1725	1718	1725	1718	1725	1718	1725
Speranze godete	Elisa	I/2	allegro	allegro	C	¢	C	A	2	2
Senza core	Agenore	I/3	—	allegretto	1/2	3/8	G	d	4	3
Care labbra	Nino	I/4	—	allegro	3/8	2/4	B♭	G	3	2
Vi sento, si	Sidonia	I/5	allegro	allegro vivace	C	3/8	c	B♭	3	2
Stelle ingrate	Clearco	I/9	allegro	larghetto	3/4	C	F	c	2	3
No, pietoso esser	Fenicio	I/10	andante	risoluto	C	C	d	C	3	4
Care pupille	Clearco	I/12	allegro	allegro moderato	3/8	2/4	C	a	3	2
Su cor mio	Elisa	I-13	allegro	risoluto	C	C	G	C	3	3
Amo, e bramo	Sidonia	I/14	allegro	allegro moderato	C	¢	a	F	1	2
Benche tarda	Nino	I/15	allegretto	allegro	3/4	3/4	d	F	2	2
Torni Astarto	Geronzio	II/1	adagio; presto	allegro	C	C	b	B♭	4e	2
Perche labbro	Clearco	II/4	vivace	larghetto	C	C	e	c	3	2

Text incipit	Character	Act/scene	Tempo where indicated 1718	Tempo where indicated 1725	Meter 1718	Meter 1725	Key 1718	Key 1725	Instrumentation 1718	Instrumentation 1725
Peno amando	Elisa	II/5	largo	—	3/8	2/4	f	a	4	2
Basta la speme	Agenore	II/9	allegro	allegretto	C	¢	a	G	3	2
Se vuoi, che in pace	Clearco	II/10	largo	larghetto	C	C	D	g	4f	3
Pari a me	Elisa	II/11	allegro	allegro assai	C	3/8	C	F	3	2
Non è poco	Sidonia	II/12	allegro	allegretto	1/2	12/8	B^b	C	1	2
Era meglio	Nino	II/13	vivace	allegro	C	C	d	G	3	1
Bella prova	Geronzio	II/15	allegro	allegro	3/4	¢	g	A	3	2
Come potesti	Geronzio	III/2	—	risoluto	C	C	d	C	1	3
Puniro nel vostro	Elisa	III/4	allegro assai	risoluto	C	C	F	B^b	2	3
Occhi vezzosi	Clearco Elisa	III/6	allegro	allegretto	3/8	C	B^b	d	2	2
Sciola da le ritorte	Fenicio	III/7	andante	allegro	C	¢	a	G	1	4
Veggo begli occhi	Sidonia	III/9	—	allegro assai	3/8	2/4	G	g	3	2
Finche spera	Elisa	III/12	allegro	allegro	1/2	¢	G	D	4g	2

Questo è tempo	Nino	III/13	—	allegro	3/8	3/4	D	F	3	3h
Se tu m'inganni	Agenore	III/15	presto	allegro	1/2	C	F	d	4e	2
Qual fra'l porto	Clearco	III/16	allegro	allegro assai	3/4	C	C	B♭	3	2
Se ha per guida	Chorus	III/19	—	—	1/2	3/8	F	G	3	2

Appendix F

"Dovresti haver" and "Vanne tosto"

"Dovresti haver" from A. Scarlatti's opera *L'Amazzone*, I/1, I-Rsc

"Vanne tosto," from A. Caldara's *L'Atenaide*, III/6, A-Wn 17192

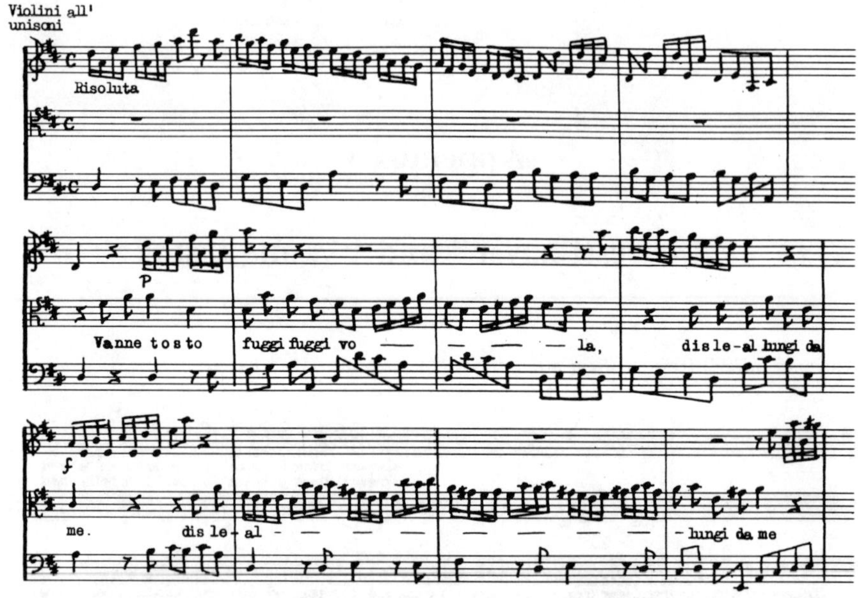

FINE

DA CAPO

Appendix G

Comparisons of Parallel Arias
in Caldara's *La verità nell'inganno*

I/1 Atalo

La di Cerbero a la soglia
Ombra vil non passerò.
Io trarrò
Dentro a l'Erebo profondo
Il velen del nostro mondo,
E le furie accrescerò.

1717 ritornello ab b/2—b/2 rit. ab b/2—b/2 b b/2 rit.⌒ ‖ c d e f—f f/2 ‖ DA
      I ——— I ———→ V — V ————————→ I ——— I ‖ I → VI→IV→IV ‖ CAPO
no.of   11
bars └─ 6 ──── 6 ──── 3 ──────── 11 ──────── 4 ─┘
              └──────────────── 30 ────────────────┘

1727 ritornello a b b/2—b/2 rit. a b b/2—b b/2 b/2 b/2 rit.⌒ ‖ c d e f f/2 f f/2 f ‖ DA
      I ——— I ———→ V — V I ————————————————→ I ‖ VI→III→ V ——→ VI ‖ CAPO
m.of   12
bars └─ 6 ──── 7 ──── 2 ──────── 9 ──────── 6 ─┘
              └──────────────── 30 ────────────────┘

I/2 Atalo

Per abbattere la sorte
Alma forte ancor m'avanza.
Solo amore è qual tormento,
Per cui sento
Vacillar la mia costanza.

1717 ritornello* a b rit. a b b/2—b/2 rit. a b b/2—b/2 rit.⌒ ‖ cde ——cde rit. ‖DS
      I ——— I ——— I ———→ V — V ————————→ I — I ‖ II→ IV ——→ IV→V ‖ *
no.of   21
bars └─ 8 ── 4 ── 3 ── 10 ── 4 ── 14 ── 8 ─┘
              └──────────── 51 ────────────┘

1727 ritornello a—b rit. a—b b/2—b/2 rit. a a b/1—b/2 b/2 b rit.⌒ ‖ Largo
                                                                      cde — cde
      I ——— I ——————————→ V — V I ——————————————→ I ‖ VI ———→ IV ‖
no.of   9
bars └─ 13 ──────── 22 ──────── 3 ──────── 16 ──────── 13 ─┘

67

I/4 Nicomede

Quanta empietà
Ne'mostri e accolta,
L'alma rubella
Soffrir saprà;
Questa sarà
La prima volta,
Che apparve bella
La crudeltà.

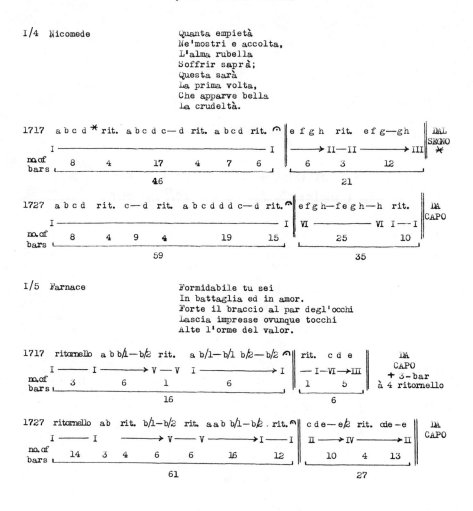

I/5 Farnace

Formidabile tu sei
In battaglia ed in amor.
Forte il braccio al par degl'occhi
Lascia impresse ovunque tocchi
Alte l'orme del valor.

I/6　Laodicea

Ah! se tu fossi amor,
Che serpe nel mio cor,
Sei troppo folle.
Pietà, ch'è un dolce affetto,
Si forte in regio petto mai non bolle.

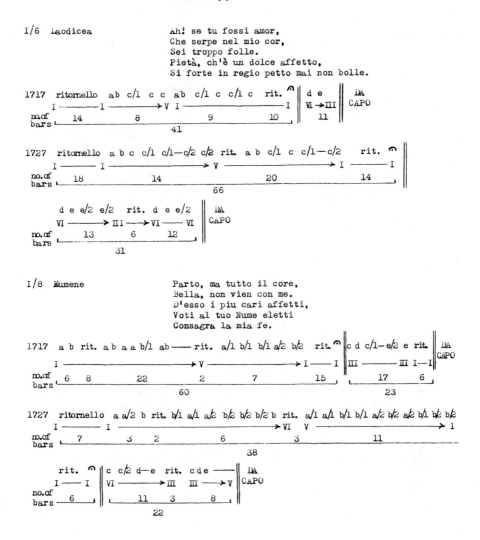

I/8　Eumene

Parto, ma tutto il core,
Bella, non vien con me.
D'esso i piu cari affetti,
Voti al tuo Nume eletti
Consagra la mia fe.

I/10   Tiridate   Empio, vivi, e per tua pena
                                    Pensa ogn'or, che fosti Re.
                                    Peso accresca alla catena
                                    Il perduto onor del pio.

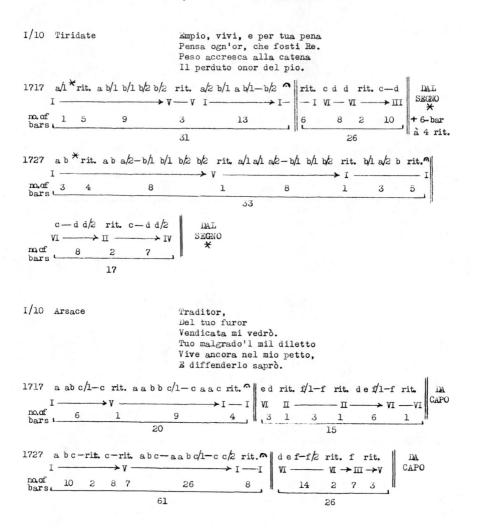

I/10   Arsace   Traditor,
                                    Del tuo furor
                                    Vendicata mi vedrò.
                                    Tuo malgrado'l mil diletto
                                    Vive ancora nel mio petto,
                                    E diffenderlo saprò.

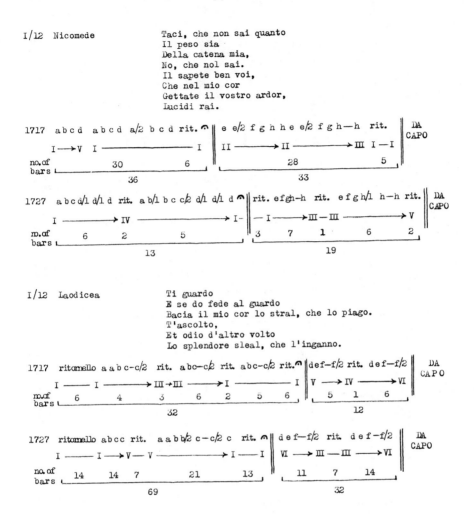

I/12 Nicomede

Taci, che non sai quanto
Il peso sia
Della catena mia,
No, che nol sai.
Il sapete ben voi,
Che nel mio cor
Gettate il vostro ardor,
Lucidi rai.

1717   a b c d   a b c d   a/2 b c d   rit. ⌒ ‖ e   e/2 f g h h e   e/2 f g h—h   rit. ‖ DA CAPO

I ⟶ V   I ————————————— I ‖ II ————⟶ II ————————⟶ III   I — I

no. of bars   30   6   ‖ 28   5

36   33

1727   a b c d/1 d/1 d   rit.   a b/1 b c c/2 d/1 d/1 d ⌒ ‖ rit. e f g h—h   rit.   e f g h/1 h—h   rit. ‖ DA CAPO

I ————————⟶ IV ———————————⟶ I-   — I ———⟶ III — III ————————⟶ V

no. of bars   6   2   5   3   7   1   6   2

13   19

I/12   Laodicea

Ti guardo
E se do fede al guardo
Bacia il mio cor lo stral, che lo piago.
T'ascolto,
Et odio d'altro volto
Lo splendore sleal, che l'inganno.

1717   ritornello   a a b c—c/2   rit.   a b c—c/2   rit.   a b c—c/2   rit. ⌒ ‖ d e f—f/2   rit.   d e f—f/2 ‖ DA CAPO

I ————— I ————————⟶ III ⟶ III ————⟶ I ————————— I ‖ V ——⟶ IV ————————⟶ VI

no. of bars   6   4   3   6   2   5   6   5   1   6

32   12

1727   ritornello   a b c c   rit.   a a b b/2 c—c/2 c   rit. ⌒ ‖ d e f—f/2   rit.   d e f—f/2 ‖ DA CAPO

I ————— I ⟶ V — V ————————⟶ I — I ‖ VI ——⟶ III — III ————⟶ VI

no. of bars   14   14   7   21   13   11   7   14

69   32

I/13　Arsace and Atalo

Arsace	-	Ah no; vivi.
Atalo	-	Si, cuor mio.
Arsace	-	Vivi a me.
Atalo	-	Vivro per te.
		E s'io muoro,
Arsace	-	Ah, se tu muori,
à due	-	Morro teco:
Atalo	-	A i nostri amori
		Serba almeno la tua fe.
Arsace	-	Tutta amore, e tutta fe.

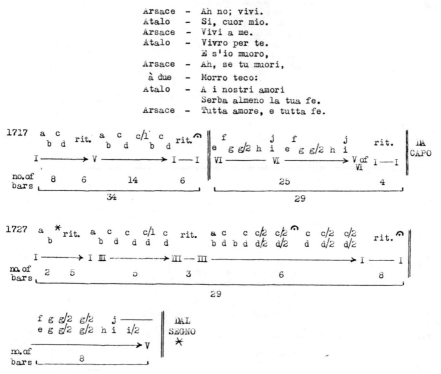

Appendix H

Examples of Caldara Arias
Employing Instrumental *Obbligato* Parts

(Those abbreviations in use are the same as those
introduced on page 248 of the text.)

Opera pastorale (1701)

   II/14 Aminta   𝄞 𝄞 𝄡 𝄡 (tenor) 𝄢   "Violino solo," violini ripieni,
                                                 violette, "violoncello," continuo
                                               e minor; $\frac{3}{8}$; ------

Venticelli che tra le ronde
Cosi placidi sussurrate
Deh fermate i vanni erranti.
E se mesta compagnia
Nel ardor scema il dolore
Noi con flebile armonia
Rispondete ecco a miei pianti.

Atenaide, Act II (1709)

   II/3 Eudossa   𝄡 (tenor) 𝄢   "Violoncello solo," continuo
                                                 F major; C ; larghetta cosi cosi

Son colpevole a'tuoi lumi,
Ma innocente è il mesto cor.
Giusti Numi, il vostro sguardo
Ben lo vede
Pien di fede, e di dolor.

L'inimico generoso (1709)

   II/4 Teodosio   𝄞 𝄞 𝄡 𝄡 (tenor) 𝄢   upper and middle strings,
                                                 "violoncello," continuo
                                             a minor; $\frac{2}{4}$; allegro

Il mirarti è non amarti
Bella mia, non non si può.
Sin che tu si vaga sei,
Non han colpa gl'occhi miei
Se il mio cor poi t'adorò.

(L'inimico generoso)

III/3 Valentiniano   (Violino) "solo," upper and middle
strings, "violoncello," "teorba,"
continuo

C major; $\frac{3}{4}$; ------

A pugnar, a trionfar,
Da begl'occhi apprenderò.
Anco amor dal loro esempio
A piagar forse imparò.

III/5 Pulcheria   "violini" (2 parts on 1 staff),
violette, "teorba," continuo

a minor; C ; andante

Deh lasciatemi, o pensieri
Di riposo un sol momento.
Agitata dall'amore
Tormentata dal timore
Vò sperando ma pavento.

La verità nell'inganno (1717)

II/2 Eumene   (tenor)   "Violoncello," continuo

F major; C ; allegro

Gran difesa è il pentimento
Dove giudice è l'amore.
Mi punise quel tormento,
Che l'error mi getta al cuore.

Ifigenia in Aulide (1718)

II/7 Teucro   "Violino concertato," violini,
violette, continuo

e minor; $\frac{3}{4}$; ------

Tutto fa nocchiero esperto
Nell'incerto ondoso regno,
Onde il frale errante legno
Scorra il mare, e afferri il porto.
Ma che può, se avversa stella,
O furor di ria procella
Fa, ch'ei rompa a duro scoglio,
E dall'onde ei resti assorto?

Lucio Papirio (1719)

III/3   Quinto Fabio   𝄢 ℭ: "Scialmo," continuo
                                        d minor; $\frac{12}{8}$; largo

Dammi un amplesso, o padre.
Forse tra ceppi avvinto
Più non tel renderò.
Perdonami il dolore,
Che avrai se cado estinto;
E degno del tuo amore
Anche in morir sarò.

III/4   Marco Fabio   𝄢 𝄢 𝄢 ₵ ℭ: "Violino di concerto," violini,
                                        violette, continuo

                                        D major; $\frac{3}{4}$; allegro

A torrente che cresce, ed inonda,
Poi argine, o sponda,
Lo fa piu orgoglioso.
Mi trae seco que'faggi, e que'sassi;
E tumido vassi,
Sinche in piano piu libero e aperto,
Spande l'onda, men gonfio e spumoso.

Ormisda (1721)

I/14   Cosroe   𝄢 𝄢 ℭ: 𝄢 𝄢 ₵ ℭ: "Oboe" (2 staves), "fagotti,"
                                        violini, violette, continuo

                                        G major; $\frac{3}{8}$; allegro

Vede quel pastorello
L'avido lupo ingordo,
Che nel piu scelto agnello
Cerca sfamar il dente; e sel difende.
Tal per difesa anch'io
Del ben, che solo è mio,
Senno userò, e valor
Contra quel rio furor, che mel contende.

(Ormisda)

II/2   Artenice   𝄢 (tenor) ℧:   Violoncello (concertante?), continuo

C major; C ; allegro

M'occupa il core
La gloria mia.
Fato, od amore
Nol vincerà.
La mia fortezza
Non cederà,
Ne al genio altero
Della grandezza,
Ne al dolce impero
Della beltà.

II/13 Palmira 𝄞𝄞 ℧: 𝄞𝄞𝄢 ℧:   "V. V. Concertini," "Violoncello obbligato," "V. V. Ripieni," violette, continuo

D major; $\frac{3}{8}$; -------

Vedi la navicella
Che senza la sua stella
Erra fra rupi, e sassi, e resta assorta.
Torbida e l'aria, e l'onda;
Ma afferrerai la sponda,
Se presso a me verrai, tua fida scorta.

II/14 Arsace 𝄞 𝄞 𝄞 𝄢 ℧:   "Chalumeaux" (2 staves), violini, violette, continuo

d minor; C ; ------

Che vuoi far, povero Arsace?
Dei pugnar contra il tuo core.
Dei nimico alla tua pace
Cerca danno, e amar dolore.

Scipione nelle Spagne (1722)

   II/16 Scipione   𝄢 𝄐:   "Mandolino solo," "cembalo e
                                                violoncelli"

                                                C major; C; allegro

                    Lieti amori,
                    Mirti, e rose a'verdi allori
                    Intrecciatemi sul crine.
                    Le soavi mie speranze
                    A goder son già vicine.

Gianguir (1724)

   IV/7 Asaf   𝄢𝄢𝄚𝄚 (tenor) 𝄐:   "Gli Strumenti," "violoncell',"
                                                  "contrabasso solo, e cembalo"

                                                D major; C ; andante

                    Tanto, e con si gran piena
                    Non vi affrettate, o gioje,
                    A rendirmi contento.
                    Voi mi opprimete; e parmi
                    Un genere di pena
                    Il troppo godimento.

   IV/11 Cosrovio   𝄢𝄢𝄢𝄚𝄐:   "Tromba," "Violini," "Viole,"
                                                  continuo

                                                C major; C ; -------

                    Date, o trombe, il suon guerriero,
                    Certo invito alla vittoria.
                    Cara, addio. Mio cor tu sei.
                    Dammi un guardo, e vincerò.
                    Sguardo egli è tutto amoroso:
                    Ma più lieto anche il vorrei.
                    Non temer: che pien di gloria,
                    E d'amor ritornerò.

Euristeo (1724)

II/2   Aglatida   ₵ ℭ: "Violino solo," continuo

B♭ major; C and $\frac{3}{8}$; andante

Di mie catene pur son contenta;
Ne mi tormenta
La rimembranza di libertà.
So che nel caro mio bel tiranno
Uniti stanno
Virtù, ed amore con fedeltà.

III/1   Erginda   ₵ ₵ ℭ: "Scialmo," "traverso," "fagotto"

g minor; $\frac{3}{4}$; andante

Sotto un faggio, o lungo un rio
Spero ancor con l'idol mio
Starmi assisa, o selve amate.
E con lui di quando in quando,
Or ridendo, or sospirando,
Rammentar le pene andate.

I due dittatori (1726)

III/4   Quinto Fabio   ₵ ₵ ₵ 𝄡 ℭ: "Tromba," violini, violette, continuo

C major; $\frac{3}{4}$; allegro assai

Nulla bada destrier generoso,
Se suon strepitoso,
D'oricalco lo sfidi, o lo desti.
Corra ardito ad invito d'onore,
Magnanimore core;
E da gloria altro amor non l'arresti.

IV/2   Osidio   ℭ: ℭ: ℭ: "due Fagotti," continuo

d minor; C ; ------

Non dovria chi impera, e regge,
Con la forza, e con la legge
In suo oltraggio vendicar.
Non è zelo il suo rigore,
Ma furore,
Che a se fa, non un dovere,
Ma un piacere in condannar.

(I due dittatori)

IV/9   Velia   ♄♄ КК (tenor) ℭ: Violini, violette, "violoncello,"
                                    "cembali soli e contrabasso"

                                    D major; $\frac{6}{8}$; allegro

A te basti, o degno amante,
Che in mercede alla tua fede
Volli amarti, e non potei.
Che costretti dal dovere,
Più non erano in potere
Del voler, gli affetti miei.

V/1   Fabio Massimo   ♄♄ КК (tenor) ℭ: ♄♄ К ℭ:

                      "Clarini" (2 staves), "trombe"(2
                      staves), "Timpani," "V.V." (2 staves),
                      "viole," continuo

                      C major; C ; allegro

Il suon delle trombe
Si alto rimbombe,
Che rechi al Numida
Il primo spavento.
E i nostri in udirlo
Compagni guerrieri,
Ripiglin più fieri
L'usato ardimento.

La verità nell'inganno   (1727)

I/10   Arsinoe   К (tenor) ℭ: "Violoncello," continuo

                                 B♭ major; $\frac{3}{8}$; presto

Traditor, del tuo furor
Vendicata mi vedrò.
Tuo malgrado'l mio diletto
Vivrà ancora nel mio petto,
E diffenderlo saprò.

(La verità nell'inganno)

I/13 Arsinoe and Atalo   𝄢   "Scialmo," continuo

                                                                c minor; C ; largo ed amoroso

Arsinoe	-	Ah No; vivi.
Atalo	-	Si, cuor mio.
Arsinoe	-	Vivi a me.
Atalo	-	Vivrò per te.
		E s'io muojo,
à due	-	Morrò teco:
Atalo	-	A i nostri amori
		Serba almeno la tua fe.
Arsinoe	-	Tutta amore, e tutta fe.

II/7 Eumene   𝄢 𝄢 𝄢 𝄢 (tenor) 𝄢   Violini, violette, "violoncello"
                                                      (obbligato), continuo

                                                      D major; C ; -----

No, che un cieco non è la mia guida,
Quando io servo d due fulgide stelle.
Non sarà mai quest'anima infrida
A due luci languenti, ma belle.

III/5 Nicomede   𝄢   "Violino" (solo), continuo

                                                      B♭ major; $\frac{3}{4}$; largo ed amoroso

Non mi giova aver il piede
Fuor del carcere penoso,
Se gia il core è fra catene.
Prigionier della mia fede,
Spero solo il mio riposo
Negl'affetti del mio bene.

Imeneo (1727)

II/6 Imeneo   𝄢 𝄢 𝄢 𝄢   Violini, violette, continuo; in the
                                                    aria's B section the uppermost staff
                                                    is marked "scialmo solo."

                                                      B♭ major; C ; andante

Sulle sponde di placido fiume
Anche augello di candide piume
Dolce canta, vicino a morir.
Ed un eco pietosa, e dolente
Fin da tronchi, e da rupi si sente
Al suo canto compagna languir.

Bibliography

This bibliography supplements the comprehensive operatic bibliography contained in the second edition of Donald J. Grout's *A Short History of Opera* (New York, 1965).

Abert, A. A., "Zum metastasianischen Reformdrama," *Kongressbericht der Gesellschaft für Musikforschung: Lüneburg 1950* (Kassel, n.d.), pp. 138–39.

Abert, H., "Einleitung [to Carlo Pallovicino's *La Gerusalemme liberata*]," DDT, Series I, Vol. LV (1916), v–xlvi.

Amadei, F. *Cronaca universale della Città di Mantova*, 4 vols., Mantua, 1954–55.

Anonymous, *Mémoires de la Cour de Vienna*, Cologne, 1705.

————, *Riflessioni sopra i drammi per musica*, Venice, 1757.

Aristotle, *On the Art of Poetry*, trans. Ingram Bywater, Oxford, 1959.

Arlt, W., "Zur Deutung der Barockoper: 'Il trionfo dell'Amicizia e dell'Amore' (Wien 1711)," *Music and Society* (Cologne, 1963), pp. 96–145.

Barnes, M., "The Trio Sonatas of Antonio Caldara," Florida State University dissertation, 1960.

[Becelli, G. C.], *Della novella poesia cioè del vero genere e particolari bellezze della poesia italiana*, Verona, 1732.

Bedarida, H., and Hazard, P., *L'influence française en Italie au dix-huitième siècle*, Etudes françaises XXXIV, Paris, 1935.

Bellaigue, C., "Antonio Caldara," *Etudes musicales*, series II (Paris, n.d.), 471–75.

Belloni, A., *Il seicento*, Milan, 1929.

Bernardoni, P. A., Poemi drammatici, 3 vols., Vienna, 1706–1707.

Bertana, E., *Il teatro tragico italiano del secolo XVIII prima dell'Alfieri*. Giornale della storico letteratura italiana, supplementary series, IV (Turin, 1901).

Biagi, G., "Lettere di Lodovico Antonio Muratori," *Rivista delle biblioteche e delle archivi* VII (1896), 38–61.

Bonta, S., "The Church Sonatas of Giovanni Legrenzi," Harvard University dissertation, 1964.

Bouhours, D., *La manière de bien penser dans les ouvrages d'esprit*, Paris, 1687.

Breggi, P., *Serie degli spettacoli rappresentati al Teatro Regio di Torino dal 1688 al presente*, Turin, 1872.

Caffi, F., Storia della musica teatrale in Venezia; four-volume manuscript (no. 10465) in the holdings of the Biblioteca Marciana, Venice.

Calcaterra, C., *Il Barocca in Arcadia*, Bologna, 1950.

————, *Il Parnasso in rivolta*, Milan, 1940.

Calsabigi, R. de', "Dissertazione su le poesie drammatiche del Sig. Abate Pietro Metastasio," *Poesie del Signor Abate Pietro Metastasio*, Paris, 1755.

Campanini, N., *Un precursore del Metastasio*, Biblioteca critica della letteratura italiana XLIII (Florence, 1904).

Careri, D. F. G., *Aggiunta a viaggi di Europa*, Naples, 1711.

Carini, I., *L'Arcadia dal 1690 al 1890*, Rome, 1891

Carreras y Bulbena, J. R., *Carlos d'Austria y Elisabeth de Brunswick-Wolffenbüttel*, Barcelona, 1902.

──────, "Les primeras operas cantadas a Barcelona en la Llotja de Mar," *Revista Musical Catalana* II (May, 1905), 95–97.

Carse, A., *The Orchestra in the 18th Century,* London, 1940.

Chiuppani, G., *Apostolo Zeno in relazione all'erudizione del suo tempo*, Bassano, 1900.

Coulanges, M. de, *Mémoires de M. de Coulanges*, ed. M. de Monmerqui, Paris, 1820.

Crescrimbeni, G. M., *L'Arcadia*, Rome, 1711.

──────, *La bellezza della volgar poesia*, Rome, 1700.

──────, *Comentarii alla sua istoria della volgar poesia*, 5 vols., Rome, 1702–11.

──────, *L'istoria della volgar poesia*, 6 vols., Rome, 1698.

──────, *Notizie istoriche degli Arcadi morti*, 3 vols., Rome, 1720.

──────, *Le vite degli Arcadi illustri*, 5 vols., Rome, 1708–29.

Croll, G., "Vorwort [to Agostino Steffani's *Tassilone*]," Denkmäler rheinischer Musik VIII (1958), v–viii.

Déjob, C., *Etudes sur la tragedie*, Paris, n.d.

Fehr, M., introduction to *Zeno, Drammi scelti*, Bari, 1929.

Feind, B., *Gedancken von der Opera*, Hamburg, 1706.

Fischer, W., "Zur Entwicklungsgeschichte des Wiener klassischen Stils," *SzMw* III (1915), 24–84.

Fochessati, G., *I Gonzaga di Montova*, Milan, 1930.

Frugoni, F. F., *L'Epulone*, Venice, 1675.

Fux, J. J., *Gradus ad Parnassum*, Vienna, 1725.

Galletti, A., *Le teorie drammatiche e la tragedia in Italia nel secolo XVIII*, Cremona, 1901.

Gigli, G., *Opere*, 3 vols., Siena, 1797.

Il Giornale dei letterati d'Italia, 38 vols., Venice, 1710–27.

Goldschmidt, H., "Zur Geschichte der Arien- und Symphonie-Formen," *MfMg* XXXIII (1901), 61–70.

Gravina, G., *Della ragion poetica*, 2 vols., Rome, 1708.

──────, *Della tragedia*, Naples, 1715.

──────, *Discorso sopra L'Endimione*, Rome, 1692.

──────, *Tragedie cinque*, Naples, 1712.

Gray, C., "Antonio Caldara," *Contingencies and other Essays* (London, 1947), pp. 132–43.

Hüber, K., "Die Wiener Opern Giovanni Bonocinis von 1697–1710," University of Vienna dissertation, 1955.

Jander, O. H., "Alessandro Stradella and his Minor Dramatic Works," Harvard University dissertation, 1962.

Keysser, J. G., *Travels through Germany, Bohemia, Hungary, Switzerland, Italy, and Lorrain*, 4 vols., London, 1756 (2nd ed.).

Kirkendale, U., "The War of the Spanish Succession Reflected in Works of Antonio Caldara," *Acta* XXXVI (1964), 221–33.

Kraus, F., "Biographie des K. K. Vice-Hof-Kapellmeisters, Antonio Caldara (1670–1736)," University of Vienna dissertation, 1894.

Küchelbecker, J. B., *Allerneueste Nachricht vom Römisch-Käyserl. Hofe*, Hanover, 1730.

LaBorde, J. B., *Essai sur la musique*, 4 vols., Paris, 1780.

Landau, M., *Die italienische Literatur am österreichischen Hofe*, Vienna, 1879.

Livingston, H., "The Italian Overture from Alessandro Scarlatti to Mozart," University of North Carolina dissertation, 1952.

Luin, E. I., "Unbekanntes aus der Blütezeit der Salzburger Operngeschichte," *Alpenjournal* (July, 1946), pp. 5-8.

————, "Sulla vita e sulle opere di Antonio Caldara," *La scuola veneziana*, Siena, 1941, pp. 38-48.

Maffei, S., *Teatro italiano*, 3 vols., Verona, 1723.

Malipiero, G. F., *I profeti di Babylonia*, Milan, 1924.

Mando, F., *Il più prossimo precursore di Carlo Goldoni, Jacopo Angelo Nelli*, Florence, 1904.

Mantuani, J., *Tabulae codicum manuscriptorum*, IX–X, Vienna, 1897–99.

Martello, P. J., *Della tragedia antica e moderna*, Scrittori d'Italia CCXXV, 187–316.

Maugain, G., *L'évolution intellectuelle de l'Italie de 1657 à 1750 environ*, Paris, 1909.

Maylender, M., *Storia delle accademie d'Italia*, 5 vols., Bologna, 1926.

Menegatti, P. F. H., *In funere Illustrissimi Domini Apostoli Zeni*, Venice, 1750.

Menghi, L., *Lo Zeno e la critica letteraria*, Camerino, 1901.

Metastasio, P., *Tutte le opere*, 5 vols., ed. B. Brunelli, Milan, 1943–54.

Moncallero, G. L., *L'Arcadia*, Florence, 1953.

Moniglia, G. A., *Poesie drammatiche*, 3 vols., Florence, 1689–90.

Montalto, L., "Tra virtuosi e musici nella corte del Cardinale Benedetto Pamphili," *Rivista italiana del dramma* V (1941), 81–97, 193–209.

————*Un cardinale in Roma barocca*, Florence, 1955.

Napoli-Signorelli, P., *Storia critica de'teatri antichi e moderni*, Naples, 1777.

Nelson, P. F., "Nicholas Bernier (1665-1734): a Study of the Composer and his Sacred Works," University of North Carolina dissertation, 1958.

Neumann, F. H., "Die Theorie des Rezitative im 17. und 18. Jahrhundert unter besonderer Berücksichtigung des deutschen Musikschrifttums des 18. Jahrhunderts," University of Göttingen dissertation, 1955. The first chapter of the dissertation, "Die Aesthetik des Rezitative," was published as a monograph in 1962 by Heitz of Strasbourg.

Orsi, G. G., *Considerazioni sopra la maniera di ben pensare*, Bologna, 1703.

Pauly, R. G., "Benedetto Marcello's 'Il teatro alla moda,' a Critique of Early *Settecento* Opera," Columbia University master's thesis, 1947.

Pavan, G., "Il teatro Capranica," *RMI* XXIX (1922), 425–44.

Perrucci, A., *Dell'arte rappresentativa premeditata ed all'improviso*, Naples, 1699.

Pietzsch, W., *Apostolo Zeno in seiner Abhängigkeit von der französischen Tragödie*, Leipzig, 1907.

Pistorelli, L., *I melodrammi di Apostolo Zeno*, Padua, 1894.

Preussner, E., *Die musikalischen Reisen des Herrn von Uffenbach*, Kassel, 1949.

Renda, U., and Operti, P., *Dizionario storico della letteratura italiana*, ed. V. Turri, Turin, 1959.

Ricci, C., *I teatri di Bologna nei secoli XVII e XVIII*, Bologna, 1888.

Riccoboni, L., *De la réformation du théâtre*, Paris, 1743.

Riemann, H., "Einleitung [to Agostino Steffani's *Alarico*]," DDT, Series II, Vol. XI/2, vii–xxii.

[Riva, G.], *Advice to the Composers and Performers of Vocal Musick*, trans. from Italian, London, 1727.

Rolandi, U., " 'Il teatro alla moda' di B. Marcello e le sue propaggini," *La scuola veneziana*, Siena, 1941, pp. 51–56.

Roncaglia, G., *L. A. Muratori e il maggior compositore modenese del suo tempo*, Modena, 1933.

Salvadori, G. G., *Poetica toscano all'uso*, Naples, 1691.

Salzer, E.C., "Teatro italiano in Vienna barocca," *Rivista italiana del dramma* II (1938), 47–70.

Scheib, W., "Die Entwicklung der Musikberichterstattung im Wienerischen Diarium von 1703–1780, mit besonderer Berücksichtigung der Wiener Oper," University of Vienna dissertation, 1950.

Schneider, C., "Einleitung [to Antonio Caldara's *Dafne*]," DTO XCI (1955), xiii-xv.

————, *Geschichte der Musik in Salzburg*, Salzburg, 1935.

Schneider, J., "Francesco Conti als dramatischer Componist," University of Vienna dissertation, 1902.

Silvani, F., *Opere drammatiche*, 4 vols., Venice, 1744.

Soccii Filopatrii, *Serie cronologica de'drammi recitati ne'pubblici teatri di Bologna dall'anno 1600 fino al 1737*, Bologna, 1737.

Sonnleithner, L., "Zur Lebensgeschichte des Antonio Caldara," *Recensionen und Mittheilungen über Theater und Musik* XI (1865), 225.

Tirinelli, G., "Silvio Stampiglia," *La scuola romana*, Rome, 1882, pp. 6–10.

Toscani, B., "Antonio Caldara," Columbia University master's thesis, 1958.

Valsecchi, A., *Orazione in morte di Apostolo Zeno*, Venice, 1750.

VanderMeer, J. H., *Johann Josef Fux als Opernkomponist*, 3 vols., Bilthoven, 1961.

Vetter, W., "Zur Stilproblematik der italienischen Oper des 17. and 18. Jahrhunderts," *SzMw* XXV (1962), 561–73.

Volkmann, H., *Emanuele d'Astorga*, 2 vols., Leipzig, 1911–19.

Wellesz, E., "Einleitung [to J. J. Fux's *Costanza e Fortezza*]," DTÖ XVII (1910), vii–xxv.

Winterfeld, C. von, *Allegorisch-politische Festopern am kaiserlichen Hofe zu Wien in der letzten Hälfte des siebzehnten Jahrhunderts*, Berlin, 1852.

Zeno, Apostolo, *Oeuvres dramatiques . . . traduites de l'italien*, 2 vols., Paris, 1758.

————, *Poesie drammatiche*, 10 vols., Venice, 1744.

Index